DUE DUE

Behavioral Finance and Capital Markets

Behavioral Finance and Capital Markets

How Psychology Influences Investors and Corporations

Adam Szyszka

palgrave
macmillan

BEHAVIORAL FINANCE AND CAPITAL MARKETS

Copyright © Adam Szyszka, 2013.

First published in 2013 by
PALGRAVE MACMILLAN®
in the United States—a division of St. Martin's Press LLC,
175 Fifth Avenue, New York, NY 10010.

Where this book is distributed in the UK, Europe and the rest of the world,
this is by Palgrave Macmillan, a division of Macmillan Publishers Limited,
registered in England, company number 785998, of Houndmills,
Basingstoke, Hampshire RG21 6XS.

Palgrave Macmillan is the global academic imprint of the above companies
and has companies and representatives throughout the world.

Palgrave® and Macmillan® are registered trademarks in the United States,
the United Kingdom, Europe and other countries.

ISBN: 978–1–137–33874–7

Library of Congress Cataloging-in-Publication Data is available from the
Library of Congress.

A catalogue record of the book is available from the British Library.

Design by Newgen Knowledge Works (P) Ltd., Chennai, India.

First edition: September 2013

10 9 8 7 6 5 4 3 2 1

*To those who encouraged, motivated, and supported me greatly
in the effort to prepare this book. Your inspiration,
friendship, and love made this possible*

Contents

Figures and Exhibits

Figures

Exhibits

Introduction

The neoclassical financial theory made various strong assumptions including decision makers' rationality, common risk aversion, perfect markets with no frictions such as transaction costs or taxes, and easy access to information for all market participants. Although many of the assumptions of the neoclassical theory were unrealistic, financial economists initially accepted it because its predictions seemed to fit reality. It was not until much later that contradictive evidence started to pile up and behavioral finance emerged in response.

First, the neoclassical financial economics assumed that all decision makers, or at least a large majority of them, behave rationally. This means that they know how to interpret incoming information and correctly estimate the probability of future events on that basis. Rational decision makers evaluate different levels of wealth following the subjective utility function, which meets all the axioms suggested by Von Neumann and Morgenstern (1944). Making risky decisions, they will try to maximize the total expected utility, while displaying general risk aversion (Friedman and Savage, 1948).

Markowitz (1952) developed the portfolio theory according to which rational investors should create well-diversified investment portfolios. This reduces the impact specific factors have on total investment value and makes for an optimal relation between the expected return and the level of risk. Hence, in the long run, expected returns on securities should depend only on the level of systemic (market) risk. This was reflected, inter alia, in the Capital Asset Pricing Model (CAPM) put forward by Sharpe (1964), Lintner (1965), and Mossin (1966).

The neoclassical theory also assumed that if there are instances of irrationality on the part of some investors resulting in asset mispricing, this is quickly corrected by actions taken by rational market players who may apply efficient and unconstrained arbitrage strategies. Consequently, capital markets is always efficient in that it prices assets correctly and reflects all the available information, offering the best approximation of the intrinsic value of assets (Fama, 1965, 1970).

The main advantage of the neoclassical approach is that it constitutes a consistent and comprehensive system providing normative models. On the other hand, its major disadvantage is that it adopts unrealistic assumptions as the basis for its different component theories. Such assumptions, however, are necessary in order to quantify and simulate different processes and phenomena so that the developed models may be normative. Actually, one of the real-life aspects that the neoclassical financial theory largely ignored is the fact that there might be serious disruptions to decision makers' rationality. The traditional approach dismissed irrational behavior as irrelevant for the asset-pricing process.

Unrealistic assumptions are often a necessary compromise made in order to construct formalized models. They do not depreciate the importance of the theoretical approach, especially when a model is able to explain the reality well. This was initially the case with the cornerstones of the neoclassical financial economics. Early empirical evidence was indeed supportive of the Efficient Market Hypothesis (Fama, 1970) and the CAPM model (Black et al., 1972; Fama and MacBeth, 1973).

It was not until a decade or two later that many studies yielded results that flatly contradicted the traditional paradigm. In response to a growing number of anomalies, behavioral finance emerged. Its key concept is that the behavior of irrational investors may impact asset pricing and will not always be eliminated quickly by rational arbitrageurs. There are limits to arbitrage resulting from additional risks and real-life institutional and organizational context. As a result, markets will not always be efficient and asset pricing may deviate from predictions of traditional market models. Highly intuitive and convincing explanations referring to irrational behavior and psychological biases of investors have gained popularity among professionals and academics.

Yet, behavioral finance is affected by an ailment typical of relatively young and scarcely penetrated areas of knowledge. That is, a plethora of research carried out in an uncoordinated manner produced fragmentary outcomes that are difficult to cohere into a comprehensive theory. Issues related to investors' behavior and the way it affects valuation of assets are complex. Thus, researchers face much difficulty in specifying all the factors and relationships that describe the phenomena taking place in the capital market. However, focusing only on selected aspects of the market leads to behavioral models that appear fragmentary and designed only to fit selected peculiarities. Prevailing in the literature so far are studies identifying some market peculiarity and then attempting to explain it. Alternatively, other works provide evidence for a specific attitude of market participants and try to establish its potential market outcome. Some papers focus on a given irrational behavior and its impact on asset pricing, being less interested in the psychological background of the behavior itself. Other authors concentrate more on the psychology of decision making and risk taking, but to a lesser extent on its inference for aggregated market data. Rare are those works that take a comprehensive look at multidimensional relations between various anomalies. Few authors apply a wider approach to study the whole story starting with psychology, to irrational behavior of market participants and anomalous results of such behavior in asset pricing, to the implications for real-life practice.

Behavioral corporate finance is one of the newest areas within the behavioral framework. Traditional corporate finance made a general assumption that rational corporate managers operate in efficient markets in order to maximize shareholders' wealth. Incentives shaped by adequate compensation contracts, the market for corporate control, and other governance mechanisms were said to minimize potential agency costs. The CAPM has been typically used to determine the cost of equity, which is of course the same figure as the expected return for investor, just seen from a different perspective. Under the Efficient Market Hypothesis, the cost of firm financing should always be adequate and dependent solely on how risky the company is. When considering an acquisition, managers could take for granted that other assets are also always correctly priced. As behavioral finance changes the way we look at investor behavior and asset pricing in capital markets, it must naturally also have implications for the second group of capital market participants, that is, for corporations. Behavioral corporate finance takes two distinctive approaches. The first one emphasizes the effect of market inefficiency on corporate polices, assuming that executives act as rational professionals. In other words, it focuses on how a smart manager adapts corporate policy in order to exploit investor irrationality and market inefficiency. The second approach replaces the assumption of managers' rationality with evidence-driven psychological foundations. It shows how managerial biases may impact managerial practice, and if particular distortions are actually beneficial or detrimental to shareholders' wealth.

Finally, the behavioral approach is entering macroeconomics. For example, it may be applied to help understand the recent economic turmoil, that is, the credit crunch in the United States in 2008 and the later crisis in Europe. Although, problems in the United States and in the Eurozone were mainly due to vast macroeconomic imbalances, behavioral biases and inclinations of market participants helped to build up the crisis exacerbating its scope and dynamics.

The purpose of this book is to fill in the identified gaps and to address the aforementioned issues in the current state of behavioral financial research. First, the rich polemic between traditional and behavioral finance is presented and systematized. A comprehensive overview of the psychological foundations and their applications to finance is provided in such a way as to demonstrate a three-stage continuity among psychological factors, the behavior of investors who are influenced by them, and asset-pricing anomalies as a result of these irrational attitudes. The book also offers a multidimensional view on relations between various anomalies. This is supplemented by a discussion on practical implications for investment strategies. In the next step, the market-wide consequences of behavioral biases and attempts to model the aggregate market behavior are extensively discussed. The Generalized Behavioral Model (GBM) developed by Szyszka (2007, 2010) is proposed as the one that is able to explain, albeit at a general level and in a descriptive manner, the broadest possible range of market phenomena. The recent economic turbulence in the United States and Europe is discussed in detail both in the framework of macroeconomics and from the behavioral perspective. The book also includes a comprehensive review of the most recent findings in the field of behavioral corporate finance. It addresses both the cases of rational managers operating in inefficient markets, as well as the possibility of managerial biases. This part is also supplemented with original results of the survey among executives of publicly listed companies.

Such an extensive and multidimensional scope makes the book unique. Its preparation required appropriate methodology and sources. The book drew on over 700 academic papers and books. The collected and systematized literature sources are a digest of the current global state of knowledge on capital markets and corporate finance seen from the behavioral perspective. When necessary, references were also made to older historical sources. The author has used his own previous work as well. Most of the publications cited relate to the American market and, to a lesser extent, the British and Canadian ones. Some papers also refer to other markets in Europe, Australia, and Asia. Systemization, classification, and comparative analysis were all used to develop a deductive and inductive line of argument. Specific problems were most often discussed starting from general statements to reach detailed conclusions, which allowed for a thorough analysis and made it possible to present the issues in an exhaustive, systematic way. Next, wherever it was possible and reasonable, the author tried to combine the different strands of knowledge and synthesize them in order to arrive at generalized conclusions. The empirical part contains a specially designed survey. Adequate statistical methods were used to process the obtained results and reach conclusions where it was possible.

The book consists of four major parts totaling ten chapters altogether. The first part is dedicated to foundations of behavioral finance. Chapter 1 confronts the principles of the neoclassical financial theory and traditional corporate finance. Chapter 2 covers selected elements of psychology financial behaviorists refer to when they explain how people construct their beliefs, how preferences emerge, and how emotions influence the decision-making process. These two chapters constitute the basic framework for further deliberations in later parts of the book.

Part II of the book focuses on investor behavior and anomalies in asset pricing. Chapter 3 describes attitudes investors adopt when making investment decisions. It shows how psychological factors described in the previous chapter may impact investors' beliefs about future price changes, influence the perception of company value and investment selection criteria, as well as determine the way portfolios are managed. Chapter 4 systematizes and thoroughly discusses a number of phenomena observed in the capital market. It also demonstrates how the anomalies are linked with irrational investor behavior and its psychological background. Practical implications and profitability of various investment strategies based on asset-pricing anomalies are also discussed.

Part III takes a comprehensive look at market behavior as a whole. Chapter 5 begins with the discussion of two puzzling anomalies related to aggregated market data—the equity risk premium puzzle and excessive volatility of stock prices. It is followed by an overview of behavioral models developed to explain various market phenomena that the neoclassical financial theory struggles with. It is shown that the most popular behavioral models account for some peculiarities, but usually are not able to explain all of them. The GBM is proposed as the one that is broad enough to be able to explain the whole range of market phenomena. The model is general and only descriptive, but it can roughly describe when, how, and what kind of psychological factors may distort correct asset pricing and influence returns observed on the market. Chapter 6 is dedicated to behavioral insights into the recent financial crisis. It offers both macroeconomic and behavioral perspective on the credit crunch in the United States in 2008 as well as on the turbulence in the Eurozone.

Part IV deals with corporate behavioral finance. Chapter 7 shows how rational managers may decide to amend their corporate policy in order to take advantage of investors' irrationality and temporary market anomalies. On the other hand, chapter 8 discusses potential psychological biases among managers themselves. As behavioral corporate finance has been studied much less than investor behavior and asset-pricing anomalies, we decided to carry out our own original research in this area based on the survey of top executives of publicly listed companies. Chapter 9 presents results that relate directly to corporate managerial practice. It documents cases of rational managerial behavior attempting to exploit market inefficiency, as well as examples of erroneous managerial practice. Chapter 10 focuses on managerial psychology and verifies if similar heuristics and biases that were earlier documented for investors may be found also among corporate executives.

The book concludes with final remarks that recapitulate its main findings as well as open issues for further discussion and potential research.

This book is unique in that it surveys all facets of behavioral finance and offers exceptional breadth and depth of discussion. Its target audience includes academics, capital market and corporate practitioners, regulators, students, and other people interested in behavioral finance and economic psychology. The book is appropriate as a stand-alone material for undergraduate or graduate courses in behavioral finance, or as supplementary reading for more general courses in areas of financial economics and corporate finance. Given the scope of the work, doctoral students in this field may also find it helpful.

PART I

———

Foundations

CHAPTER 1

Behavioral Approach versus Neoclassical Finance

This chapter confronts the main foundations of the neoclassical theory of finance with allegations of the behavioral approach. Theoretical models of classical financial economics do not take into account the possibility of decision maker irrationality. It is often assumed that irrational investors are not coordinated and therefore their behavior cancels out. And even if irrationality becomes strong and common among a large group of investors, it will be voided by rational actions of arbitrageurs. However, behavioral finance points out limits to arbitrage. It is argued that irrationality of investors may indeed influence asset pricing. This position challenges the main theoretical foundations of the neoclassical paradigm, including the Markowitz's portfolio theory, traditional asset pricing models, and the Efficient Market Hypothesis. The behavioral approach is of high importance also for the second side of capital market, that is issuers. A discussion on key elements of corporate finance policy in the light of behavioral implications concludes the first chapter.

1. Decision-Maker Rationality and the Expected Utility Theory

One of the key concepts in the neoclassical theory of finance is decision-maker rationality. A rational person correctly interprets the information he receives and knows how to estimate the probability of future events on its basis. He prioritizes various alternatives according to his own utility function and tries to optimize subjective expected utility. It is assumed that rational market participants are so strong and dominant as a group that they are able to quickly and efficiently eliminate any symptoms of irrationality on the part of other traders. As a result, the market will behave as if all participants acted rationally.

Determining decision-maker preferences and the way in which he assesses investment options is a point of departure for any traditional capital asset-pricing model. In the classical approach, these issues were comprehensively described by the expected utility hypothesis commonly believed to have been put forward by John von Neumann and Oscar Morgenstern (1944) although it could be traced as far back as the eighteenth-century writings of Daniel Bernoulli (1954).

According to the neoclassical theory of finance, a rational decision maker follows two general rules. First, he displays so-called risk aversion in that he is willing to take risk only when it may lead to further benefits, that is, only when he stands a chance of being rewarded with a risk premium (Friedman and Savage, 1948). Risk aversion is a general and common phenomenon even though its degree may vary for each individual decision maker. Second, decision makers always make choices in such a way as to maximize total expected utility, given that the marginal utility of each additional benefit unit is positive.

The behavioral approach challenges both these assumptions on the grounds that risk aversion depends primarily on the context in which decisions are made. Moreover, decision makers attach greater importance to changes in the affluence level when measured against a specific reference point rather than its total value. Many behavioral experiments showed that subjects display risk aversion when they make choices between alternatives leading to lower or higher gains. However, when faced with a decision problem in the domain of losses, they are more prone to take risks. All of these observations lay at the foundation of the prospect theory developed by Kahneman and Tversky (1979).

Von Neumann and Morgenstern (1944) formalized the classical theorem on the existence of the utility function on the basis of a series of assumptions determining preferences of rational decision makers. What follows is a discussion of four fundamental axioms that cause the most controversy among representatives of behavioral finance.

1.1. Axiom of Completeness

The axiom of completeness assumes that a rational decision maker knows how to compare different options and has well-defined preferences. Comparing available information and guided by the constant set of preferences, he either prefers variant A to B, or B to A, or is indifferent between A and B.

However, Tversky and Kahneman (1981, 1986) point to results of experimental studies showing that people are often not able to correctly interpret the problems they face. Because of their limited perception of information, they are not always in a position to recognize repeated decision problems even if they are logically the same, but formulated in a different way. Depending on how the information is framed, decisions makers may exhibit different preferences in the same situations. We focus on mistakes in perception and information processing in greater detail in chapter 2.

1.2. Axiom of Transitivity

According to the axiom of transitivity, if a decision maker prefers variant A to B and rates variant B higher than C, then he will also prefer variant A to C. Even though this rule seems obvious, at least at first glance, it is also undermined by representatives of behavioral finance. The argument goes that, under real-life economic conditions, decision makers may make intransitive choices because they are motivated by several criteria of variant assessment. For example, depending on the situation in which a decision needs to be made, a decision maker may be motivated by the amount of the reward in one case but the probability of success in another.

Tversky (1969) conducted an experiment where a group of subjects were to choose from several pairs of lotteries, but the expected value of each lottery within a pair was equal. In some games the potential payoff was large but with small probability assigned. In others, the payoff was small, but the probability of winning was very high. Tversky noted that when two lotteries are relatively similar in terms of gain probability (e.g., winning is possible, but very unlikely), decision makers will choose the game offering a higher payoff disregarding the risk criterion. However, when the difference in gain probability between each of the lotteries is considerable (e.g., winning is probable in both cases, but the probability is much higher in one of them), people will choose the lottery that offers higher chances of winning, paying less attention to the actual amount to be won.

So let us imagine three possible investments, I_1, I_2, I_3, each of which has a different expected return, $E(R)$, and different risk level measured by variance V. Let us also assume the following relations between the expected return and risk of individual investments:

$$E(R)_1 > E(R)_2 > E(R)_3 \qquad (1.1)$$

and

$$V_1 > V_2 > V_3 \qquad (1.2)$$

If the decision maker believes that differences between risk levels V_1 and V_2 as well as between V_2 and V_3 are relatively small, he will be motivated by the criterion of higher expected return when comparing investments in such pairs. Consequently, he will prefer investment I_1 to I_2 and I_2 to I_3. According to the axiom of transitivity, the investor should also prefer investment I_1 to I_3. This does not necessarily have to be the case. The difference between risk levels V_1 and V_3 may be assessed by the investor as much larger than the difference in the level of risk for the two other pairs of investments. In such a case, the investor may make decisions following the criterion of risk reduction instead of trying to maximize the expected return. He will then prefer investment V_3 to V_1 which is plainly against the rule of transitivity.

1.3. Axiom of Continuity

The axiom of continuity says that the choice between two variants should only depend upon differences between them or conditions under which the two variants lead to different results. If both options are changed in the same way, decision maker's preferences should remain as they were. Hence, in accordance with the axiom, the investor should not change his mind if, for example, the risk level is changed for both variants in the same way (i.e., when the probability of each variant taking place will equally increase or decrease). However, psychological experiments have shown that people do modify their behavior in response to the level of risk. This has to do with the so-called certainty effect—decision makers tend to overestimate the value of a lottery where the reward is certain compared to a lottery with a higher expected reward but involving even a marginal level of risk (Allais, 1953; Kahneman and Tversky, 1979, 1984; Tversky and Kahneman, 1986).

Let us consider the following example. A decision maker is faced with a choice between the following investment strategies: strategy A offers certain income in the amount X, strategy B offers a possibility to earn a much higher income Y with the probability determined in such a way that the expected value of the strategy exceeds the value of income X, albeit only slightly. It turns out that in such situations decision makers usually choose strategy A, even though its value of expected reward is slightly lower. Let us now imagine that both strategies are changed in the same way, that is, they are burdened with identical additional risk, for instance, by reducing the probability of profit in each of them fourfold. Following the change, none of the strategies offers a 100 percent certainty of income. Faced with this choice, the decision maker will change his preferences choosing strategy B as the one that offers higher expected value. Naturally, the change in investor preferences contradicts the axiom of continuity.

Another aspect putting the axiom into question is the issue of sensitivity to the way in which a decision problem is presented. In other words, dependence on information framing. Kahneman and Tversky (1984) give the example of choosing a strategy to fight an epidemic involving the total of 600 people infected. The choice to be made is between two alternative treatment programs:

- program A that gives a 100 percent certainty of saving 200 of the infected, and
- program B that gives a one-third probability of saving all 600 infected people and a two-thirds probability of failing to save a single person.

Most respondents (72%) decided to opt for program A. Then, the same respondents had to choose between "other" possible programs:

- program C that will cause the death of 400 of the infected, and
- program D that gives a one-third probability that no one will die, but a two-thirds probability that all 600 people will perish.

In the second task, most of the respondents (78%) preferred program D. However, logically speaking, programs A and C as well as B and D are identical, the only difference being that the results of each of them are presented first in the context of the number of people saved, and then in the context of people who will have to die.

1.4. Axiom of Independence

According to the axiom of independence, if the decision maker treats two options X and Y indifferently, he should also be indifferent about the following two variants for any option Z:

(a) option X with probability p and option Z with probability $(1 - p)$,
(b) option Y with probability p and option Z with probability $(1 - p)$.

It is enough to take the example of complementary goods to show that this assumption will not always work in reality. The reason is that if any option Z turns out to be complementary in relation to X but not Y, the decision maker may be more inclined to prefer the simultaneous occurrence of X and Z to Y and Z, even though he would be indifferent toward X and Y if he considered them separately.

Considering the axiom of independence in the context of the stock market, let us imagine two assets X and Y with exactly the same amount of risk and the same expected return. Theoretically, when assessed individually, they will be perceived by the investor as equally good investment opportunities if he adopts the criterion of risk premium only. It may, however, happen that the return for asset Y will be strongly correlated with the return for asset Z while fluctuations in the value of asset X will be relatively independent of changes in the value of Z. According to classical portfolio theory, in such a case, the investor will prefer to simultaneously invest in X and Z rather than Y and Z because the first option leads to more benefits from diversification. Thus, the axiom of independence falls before it is even necessary to remove the assumption of decision-maker rationality.

1.5. Probability Assessment

According to the traditional theory of finance, before decision makers can rationally apply the criterion of maximizing expected utility when making decisions under risk, they must first estimate the probability of different scenarios and then correctly modify their beliefs in the light of new information. Theoretically, such verification of probability should be done according to Bayes's rule.[1]

Probability of event A given the occurrence of observation B may be defined in the following way:

$$P(A|B) = \frac{P(A \cap B)}{P(B)} \qquad (1.3)$$

where:

$P(A|B)$ is conditional probability of event A given B,
$P(A \cap B)$ is joint probability of events A and B,
$P(B)$ is probability of event B.

As the probability of the product of events A and B is hard to estimate, we need to make several transformations. Conditional probability of event B given A, that is, $P(B \mid A)$ amounts to:

$$P(B \mid A) = \frac{P(B \cap A)}{P(A)}$$

(1.4)

Transforming equation (1.4) we arrive at:

$$P(B \cap A) = P(B \mid A) \cdot P(A)$$

(1.5)

Let us note that $P(A \cap B) = P(B \cap A)$ and so

$$P(A \cap B) = P(B \mid A) \cdot P(A)$$

(1.6)

Plugging in equation (1.6) to equation (1.3), we arrive at the best-known, so-called simplified version of Bayes's rule

$$P(A \mid B) = \frac{P(B \mid A) \cdot P(A)}{P(B)}$$

(1.7)

The most important advantage of this transformation is that, unlike equation (1.3), equation (1.7) refers directly to information that is theoretically either available to the decision maker or pose no problems when it comes to assessing it.

Extended Bayes's rule shows how to calculate the value of $P(B)$. The denominator in equation (1.7) is a normalizing constant that can be derived from the total probability formula with the use of the marginalization principle:

$$P(B) = \sum_i P(B \cap A_i) = \sum_i P(B \cap A_i) \cdot P(A_i)$$

(1.8)

We can now write Bayes's rule in its full version, that is:

$$P(A \mid B) = \frac{P(B \mid A) \cdot P(A)}{\sum_i P(B \mid A_i) \cdot P(A_i)}$$

(1.9)

Bayes's rule is a mathematical tool describing how rational investors should modify their opinions in the light of new facts.

Proponents of behavioral finance provide many arguments proving that investors struggle to correctly estimate probability, finding it especially difficult to apply Bayes's rule properly. People overreact to powerful information of a descriptive nature downplaying the importance of underlying statistical data.

Kahneman and Tversky (1982) devised the following task: A taxicab was involved in a hit-and-run accident in a certain city. There are two cab companies operating in the city—one has only green cars, the other only blue. We know that 85 percent of the cabs in the city are green and 15 percent are blue. A witness found in the course of the investigation identified the cab as blue. It was tested, however, that, under the same circumstances that existed on the night of the accident, the witness was able to identify correctly each one of the two colors eight out of ten times, that is with 80 percent probability of a correct answer. What is the probability that the cab involved in the accident was blue?

To solve this problem, we will use formula (1.9). First, let us assign symbols to each of the events mentioned in the task:

A_1—event of a blue cab causing the accident,

A_2—event of a green cab causing the accident,

B—event of the witness recognizing the cab as blue,

$P(A|B)$ —probability of a blue cab causing the accident given that the witness recognized it as blue,

$P(A)$ —prior probability of a blue cab causing the accident,

$P(B|A_1)$—probability of the witness recognizing the cab as blue given that the cab was in fact blue; in other words, probability of the witness correctly recognizing the color in a certain light,

$P(B|A_2)$ —probability of the witness recognizing the cab as blue when the accident was in fact caused by a green cab; in other words, probability of the witness being wrong.

Plugging in relevant values to formula (1.9) we arrive at:

$$P(A \mid B) = \frac{0.80 \times 0.15}{0.80 \times 0.15 + 0.20 \times 0.85} \approx 41\% \qquad (1.10)$$

However, the median of answers given by respondents in the Kahneman and Tversky's experiment was as high as 80 percent. People involved in the survey usually did not attach importance to the low percentage of prior probability ($P(A) = 15\%$) and so overestimated their general assessment.

Another demonstration of problems with base probability and application of Bayes's rule is a judgment based on a stereotype. Having noticed a clear personal trait corresponding to a common stereotype, respondents are overconfident about the probability that the person will follow the stereotype and underestimate base probability. They frequently disregard the fact that, statistically speaking, it is more probable that the analyzed person belongs to a different group only because this other group is larger than the set of people conforming to the stereotype.

Tversky and Kahneman (1982) conducted the following experiment. A group of subjects was given the following personality sketch of a woman: "Linda is 31 years old, single, outspoken, and very bright. She majored in philosophy. As a student, she was deeply concerned with issues of discrimination and social justice, and also participated in anti-nuclear demonstrations." The subjects were then asked to identify which was more probable:

(a) Linda is a bank teller,
(b) Linda is a bank teller and is active in the feminist movement.

Over 86 percent of the respondents said that statement B was more probable. However, it is obvious that, statistically speaking, option A is more probable as there are more women who are bank tellers than women who are bank tellers and feminists at the same time.

On the other hand, if the information received cannot be assigned to any specific pattern already familiar to the decision maker—for example, there is no stereotype—the opposite phenomenon may take place—the so-called conservatism bias (Edwards, 1968). It consists in overweighing prior distribution and failing to correctly update probability estimates when faced with new information.

In addition, decision makers do not pay enough attention to the size of the sample on the basis of which they estimate probability (Bar-Hillel, 1982). They overemphasize information derived from small samples to the detriment of signals generated by samples containing a lot of observations. Ignoring the size of the sample when the real process of data generation is unknown, respondents may jump to conclusions or construct ungrounded rules or patters. On the other hand, when the processes governing data generation are known, underestimating the importance of sample size may result in the so-called gambler's fallacy.

Another obstacle to estimating probability correctly is overconfidence observed in the form of the calibration error. When asked to provide information or make a forecast without being precise but staying within a certain confidence interval, respondents usually give answers which indicate that they are overconfident as to the precision of their knowledge (Lichtenstein et al., 1982; Alpert and Raiffa, 1982; Yates, 1990; Keren, 1991; De Bondt, 1998).

Kahneman and Tversky (1979) claim that, in general, people attach too much importance to highly unlikely events, underestimating those where the probability is relatively high. This is reflected in the shape of the so-called weighting function in the prospect theory Kahneman and Tversky developed to counter the classical utility hypothesis of von Neumann and Morgenstern.

Detail presentation of behavioral biases mentioned earlier will follow in chapter 2.

2. Limits to Arbitrage

2.1. Role of Arbitrage in Asset Pricing

Theoretical models of traditional financial economics are based on the notion of *homo oeconomicus*, an idealized fully rational agent who has unlimited access to information, is capable of processing correctly all signals, and makes right choices that maximize his expected utility based on perfectly unbiased perception of reality and estimation of future events. The existence of irrational investors was not ruled out in the traditional financial economics. However, it was assumed either that irrational investors are not coordinated and therefore their behavior cancels out or that the actions of rational arbitrageurs efficiently correct market pricing, as soon as irrational traders happen to drive them away from fundamentals.

Friedman (1953) points out the use of arbitrage on the currency market suggesting full liberalization of exchange rates. Ross (1976) develops the theory of arbitrage in respect to capital asset pricing. Arbitrage may be defined as the simultaneous purchase and sale of the same, or essentially the same, security in two different markets for advantageously different prices. Its role in capital asset pricing is to sustain asset prices at fundamentals.

Let us assume that a large group of irrational investors too optimistically assess the fundamental value of a security, which leads to temporary market overvaluation. A rational arbitrageur should then sell or even short-sell the security and simultaneously buy the same security on another market. He might also purchase a sufficiently similar security whose fundamental value is sensitive to the same factors that influenced the original one. Doing this, the arbitrageur will hedge his position against the risk of new information that could change the actual value of his investment. He will also generate profit in the form of a difference between the amount obtained from the sale of the security and the amount he will spend to buy an "almost identical" stock. Following the same logic, arbitrageurs will buy an underestimated security and hedge against risk by short-selling the same security on a different market or short-selling an "almost identical" security. Thus, perfect arbitrage may generate profit without incurring risk. When arbitrageurs take short and long positions for "identical" securities simultaneously, future flow of funds following this type of investment will amount to zero. Because an arbitrageur takes a long position for the cheaper security and sells the more expensive one, he collects arbitrage profit upfront.

In the traditional view, active arbitrage triggers the market adjustment mechanism, which quickly brings asset prices back to their real values through changing demand and supply. Higher demand for the cheaper asset pushes the price up while higher supply for the same or essentially the same asset pushes the price down. Eventually, prices on both markets or of both similar assets reach an equilibrium.

Behavioral finance does not negate the principle of arbitrage itself. However, in practice, arbitrageurs face a series of limitations that partly or totally constrain their actions contributing to market inefficiency and incorrect asset pricing. The reason is that arbitrage may be not only risky but also costly and so the market is not always able to eliminate the effects of irrational behavior.

2.2. Fundamental Risk

Fundamental risk in arbitrage is due to the fact that financial markets do not always offer an ideal substitute whose price will react to news in exactly the same way as the price of the security to be initially mispriced. Usually, if a stock is priced incorrectly, derivative instruments based on this stock will also be mispriced. This is why arbitrageurs must often look for further substitutes such as stock of other companies with a similar activity profile and similar (although, unfortunately, not identical) parameters compared to the original security.

The use of such imperfect substitutes exposes arbitrageurs to fundamental risk related to the possibility of new information emerging on the market. The information could be specific for one company only and have considerable impact on the price of one security, but not on the price of the other instrument (or, worse, impact the other position in the opposite direction). In cases like this, the most important principle of arbitrage does not apply. The principle is that after arbitrage positions have been open, losses on short positions are compensated by the same revenue from long positions and vice versa.

Fundamental risk may trigger severe losses for arbitrageurs, which potentially are much higher than initial profits from the difference between prices of both securities at the moment when positions are taken. This is why, when perfect substitutes are missing, professional arbitrageurs are often less inclined to exploit instances of mispricing.

2.3. Noise Traders Risk

In reality, even when there is a perfect substitute for a security, arbitrage is still not free of risk, contrary to what the classical approach claims. De Long, Shleifer, Summers and Waldmann (1990a, 1991) and Shleifer and Summers (1990) point out the risk related to activities of noise traders. The idea was then further developed by Shleifer and Vishny (1997) and Shleifer (2000). Basically, the risk that arbitrageurs incur here stems from the danger of more intense activities on the part of noise traders who may cause the price of the security to deviate even further from its fundamental value. Once the price of a security has been decoupled from its real value, further price deviations cannot be ruled out, at least not in the short term.

The fundamental assumption to make when identifying this type of risk is that arbitrageurs need to act in a narrow time window. In the longer perspective, there is practically no risk related to further deviations from the real value as actions taken by more and more rational traders will eventually bring prices back to their fundamental values. However, many professional arbitrageurs do not have the comfort of waiting.

Professional investors usually manage funds that are not in their possession but have only been entrusted to them. Capital owners assess their investment performance at least once a year or, as often happens, at shorter intervals on the basis of reports and current asset pricing. Further deviation of the price from the fundamental value caused by activities of noise traders may expose the arbitrageur to severe losses in the short term, but the losses will not be final until he keeps his positions open. Nevertheless, poor results reported by the arbitrageur over a short time period may mean that capital owners, especially those who are not competent specialists and do not understand the strategies employed by the arbitrageur, will take their funds back to entrust them to someone whose performance is better at the moment. When funds are withdrawn by capital owners, arbitrageurs are forced to close their positions prematurely and realize a loss even though it might result from market deviations that are only temporary. Arbitrageurs are often forced to close their positions at the very moment when the deviation of the price from the fundamental value of the security is at its greatest creating the best opportunities for arbitrage.

The attitude of creditors may exacerbate the situation further. When making a transaction, arbitrageurs borrow money (to be able to take long positions) and securities (for short positions). As short-term losses accrue, lenders of capital and securities may want their loans back because they no longer perceive the arbitrageur as credible. Such reactions are commonly triggered by a fall in the value of shares in a long position given as a collateral to hedge short-selling. This usually requires that the arbitrageur present additional margin or else he is automatically forced to close his position immediately, which means realizing accrued losses even though it might turn out later on that the price of the security starts returning to the fundamental value.

In the case of short-selling, the obligation to return the borrowed security does not necessarily have to be related to damaged credibility of the arbitrageur. It might simply derive from the fact that the deadline specified in the loan contract has expired. If the activity of noise traders persists preventing prices of a security from going back to their fundamental value and the arbitrageur is not able to find another source from which he could borrow the same shares, he will be forced to close his positions prematurely in order to return borrowed stocks to their owner in time.

All of the aforementioned risk elements related to unpredictability of actions undertaken by noise traders may hamper professional and rational investors from getting involved in arbitrage transactions or, at the very least, limit the scope of such endeavors. If arbitrage is limited, instances of incorrect pricing that had not been acted upon may linger on the market for some time, making it inefficient.

2.4. Risk of Synchronization

Abreu and Brunnermeier (2002) point out another obstacle to immediate and full arbitrage. They believe that arbitrageurs are exposed to the so-called risk of synchronization stemming from uncertainty on the part of individual arbitrageurs as to when other rational traders will notice the incorrect pricing of the security and take steps to eliminate it. Abreu and Brunnermeier (2002) propose a model based on three main assumptions. First, it is assumed that actions taken by a single arbitrageur cannot influence the market strongly enough to correct incorrect pricing on their own. Achieving this requires coordinated actions of a larger number of traders. Second, it is assumed that the community of arbitrageurs notices a specific instance of inefficiency only gradually, that is, some arbitrageurs detect the inefficiency quicker than others. Importantly, when he notices an opportunity for arbitrage, a trader does not know how soon he managed to do so compared to other rational traders. This means he is not aware when other arbitrageurs will start acting. The third assumption has to do with costs related to applying arbitrage and keeping arbitrage positions open. The longer it takes to eliminate incorrect pricing, the longer the trader is forced to keep arbitrage positions open incurring higher related costs.

Hence, on the one hand, arbitrageurs are afraid to open their arbitrage positions too soon not to incur excessive costs; on the other, they are motivated by a desire to benefit from the opportunity they noticed before other traders manage to do the same. Abreu and Brunnermeier have demonstrated that when arbitrageurs are faced with this dilemma, they usually eventually decide to postpone their actions. The model proposed by Abreu and Brunnermeier suggests that this period of restraint will last longer the higher the costs related to keeping arbitrage positions open. Conversely, the more the price of a security deviates from its fundamental value, the more motivated arbitrageurs are likely to be and the sooner they start acting.

The risk of synchronization is a specific obstacle that is not caused by actions taken by noise traders. Instead, it is triggered by uncertainty related to decisions to be made by rational investors themselves.

2.5. Implementation Costs and Regulatory Barriers

Discussing synchronization risks, we mentioned the problem of costs needed to keep arbitrage positions open. These include first of all costs related to borrowing stocks for short-selling. Other costs include typical transaction costs such as commissions, bid-ask spreads, and costs of information services and analysis. Obviously, the higher the total costs of implementing and maintaining an arbitration strategy are, the less willing rational investors are to benefit from incorrect pricing on the market.

Finally, we should not forget about legal requirement and internal regulations that are binding for a large group of institutional investors. In the case of many traders, especially pension funds, safe mutual funds, and other institutions following rigorous safety regimes and so-called prudent man rules, it is forbidden to short-sell or invest in derivative instruments. Naturally, this constitutes a major obstacle for arbitrage strategies.

3. Fundamentals of the Neoclassical Financial Economics

3.1. Portfolio Theory

Classical portfolio theory, which was developed primarily by Markowitz (1952), is based on the concept according to which every investment in securities is accompanied by two kinds of risk: systemic (market) and nonsystemic (unique, specific). Nonsystemic risk is related to a specific asset individually and may be eliminated through correct diversification of stock in the portfolio. Benefits from diversification will increase with the rise in the number

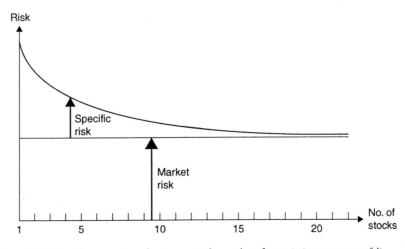

Figure 1.1 Risk reduction against the increase in the number of assets in investment portfolio.

of different financial instruments in the portfolio and the fall in correlation between returns on these instruments. However, marginal benefits of diversification (i.e., risk reduction resulting from the addition of another investment to the portfolio) decrease until they reach the level of systemic risk (Figure 1.1). Systemic risk is related to the market as a whole and cannot be eliminated because returns on stock in the market are correlated to a certain extent.

In the well-developed mature capital markets, it is commonly assumed that an optimally diversified portfolio should contain about 20–30 different assets given transaction and investment monitoring costs (Bloomfield et al., 1977; Statman, 1987). Nevertheless, Campbell, Lettau, Malkiel, and Xu (2001) point out a strong tendency on the American market whereby the correlation between returns on individual stocks decreases, which suggests an increase in potential benefits to be derived from diversification. Statman (2004) claims that, taking account of transaction costs available for big professional players, marginal benefits from increasing diversification are present even for up to 300 different assets in an investment portfolio.

According to classical portfolio theory, investors are always risk averse, try to maximize the single-period expected utility, estimate portfolio risk on the basis of expected returns, and can parameterize each individual investment alternative with the use of probability distribution for expected returns. If the choice between alternative investment portfolios is to be made solely on the basis of the comparison between expected returns and variance, we need to make the additional assumption that returns are generated following normal distribution. Knowing only the expected return and variance, we are now in a position to describe alternative investments in detail and compare them.

Acting in line with the aforementioned assumptions, rational investors should diversify their investments in such a way as to eliminate nonsystemic risk and create efficient portfolios displaying minimal variance (risk) for specific expected returns or guaranteeing maximum expected return for a given

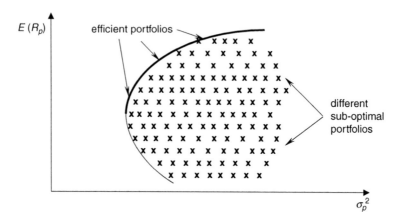

Figure 1.2 Efficient frontier.

risk level. The set of efficient portfolios is known as the efficient frontier (Figure 1.2). Each point at the efficient frontier represents the best possible combination of risk and expected return.

Expected return from the portfolio is a weighted average of expected returns on the assets it contains:

$$E(R_p) = x_i \cdot E(R_i) + x_j \cdot E(R_j) + \ldots + x_n \cdot E(R_n)$$ (1.11)

where

$E(R_p)$ is expected return from the investment portfolio,
$E(R_i)$ is expected return on asset i,
$E(R_j)$ is expected return on asset j,
$E(R_n)$ is expected return on asset n,
$x_i, x_j, \ldots$, xn are percentage share of assets $i, j, \ldots n$ in investment portfolio given that the total of $x_i + x_j + \ldots + x_n = 100\%$.

As for portfolio variance, it may be described by the following formula:

$$\sigma_p^2 = \sum_{i=1}^{n} x_i^2 \sigma_i^2 + \sum_{i=1}^{n} \sum_{j=1 \neq i}^{n} x_i x_j \sigma_{i,j}$$ (1.12)

where

$\rho_{i,j}$ is a correlation coefficient between returns on assets i and j.

Selecting stocks for the new portfolio out of the whole universe of assets available in the market, investors should not consider the risk associated with an individual asset as if it was held in isolation. They should rather focus on its covariance with other assets and, consequently, on how much it contributes to the risk of the entire portfolio. If all traders create efficient portfolios, then the whole market portfolio will also be efficient being a function of all investments run by investors at a given moment. In other words, it should not be possible to make investments that would offer a higher (abnormal) return than the overall market portfolio with the level of risk equal to market risk. Higher-than-market returns are possible, but only from portfolios that have higher-than-market level of risk, that is, their beta is greater than one.

Proponents of behavioral finance challenge the classical portfolio theory. First, they raise the already mentioned arguments to undermine the standard utility hypothesis and show that probability is incorrectly estimated. This suggests that fundamental assumptions behind Markowitz theory are not fulfilled. Since investors have unstable preferences and are not in a position to estimate risk correctly, one cannot expect that they should always take appropriate steps to maximize expected utility and be motivated in their investment choices only by the relation between the level of systemic risk and expected return. Another assumption that does not work in practice is the one related to normal distribution and the ability to precisely describe the process whereby returns are generated. Achieving the latter means that one must look beyond expected utility and variance at such parameters as distribution skewness.

Much more important objections raised by the proponents of behavioral finance are derived from empirical studies. These show that, in real life, investors remarkably often do not follow the rule of minimizing nonsystemic risk, running portfolios that are not diversified enough (De Bondt, 1998; Statman, 2002a, 2002b; Polkovnichenko, 2005; Goetzmann and Kumar, 2008). In addition, they do not attach enough importance to the issue of correlation between different kinds of assets (Kroll et al., 1988). We develop this discussion more in section 3.1 in chapter 3.

Shefrin and Statman (2000) claim that if people optimize the structure of their investments at all, they do it in a gradual fashion. Investors set up investment portfolios consisting of many layers, that is, they use sub-portfolios, each of which has a different purpose and relation to risk. For example, one sub-portfolio may serve as a pension scheme, another might be used to fund children's education, and yet another, burdened with a lot of risk, could be opened with a view to get rich quickly. Shefrin and Statman say that as investors take care of subsequent layers in the pyramid of needs to be fulfilled through investment, they disregard the problem of covariance between individual "layers." If they pay attention to covariance at all, it is limited to assets contained within one sub-portfolio. What is more, Shefrin and Statman argue that problems with correct application of Markowitz's theory relate not only to individual investors, but also to institutional ones. Even if professionals apply the classical portfolio theory more often and in a more sophisticated manner than individuals do, they still do not factor in the covariance between all the assets they manage, treating portfolio optimization fragmentarily, that is, only when it comes to individual asset categories (e.g., different types of investment funds, sectoral funds, style investing, etc.).

Low level of diversification and underestimating the importance of mutual correlation between returns on individual assets or group of assets blatantly undermine Markowitz's classical portfolio theory and may have far-reaching consequences. If some investors create inefficient portfolios, which sometimes leads to overweighting one group of assets to the detriment of others, the entire market portfolio might turn out to be inefficient. As a result, it turns out to be possible to make higher return at market risk or the same return as the market portfolio, but at smaller risk. The contention is vitally important when assessing validity and correctness of classical capital asset pricing models that are generally based on the pricing of market risk premium.

3.2. Capital Asset Pricing Model

Markowitz's portfolio theory paved the way for the Capital Asset Pricing Model (CAPM) formulated by Sharpe (1964), Lintner (1965), and Mossin (1966). In its general and most widely known form, the model posits that the risk premium on the capital market is directly proportional to the level of systemic risk:

$$E(R_i) - R_f = \beta \cdot [E(R_m) - R_f] \tag{1.13}$$

where:
$E(R_i)$ is expected return on asset i,
R_f is return from a risk-free instrument,
$E(R_m)$ is expected return from the market portfolio,
β is systemic risk measure calculated as:

$$\beta = \frac{\text{cov}(R_i, R_m)}{\sigma^2(R_m)} \tag{1.14}$$

where:
$\text{cov}(R_i, R_m)$ is the covariance between the return on asset i and return on market portfolio, whereas $\sigma^2(R_m)$ is the variance of the return on market portfolio.

The CAPM model was put forward based on a series of assumptions. Investors are risk averse and try to maximize utility, shaping their preferences in accordance with Von Neumann and Morgenstern's theory. They create efficient portfolios on the basis of Markowitz's portfolio theory, assessing them only from the angle of expected value and variance of returns, which are characterized by normal distribution. All market players are homogeneous, that is, they adopt the same single-period investment perspective, have the same amount of information, perceive reality in the same way, and harbor the same expectations. Capital market is perfect. There are no obstacles hampering the flow of capital and information (e.g., transaction costs, taxes). All assets may be bought and sold, including through short-selling. Finally, there are unlimited possibilities to borrow and lend funds at the same risk-free return with no market player being able to influence prices.

Most of the aforementioned assumptions are disproved in real life.[2] Let us not forget, however, that models are nearly always an idealized approximation of reality and cannot be dismissed only because their theoretical assumptions have not been met. We need to ask two questions at this point. First, can the standard CAPM model be developed in such a way as to remove at least some of the unrealistic assumptions? Second, how well does the model work in practice in spite of its restrictive conditions and how good is it when it comes to predicting return trends? (Szyszka, 2001).

Over the last decades, representatives of the classical theory of finance have published many theoretical papers in an attempt to modify the CAPM model with some of the assumptions removed. Lintner (1971) provided formal proof that the CAPM works correctly without the assumption of short-selling. Brennan (1971) analyzed the situation where risk-free loans are taken out and granted at different returns as well as where the returns available for individual investors are different. Black (1972) argued that CAPM does not require a risk-free asset as it may be successfully replaced by a synthetic zero market risk portfolio (beta = 0), that is, a portfolio with minimal variance and zero covariance with the market. Mayers (1972) showed that the idea behind CAPM may be expanded to include situations where investors are forced to keep also those assets that are nonmarketable. In such cases, the expected return is still the total of the risk-free rate and the expected premium for undiversified risk. Nevertheless, risk will be measured not just by means of covariance with the market portfolio. The measure will be broader—covariance between an individual asset and two portfolios: the one made up of marketable assets and the one with nonmarketable assets. Several researchers, including Lintner (1969), Sharpe (1970), and Gonedes (1976), analyzed the structure of the model with the assumption that investors do not have homogeneous expectations. In such cases, the condition of market balance can still be described in terms of expected returns, variance, and covariance. The problem, however, is that these values are weighted averages of expectations and preferences of individual people, which are always complex and difficult to determine. Lindenberg (1979) considered a theoretical possibility that there might be a trader who influences prices and showed that the CAPM model can still be used in such cases although the market risk premium will be lower. Another issue to consider was related to the multi-period version of the CAPM model. Fama (1970) analyzed conditions for which a multi-period selection between consumption and investment can be reduced to the goal of maximizing a single-period utility function. This means that the classical CAPM model can be used. Merton (1973a) suggested a multi-period version of the model that allows for many sources of systemic risk and many beta coefficients measuring individual risk components. Rubinstein (1976) and Breeden (1979) put forward a consumption CAPM in which investors maximize their utility function taking account of consumption levels at different stages of life. The return should be linearly dependent on fluctuations in the overall consumption level.

Removing some restrictive assumptions does not change the general nature of the CAPM, whereas adapting others leads to modification or addition of new elements. Still, the obvious common characteristic for all versions of the model is the fact that investors are risk averse and returns are dependent on the amount of the market risk accepted. According to the classical theory of finance, one should not expect higher average profit than what is indicated by the level of undiversified risk accompanying the investment.

Pioneer empirical tests of the CAPM were carried out by Black, Jensen, and Scholes (1972), and Fama and MacBeth (1973). The former group performed a time-series regression for returns of portfolios listed at the New York Stock Exchange (NYSE) in the years 1931–1965; the latter studied the period of 1926–1968. Results of their analysis generally confirmed that the CAPM works well as a tool describing the process shaping returns on the American market.[3]

However, later studies into a longer time period led to many controversial results. It was more and more often said that returns could be predicted not only on the basis of the beta coefficient, which was supposed to be the sole measure of systemic risk and, consequently, the only determinant of the expected risk premium. Other company characteristics could be used for that purpose. Banz (1981) and Reinganum (1981) were the first to document that stocks of small-capitalization companies yield higher returns than one might expect judging from the level of systemic risk measured by beta coefficients. Basu (1983) pointed out that shares with a low price-to-earnings ratio (P/E) offer higher returns compared to securities for which the ratio is high. Jaffe, Keim, and Wasterfield (1989) confirmed this relationship although they also noted the paradox that loser shares offer higher average returns too. Lanstein, Reid, and Rosenberg (1985) as well as Lakonishok, Shleifer, and Vishny (1994) indicated that it is possible to predict returns also on the basis of such parameters as cash-flow-to-market-equity ratio and historic sales growth rate.

Fama and French (1992, 1993, 1996) argue that the wide range of identified relationships may be in fact reduced to two important phenomena—the size effect and the book-to-market equity effect. They suggest a Three Factor pricing model (determined empirically instead of theoretically) in which the traditional market risk premium is supplemented by two additional elements related to the size of the company and the book-to-market equity ratio, elements not taken into account by the previously used beta measure of risk. Coming from the classical theory of finance, they argue that returns for small companies or companies with a high book-to-market equity ratio are higher than might be expected from the traditional CAPM because they represent a rational premium for unidentified elements of undiversified risk. Fama and French (1993, 1996) believe that the model they suggested might be considered to be a version of the intertemporal model of capital asset pricing put forward by Merton (1973a) or the arbitrage pricing theory (APT) developed by Ross (1976).

Proponents of behavioral finance do not negate the empirical observations made by Fama and French (1992, 1993, 1996), but they reject their interpretation. The only thing the Three Factor model demonstrates is that some earlier found relationships overlap, capitalization and the book-to-market equity ratio being the most effective in explaining returns. They account for the company size effect by the presence of individual noise traders and explain higher returns for companies with high book-to-market equity ratios as related to market overreaction. They challenge the classical school of thought, which says that if there were higher average returns for a given category of companies, they must have represented a rational premium for extra risk.

In the light of behavioral observations, asset pricing and market equilibrium models assuming that investors are risk averse and rational and the portfolios they hold efficient must fail. Since the level of risk aversion is different depending on arbitrarily chosen reference points and if risk aversion may change to risk propensity in a situation where investors want to postpone losses, they will not always require a risk premium. Given that decision makers cannot always interpret information they receive correctly and do not always know how to estimate probability, it would be difficult to expect them never to make mistakes when assessing risk and expected returns. If they do not create investment portfolios according to Markowitz's theory, it is likely that their portfolios offer the best possible combination between expected returns and variance. As a result, the market portfolio will not be efficient either. As you can see, the behavioral approach undermines the entire theoretical foundation on which proponents of the classical theory of finance build their asset-pricing models.

Empirical verification of any asset-pricing model is related to the problem of the so-called dual hypothesis. When empirical data do not confirm certain theoretical predictions, it is difficult to say with certainty whether this is due to a mistake in the model and its assumptions or not. After all, the model might be correct and justified from the perspective of theory, but irrational trading activity could make it ineffective as a tool for information processing and asset pricing.

3.3. Efficient Market Hypothesis

The Efficient Market Hypothesis (EMH) has been one of the key and hotly debated issues in the field of finance for almost half a century. According to the classical definition suggested by Fama (1970), an efficient market is a market in which prices always fully reflect available information. Market prices incorporate both information based on events that have already occurred and on events that, as of now, the market expects to take place in the future.

Roberts (1967) first distinguished, and then Fama (1970) adopted and wildly publicized, three basic forms of informational efficiency of capital market depending on the scope of information to be reflected in asset prices. Weak efficiency assumes that stock prices reflect all important information from historical pricing. Investors cannot predict how asset prices will behave in the future solely on the basis of past price changes. Semi-strong efficiency broadens the scope of information taken into account when pricing assets. It assumes that stock prices do not only reflect the information that can be obtained from historical prices, but also all other publicly available information such as company financial statements or earnings forecasts. Finally, strong efficiency means that no matter whether information is publicly available or private, confidential, and available to a small group of people, it is quickly reflected in stock prices only because it can be induced by observing actions of insiders.

Adopting one of the aforementioned levels of the efficiency hypothesis will have far-reaching consequences for market players, including investors and issuers because it means that assets are always correctly priced by the market on the basis of available information (depending on the level of the hypothesis, "available information" will be defined differently). However, the efficiency hypothesis does not imply that the asset price will always be exactly equal to its current fundamental value. In a world of uncertainty, exact intrinsic values are unknown. In an efficient market, at any point in time, the actual price of a security is a *good approximation* of its intrinsic value. The words "good approximation" need to be highlighted. At any given moment, it is equally probable that the asset is under- and overestimated with deviations from the real value being independent of any variables. Even the most professional investors cannot expect that they will always obtain results that are above normally expected returns for a given level of risk.

The EMH rests on three main assumptions. Each of them is progressively weaker. First, investors are assumed to be rational and hence to value assets rationally. They should value each security for its fundamental value: the net present value (NPV) of future cash flows, discounted by a rate appropriate to the risk level. When investors learn something new about future cash flows or risk attached to a particular security, they should quickly and appropriately (no under- and no overreaction) respond to the new information by bidding up prices when the news is good or bringing them down when the news is bad. As a consequence, asset prices should incorporate all the available information almost immediately. If anyone wanted to make consistently more money than the market average based only on publicly available information, they would always have to react to news quicker than the rest of market participants, and this is obviously not possible every time.

However, markets may remain efficient even if not all investors are rational and some of them make mistakes in perceiving and reacting to information. In such a case, it is assumed that irrational investors in the market trade randomly. When their trading decisions are uncorrelated, their impacts are likely to cancel out. Altogether they will not generate a market force that could influence the equilibrium prices. Their transactions only increase the trading volume. This argument relies crucially on the lack of correlation in the behavior of irrational investors.

However, even if irrationality becomes common for a relatively large group of investors who act in a correlated manner, and therefore are able to move prices away from fundamental levels, it is assumed that rational arbitrageurs quickly notice the mispricing and act appropriately. By selling the overpriced asset on one market and buying the same or similar asset on the other cheaper market, they create additional market forces that bring asset prices back to fundamentals. It is assumed that there are many rational arbitrageurs who act quickly and without any constraints. Abnormal arbitrage profits are reaped by the fastest players, and are difficult to be repeated constantly by the same players.

At first glance, the argumentation in favor of the EMH seems quite appealing. Until the mid-1980s, the EMH turned into an enormous theoretical and empirical success. Academics from the most prestigious universities and business schools developed powerful theoretical reasons why the efficient paradigm should hold. This was accompanied by a vast array of early empirical research—nearly all of them supporting the EMH. The idea that the market knows best was promoted in business press and taught at various MBA and other courses. It strongly influenced the investment community (increased popularity of index funds and the buy-and-hold strategy), but luckily not everybody. From the beginning of the 1980s, and more and more in the 1990s, new empirical studies of security prices have reversed some of the earlier evidence favoring the EMH. The traditional finance school named these observations anomalies, because they could not be explained in the neoclassical framework.

Behavioral finance questions all of the aforementioned assumptions as well as the very hypothesis of market efficiency, of course. The human mind is often imperfect in the way it perceives reality and processes information. Investors cannot price securities correctly and their preferences may change without any reason. Irrational behavior is far from being individual. It is often shared by specific groups of investors, which may lead to periodic problems with correct pricing. Market players, including the rational ones, may display symptoms of the so-called herd behavior in that they obtain information by observing how others behave, underestimating the results of their own analyses. This leads to a situation where they copy actions taken by others so that the market does not reflect part of private information known to its players. In extreme cases, investors may not be in the least interested in searching for and processing fundamental information about companies, adopting a purely speculative approach. They buy specific securities not because they are motivated by a rationally calculated ratio of risk and expected return, but most of all, because they expect that other market players will price the same instruments even higher in the near future. With this kind of approach, current market prices may naturally deviate from the real value of the securities. Even though rational arbitrageurs will have no problems noticing such deviations from correct pricing, they will not always be able to take active part and bring prices back to their fundamentals. The reason is that even rational investors often face limitations that do not allow them to benefit from the mispricing they notice.

3.4. Practical Implications to Investors

The EMH rules out the possibility of repeatable investment strategies based on currently available information that have expected returns in excess of the market expected return for a particular level of systematic risk. In other words, an average investor—whether individual or professional—should not hope to consistently beat the market. In the short term, achieving abnormal returns is possible, but only as a simple result of luck, and not due to whatever trading strategy used or resources spent on analysis. In the light of the EMH, the best investment strategy is the passive "buy & hold" approach—investors should hold well-diversified portfolios, allowing only for the systematic risk in the amount adjusted to a subjective degree of risk aversion. Frequent changes to the portfolio are not recommended, as active trading only generates transaction costs and cannot help at all to achieve long-term abnormal returns.

Behavioral finance challenges this view, a natural consequence of confronting the EMH. Because market is not always efficient, investors who make better than average use of available information are capable of making abnormal returns. In this light, it might be worth to seek good investment opportunities and to spend resources on the investigation of the mispricing that occur from time to time in the market. Active trading strategies might be indeed better than passive "buy & hold." This is a rationale for hedge funds, opportunity funds, and other examples of active portfolio management. However, active investors should bear in mind that they also may be subject to behavioral biases and heuristics. Therefore, achieving higher returns is possible, thanks to better analysis and strategies, but also requires better self-control.

Behavioral finance does not rule out completely the utility of traditional analytical tools and pricing methods derived from traditional finance. However, these models should not be treated dogmatically as the only precise way to judge investment choices. In the end, they are only a simplification of complex processes at work on real capital markets. Traditional finance should be seen more like a theoretical benchmark that needs to be enriched by various aspects of investors' psychology and human actions. Behavioral market models concentrate on predicting deviations from traditional models. They focus on investors' irrationality and attempt to identify factors responsible for its direction and strength. When mispricing is noticed, investors should ask themselves about the reasons for the situation and try to predict its future development. If behavioral analysis indicates a high probability of a further increase in irrationality, which may potentially lead to even more pronounced mispricing, then also for a rational investor it might be worth to "hop on the train" and buy assets that might seem overpriced according to traditional valuation methods. In the light of traditional finance, such a decision would be irrational, but in the framework of the behavioral approach, it is acceptable. It might bring abnormal returns as long as the investor is able to sell these assets for a higher price before irrationality gets weaker and the stocks are finally brought back to fundamental levels. Obviously, such practices of rational speculators do not contribute to market efficiency and stabilization.

4. Cornerstones of Corporate Finance

Corporations, being issuers of stocks and other securities, are naturally the other side of capital market in relation to investors. Traditional corporate finance theory shares many assumptions with the neoclassical financial economics and relies to a large extent on the foundations presented earlier. Corporate executives are assumed to act rationally and to maximize the expected utility of their decisions. The agency theory points out the possibility that the interest of a manager is sometimes different from the interest of shareholders; hence, a manager's utility maximization does not have to be identical with making most of the firm's value. However, incentives shaped by adequate compensation contracts, the market for corporate control, and other governance mechanisms are said to minimize potential moral hazards. As a result, traditional corporate finance typically assumes that managerial performance is targeted at maximization of shareholder wealth. The CAPM has been typically used to determine the cost of equity, which is of course the same figure as the expected return for investors, just seen from a different perspective. Under the EMH, the cost of firm financing should be always adequate and depend solely on how risky the company is. When considering an acquisition, managers can take for granted that other assets are also always correctly priced in an efficient capital market.

As the behavioral approach changes the way we look at investor behavior and asset pricing in capital markets, naturally it must also impact financial contracts and real investment that emerge from the interaction of corporations and investors. Behavioral corporate finance can be divided into two main areas based on distinctively different assumptions. The first approach emphasizes the effect of market inefficiency on corporate polices, assuming that executives act as rational professionals. In other words, it focuses on how a smart manager modifies corporate policy in order to exploit investor irrationality and market inefficiency. We explore this path in detail in chapter 7.

The second approach replaces the assumption of managers' rationality with evidence-driven psychological foundations. It shows how managerial biases may impact managerial practice, and if particular distortions are actually beneficial or detrimental to shareholders' wealth. This approach is discussed in depth in chapter 8.

While the existing literature has generally considered the two approaches separately, in practice, both managerial and investor irrationality may, of course, coexist. Let us now see how these behavioral frameworks affect the traditional aspects of corporate finance, that is the key problems of which assets to invest in and how to finance them.

4.1. Capital Budgeting and Investment Policy

Capital budgeting is the process by which a company determines how to invest its capital. Included in this process are the decisions to invest in a new project, reexamine the effects of the capital already invested in existing projects and reconsider the sense of project continuation, allocate capital across corporate divisions, or engage in mergers and acquisitions.

Under the assumption of a manager acting rationally in the best interest of shareholders, a decision to invest in a new project should be made according to whether the project increases the firm's value. Dean (1951) formally introduced the NPV rule that has been commonly advised by corporate finance textbooks for over half a century as the most comprehensive way a firm can assess the value that new investments are expected to create. It is based on discounting a project's cash flows, starting with initial investment expenditures and later hopefully positive revenues after the investment phase is completed. Forecasted cash flows should be discounted at the rate appropriate to the amount of risk that the project involves. Only if the project is not substantially different from the average risk of the firm, the overall corporate weighted cost of capital (WACC) can be applied as the discount rate. When the sum of project's cash flows discounted at the adequate rate is positive, then the project is worth undertaking. If a firm considers two projects with a positive NPV, but faces budgetary or organizational constrains to take up both, the one with a higher NPV should be chosen.

Because the estimation of a project's future cash flows and the rate at which they should be discounted is complex and difficult, but still relatively subjective, the evaluation process may be affected by managerial personal traits and psychological biases. Excessive optimism is likely to lift upward the forecasted cash flows, and overconfidence, understood as too narrow calibration of possible outcomes, leads to the underestimation of the project's risk, hence application of too low a discount rate. As a result, overconfident and optimistic managers tend to invest too much and often waste the resources in the way that does not contribute value to the firm. There are also various heuristics or often even plain errors that impact the NPV analysis. The residual value of the project is calculated under the assumption that cash flows are constant or growing at a stable rate after the early implementation phase. Calculating the residual value of the project with the annuity formula saves a lot of effort. However, projecting a constant growth rate into the indefinite future might be a really tricky part of the exercise given the NPV analysis is often highly sensitive to the residual value of the project. Another heuristic is related to applying the overall firm's WACC to a project that significantly differs from the average risk profile of the company. Mistakes between nominal and real interest rates constitute yet another frequent problem in the practical application of the NPV rule. The common error is to prepare cash flow forecasts in inflated nominal figures while applying a real discount rate or vice versa.

In chapters 8 and 10, we argue that managers not only commit mistakes when appplying the NPV, but often they use simpler tools, including various rules of thumb, when making investment decision. For example, a relatively common habit of calculating the payback period totally neglects the meaning of the project's risk.

Managerial biases and mistakes in project evaluation coexist with intentional nonoptimal investment decisions. These may be motivated by catering for investor expectations resulting from temporary fads. Some investments might be taken up simply because they are fashionable and well-perceived by investors. Catering is short-term oriented. It is intended to boost the stock price temporarily above the fundamental value at the possible expense of the long-term shareholders.

Under some special circumstances, managerial overconfidence and excessive optimism in investment might be advantageous. It is argued in chapter 8 that those biases sometimes allow to overcome risk aversion and to take up some valuable projects that otherwise would be rejected. Perhaps, many sparking ideas would have never materialized if their chances of success had been diligently and rationally scrutinized. For example, the underdiversified nature of entrepreneurial engagement, both financial and personal (time, effort, reputation, opportunity costs), might not have been offset by the vision of potential high rewards, if the probability of success had not been biased upward by overconfidence and optimism.

Mergers and acquisitions are theoretically justified as long as they create synergy that is shared by both the target's and the bidder's shareholders. However, there is a lot of evidence indicating that it is typically only the target's shareholder who benefits from acquisitions by securing high takeover premiums. In the latter part of this book, we discuss the evidence on merger activities in more detail. We present evidence that managers attempt market timing as well as fall victim to individual psychologically driven mistakes. For example, rational managers observing that their stock is overvalued may decide to engage in a merger and pay for the acquisition with their overpriced equity. This might be interpreted as beneficial to long-term investors of the bidding firm. Alternatively, overconfidence, narcissism, and excessive optimism may incline the manager to heavily overpay for the targeted firm. In this case, bidder's shareholders are likely to be harmed.

Overall, behavioral distortions in corporate investment policies may result not only from market inefficiency but also directly from managerial biases. Both sources lead to serious consequences for the real economy. Asset mispricing or inadequate project valuations result in inefficient use of resources and the general misallocation of capital in the economy as a whole.

4.2. Financing Policy and Capital Structure

Financing policy determines how corporations secure funds for the investment projects they undertake. It consists of a mixture of decisions that in the end results in a given corporate capital structure. Within the scope of their financial policy, companies make decisions to issue new equity, go public, pay out dividends or repurchase shares, take more or less debt of short- or long-term maturity, and so on.

Modigliani and Miller (MM, 1958) formulated their famous theorem of capital structure irrelevance to corporate value. In a perfect capital market, the value of a company depends simply on its income stream and the degree of attached business risk, regardless of the way in which its income was split between providers of financing, that is, between shareholders and lenders. Higher returns from leveraged equity are just a compensation for a higher level of financial risk resulting from more debt in capital structure. In a similar framework of a perfect capital market, MM (1961) and Lintner (1962) formulated the theorem that dividend policy is irrelevant to company value. The capital loss on stock price just offsets the cash dividend shareholders receive. The logic of MM arguments, both related to capital structure and dividend policy, rests on the principle of arbitrage eliminating any returns that would not be justified by risk. They assumed that firms can be grouped into homogeneous risk classes such that the market seeks the same return for the same risk category, investors formulate similar expectations about future company earnings that are described by a normal distribution, players are price-takers (no individual can influence market prices) and act rationally to maximize their wealth, all market participants, firms, and investors can lend and borrow at the same risk-free rate, all information is free and easily available, and there are no personal or corporate taxes, transaction costs, or other market frictions. The assumption of a perfect capital market is actually much stronger than the assumption of market efficiency. These restrictive conditions were necessary to isolate the critical variables affecting the firm value. Even if their setting was unrealistic, MM contributed enormously to understanding the links among capital structure, risk, payout policy, and corporate value. Their work provided a systematic basis for traditional corporate finance to develop further concepts in which at least some of the unrealistic assumptions are repealed.

MM (1963) extended their initial model by introducing personal and corporate taxation. In the presence of taxes, the capital structure may actually matter to corporate value. They demonstrated that debt financing is preferable due to the fact that under most of the taxation regimes, interest payable on debt constitutes a tax-deductable cost (so-called tax shield). However, too much of debt increases the risk of bankruptcy and incurs financial distress costs. This consideration paved the way for the trade-off theory of capital structure (Kraus and Litzenberger, 1973). In the trade-off model, managers choose the mix of debt and equity that strikes the balance between the tax advantages of debt and various costs related to financial distress. In other words, in the optimal capital structure, the marginal tax shield benefit equals marginal costs associated with potential insolvency. Although this optimal point is easy to draw on theoretical function curves, it is extremely difficult to estimate in practice. Under the trade-off model, one might expect to find that firms enjoying higher profits and more stable cash flows should use debt financing more extensively. However, this prediction is inconsistent with empirical findings (Fama and French, 2002b).

The pecking order theory, first suggested by Donaldson (1961) and later formally developed and popularized by Myers and Majluf (1984), predicts that firms tend to use their accumulated internal funds first, then debt financing, and decide to raise money from new equity issuances only as a last resort. Myers and Shyam-Sunder (1999), and Fama and French (2002b) confirm such preferences of financing sources empirically. However, Frank and Goyal (2003) find contradictive evidence, particularly among smaller firms. The pecking order theory is based on two main assumptions. First, managers are better informed about the investment opportunities faced by their firms than are outside investors. Second, managers rationally act in the best interest of existing shareholders. Myers and Majluf demonstrates that under these conditions, a firm will sometimes forgo positive-NPV projects if accepting them means that the firm will have to issue new equity at a price that does not reflect the true value of the company's investment opportunities. This, in turn, provides a rationale for maintaining financial slack, such as large cash and marketable securities holdings or unused debt capacity. Asymmetric information also gives grounds to the signaling hypothesis. Debt financing is favored over equity as the issue of debt signals managerial confidence that the firm's investment opportunities are profitable and that the current stock price is undervalued.

Signaling hypothesis was also applied to market reaction to dividend announcement. Contrary to MM (1961) proposition, Healy and Palepu (1988) document a positive reaction to dividend initiations and much stronger negative reaction to dividend omissions. They interpret this not as a indication of investor preference of dividends over capital gains, but as the sign that dividend initiations and omissions convey information about future company earnings and that the market can efficiently read these signals.[4]

Behavioral finance argues that the same capital structure preference as predicted by the pecking order theory may result from managerial overconfidence and excessive optimism. As discussed in more detail in chapter 8 and empirically confirmed in chapter 10, an overconfident and optimistic manager overestimates the value of his firm's investment opportunities and considers his stock to be undervalued. Hence, he is strongly reluctant to issue new equity. Overconfidence and excessive optimism also make him underestimate the risk of new projects; so he will subjectively consider available debt financing as too costly. As a result, he will depend on internal funds first. Graham and Harvey (2001) and Shefrin (2005) argue that surveys of managers give little support to the information asymmetry or signaling hypotheses. Instead, there is some direct evidence that the standard pecking order preference seems to be actually driven by managerial overconfidence and excessive optimism.

Another approach within the context of behavioral reasoning relates to market timing. In this framework, managers are assumed to act rationally in the interest of long-term shareholders and to exploit temporary market mispricing and investor irrationality. Rational managers acting in inefficient markets tend to issue equity when market valuations are high and announce repurchase programs usually after the stock has been severely downpriced. They also engage in timing the debt market, not only in respect to issuing more debt when interest rates seem to be particularly low, but also balancing between short-term and long-term maturity of debt.

Finally, behavioral finance argues that in some cases, rational managers may cater to investor tastes. In other words, managers respond to temporary fads and changing investor preferences, adapting the corporate policy so that it looks favorable in investors' eyes and fits the current market sentiment. Catering is targeted at boosting the current stock price above its fundamental value. As market fads are typically short-lived and investor preferences tend to change over time, the effect of catering is also likely to be short term. Baker and Wurgler (2004a) argue that the dividend puzzle is one of the main candidates to be explained by the catering theory. Market timing and catering to investor tastes are discussed in detail in chapter 7.

4.3. Practical Implications to Corporate Managers

If markets are efficient, then the cost of alternative sources of financing is always priced correctly. Current market situation should not influence corporate capital structure. Companies should not be extra motivated to make equity offerings in a bull market when they are potentially overpriced, nor to repurchase their stocks in a bear market when they seem to be undervalued. Resources should be always allocated to best investment projects and these projects should be taken up only if they add value to the firm. Mergers and acquisitions should only happen if they generate real synergy.

Behavioral finance offers a different view. High market valuations are motivation for issuing new equity. Relatively low cost of equity lowers total weighted average cost of capital (WACC) for the company, as well as financing cost for a given project (if this is considered individually at all). Cheaper financing boosts investment, as more projects have positive NPV. On the other hand, when the market is bearish, the company will tend not to make new equity offerings. New investment projects will be financed with a higher leverage or put on hold. More debt will be allowed in the capital structure. Low market valuation may also stimulate the company to repurchase its stocks.

In the behavioral approach, it makes sense to seek an optimal moment for a new equity offering or a buyback transaction. It is also helpful when planning a takeover of another firm, particularly in the form of a public tender offer. Knowledge of investors' preferences is necessary when structuring the transaction and trying to set the price right. For example, even if a price in a tender offer is higher than the current market price (takeover premium), but the tender offer takes place after a series of negative returns, the reply to the offer may not be sufficient. This may happen, because investors are stopped by a strong aversion to losses, if the tender price is set below their reference point that usually is their purchase price. In fact, tender offer prices tend to cluster around historical peaks, particularly the 52-week peak. We elaborate more on this in section 3.4 in chapter 8.

Psychological aspects are also important when communicating with the market. The way the news is framed, that is, how it is put into words or numbers, may influence the strength and sometimes even the direction of market reaction to it. People usually overreact to good information and underreact to bad news. They pay more attention to a descriptive report than to statistical or numeric data. They are sensitive to the context in which the information is given. For example, assume that the current firm's performance is better than last year, but worse than earlier forecast and market expectation. News like "Current profit is higher than last year's profit by" will be definitely better received than the same information formulated like this: "Current profit is lower than expected by"

Finally, we should not forget that a corporate manager may also be subject to behavioral biases. Wrong judgment of probability accompanied by overconfidence may lead to underestimating the risk of an investment project. A particularly strong and dangerous inclination is associated with so-called sunk costs. Decision makers are usually unwilling to give up a project that has already consumed a lot of money and effort. Even if it becomes more and more obvious that the project has little chance to be profitable, managers are often ready to throw more and more money into it. They do not want to admit their mistake and attempt to delay the moment they have to report a loss on the investment. This is similar to the disposition effect observed among stock market investors. The sunk cost effect and the disposition effect have both their roots in the strong human aversion to accept final losses. We discuss managerial biases in chapter 8 and provide some empirical evidence in chapters 9 and 10.

CHAPTER 2

Psychological Aspects of
Decision Making

In its quest to explain the phenomena taking place in the capital market, behavioral finance has drawn a lot on psychological findings applying selected insights of this branch of science to the study of investor behavior. The great majority of these insights do not provide theoretical background as such. Rather, they concern certain phenomena previously described by psychology which were later transposed onto economics and finance. Only then were they used to construct models of investor behavior and develop a new school of thought in the theory of finance.

What follows is a presentation of selected elements of psychology which behavioral finance refer to when explaining how people construct their beliefs, how preferences emerge and how emotions influence the decision making process.[1]

1. Beliefs Formation

1.1. Perception of Information

Psychologists believe that the human mind is limited in its ability to focus and process all the incoming information. They also stress that the final form our decisions take is often strongly influenced by the signals received by our subconscious.

One of the widely discussed psychological phenomena is the so-called *framing effect* (Kahneman and Tversky, 1984, 2000; Kahneman and Lovallo, 1993; Read et al., 1999). This consists in analyzing problems without paying attention to their wider context or even in an extremely isolated way. Experiments carried out by Tversky and Kahneman (1981, 1986), among others, showed that, because of such narrow perception, decision makers may display changing preferences and make radically different choices depending on the way in which the same, logically identical problem was presented to them.

One version of the framing bias is the so-called *money illusion*. Even though people generally know the difference between the real and nominal value of money, there is a lot of evidence suggesting that their perception is remarkably often dominated by nominal values. For example, a pay rise of 2 percent with inflation running at 4 percent will be much better perceived by the employee than a reduction of 2 percent when there is no inflation (Shafir et al., 1997).

Another instance of framing is *mental accounting* in which individual aspects of financial decisions are perceived in isolation (Thaler, 1985, 1990, 1999). People create different "accounts" in their mind for various expenses or revenues. They also link together specific categories of inflows and outflows. To illustrate, people are easier about spending money won at a lottery but more careful with their hard-earned savings, even though, objectively speaking, the economic value of 1 dollar won at a lottery is the same as 1 dollar earned at work. They will have one "account" where they post savings kept "just in case," another for savings made in order to buy an apartment, and still another for a loan taken out to purchase a car. Yet, it is not economically rational to keep low-interest deposits and take out a usually more expensive loan at the same time. From the psychological perspective, however, such choices made by decision makers are justified. The reason is that savings are earmarked for a different purpose (posted to a different "account") than the loan.

What may be especially important is separate accounting for profit and loss because decision makers usually have different preferences depending on whether they relate to gains or losses. We may assume, therefore, that people will take a different view of profit and loss considered separately than they would at the aggregated level. This notion is one of the key concepts of the prospect theory by Kahneman and Tversky (1979) that will be presented in section 2.1 later in this chapter.

Another widely discussed distortion of perception and information processing is the *anchoring bias*. Kahneman and Tversky (1974) pointed out that when people try to estimate a parameter or quantity, they start their thought process by adopting a value that is sometimes completely arbitrary. It is only later when they process more information and look for the right answer that they gradually move away from the initially assumed figure. Nevertheless, there is overwhelming empirical evidence to suggest that people become very strongly attached to the initial value (the "anchor") and are not able to adjust their final estimates correctly. It is a paradox that the initial value may be suggested to the decision maker in different ways and will often influence the process of estimating the right answer even though it might be totally disconnected from the problem at hand and completely irrelevant to it (Chapman and Johnson, 1994; Strack and Mussweiler, 1997).

The anchoring bias is most often illustrated by the following experiment conducted by Tversky and Kahneman (1974). In the experiment, subjects were asked to estimate the percentage of African countries in the United Nations (UN). The study was carried out following a specific procedure: First, respondents were requested to spin a "wheel of fortune" to generate a number between 0 and 100. Next, they had to say whether they believe the percentage of African countries in the UN is lower or higher than the randomly selected number. It was only after they did this that they were asked to estimate the actual percentage of Africa's representatives among all UN members as precisely as possible.

It turned out that the initial, totally arbitrary anchor value significantly influenced participants' responses. For example, the median estimates were 25 for the group that received 10 as a starting point and 45 for the group that started the study with 65.

The anchoring effect is valid for both laypersons and experts in a given field. Northcraft and Neale (1987) proved that, when estimating the value of a house, professional real estate appraisers are very much influenced by the price suggested by the owner. Most probably, the anchoring effect works on the subconscious level if over 90 percent of the experts in the study insisted that the owner's expected price had no impact on the value they estimated.

Stephan and Kiell (2000) asked two groups of professional financial analysts to forecast the value of the German Stock Index (DAX) for the next 12 months. First, respondents were only asked if they thought that next year the index was going to be below or above the threshold of 4,500 points (question in group one) or 6,500 points (question in group two). Next, they were asked to provide an accurate forecast. The value suggested in the first question proved to be an important "anchor" for the forecasts as a result of which the average forecast value in group one was significantly lower than the same value in group two.

Trying to estimate the probability of an event, people often rely on their memory and search for relevant information from the past. But memory might be selective and our consciousness is most responsive to those signals that can be remembered most easily. Constructing our beliefs, we usually attach too much importance to information that is readily available, extreme, and often repeated, for example, in the media. We also overemphasize things we know from our experience and generalize events that became lodged in our memory simply because they happened to us or in our direct environment. The tendency to overestimate probabilities or frequency of events we can remember easily is called the *availability bias* (Tversky and Kahneman, 1973; Taylor, 1982).

A version of the availability bias is the so-called *halo effect* (Thorndike, 1920; Nisbett and Wilson, 1977a; Rosenzweig, 2007). It is a form of bias in which, having perceived a distinctive characteristic they like in others, people tend to extend their positive judgment and are convinced that the evaluated person, thing, or phenomenon has many more desired features.

According to the theory of *self-perception* (Bem, 1972), people get to know themselves by observing their own behavior in different situations. When taking action or deciding how to treat new information, they remember what they did in various other situations. This approach facilitates the formation of *habits* or self-imposition of *rules of behavior*, including various rules of thumb used by investors or corporate managers.

Reception and assessment of incoming information is also frequently influenced by its clarity to the recipient and the ease with which he can take in and process new messages. Our perception is often marred by the so-called *illusion of truth*, whereby we are more willing to accept as true those statements that seem clear to us even though they might be in fact false. At the same time, we reject as untrue the information that we perceive as complicated and difficult to decipher (Reber and Schwarz, 1999).

The illusion of truth is also at work when oft-repeated statements are identified as true after a time regardless of their factual quality (Hawkins and Hoch, 1992; Skurnik et al., 2005). What is more, Gilbert, Krull, and Malone (1990) and Begg, Anas, and Farinacci (1992) showed that even those statements that are initially perceived as blatantly false are accepted as the truth if they have been repeated many times. In other words, an untrue rumor that is widely disseminated and will be repeated often enough may eventually be considered by the investors to be valuable information.

Furthermore, when people receive incoming information, they sometimes link it irrationally with totally unrelated factors. Such *magical thinking* is present in a belief in astrology, different superstitions, reliance on lucky numbers, and other similar attitudes that are sometimes important aspects of decision making and constructing beliefs (Tambiah, 1990).

1.2. Overconfidence, Optimism, and Narcissism

A lot of evidence suggests that decision makers are generally overconfident. This can be manifested in three basic ways: above-average effect, calibration effect, and illusion of control. Overconfidence is usually closely linked with excessive optimism and unrealistic wishful thinking. It is also related to narcissism, which, however, is more a personal trait than a cognitive bias.

First, when making assessments and constructing beliefs about reality, people consider their knowledge and skills to be *above the average*. They rate themselves better than the average man. For example, in different surveys, 60 percent to 90 percent of the respondents claimed that they had above-average driving skills or better-than-average sense of humor. They also said that they stood less-than-average chance of developing a specific disease and were less-than-average likely to be victims of mugging, and others (Weinstein, 1980; Svenson, 1981; Barberis and Thaler, 2003). Yet, if we were to divide the entire population in two by each of these criteria, those who are better than average cannot possibly constitute more than 50 percent. This means that a large group of people overestimate their capabilities.

Overconfidence is also evident in the so-called *calibration bias* (Lichtenstein et al., 1982; Yates, 1990; Keren, 1991). When asked to provide information or make a forecast without being precise but estimating within a certain confidence range, people usually give answers which indicate that they are overconfident as to the precision of their knowledge. Alpert and Raiffa (1982) demonstrated that responses given by respondents with an alleged 98 percent certainty actually turn out to be correct only in about 60 percent of cases. Fischhoff, Slovic, and Lichtenstein (1977) showed that events that respondents claimed would certainly occur in reality took place in only 80 percent of cases on average, whereas events classified as impossible occurred in 20 percent of cases. De Bondt (1998) confirmed the existence of the calibration error among stock exchange investors.

In certain cases, expertise or experience are helpful for the right calibration (Oskamp, 1962; Sieber, 1974); however, experts who are aware of their know-how in a given field may often fall into the trap of overconfidence to a much higher degree than nonexperts (Lichtenstein and Fischhoff, 1977). Overconfidence is a characteristic of representatives of numerous professions, including physicians (Christensen-Szalanski and Bushyhead, 1981); psychologists (Taft, 1955; Oskamp, 1982), engineers (Kidd, 1970), negotiators (Neale and Bazerman, 1990), and financial analysts (Stael von Holstein, 1972). Barber and Odean (2001) document overconfidence among investors and March and Shapira (1987), and Ben-David, Graham, and Harvey (2007) provide evidence on overconfidence among corporate managers.

Professionals are exposed to a particular risk of overconfidence if a specific task is vague and does not carry unambiguous premises that suggest the right solution (Griffin and Tversky, 1992). In such circumstances, they often follow patterns and stereotypes instead of processing the information and clarifying the problem. It is astonishing that having made the wrong assessment once, when subsequent information appears that gradually clarifies the problem, experts become increasingly convinced that they have examined the case properly, and they tend to not change their initial opinion. The conviction of being right increases despite the inflow of an increasing amount of data that indicate the contrary (Oskamp, 1982).

Overconfidence grows with the degree of difficulty of the tasks and if there are no prompt signals from the environment that confirm or negate previous information or previously made decisions (Fischhoff et al., 1977; Einhorn, 1980; Lichtenstein et al., 1982; Yates, 1990; Griffin and Tversky, 1992). Lichtenstein and Fischhoff (1977) show that, paradoxically, people demonstrate underconfidence in very easy tasks. De Bondt (1998) argues that investors exhibit more overconfidence when asked for long-term predictions than in short-term forecasts. Gender is also a factor in the degree of people's self-confidence. Usually, men are more confident than women, although differences in this respect also depend on whether a specific task is perceived as a man's or woman's domain (Deaux and Emswiller, 1974; Lenney, 1977; Lundenberg et al., 1994).

Overconfidence also manifests itself in the *illusion of control*: People are frequently convinced that their actions may positively affect totally random outcomes. Langer (1975) documents that lottery players place a higher value on the tickets for which they themselves picked the numbers than on the tickets filled in by the quick-pick lottery machine. Strickland, Lewicki, and Katz (1966) show that the illusion of control may incline decision makers to accept higher stakes of risks.

Overconfidence is also related to *excessive optimism* and unrealistic wishful thinking, resulting in various kinds of planning errors due to the underestimation of negative factors and overestimation of positive outcomes. Buehler, Griffin, and Ross (2002) give numerous examples of the improper estimation of the time required to complete planned assignments. The problem concerns both plans related to large-scale public investment (e.g., construction of buildings, infrastructure projects) and matters of everyday life (e.g., shopping, car washing, writing another article). Failing to meet the deadline often results in the additional problem of overstepping the planned budget. Merrow, Phillips, and Myers (1981) compare forecast and actual construction cost for investment projects in the energy sector. Statman and Tyebjee (1985) survey several other studies of this sort in the design of military hardware, drugs research, chemicals, and other development projects, and conclude that optimistic biases in cost estimation and sales forecast are fairly widespread. Moreover, it seems that planners do not learn from previous mistakes. Although aware that previous forecasts were very often too optimistic, they still unrealistically believe that, next time, their predictions will actually prove to be accurate.

Problems with proper planning are not only related to incorrect estimation of time or costs of a specific project or task, but also to forecasting of more general economic figures. For example, Montgomery (1997) collected macroeconomic forecasts about inflation, gross domestic product (GDP) growth, unemployment, and so on, estimated by various experts over many years. He then performed an ex post comparison of the forecasts with the values actually observed. It turned out that the forecasts of unfavorable effects (e.g., inflation, unemployment) were systematically underestimated, whereas predictions of positive effects were generally overestimated. Olsen (1997) similarly demonstrated excessive optimism among financial analysts.

Narcissism is a personal trait that is related to but distinct from overconfidence. The central idea of narcissism is that individuals are not only convinced about their superiority but also have a need to maintain a positive sense of self by engaging in ego-defensive high-stake activities. Campbell, Goodie, and Foster (2004) document in experimental studies that narcissists display greater overconfidence and more willingness to bet. Liu (2009) and Aktas, de Bodt, Bollaert, and Roll (2012) investigate narcissism among corporate executives in the real setting of mergers and acquisitions.

Overconfidence is supported by the *selective-attribution bias*, which consists in people attributing successes (even random ones) to themselves and their capabilities while explaining failures by independent factors, such as bad luck, mistakes made by others, and so on (Langer and Roth, 1975; Miller and Ross, 1975; Fischhoff, 1982; Taylor and Brown, 1988). Lack of objectivity in the assessment of successes and failures limits the ability to learn from one's own mistakes and supports the persistence of overconfidence. Another paradox related to overconfidence is the *hindsight bias*, which consists in people being erroneously convinced that a specific unexpected event could have been predicted. The possibility and importance of random events are systematically underestimated (Fischhoff, 1982). For example, following a totally unexpected event a lot of people will say: "It didn't come as a surprise at all, I knew this before," which only increases their faith in their capability to correctly predict and assess all situations (Hawkins and Hastie, 1990).

What is especially dangerous is a combination of different forms of overconfidence as it results in people overestimating the breadth of their knowledge, underestimating risk, and exposing themselves to unpleasant surprises, which, to make matters even worse, will not teach them to know better in the future. Hegel, the German philosopher, once said: "We learn from history that man can never learn anything from history."

1.3. Representativeness, Short-Series Problem, and Regression toward the Mean

Representativeness heuristic is a mental shortcut where the probability of an event or a state is estimated through assessing the degree to which incoming information is similar to a specific remembered pattern (Kahneman and Tversky, 1973; Tversky and Kahneman, 1974; Grether, 1980). In other words, if we want to know whether a given set of data X was generated by model Y or whether object X belongs to a certain class Y, we should look for similarities between X and crucial features of Y. The approach itself might make sense, but its practical application is often fraught with serious mistakes that have impact on the final decisions.

People overreact to information of a descriptive nature downplaying the importance of base probability resulting from statistical data (Kahneman and Tversky, 1973; Tversky and Kahneman, 1982; Griffin and Tversky, 1992). Having noticed a distinct quality, which is usually typical of a specific category, respondents are overconfident about the probability that the case they are dealing with belongs to the category of events, objects, or people represented by this quality (e.g., reliance on stereotypes). They underestimate the fact that, statistically speaking, it is more likely that the case belongs to another category, for example, one which is more frequent in real life.

People do not pay enough attention to the representativeness and size of the sample on the basis of which they estimate probability and draw conclusions (Bar-Hillel, 1982). They often overemphasize information derived from small samples to the detriment of signals generated by samples containing a lot of observations. Ignoring the size of the sample when the real process of data generation is unknown, respondents may jump to conclusions or construct ungrounded rules or patters based on too few observations. Gilovich, Vallone, and Tversky (1985) describe the so-called hot hand phenomenon in basketball. It occurs when, after three successive hits by one player, both the spectators and coaches become deeply convinced that the player is more likely to score a fourth hit than other players on the court. It turns out, however, that hard data do not confirm this pattern.

On the other hand, when the decision maker is familiar with the process governing data generation (e.g., occurrence of heads or tails when tossing a coin), underestimating the importance of sample size may result in the so-called *gambler's fallacy*. For example, if four consecutive tosses of a coin give four heads, many people will expect that they will get more tails in the following tosses to "catch up with" and even out the number of heads. Expecting more tails stems from the erroneous belief that even in a small sample, the number of results should reflect the probability distribution.[2] But the chances of getting tails are the same each time. Only in a large sample of, for example, 1,000 tosses, a considerable advantage of heads over tails could suggest that there is something wrong with the coin and the randomness of the process generating results.

Incorrect perception of randomness results in the so-called *short-series problem* where people underestimate the possibility of relatively long series of results generated completely at random. Shefrin (2000) conducted an experiment in which he asked one group of subjects to toss a coin 100 times and record the sequence of results while another group was asked only to imagine the tosses and put down their imagined sequence of heads and tails. It turned out that empirical series from group one was much longer than the other group imagined it to be. People believe that randomness must entail frequent changes of results. In fact, getting five heads in a row is as probable as a sequence of three heads and two tails. It is easy to imagine that the short-series mistake may be behind attempts to find trends and patters in totally random sequences.[3]

Kahneman and Tversky (1973), and Tversky and Kahneman (1974) point at another problem that is related to the short-series bias. People often misinterpret the *principle of regression toward the mean*. According to the principle, the values of successive observations get closer to the mean of a given feature in the entire population. Reoccurrence of extreme observations is not likely. One example of failing to account for the principle of regression toward the mean is excessive extrapolation of good and bad average student grades (Shefrin, 2000). We must remember that good grades obtained by a student are partly a reflection of his actual knowledge and partly a function of luck. Similarly, bad grades of another student were certainly caused by his ignorance, but could also be a product of independent factors (unlucky questions, bad physical condition on the day of the exam, etc.). As a result, one might assume that in the following academic year, the gap between the average grade of the student who was best the previous year and the average grade for the entire population will narrow. By the same token, the average grade of the worst student will most probably be closer to the average for all students the following year. However, the principle of regression toward the mean must not be overinterpreted. It does not say that where there have recently been values above the average, we should expect result *below* the average in the future. We can only suppose that subsequent observations will be *closer* to the average value for the entire population calculated on an ongoing basis. The principle does not therefore mean that the best student from last year will suddenly have results below the average.

1.4. Beliefs Updating

The reality surrounding us is very dynamic. Almost every moment brings new information that forces us to constantly revise our previous beliefs and forecasts. The key question though is whether the human mind is capable of catching up with this multitude of news. Also, can such information be correctly received and processed in the context of preconceived notions? There is a lot to suggest that we cannot properly update our forecasts in the light of new facts and that we often treat such facts in a selective manner.

Theoretically, verification of probability in the context of new information should be done following the Bayes's rule, as discussed in section 1.5 in chapter 1. Edwards (1968) proved that even though new information usually triggers a change in opinion in the direction predicted by the Bayes's rule, the value of the change is far from satisfactory. People usually display excessive *cognitive conservatism* and are slow to react to new information. Edwards (1968) conducted the following experiment: There are 1,000 chips in each of two identical bags. One bag contains 700 red and 300 blue chips, the other 300 red and 700 blue chips. A coin is tossed to select the bag from which chips will be drawn. So the probability that chips will be drawn from the bag in which the great majority of them are red is 50 percent. Next, 12 chips are drawn. It turns out that there are 8 red and 4 blue. Acting on this information, respondents were to estimate the probability that the bag chips were drawn from was predominantly red. Most respondents gave answers in the range of 70–80 percent when the correct probability estimated on the basis of Bayes's rule should amount to as much as 97 percent.

On the face of it, cognitive conservatism might seem to contradict the tendency described in the previous section whereby people jumped to conclusions on scant information. However, although representativeness bias may stem from such factors as overreaction to clear, descriptive signals conforming to a stereotype, cognitive conservatism occurs when such signals cannot be assigned to any specific pattern familiar to the decision maker. In such cases, the new information is likely to be underestimated, and the decision maker will focus on his initial assessments (Barberis and Thaler, 2003).

Revising their beliefs, people are not only slow to react to the new signals, but also often fall victim to the so-called *confirmation bias*. This consists in a tendency to look for information confirming a previously adopted hypothesis while avoiding confrontation with facts that could contradict one's current opinions or disturb a previously developed attitude toward a problem (Wason, 1966; Lord et al., 1979). Assessing the validity of the cause-and-effect relationship between two variables (e.g., between implementing a specific investment strategy and realized returns), people focus on cases where both variables were observed simultaneously (e.g., a specific rule was followed giving better-than-average results). At the same time, they seem not to notice examples of only one variable occurring without the other (e.g., the strategy did not yield abnormal results or abnormal returns were obtained without following the rule). Adopting this selective approach, the decision maker may fall victim to the *illusion of validity*, that is, he will persist in his erroneous beliefs or even become more entrenched demonstrating overconfidence (Einhorn and Hogarth, 1978; Shefrin, 2000).

If there is no information that could even partially confirm previous convictions or decisions, people sometimes resort to *rationalization*—they construct ex post a credible justification for the choices they made (Nisbett and Wilson, 1977b). Just like the confirmation bias, rationalization may also contribute in part to the already described overconfidence in belief formation.

Finally, Newman, Wolff, and Hearst (1980) argue that people attach greater importance to events that have occurred than events that did not happen even though they had been expected to happen. Yet, the lack of an event may be equally or sometimes even more significant than its occurrence.

2. Preferences

What we have presented so far are selected psychological phenomena illustrating how people perceive reality, construct their beliefs, and revise them. Let us now focus on those factors that may contribute to shaping a decision maker's preferences.

2.1. Prospect Theory

Probably the biggest contribution psychology made into the development of behavioral finance is the prospect theory put forward by Kahneman and Tversky (1979) to explain how people attribute subjective values (utilities) to objective results of their choices. The prospect theory counters the standard utility theory of Von Neuman and Morgenstern (1944), which had previously dominated classical economics even though it was often criticized in the literature because of the restrictive and unrealistic axioms it was based upon.[4] However, while Von Neuman and Morgenstern's theory is normative, the prospect theory is supposed to be descriptive in nature. Tversky and Kahneman (1986) go as far as to argue that the normative approach is doomed to fail as people routinely make choices that cannot be justified by normative axioms. Instead of the normative model, they suggest a descriptive theory based on a series of experiments conducted by themselves and other psychologists.

In the initial version of the prospect theory, Kahneman and Tversky (1979) limited themselves to lotteries with the maximum number of two non-zero results. Later, Tversky and Kahneman (1992) generalized the prospect theory for any number of possible results. For the sake of clarity of presentation, let us focus on the earlier simpler version. Kahneman and Tversky (1979) suggest that if a decision maker is offered the following prospect (lottery)

$$(x, p; y, q),$$

that is, a lottery as a result of which he may achieve result x with probability p and result y with probability q or nothing with probability $1 - p - q$, where $p + q \leq 1$ and $x \leq 0 \leq y$ or $y \leq 0 \leq x$, he will make estimates based on two subjective functions: value and weighting. Out of many prospects (lotteries), the decision maker will prefer the one that will have the highest total value (utility) V understood as in equation (2.1)

$$V(x, p; y, q) = \pi(p)v(x) + \pi(q)v(y), \tag{2.1}$$

where π is the weighting function, whereas v is the value function and $v(0) = 0$, $\pi(0) = 0$, $\pi(1) = 1$. Both weighting function π as well as value function v have specific qualities that will be discussed later.

Kahneman and Tversky posit that a decision maker analyzes the value of an alternative through the prism of profit and loss in relation to a reference point he adopted rather than from the perspective of absolute wealth. They argue that the human mind is naturally more focused on assessing ongoing changes than evaluating final states.

Kahneman and Tversky (1979) illustrate this describing results of the following experiment in which respondents were faced with two decision problems.

In the first one, each of the respondents "got" 1,000 as an addition to everything he had. Next, respondents were asked to choose between two alternatives: A—win another 1,000 with the probability of 50 percent or win nothing, B—be sure to get 500. Most of the respondents chose alternative B. The same people were then faced with another problem. This time round, each "got" 2,000 as an addition to everything he had. Next, they had to choose between option C—lose 1,000 with the probability of 50 percent or lose nothing of the 2,000, option D—be sure to lose 500 from the 2,000. Most of the respondents chose option C. This means that, in the former case, most subjects were risk averse—in the latter, they were prone to take risks. Yet, options A and C as well as B and D in both cases result in identical final wealth.

Value function v attributes to each result x, that is, each change in relation to the adopted point of reference, value $v(x)$. Of course, the exact shape of the value function will be subjective for each decision maker. Nevertheless, Kahneman and Tversky believe that some properties of value functions are shared by most people. They argue that the value function will be concave above the reference point in most cases ($v''(x) < 0$ for $x > 0$) and convex below the reference point ($v''(x) > 0$ for $x < 0$) (Figure 2.1). This means, for example, that decision makers will be more ready to appreciate the difference between the profit of 100 and 200 than the one between the prospect of the profit of 1,100 and 1,200. Similarly, the difference in the amount of loss between 100 and 200 will be more painful than the difference between losses of 1,100 and 1,200. Consequently, people are usually risk averse when faced with alternatives of earning profit and prefer risky strategies when they have to choose between lotteries generating losses.

Exceptions from this general rule may happen in special cases: First, when an individual decision maker needs a given amount of money very much, or,

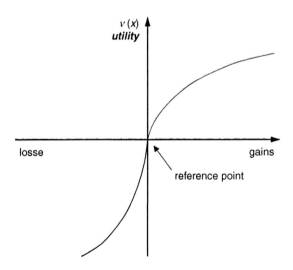

Figure 2.1 Shape of a hypothetical value function v according to the prospect theory.
Source: Own work based on Kahneman and Tversky (1979).

second, when the loss above a specific value would be unacceptable for him as it could, for example, drastically diminish his quality of life. It is in these exceptional situations that the shape of the value function in the vicinity of critical values may run counter to the general rule. To recapitulate, in order to obtain an amount of money that is really indispensable, the decision maker may pursue very risky strategies (value function is convex for profits!). On the other hand, if potential losses are close to the critical value that the decision maker is ready to accept, he may display aversion to such risky strategies (value function is concave for losses!). However, such situations are exceptional.

Another property of the value function is its steeper slope (higher values of the first-derivative function) for losses (i.e., for $x < 0$) than profits (i.e., for $x > 0$). In other words, satisfaction (positive value of function v) caused by earning profit on the amount of x will be lower than dissatisfaction (negative value of function v) caused by the loss of the same absolute value. The combined convex shape and steeper slope of the value curve for $x < 0$ translate into a phenomenon known as *loss aversion*. Tversky and Kahneman (1992) attempt to experimentally estimate the loss-aversion coefficient. They claim that it amounts in most cases to 2.25. Hence, in order to compensate for the "discomfort" of suffering a loss of, say, 100 units, one needs to generate a profit that is more than twice as high, that is 225 units.

The other function influencing the assessment of total prospect utility is the weighting function π that attributes weight $\pi(p)$ to each probability value p (Figure 2.2). Kahneman and Tversky are very clear that function π is by no means a measure of probability and does not fulfill probability axioms. This could only be the case if people were always correct in formulating their preferences on the

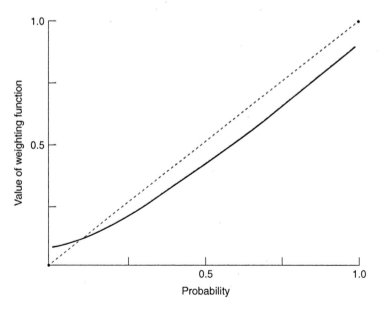

Figure 2.2 Shape of a hypothetical weighting function π according to the prospect theory.
Source: Own work on the basis of Kahneman and Tversky (1979).

basis of probability distribution and could determine such distribution precisely. In practice, both are very difficult.

Naturally, π is an increasing function p ($\pi'(p) > 0$), assumes the value of $\pi(0) = 0$ and $\pi(1) = 1$, but is not a linear function. Kahneman and Tversky claim that people usually attach too much importance to very small probability values, that is, $\pi(p) > p$ for small p. They stress that, in their theory, a decision maker can precisely estimate probability p, so if he overweights small p values, it is not because he estimated probability incorrectly, but because he has specific preferences that are reflected in the weighting function π. In real-life situations, however, if a decision makers often finds it difficult to estimate p correctly, we may assume that prospects with small probability might be overweighted even more resulting from the combination of weighting function values and the overestimation of p itself.

Overweighting small probabilities has been confirmed by experiments showing that people prefer lotteries in which they can win a large amount with very small probability to a safe alternative guaranteeing the expected value of the lottery. Furthermore, people will usually prefer to suffer a relatively small loss than expose themselves to a highly unlikely possibility of a major loss (e.g., they will pay insurance premiums).

Kahneman and Tversky (1979) give the following example. A decision maker needs to choose from: option A—take part in a lottery offering 5,000 with the probability of 0.001; or option B—be sure to get 5. Most respondents choose option A. Next, the following choice is offered: option C—take part in a lottery where 5,000 may be lost with the probability of 0.001; or option D—be sure to lose 5. This time round, most respondents choose option D.

Another property of weighting function π is the so-called subcertainty where for all $0 < p < 1$ the weighting function assumes such values as $\pi(p) + \pi(1- p) < 1$. This means that people are more sensitive to differences in the degree of probability on higher levels, that is, in the case of relatively probable events. The property has been confirmed by experiments demonstrating the *certainty effect*. It occurs when people prefer to be certain of getting a specific value to participating in a lottery offering a slightly higher expected value, but at a small risk.

The weighting function is also discontinuous near points $p = 0$ and $p = 1$ as people are often limited and inconsistent in the way they perceive extreme probability values. Highly unlikely events are once treated as impossible only to be overweighted a moment later. Similarly, very probable variants are sometimes perceived in a simplified way as events that are certain—at other times, they are underestimated.

To sum up, the most important tenets of the prospect theory are the following. First, a decision maker assesses different alternatives focusing first and foremost on changes in relation to a specific reference point rather than on final values resulting from such changes. Therefore, he is sensitive in his preferences to the context (reference point) against which alternatives were presented to him. If the context changes, the preferences may change as well. Second, decision makers are usually risk averse in the area of profit and risk-prone in the area of losses. Third, people dislike losses much more than they want profits (loss aversion).

Finally, decision makers attach too much importance to highly unlikely events, underestimating those where the probability is relatively high. On the one hand, overestimating unlikely events may override general aversion to risk in the area of profits and, for example, make a decision maker buy a lottery ticket. On the other, the same phenomenon may dissuade a decision maker from habitual risk aversion in the area of losses and convince him to buy an insurance policy.

Prospect theory can explain a raft of irrational actions taken by decision makers, actions blatantly contradicting the classical utility hypothesis. Most importantly, it allows for the instability of decision maker's preferences, a phenomenon that is very often observed empirically (Allais, 1953; Lichtenstein and Slovic, 1971, 1973; Kahneman and Tversky, 1979, 1984; Grether and Plott, 1979; Tversky and Kahneman, 1986; Tversky and Thaler, 1990).

2.2. Ambiguity Aversion

So far, the discussion was based on the assumption that decision makers face choices between alternatives whose probability distribution is objectively known. In reality, however, the probability of many events is not defined precisely and must usually be estimated subjectively when making a decision.

When it comes to analyzing cases with undefined probability distribution, the equivalent of the classical utility hypothesis of Von Neumann and Morgenstern (1944) is the theory of subjective utility proposed by Savage (1954). According to the theory, preferences stem from utility function expectations weighted by probability estimates made individually by the decision maker. The theory was also based on a number of restrictive axioms, one of which is the assumption of additivity imposing a condition that the total of all probabilities estimated by the decision maker for different alternatives must be equal to one.

Comprehensive empirical psychological studies suggest that most people try to avoid lotteries with undefined probability distribution. In other words, they display *ambiguity aversion* (Ellsberg, 1961; Fox and Tversky, 1995; Rode et al., 1999). Making decisions under ambiguity is tantamount to making choices of uncertain result and undefined risk level. In such cases, people often take actions that belie the principle of rational expectations and run counter to the theory of subjective utility. The choices they make undermine the axiom of additivity, among others. The most often cited example of such irrationality is the Ellsberg's paradox.

Ellsberg (1961) conducted the following experiment. Subjects are presented with two urns. Urn 1 contains 100 balls, some of which are red, some blue. The ratio of blue and red balls is not known. Urn 2 contains the total of 100 balls—50 red and 50 blue. Respondents are asked to choose one of the following lotteries:

a_1—you draw a ball from urn 1 and get 100 dollars if the ball you drew is red or get nothing if the ball is blue,

a_2—you draw a ball from urn 2 and get 100 dollars if the ball you drew is red or get nothing if the ball is blue.

The great majority of respondents choose lottery a_2 where the ball is drawn from the urn with defined probability distribution. The same people are then required to make another choice between lotteries with contradictory rules:

b_1—you draw a ball from urn 1 and get a 100 dollars if the ball you drew is blue or get nothing if the ball is red,

b_2—you draw a ball from urn 2 and get a 100 dollars if the ball you drew is blue or get nothing if the ball is red.

Again, the great majority of the subjects prefer to draw from the urn with defined probability distribution choosing lottery b_2. Such behavior is irrational. Theoretically, choosing lottery a_2 in the first case is logically justified only if the decision maker subjectively believes that urn 1 contains less than 50 red balls and so urn 2 offers higher probability of drawing red. But if this was the case, why does he still want to draw from urn 2 in the second stage? After all, this time round, he gets a reward if he draws a blue ball.

Heath and Tversky (1991) suggest that the degree of ambiguity aversion may depend on how competent a decision maker feels in the field where he is supposed to estimate probability. The higher qualifications he thinks he has, the less concerned and more ready to accept the ambiguous situation he will be. Conversely, if someone feels incompetent in a given field and does not know clear rules of the game (i.e., its probability distribution), he might be concerned that he will be abused by players having more expertise and better judgment (Frisch and Baron, 1988). In a similar vein, Fox and Tversky (1995) demonstrate that making decision makers aware of their incompetence will typically increase ambiguity aversion. The lack of competence may be shown by pointing out other people who are better placed to assess the ambiguous situation or by indicating to the decision maker other areas in which it is more competent. In such a case, the decision maker will usually decide to choose the lottery with defined probability distribution (if it is available) or a lottery in the field where he is more competent. As a result, he will stand a better chance of estimating probability correctly, at least in his own opinion.

2.3. Status Quo Bias and the Endowment Effect

Samuelson and Zeckhauser (1988) documented that preferences may be heavily dependent on the status quo present when making a decision. It turns out that we are incredibly often reluctant to take steps that would change the current situation. We are biased toward maintaining the status quo even though our preferences would be completely different if we were to make the same choices without any information on the current state of affairs. Samuelson and Zeckhauser conducted an experiment in which they asked different groups of respondents to specify their investment preferences given various alternatives of investing a hypothetically inherited sum of funds. Each time, the respondents were to choose whether to invest in: stock of a moderate-risk company and moderate expected return, stock of a high-risk company and high expected return, treasury bills. The task was slightly modified for each group, that is, one group did not get any additional information about the form in which the funds were inherited, whereas other groups were told that at the moment of inheritance, the funds were in the form of one of investment opportunities. For example, one group learned that the funds consisted of moderate-risk stocks, while for another, they were treasury bills. Respondents were asked to state their investment preferences given that they are free to manage the funds as they want and there are no transaction costs. It turned out that average preferences in each of the groups were markedly different displaying the status quo bias. Respondents showed a strong inclination to keep the funds in the form they had inherited them.

Related to the status quo effect is the so-called *endowment effect*. It consists in people attaching more value to things they currently have than to identical objects that are not in their possession (Thaler, 1980; Knetsch and Sinden, 1984; Knetsch, 1989; Kahneman et al., 1990, 1991; Loewenstein and Kahneman, 1991). This leads to such phenomena as a considerable discrepancy between the sales price for which the owner of a thing would be willing to sell it and the purchase price he would be prepared to pay for the same thing. In one of their experiments conducted on an artificial market without transaction costs and other frictions, Kahneman et al. (1990) demonstrated that the required sales price might be even two times higher than the acceptable purchase price. It was documented that the discrepancy of this size occurred not because the suggested purchase price was deflated but because owners inflated the sales price. Similarly, Loewenstein and Kahneman (1991) argue that the endowment effect does not result from assessing a given thing as particularly attractive, but first and foremost from the discomfort related to parting with something we already received.

The endowment effect may be explained with the prospect theory. After all, dissatisfaction of having to part with a possession (suffering a loss) is much greater than potential positive feelings caused by obtaining the same object (making a profit). Therefore, decision makers require higher remuneration for more dissatisfaction (higher sales price) than they are ready to pay for positive sensations (lower purchase price) even though both situations concern the value of the same object.

2.4. Preferences in Time

Traditional economic analysis of preferences in time is based on the theory of discounted utility suggested by Samuelson (1937). According to the theory, decision makers will postpone consumption only when the level of utility for future consumption is sufficiently higher than the utility of current consumption. The required difference between the levels of current and future consumption is determined by the discount rate. One of the central axioms in Samuelson's theory of discount utility is the stationary nature of the discount rate. In other words, preferences toward two alternatives with different consumption levels will only depend on the time interval between the occurrence of one or the other alternative.

However, psychological literature on decision making records many cases when the discount rate is not constant. Thaler (1981) and Benzion, Rapoport, and Yagil (1989) documented three basic properties of the discount function that contradict stationarity. First, the further compared alternatives are in time from the moment of making a decision, the lower the discount rate required by the decision maker. This phenomenon has been named *hyperbolic discounting* (Kirby and Markovic, 1995; Azfar, 1999; Hirshleifer, 2001). For example, a decision maker will give up on immediate consumption of one apple on the condition that there is an alternative of eating at least three apples on the following day. However, if he were to choose between eating one apple in a week or in eight days, he would require only one additional apple to decide to wait. In both cases, the decision maker postpones consumption by one day but the required "premium for waiting" is different. Studies have shown that decision makers apply particularly high discount rates when they forgo immediate consumption having a strong preference for consuming results right away.

The second property highlighted by Thaler (1981) and Benzion et al. (1989) is the fact that decision makers use different discount rates in the case of choices where alternatives differ only in terms of the nominal value. People discount small values by significantly higher discount rates compared to large values analyzed in the same time period. For example, faced with the choice between 10 dollars immediately and 15 dollars in the future, the decision maker may decide to wait, but not longer than, say, two days. However, if the same person were to chose between getting 1,000 dollars immediately and 1,500 dollars in the future, he would decide to wait for, for example, a month. In Thaler's experiment (1981), respondents attached the same value to the prospect of getting 15 dollars immediately or obtaining 60 dollars in a year (sic!—discount rate of 400%). Next, the same respondents were ready to postpone consumption of 250 dollars when offered the prospect of getting 350 dollars in a year (the discount rate of 40%) and delay the consumption of 3,000 dollars with a view of getting 4,000 dollars in a year (the discount rate of 33%). Please note the unrealistically high discount rates, especially in the first case.

Another observed inclination is the one of applying various discount rates for gains and losses (Thaler, 1981; Benzion et al., 1989; Loewenstein and Prelec, 1992). It turns out that profits are much more discounted than losses. People will usually require a higher premium for refraining from consuming profit than they are prepared to pay for postponing a loss. Slower discounting of losses is related to loss aversion from Kahneman and Tversky's prospect theory (1979). A unit of loss is more important to the decision maker (hurts more) than a unit of profit earned at the same time.

The prospect theory is also in the background of discounting future utilities in relation to a previously adopted reference point combined with loss aversion. People who already know the date (reference point) when they are supposed to get a given amount of consumption will require a much higher premium for exceeding that date than they themselves would be willing to pay in order to speed up the consumption before the planned date by the same number of days (Loewenstein, 1988; Loewenstein and Prelec, 1993). In other words, getting something faster (i.e., profit in relation to the reference point) is less appreciated than the equivalent delay (loss in relation to the reference point).

Loewenstein and Prelec (1993) show that the fact that a decision maker uses reference points may in some special cases result in negative discount rates, a phenomenon that is totally irrational from the perspective of the traditional utility theory. It means that decision makers may prefer to postpone favorable events choosing disadvantageous events first. This may happen in such cases as preferring sequences with a growing trend in the level of consumption or choosing a sequence where advantageous and disadvantageous events take place alternately.

Thaler and Johnson (1990) point out the instability of a decision maker's preferences depending on the results of previous choices. In particular, they document changeability in the attitude to risk caused by previous experiences. A previous win will decrease the degree of risk aversion and encourage decision makers to take part in a new lottery. A loss suffered in the past, on the other hand, makes people more sensitive to risk. They will often not take up another challenge even if they would have accepted it under normal conditions, that is, without previous experiences. Importantly, unlike the prospect theory, which is static and concerned with a decision maker's choices in a single lottery, Thaler and Johnson's suggestions are dynamic and describe changes in the attitude to risk in the case of subsequent choices made for an entire sequence of lotteries.

3. Emotions

3.1. Mood and Weather

Psychologists argue that the decisions we make may be heavily dependent on emotional states. In general, people in good mood are more optimistic in their judgments and more willing to take risks (Johnson and Tversky, 1983; Wright and Bower, 1992, inter alias). On the other hand, in a bad mood, incoming information is usually assessed more thoroughly and critically (Petty et al., 1991). Mood swings have an especially strong impact on how decision makers evaluate abstract, temporarily distant phenomena about which they do not have any specific or precise information (Forgas, 1995). The role of emotions in risk perception and decision making was systematically expanded on by Loewenstein et al. (2001). They argue that each element of the decision process is influenced by emotions. Dowling and Lucey (2005) also provide an overview of literature on the role of emotions and feelings in decision making.

People shape their preference depending on their mood even when the reason for the good or bad feeling is completely unrelated to the area in which they need to make a decision. For example, Arkes, Hercen, and Isen (1988) noticed a significant rise in the sale of state lottery tickets in Ohio in the days directly following a victory by a local football team.

It is widely documented that mood depends on weather conditions. More daylight means less depression (Eagles, 1994); less skepticism (Howarth and Hoffman, 1984); and more optimism, happiness, and well-being (Persinger, 1975; Schwarz and Clore, 1983).

Observations made by psychologists inspired studies into weather's influence on stock market returns. Saunders (1993) proved that there is a statistical relationship between the level of cloud cover over New York City and changes of the *Dow Jones Industrial* index as well *NYSE/AMEX* indexes. With total cloud cover, returns for the indexes were usually below average. On sunny days (cloud cover up to 20%), indexes usually increased more than on average. Trombley (1997) confirmed the relation between extensive cloud cover and lower rates of return on indexes, but was not able to find a statistically significant interdependence that would suggest higher rates of return on sunny days. Similar results were obtained by Kramer and Runde (1997) when it comes to the German *DAX* index and the weather over Frankfurt am Mein. Hirshleifer and Shumway (2003) carried out more comprehensive studies to analyze the influence of weather on index changes on 26 stock markets all over the world. The negative correlation between the level of could cover and rates of return was basically confirmed on 22 stock markets, although with relatively low statistical significance.

One general remark about testing weather impact on stock returns relates to the implicit assumption that traders are geographically concentrated in the area where the exchange is located and the weather is observed. However, in the era of convenient telecommunication means, and particularly having a possibility of placing orders over the Internet, investors might actually be located far away from the physical place of transaction. Hence, the relationship between weather and returns may not be so much evident. This is especially likely in the case of those national exchanges where turnover volume is dominated by foreign investors residing in major financial centers worldwide.

3.2. Regret and Disappointment

Regret is a psychological reaction to making a choice whose outcomes proved disadvantageous (Bell, 1982). The feeling of regret will be especially strong when it turns out that an alternative, previously rejected in favor of the wrong decision, would have brought desired results. For example, we will regret less having invested in company X stocks whose price has decreased if the alternative investment in stocks Y we had considered would also have generated a loss. However, our regret will be much more acute if the price of stocks X falls while the market is bullish (Nofsinger, 2001).

We usually are less regretful of lost profits we have not earned because we did not decide to act than of the same losses suffered as a result of a wrong decision. Kahneman and Repie (1998) give the following example: Investor X had company A stocks and was thinking about selling them to invest the proceeds in stocks B. Finally, he decided not to sell A stocks. Investor Y had company B stocks and decided to sell them to invest in company A stocks. It then turned out that the price of company B stocks went up while stock price of company A remained constant. Which of the two investors will regret more? Most respondents mention investor Y. This is of course in line with the previously discussed loss aversion derived from Kahneman and Tversky's prospect theory (1979).

The feeling of regret will also be much greater if the wrong decision is taken as an exception from rules or habits normally adhered to. The regret of a man who usually invested his savings in safe treasury bills but made a loss because he invested in stocks by way of exception will be much deeper than the regret felt in the same situation by a seasoned stock market speculator who is used to ups and downs (Shefrin, 2000).

Regret will also be exacerbated if the wrong decision was made individually. When this happens, one cannot put the blame on anyone else or identify external factors that could be made responsible for the failure. A decision maker's ego will suffer all the more if he is a narcissistic or reputation-conscious person as it is often the case with fund managers or financial analysts (Harbaugh, 2002). Regret for not having obtained a desired result will be especially painful if it was relatively easy (probable) to achieve the outcome. We usually feel less regretful if it was evident from the outset that chances for a positive solution were rather slim.

Feeling regret because of a wrong decision may lead to being passive in the same situation in the future. Tykocinski and Pittman (1998) demonstrated that people who reject an attractive purchase offer first time round and regret doing so are usually not interested in the second, slightly worse offer either even if it is still more attractive than the market price. The same applies to sales. In one of the experiments carried out by Tykocinski and Pittman (1998), two groups of respondents purchased stocks whose price subsequently rocketed. After the sharp increase stopped and the prices started to fall slightly, one group of "investors" was given the possibility to sell its stocks and earn a considerable profit. The other group was not allowed to do so. As often happens in real life, part of the people making up the first group chose to sell their stocks while others decided to wait believing that a slight drop in prices was just a small adjustment and the price will start rising again soon. Unfortunately, the downward trend continued; so those who rejected the offer to sell must have regretted it later. Next, when the price was just slightly higher than the one of initial purchase, all respondents were given the possibility to sell. Almost all "investors" from the second group, which was not allowed to dispose of stocks previously, decided to sell and make even a small profit. However, those who belonged to the first group and did not decide to sell previously, did not want to sell the stocks the second time round even though it was evident at this point that stock prices are not likely to rise. Regret for not having benefited from the first offer hampered "investors" from taking up the second one, which, while less attractive, still guaranteed some profit.

However, it is not only the feeling of *experienced* regret that may influence decisions people make. Concern about *future* regret may also play a part. In general, people are averse to regret, both realized and potential. The theory of regret in decision making was developed in a structured way independently by Bell (1982) as well as Loomes and Sugden (1982). According to the theory, the final utility of a given alternative is influenced by two functions: a value function and a separate regret function increasing with the difference between outcomes of selected and rejected alternatives. Hence, final utility does not only depend on the proceeds from the actual decision, but also on results of alternatives that were skipped when making the choice. The profit earned following the choice will have less utility if it turns out that an alternative could have been more beneficial. On the other hand, achieving the same result being aware that the other option would have brought a loss generates much more utility for the decision maker. Therefore, in the light of the regret theory, an investor may be motivated to purchase a lottery (stocks) also because he wants to avoid the regret of missing an opportunity for a major gain. For example, Bar-Hiller and Neter (1996) present an experiment in which respondents are clearly reluctant to exchange a previously obtained ticket for a lottery. They suggest that this attitude is caused by fear of deep expected regret in the case the surrendered ticket turned out to be the winning one. Nonetheless, the same person may decide to buy an insurance policy to protect himself not only against loss but also against the feeling of regret of not having bought the policy when it turns out that it is needed. Dodonova and Khoroshilov (2005) attempt to apply the regret theory directly to asset pricing.

An emotion that is close to regret but usually has less of an impact on the decision-making process is disappointment. We have mentioned before that the feeling of regret arises when the outcome of a decision is disadvantageous to the decision maker, that is, if his loss or lost profit would not have taken place if he chose an alternative he rejected. Disappointment, in turn, is experienced when the results of a choice fall short of decision maker's expectations. Disappointment may, but does not have to, accompany regret. Just as in the case of regret, decision makers will usually try to avoid disappointment taking it into account as one of the many factors against which they assess alternatives and make choices (Bell, 1985; Gul, 1991). Aversion to disappointment may sometimes lead to attaching irrational values to alternatives depending on the assumed level of expectation. For example, a decision maker may be more satisfied with a loss of 8 dollars if he expected losing 32 dollars than with a 8 dollar gain if he expected a 32 dollar profit (Mellers et al., 1998).

3.3. Greed and Fear

Representatives of behavioral finance argue that investors experience two strong, contradictory feelings when making decisions in the capital market. Greed is related to the prospect of enrichment and it is the main causative factor for accepting risky investments. A moderate amount of greed is good in the capital market, and overall in the economy, because it makes people overcome the general risk aversion and gives motivation for many initiatives. However, too much of greed can blind people in pursuit of higher consumption.

Fear is a negative feeling triggered by the possibility of suffering a loss and it works in an opposite direction, discouraging risky behavior. It is a sort of emergency brake preventing investors from taking excessive risk when pursuing profits. The degree of fear will be the higher, the greater the loss the investor is exposed to. The loss should not be understood in absolute terms, however, but as a relative diminishing of investor's property (level of consumption) in the case the market moves against him. To illustrate, the prospect of losing 10,000 dollars may trigger terrible fear in a small investor of limited means but will ring no alarm bells for a millionaire. The feeling of fear will get especially strong if the potential loss might jeopardize the living standard enjoyed so far and force the investor to reduce consumption considerably. Under extreme circumstances, fear may turn into panic, that is, a situation when the top priority is to minimize risk, regardless of heavy losses. Panic is actually one of the few forces that can suppress general loss aversion.

Simultaneous feelings of greed and fear constantly impact investor decisions. Shefrin and Statman (2000) argue that investment portfolios are made up of two kinds of instruments. On the one hand, there are those that safeguard the minimum consumption level determined individually by the investor. On the other, there are very risky, but potentially profitable instruments that may make true an investor's hopes of quick enrichment and improve his quality of life. For example, the purchase of treasury bonds will first and foremost safeguard the real value of savings, generally offering only a small premium for delayed consumption as a potential extra benefit. On the other hand, investing part of the funds in risky stocks, especially those that are selected as a "bet" on a number of companies, without proper diversification, is a reflection of an investor's hope for high profit, which could move him from his current consumption level to the one he aspires to. So the simultaneous influence of fear and greed on the capital market leads to similar forms of behavior as the ones we can observe outside the stock exchange in people who buy insurance policies against adverse events at the same time buying lottery tickets hoping that fate will smile on them and change their lives (Statman, 2002b).

PART II

Investor Behavior and Asset Pricing

CHAPTER 3

Investor Behavior

This chapter discusses the different attitudes investors adopt when making decisions about buying securities and managing investments in the capital market. It shows how psychological factors described in the previous chapter may impact investors' beliefs about future price changes, influence the perception of company value, investment selection, and portfolio management. The discussion that follows usually focuses on individual players, but may sometimes also be relevant for professional investors.

1. Forecasting the Future on the Basis of Past Events

1.1. Extrapolation Bias

Extrapolation bias consists in overemphasizing trends observed in the past, especially over a relatively short period. Such trends are erroneously extrapolated onto future periods. One example of extrapolation bias is when investors make long-term financial forecasts assuming that the company they analyze will have same sales or profit growth rate as the one observed in the last reporting periods. Doing so, they often ignore extraordinary events whose influence on the recent level of sales and profit might have been only temporary. It is worth remembering that spread sheets are nothing more than a tool to prepare forecasts and will accept any data on dynamics entered into them. A forecast extrapolated many periods into the future on the assumption of continuously high growth rates may produce results bordering on the absurd. If the assumed growth rate is too high, financial forecasts will be overestimated resulting in overly optimistic pricing of stock.

Investors and analysts all too often forget about one of the basic microeconomic rules. If an entity earns profit which is above the average in a given sector, we should expect that sooner or later (depending on how strong barriers of entry there are) there will be other entities trying to emulate the successful strategy. More competition will decrease margins bringing profits back to the average level. This is why, barring exceptional cases (e.g., monopoly, patented know-how, very strong barriers of entry), one cannot assume that sales or profits will maintain high growth dynamics for long.

For example, a company that has just placed a new, top-quality product on the market (a bestseller) usually has high sales and profit rates. Investors extrapolate good results into the future and assign high prices to the stock of the company. Current high valuation is based on the expectation that the growth continues in next periods. But the question remains whether competitors will not offer similar products or their substitutes in the future at lower prices, which will decrease the profit margin and bring the company's profitability to the average that is typical for the sector. If investors did not account for such a possibility in the current price, they may be unpleasantly surprised in the future when the returns turn out to be disappointing. Conversely, there might be a company that, while reporting poor financial results, does have some important assets allowing it to go through a restructuring process. At present, its stock price is relatively low as investors do not believe it is possible for the company to change and extrapolate that it will keep on struggling. However, if the restructuring works, the returns on investment in the company will be exceptionally high.

Extrapolation bias is indirectly related to the representativeness error and the problem of investors not taking account of regression toward the mean. Combined with overconfidence and unrealistic optimism, this makes the market overreact. Overreaction is considered to be one of the potential reasons for the momentum strategy in the short term (Jegadeesh and Titman, 1993) as well as the contrarian strategy in the long term (De Bondt and Thaler, 1985, 1987). It is often argued to explain high price volatility in the stock market (Shiller, 1981, 1990). We discuss these aspects in detail in chapters 4 and 5.

While the extrapolation error committed when preparing forecasts of financial performance will result in current stock prices that are markedly different from the real intrinsic value and may immediately cause a hike in the price or its overestimation, the same error committed when trying to forecast future trends in stock price changes on the basis of historical data (setting aside the irrationality of such practices) may strengthen an investor's beliefs that the trend will continue.

1.2. Following Trends

Some market players are convinced that returns on stocks develop in a predictable way following a specific trend. There is even a popular market saying: Trend is your friend. This attitude contradicts the efficient market hypothesis saying that successive changes of stock prices in a time series should be independent of one another. If the market processes all new information quickly and efficiently, such information being, by definition, unknown to traders beforehand and unpredictable, changes in stock prices should remain random.[1]

Results of empirical studies using long time series of observation for individual securities seem to corroborate this hypothesis. In general, both older studies (Cootner, 1964; Fama, 1965; and King, 1966), and more recent ones benefiting from much better computing power (Campbell et al., 1997) do not confirm the presence of statistically significant autocorrelations between returns on individual assets in long observation series. The situation is different in the case of changes in stock market indexes and the returns on properly structured asset portfolios. Lo and MacKinlay (1988) and Campbell, Lo, and MacKinlay (1997) document a statistically significant autocorrelation between both changes in index values and returns on portfolios. On the one hand, this might suggest that prices can be predicted up to a point for particular groups of securities (e.g., if the price of stocks belonging to one company increases, investors become interested in stocks of other companies with a similar profile). On the other, it might be related to a series of microstructural market determinants (asynchronicity of transactions, the bid-ask spread, etc.).

Investors often observe historical stock prices very closely trying to identify patterns in totally random time series. They wrongly interpret consecutive series of rises and falls in stock prices as a trend forgetting that even relatively long strings of similar observations might be purely coincidental. Doing so, they make the so-called short-series error mistakenly expecting that historical returns continue in future periods, which, in turn, is a version of the extrapolation error.

If a sufficiently large group of investors is strongly convinced that the observed series of changes mark a beginning of a new trend, and if this conviction is buttressed by signals coming from popular strategies based on technical analyses or relevant comments made by analysts in the media, a self-fulfilling prophecy may set in and indeed trigger a further wave of rises or falls. This will convince more investors that the trend has really turned and it may be expected to continue. Actions taken by subsequent "trend observers" boarding the "leaving train" will only confirm the direction of changes. In addition, completely random series of changes may activate certain kinds of automatic orders. For example, institutional investors often apply the so-called stop-loss strategy. The strategy consists in sell orders being automatically put in when the price of stocks falls beneath a prespecified level. This is how an observed series of falls suddenly generates a large extra supply of securities, which contributes to assets being deflated even further creating the impression that the trend continues.

In his survey studies, De Bondt (1993) finds that investors are more willing to wait for the continuation of a trend when the market is bullish rather than bearish. This seems understandable in the context of the psychologically documented phenomenon of excessive optimism and wishful thinking. De Bondt also shows that investors have skewed confidence intervals. In other words, investors expect that the trend will continue, but they are also aware that, should they miscalculate, the price change in the opposite direction will be much greater than the possible underestimation of the price change following the trend. De Bondt suggests that this is a case of double anchoring—the first anchor is the recent price *changes*. These are, as it were, automatically extrapolated onto future periods. The other is price *levels*, which compel investors to set a relatively low minimum price, which may occur in the event the trend turns, a price which is close to the level from the beginning of the observed period. Importantly, the above observations are relevant most of all for small investors as De Bondt also demonstrates that it is the "novices" who usually expect that the trend will continue, experts being more often aware that it can be reversed.

On the other hand, Shefrin (2000) gives numerous examples of how renowned financial specialists were wrong in their predictions that a trend would reverse. Those predictions were most often the result of the gambler's fallacy combined with the misinterpreted principle of regression toward the mean. After a period of sharp sequences of rises or falls in the market, experts often argue that the trend must be reversed soon as the recent returns were significantly different from average historical values. Since stock prices have recently risen (fallen) more than they do on average, one should expect a reversal bringing the average value of observations closer to the long-term mean. This line of argument is wrong. The point is that the principle of regression toward the mean does not say that whatever rose (fell) more than the average is bound to fall (rise) in the future. What it does say is only that with the increase in the number of observations, subsequent returns on a given security should get closer to the average.

Expecting a trend to continue, especially if it coincides with a lot of activity from individual noise traders, may lead to herd behavior in the form of the so-called feedback trading (Cutler et al., 1990; De Long et al., 1990b). It occurs when investors make a decision on buying or selling watching how the behavior of other traders is reflected in the current pricing of assets. When they see prices rise, they decide to purchase stocks expecting further increases. Their reasoning is that the price has risen because people started buying and if others are buying, it must be because they are expecting the price to be even higher. A symmetrically equivalent reasoning takes place when a fall in the price has been observed. If the price fell, there must have been more people willing to sell. If people are selling, they must be privy to some bad news about the company and it is likely that the price will continue to fall. If the number of players trading by the above rules is sufficiently high, their actions will strengthen the direction of price changes from one period to another. This, in turn, may be a signal for more noise traders keen to identify trends and eager to believe that such trends will continue. Consequently, such herd behavior will contribute to market overreaction to fundamental information (we assume that the first price change was triggered by new information), resulting in a positive correlation of short-term returns (the momentum effect) and the reversal of long-term returns (winner–loser effect) when asset prices are finally adjusted having been initially detached from their fundamental values. Cutler et al. (1990) and De Long et al. (1990b) presented feedback trading models explaining how the phenomena discussed earlier may take place among noise traders.

In addition, De Long et al. (1990b) suggest that rational speculators may predict that there will be feedback among noise traders and destabilize prices on purpose. Their initial reaction to the fundamental signal may be stronger than the content of the information might suggest. In other words, rational speculators predict that the rise (fall) in prices triggered by fundamental factors will make the price change further because of the overreaction on the part of noise traders. This is why they decide to purchase (or sell) in advance more securities than the fundamental information itself might suggest, hoping that they will sell the securities dearer (or purchase cheaper) in the near future when herd behavior of noise traders will make assets deviate temporarily from their real value.

Doing so may cause an even stronger overreaction of the market, which will only be adjusted after a long period of time when the prevailing view, especially among experts, is that it is inevitable for future prices to be corrected soon. Just like the extrapolation bias mentioned before, such investor behavior may explain the momentum effect in a short-time perspective as well as the winner–loser effect in the longer perspective. It may also stand behind the high level of price fluctuations long observed on the stock market.

1.3. Historically Minimum and Maximum Prices

In addition to news and current commentary on the market situation, financial press or Internet pages dedicated to investing usually also publish official lists together with key indicators and statistics for each of the companies. Such statistical data most often include the minimum and maximum price listed in the last 52 weeks. It is surprising that these data are highlighted as, theoretically, they should be of no major importance to the investors. According to the efficient market hypothesis, investment decisions should be made neither on the basis of observed sequences of returns (trends), nor even extreme historical values.

One possible reason why the statistics are published is that readers want to read them. Investors might be interested to compare the current price to its historical peaks and the media simply try to satisfy their curiosity. On the other hand, the fact that this information is commonly available might make people pay more attention to it. In addition, being published in recognized sources, the statistics may suggest to the readers that they must be useful in one way or another.

It seems that investors do attach a lot of importance to whether current prices are close to their historical minimum or maximum values. Gneezy (2005) confirmed this under experimental conditions studying trader behavior during simulated sessions. Huddart, Lang, and Yetman (2005) documented a similar tendency in the real market—after the current price reached its peak from the previous year, the volume of transactions related to the securities in question rose suddenly. Higher volume was observed both at minimum and maximum levels leading in both cases to positive abnormal returns that persisted on average for up to six months. In other words, if the prices exceeded the previous maximum, the trend continued; if they fell below the minimum, the price most often rebounded. This is partly in line with De Bondt's observation (1993) that people are more likely to expect a trend to continue after a period of rises than a series of falls. Moreover, Grinblatt and Keloharju (2001) document that investor activity may depend on peaks over a period shorter than one year. Studying investor behavior on the Finnish market, they notice a significant relationship between the volume of trading and the fact whether stock prices of a given company were at their lowest or highest over the last month. Baker, Pan, and Wurgler (2012) show that historical peaks play an important role in mergers and acquisitions. They observe that offer prices tend to cluster around

13-week high, 26-week high, 39-week high, 52-week high, and 104-week high. The probability of accepting a deal increases discontinuously when the offer even slightly exceeds the 52-week high.

Such observations are difficult to explain from the perspective of the classical theory of finance. Behavioral finance, on the other hand, offers such clues as the anchoring effect combined with excessive optimism. Investors become attached to minimum and maximum price levels and treat them as natural reference points when making investment decisions. However, the way they interpret the fact of reaching the reference point is not always the same, which might be explained by their usual optimism. If the price exceeds its last maximum level, it is interpreted as a signal that the company will continue the positive trend justifying further increase in value. Conversely, reaching the minimum value will in many cases be understood as an incentive to buy as the price seems very attractive compared to historical values.

2. Perception of Value and Investment Selection

2.1. *Good Company versus Good Investment*

Investors, especially individual investors, do not always know how to tell the difference between a good company and a good investment. A good company is one that is properly managed, operates in a prospective sector, is a successful competitor, and has recognized brands and products. A company of this sort will attract the attention of market analysts and commentators and is often presented as the model of success by the media. It should therefore come as no surprise that valuation of such a company is high and it has *historically* offered high returns to its shareholders. The question, however, is whether a good company is also a good potential investment opportunity?

It might be argued that if the company has prospered as a result of good management, organization, know-how, and other unique factors, it is to be expected that it will continue to perform well and keep growing. Why then should it not be a good investment opportunity? The problem is that even if the company does continue to be successful, we must remember that this is exactly what most market observers expect. This means that the expectation of future growth is most probably accounted for in the current price of the stock. Given investors and analysts are overoptimistic by nature, we may assume that it will be extremely difficult for the company to positively surprise the market with better and better results going beyond the already high expectations. If the company does develop in a way that only meets the high expectations (a feat in itself!), future returns on its shares might be at most average for a given level of risk. In practice, analysts and investors often underestimate the probability of negative events, making forecasts that are too optimistic (extrapolation bias). Hence, it is highly likely that the company, far from performing surprisingly well, will fall short of expectations. In such cases, investing in a company that currently does very well will generate future returns much below those commonly expected for a given level of risk.

So what is a good investment? Could it be bad companies? It would of course be going too far to say that poorly managed companies that cannot find their feet on the market make for a good investment. Nevertheless, it might be a good idea to check whether some of the companies that let investors down in the past, lost much value as a result, and are not very popular have not undergone a process of restructuring, for example, which has improved their prospects for the future. Investors are usually not keen to consider investing again in companies that disappointed them, afraid that they will lose again. So it is likely that the market will be slow to correctly identify any positive changes a company went through and will underestimate its prospects. If someone manages to find such a company and purchase its stock before it is commonly perceived as a good one, then he can expect the investment to bring him extraordinary profit.

A good investment is one that generates returns which are as high as possible given the level of attached risk. The condition for achieving abnormal returns is not only to successfully predict the future standing of a company, but one must also forestall future expectations other market players have of it. In other words, one needs to invest in good companies, but do it before everyone else realizes they are good.

Investors who naively equate good companies with good investment may generate extra demand and trigger a short-term continuation of the upward trend leading to periodical overpricing. At the same time, excessive disappointment with companies that let investors down in the past may make the price of their stocks fall too low. If the two types of investor behaviors are combined, they may contribute in the short term to the so-called momentum effect. As it is adjusted in the longer perspective, it will build up the effect known as "winner–loser," which constitutes the basis for long-term contrarian strategies.

2.2. Beauty Contest

Classical theory of finance says that current stock prices are the best approximation of the underlying intrinsic value and reflect the discounted value of all expected future cash flows. As a result, changes in prices should take place only in response to changes in expectations as to the current value of the future payouts. However, given that fewer and fewer companies choose to distribute profit (Fama and French, 2001) and the fact that the period of holding securities is generally relatively short, investors pay more attention to potential capital profit than dividends. Deciding to invest, they try to predict the price for which it will be possible to resell stocks in the future. The future price will depend on the value that other market players will be ready to assign to the stocks at the time. At the moment of purchase, investors are less interested to determine the actual real fundamental value of a company, focusing more on how the company will be perceived by others. Consequently, they want to predict other players' predictions, that is, they construct higher-order beliefs.

Keynes (1936) compares this investor behavior to a newspaper beauty contest. One of the London newspapers published photographs of beautiful women asking its readers to select the prettiest. It also funded a prize awarded to the most beautiful woman selected and prizes for readers who would select the woman most often selected by other contestants. In order to win the contest, one had to choose not by following his subjective judgment, but rather by anticipating what preferences other participants will have. The situation on the capital market is similar. It does not matter what we like and what the fundamental values of a company are. What is important is that others like it in the future and be prepared to pay even more for it.

The fact that investors follow the beauty contest principle in their actions may be dangerous for informational efficiency of the market. The less investors are interested in finding out what the actual value is and the more they operate for the possibility of reselling a security with profit, the less current prices will be able to reflect fundamental values. Pricing assets through the prism of how other market players perceive or will perceive their value may lead to herd behavior and contribute to speculation bubbles. McQueen and Thorley (1994) argue that even rational investors may decide to invest in securities whose current price exceeds the fundamental value if only it is sufficiently probable that the deviation will continue. Hirota and Sunder (2002, 2007) confirm this under experimental conditions. Gerber, Hens, and Vogt (2002) present a formal model based on the beauty contest effect that can theoretically explain excessive stock price volatility as well as the momentum and winner–loser effects. Monnin (2004) uses actual market data to show that if the beauty contest effect is accounted for when modeling the market, it is possible to arrive at the level of volatility similar to the one observed empirically (see section 1.2 in chapter 5 for more information on the excessive volatility puzzle).

History knows of various "investment manias" when prices of assets first reached exorbitant levels in the heat of speculation to eventually collapse. Usually, market optimism builds up gradually, slowly increasing prices, and turns into universal euphoria only at the peak. Panic develops differently. It spreads much quicker among investors and the market reaction is much more violent. Consequences of a depression are sometimes very painful and normally affect a larger group of players than the ones who managed to withdraw their funds before the bubble burst.

Tvede (2002) and Kindleberger and Aliber (2011) provide a survey of spectacular bubbles and crashes in the history of markets. The most spectacular and well-known investment bubbles were the tulip mania in seventeenth-century Netherlands, trading in South Sea Company shares in early eighteenth century in England, and . . . trading in goods related to kite flying which took place in the Netherlands again, 130 years after the great tulip crash. More recent examples include the famous Internet bubble at the end of the last millennium and the real-estate bubble in the United States and a number of European countries that burst in 2007 and 2008.

It is possible that part of the investors involved in these speculations were aware of the absurdity of the situation and unrealistically high prices. Even so, observing collective, euphoric behavior in others, they decided to join in the dangerous gamble. They assumed that even if they buy ridiculously expensive assets, they will find even more naive optimists in the future to whom they will sell them at a better price.

Failing to be part of the general frenzy may also lead to negative psychological states. Observing how much prices have risen so far, investors often fall into the trap of regret of not having invested earlier. The more other people managed to benefit from the opportunity, the greater the regret will be. A wrong decision made against the crowd is more painful than a mistake we share with others. Therefore, in order to avoid further feelings of regret, investors might decide to join the group of speculators regardless of their own convictions as to the rationality of doing so. Keynes (1936) himself wrote that "worldly wisdom teaches that it is better to fail conventionally, than to succeed unconventionally."

2.3. Familiarity and Home Bias

People prefer to invest in companies they know. On the face of it, this seems natural and obvious. On closer scrutiny, however, one may wonder whether such behavior will always result in optimal solutions. First, the mere fact that a company is recognized, that is, people have all the information on its line of business, owned brands, products, locations and so on, does not have to mean that it enjoys information advantage over other, average market players. Second, focusing only on well-known companies without looking for new investment opportunities may lead to nonoptimal diversification and inefficient portfolios.

Active search for and assessment of new signals is one of the conditions for informational efficiency of the market. If investors concentrate only on what they are familiar with, staying clear of some sophisticated and less recognizable securities, efficiency and market pricing may be distorted at least in some segments of the market.

The familiarity bias, present both in individual and institutional investors, manifests itself in several ways. First, many studies point out that international diversification is at a very low level even at the time of progressing globalization of financial markets (Levy and Sarnat, 1970; French and Poterba, 1991; Cooper and Kaplanis, 1994; Karlsson and Norden, 2007). Regardless of whether they operate in countries with big and developed capital markets or in smaller ones, investors invest relatively little abroad, much less than what could be considered optimal given the correlation of returns in global markets. Kang and Stulz (1997), and Lewis (1999) argue that poor international diversification stems from extra costs and barriers to capital flows. Lauterbach and Reisman (2004) point out the possibility that investors are more sensitive to changes in their consumption as compared to local levels in their direct environment rather than to general fluctuations on the global scale. Adler and Dumas (1983) and Cooper and Kaplanis (1994) suggest that local investment offers better opportunities to hedge against local risk factors such as inflation. Lewis (1999), however, showed that investing in local assets will not limit risk. On the contrary, in some cases, it may even make the investor more exposed to local influences. Among other explanations, Grinblatt and Keloharju (2001) point out the role of cultural factors and language problems, whereas Morse and Shive (2011) document the importance of patriotism in deciding where to invest.

The tendency to invest in companies that are known and located nearby manifests itself not only as insufficient international diversification, but it can also be observed domestically. Huberman (2001) finds a clear preference on the part of small investors to invest in stocks of local telecom operators. Another example of home bias relates to Coca-Cola, which has its headquarter in Atlanta, Georgia. Despite the fact that it is a worldwide recognizable company, as much as 16 percent of Coca-Cola shares (according to the data from 1997) is owned by individuals or institutions from the agglomeration of Atlanta. Grinblatt and Keloharju (2001) showed that Finnish individual investors mainly focus on companies located within the radius of 100 kilometers from the place where they live. In addition, Finns prefer companies that publish their financial reports in Finnish and are run by managers of the same cultural background. Preference for local companies is also displayed by institutional investors. Coval and Moskowitz (1999, 2001) documented this for American investment funds, especially the active ones with relatively few assets under management.

Familiarity and home inclination is most often explained in psychology by referring to the availability bias and ambiguity aversion. When making a decision where to invest in, local firms or firms known from personal experience are more available to an investor's perception and more easily come up as potential investment opportunities. Beside that, nonfamiliar, remote firms are considered to be more ambiguous. Heath and Tversky (1991) showed that ambiguity aversion may be overcome if a decision maker is convinced of his expertise in a given area. Local knowledge may instill the feeling of competence. This is likely to turn into overconfidence and excessive optimism. Kilka and Weber (2000) document that surveyed students of economics in Germany were more optimistic about the development of the German economy compared to American economic prospects, whereas their American colleagues thought the exact opposite at the same time. Strong and Xu (2003) find a similarly optimistic attitude among fund managers talking about the situation on their local markets.

Coval and Moskowitz (1999, 2001) show that fund managers who decide to buy shares of local companies obtain better average results from the investment compared to other components of the portfolio. This suggests that the decision to invest locally is information driven.

2.4. Incorrect Perception of Information

Market participants sometimes find it difficult to assess particular bits of information and their reactions often depend on the way facts about the company are presented. There have been documented cases when the publication of unimportant data or media attention around facts that were already publicly known triggered investor reaction influencing stock prices (Ho and Michaely,

1988; Stice, 1991; Huberman and Regev, 2001). Tumarkin and Whitelaw (2001) document that even unverified opinions expressed by Internet users on a discussion forum are treated as information bringing about market response. Rashes (2001) finds cases of market reaction to information that was completely irrelevant for a given company, being related to another company with a similar ticker or name.

Cooper, Dimitrov, and Rau (2001) point out an interesting phenomenon from the days of the dot-com boom. The mere information about a company changing its name in such a way that the new name was associated with the Internet (e.g., *Company.com*) caused a sharp increase in the company's stock price. What is especially interesting is that the phenomenon was equally strong in the group of companies that did operate in the high-tech sector as in the group of those whose activities were far from it, the change of name being clearly a propaganda trick. It seems that, at the time of the dot-com mania, investors did not always bother to check what the company actually does. The association with the Internet by virtue of the name was enough.

Libby, Bloomfield, and Nelson (2002) and Hirshleifer and Teoh (2003) present a review of literature on limited investor perception during the processing of information included in financial reports. Many studies show that stock pricing may be influenced by the very way in which financial data are reported even if the contents of the report are exactly the same. Investors pay more attention to descriptive information than to numerical data presented without any commentary. They treat the same information differently depending on whether it is part of the main body of the report or included in a footnote. Both investor and professional analysts are sensitive to the way individual items in financial reports are grouped. For example, they are more responsive to current operational expenses than to one-off extraordinary expenses of the same magnitude, which is most likely reflected in their assessment of how profitable the company is. Their perception of company risk depends on how the same hybrid instrument is classified in the balance sheet—as equity or debt. This happens regardless of the fact that the instrument is usually precisely described at the time of its issue, so its nature should be known to investors.

Generally, people overreact to unconfirmed information while being conservative about precise and clear signals (Bloomfield et al., 2000). They also attach a lot of importance to extreme information that is in the spotlight (e.g., covered by the media) whatever its actual value might be. This sort of behavior follows the psychologically documented patterns of calibration bias and overconfidence combined with cognitive conservatism about new, precise signals as well as a version of the availability bias. Such attitudes may be reflected on the capital market as price overreaction to unreliable information and insufficient impact of confirmed signals. Pound and Zeckhauser (1990) find significant market reaction to unconfirmed gossip about a possible merger or acquisition. On the other hand, Ball and Brown (1968), Foster, Olsen, and Shelvin (1984) and Bernard and Thomas (1989, 1990) document delayed market reaction, so-called post-announcement drift, to officially reported earnings.

2.5. *Financial Forecasts and Analysts' Recommendations*

Professional analysts try to help investors in their predictions of the direction the entire market is going to take as well as anticipations of future financial results of particular companies. They prepare opinions on investment attractiveness of individual securities on the basis of information they gathered and their own analyses and then make such opinions available to individual and institutional investors. Recommendations are usually made using a popular five-point scale—"strong buy," "buy," "hold," "sell," and "strong sell."

Analysts tend to be overly optimistic when preparing forecasts and drafting recommendations. There is rich literature documenting how analysts' predictions are overestimated compared to later, actual results, especially in the case of annual and longer than annual forecasts (De Bondt and Thaler, 1990; Ali et al., 1992; Rajan and Servaes, 1997; Hansen and Sarin, 1998; Brown, 2001). The tendency is present not only in the United States, but also in the United Kingdom (Patz, 1989; Capstaff et al., 1995) and Germany (Capstaff et al., 1998). Positive recommendations are published much more often than negative ones. For example, in the sample used by Womack (1996), the ratio of recommendations to buy and sell was almost 7:1. Analysts exhibit some herding inclination, that is, their issue of similar recommendations cluster in time (Welch, 2000).

The literature offers a lot of potential explanations of excessive optimism among professional analysts. Some publications suggest that analysts might show signs of optimism on purpose as the feeling relates to the conflict of interest they have being hand in glove with financial institutions that are active on the market. For example, Michaely and Womack (1999), Dechow, Huston, and Sloan (2000), and Cliff (2004) document a significant level of optimism among analysts employed by an investment bank offering equity of a given company. Cowen, Groysberg, and Healy (2006) and Agrawal and Chen (2004) demonstrate, however, that similar consistent levels of optimism can also be observed among analysts associated with independent brokerage houses. This is explained by the role positive opinions expressed by analysts play in encouraging customers to generate higher trading volume. Irvine (2004) shows that within two weeks from the day on which a brokerage house publishes a recommendation, the value of transactions it carries out increases significantly, the volume of trading rising primarily in response to positive recommendations. Irvine, Nathan, and Simko (1998), on the other hand, point out that there is a relationship between recommendations made by analysts and changes in asset portfolios managed by companies they are associated with. They document that analysts who have a connection with asset management firms make particularly optimistic recommendations for stocks that have just been bought, while degrading the ones recently sold from the managed portfolios. Such actions are not necessarily taken in order to manipulate stock prices. They may simply be related to the fact that recommendations were first distributed internally and only then made public.

It is also sometimes argued that analysts consciously overestimate the companies they assess in order to have good relations with their management, a strategy allowing them to have access to some nonpublic information. Das, Levine, and Sivaramakrishnan (1998) and Lim (2001) find that the tendency to be overoptimistic depends on the level of uncertainty, unpredictability of the company's results, and the degree to which information is asymmetrical. In their interpretation, this confirms the hypothesis that analysts are ready to overstate their forecasts on purpose in order to have access to information from the company itself rather than be forced to rely on highly imprecise public signals. It must be noted, however, that high uncertainty and information asymmetry contribute also to psychologically driven distortions.

The consistent optimism among analysts may be due to the fact that they are not always able to interpret available information correctly (Brown, 1999; Brown and Higgins, 2001, 2005; Tan et al., 2002). Because of limited perception resulting from the framing bias, people may be sensitive to the way information is presented. The fact that companies present good and bad news in different ways may translate into analysts' reactions, as suggested by Easterwood and Nutt (1999). What may further contribute to a distorted, overly positive image of the analyzed company are unrealistic optimism, representativeness bias, and overconfidence (see chapter 2). All of these together lead to excessive extrapolation of the positive image onto future periods as well as overreaction in making long-term recommendations (De Bondt and Thaler, 1990; La Porta, 1996).

Abarbanell and Bernard (1992), Elliot, Philbrick, and Wiedman (1995), and Chan, Jegadeesh, and Lakonishok (1996) find that forecasts made by analysts consistently underestimate the most recent financial results. Although insufficient reactions can be observed when companies publish both unexpectedly good and bad results, negative surprises do lead to a much longer period of forecast adjustment. Brown (2001) and Matsumoto (2002) suggest that analysts are somewhat pessimistic when making short-term forecasts not going beyond one quarter. This may be related to practices of corporate managers who prefer to cool down analysts' optimism just before announcing results in order to be able to surprise the market positively when publishing their financial reports (see chapter 7).

From the psychological perspective, delayed analysts' reaction to the most recent information may be explained by the effects of cognitive conservatism and anchoring. The combination of underreaction to current information and analyst's excessive optimism in making long-term forecasts may potentially, although not fully, explain the so-called post-earnings-announcement drift, short-term momentum, and long-term returns reversals. The reason is that in spite of the aforementioned reservations as to the objectivism and quality of analyses, investors seem to attach a lot of importance to opinions expressed by analysts.

There are many publications documenting strong market reaction to the publication of recommendations (Stickel, 1995; Womack, 1996; Michaely and Womack, 1999; Krische and Lee, 2001; Barber, Lehavy, McNichols, and Trueman, 2001, 2003; Cliff, 2004; Jegadeesh, Kim, Krische, and Lee, 2004). Market reaction to recommendations is asymmetrical, though. Investors are more influenced when analysts recommend to sell specific securities than when they encourage to buy (Stickel, 1995; Womack, 1996). The market reacts most strongly on the announcement day. There is mixed evidence about post-announcement stock performance. Davis and Canes (1978), Liu, Smith, and Syed (1990), Beneish (1991), and Barber and Loeffler (1993) find overreaction at the moment when recommendations are published after which the accumulated abnormal return is slightly adjusted over the following two to three weeks. On the other hand, Womack (1996) and Barber et al. (2001) document abnormal returns over several months after the publication date, especially in the case of small capitalization companies. The period in which abnormal returns persist is also markedly longer for negative recommendation even though their initial impact on prices is much stronger already on the day of publication. This means that the first reaction of the market is still too weak and some investors postpone their decision to sell for too long. They may do so because of loss aversion and wishful thinking that, this time round, analysts might have been wrong. The outcome is that abnormal negative returns can be observed for up to six months after recommendations were made.

Barber et al. (2001) document that, in the years 1986–1996, portfolios held in accordance with analysts' consensus would have generated 4.13 percent of excess return per annum having factored in the related risk as well as the effects of book to market equity ratio and momentum. On the other hand, portfolios made up of stocks recommended for sale would have generated an average annual loss of -4.91 percent. It must be mentioned, though, that the aforementioned results were obtained on the assumption that all transactions were carried out on the day recommendations were made at the closing price without any transaction costs. Even minimal transaction costs or a delay of one week in investor reaction to a new recommendation would mean that above-average profits from the strategy of strictly following recommendations would be close to nil. Barber et al. (2003) repeat a similar simulation for the years 1996–1999 and for 2000 and 2001 seperately. While results based on the data from late 1990s were very close to those from earlier studies, the situation was radically different for the years of the high-tech boom. In 2000 and 2001, following recommendations to buy would have exposed investors to heavy losses. What is even stranger, buying stocks recommended for selling would have yielded abnormal positive returns. It seems that analysts were seriously wrong in their predictions during the dot-com boom.

Recommendations are a specific type of information. They do not report on concrete events that could potentially influence a company's value, but offer opinions expressed by professionals based on all the information they have. So why is the very act of making recommendations public treated as new information by investors and why does it influence asset prices? The most common explanation is a belief that recommendations are partly made on the basis of nonpublic information analysts have access to thanks to their regular contacts with companies.

Another could be the reputation of people and institutions making forecasts. Even if analyses are prepared solely from publicly available information, investors are prone to treat them as if they were new information believing that professionals have better analytical skills than they do.

After all, it may always be the case that the market's response to the publication of recommendations works as a self-fulfilling prophesy. Recommendations make specific companies stand out among many other investment opportunities and trigger general activity among investors who may engage in herd behavior. Acting on opinions expressed by analysts, investors may influence prices so that they change in line with a previously made recommendation. Barber and Loeffer (1993) and Hirschey, Richardson, and Scholz (2000) observe that the volume of trading in stocks mentioned by a recommendation increases significantly at the moment the recommendation is published. Jegadeesh, Kim, Krische, and Lee (2004) also notice that analysts are much more ready to make positive recommendations for stocks whose price have recently been on the rise. When recommendations appear in such situations, investors become even more convinced that the upward trend is going to continue and are encouraged to invest further. Jegadeesh, Kim, Krische, and Lee (2004) show that such recommendations are followed by a marked increase in trading volume and continued momentum.

3. Portfolio Management

3.1. Insufficient and Naive Diversification

Campbell, Lettau, Malkiel, and Xu (2001) document a clear tendency on the American market to narrow the correlation between rates of return on individual stocks. The average value of the correlation coefficient measured in five-year-long periods for monthly returns fell from 0.28 in the early 1960s to 0.08 at the end of the 1990s. Narrowing interdependence between returns on individual securities means more profit from portfolio diversification in this period. Bloomfield, Leftwich, and Long (1977) and Statman (1987) demonstrated that an optimally diversified portfolio should contain about 20–30 different assets given transaction and monitoring costs. For years, this suggestion has been fostered in academic textbooks, at investment courses and in many publications addressed to investors. Statman (2002a, 2004), taking account of up-to-date data on smaller average correlation between returns on individual stocks and lower transaction costs, argues that marginal profits from increasing diversification may be observed in portfolios of even up to 300 different securities.

In spite of all this, empirical studies demonstrate that, both in the past and currently, individual investors keep portfolios that are drastically under-diversified. Consumer Finance Study commissioned by the Federal Reserve in the United States showed that the average number of companies in an individual investor's portfolio in 1962 amounted to just 3.41 (Blume and Friend, 1975). By all accounts, the level has not changed significantly over the years. Analyzing data from subsequent, more recent Consumer Finance Studies, Polkovnichenko (2005) finds the median of the number of stocks individual investors kept directly in their portfolios to amount to 2 in years 1983–1998, and approximating to 3 in 2001. Goetzman and Kumar (2001), who studied 40,000 individual active brokerage accounts, showed that investors keep an average of four companies in their portfolios with the median standing at 3.

Goetzmann and Kumar (2008) also notice that the level of diversification varies significantly depending on the wealth, age, and profession of particular investors. The least diversified portfolios are kept by young people with relatively low income and professional position (workers, office staff, salespersons, etc.). The number of companies in the portfolio increases strongly in proportion to the level of income, education, and age. The observation confirms the tenets of the behavioral portfolio theory put forward by Shefrin and Statman (2000). They argue that stocks are often treated as lottery tickets. People buy a few stocks in the hope that if they bet correctly, the "wins" will let them jump to a higher level of consumption and realize their aspirations. They do not want to diversify away expected returns by holding too many assets, as, being overconfident about their selection capabilities, they overestimate the chances of their peaks to be the "winning" ones.

It does not mean, however, that investors who diversify their investment over many securities always do it optimally. Goetzmann and Kumar (2008) find that investors underestimate the meaning of cross-correlation among securities, do not apply correct weights to particular components of the portfolio, and overlook the impact of a single security on the overall variance of the portfolio. Hence, investors do not hold efficient minimum variance portfolios, contrary to Markowitz's theory. Simply investing in a variety of assets without considering their cross-correlation is known in the literature as the so-called naive diversification. This was already suggested in an experimental paper by Kroll, Levy, and Rapoport (1988).

Benartzi and Thaler (2001) observe this type of behavior in the case of allocating contributions to employee pension schemes. It turned out that the most often followed principle of allocation was "$1/n$," that is, an even spread of resources over n funds offered under a given scheme regardless of what kind of funds these were. If a scheme offered more safe funds, investors would indirectly purchase more bonds—if it included more equity funds of different kinds (e.g., various investment styles), employees allocated a larger portion of their contributions on the stock market. This was done with no attention paid to the correlation between returns on portfolios kept by the funds.

A different version of naive diversification is observed when an investor decides to spread his investment over funds of the same type. For example, he buys investment units of fund X, simultaneously investing in units of fund Y whose investment strategy is similar to X. Hence, the investor purchases the same category of assets twice, exposing himself to similar risk factors in both cases. What is in fact diversified here is not the sector-specific risk but, at most, individual skills of asset managers in the two funds.

Benartzi (2001) also finds that, in addition to investing in funds offered under a pension scheme, employees display clear preferences to invest directly in the shares of the company they work for. In many cases, their company is the only stock in their portfolio and the employees are not aware that this form of saving for their future pension is more risky than having a diversified market portfolio. On the contrary, they are often convinced that the investment is better because they know their own company well. Benartzi argues that an average employee is not privy to such private information that would allow him to gain more confidence about the prospects of the company. This is confirmed by the empirical evidence of no statistical dependence between investing in the shares of one's own company and future returns. Additionally, it might be argued that employees are already so much exposed to firm-specific risk (their compensation, employment stability, and career prospects are often related to the condition of the firm) that they should not increase their exposure additionally by voluntarily investing in the firm stock.

The inclination to invest in stocks of the employer is related, of course, to the familiarity bias. It may also result from the endowment effect. Employees feel reluctant to dispose of shares they obtained, for example, under an incentive scheme, even when they are perfectly free to do so. Not being frequent traders engaged in the capital market game, employees usually prefer the status quo and leave the received shares in their dramatically under-diversified portfolio.

However, De Bondt (1998) finds the problem with insufficient or naive diversification also among experienced individual traders. Investors who have systematically traded on the stock market have strong preferences to focus only on a few selected picks. Survey studies show that most of these investors erroneously believed that they could manage portfolio risk better by understanding a handful of companies thoroughly rather than by wide diversification. This attitude is related to the psychological phenomenon of overconfidence as well as the so-called illusion of control. Personal involvement in the process of investment selection and a good knowledge of selected companies may lead to a false feeling of control over random events. We cannot forget that more knowledge does not always bring higher returns. After all, part of the factors impacting future financial standing of the company is unpredictable even for insider-traders who have access to confidential, internal information.

Poor diversification and underestimating the mutual correlation between returns on individual assets undermine Markowitz's portfolio theory and the assumptions behind traditional asset-pricing models. Classical theory of finance assumes that all investors strive to keep efficient portfolios. As a result, the market portfolio will also be efficient as a function of all investments that are active at any given moment. In practice, however, investors routinely keep poorly diversified and inefficient portfolios, which may prevent the entire market portfolio from functioning optimally. This means that some investors are in a position to create portfolios that are more efficient than the market portfolio and hence achieve abnormal returns.

It may be that investors who do not diversify properly also contribute to irrational risk premiums present on the market. We cannot exclude the fact that such investors expect compensation in the form of higher returns not only for systemic risk but also for specific risk, which, under rational conditions, could be eliminated through diversification. If the group of such investors is sufficiently large, their expectations may translate to the higher overall risk premiums in the stock market, as observed empirically over long periods. The equity premium puzzle is discussed in detail in section 1.1 in chapter 5.

3.2. Excessive Trading

There is a lot of evidence suggesting that investors make transactions too often and too aggressively leading to an unreasonably high level of trading. For example, the average dollar volume of stock trading on NYSE amounted to 35.1 billion dollars a day in 2012. The average annualized turnover stood at 71 percent. It could be interpreted that the value of shares that changed owners within one year was equal to almost three quarters of capitalization of all companies listed on NYSE. This is still far from historical peaks. The average daily dollar volume was 82.4 billion dollars in 2008 and the average annualized turnover amounted to 137 percent.[2] This means that the total value of stock traded in a year was significantly more than the overall market capitalization in 2008.

In order for a transaction to take place on the market, both the seller and the buyer must believe that it is profitable for them to do so at the moment. Models assuming full rationality of all decision makers treat heterogeneity, that is, access to different sets of information, as a source of difference in investors' beliefs that may potentially motivate people to trade in securities. In extreme cases, however, the offer to buy or sell made by one rational decision maker may be interpreted by another as a signal that the offering person has private information motivating him to carry out the transaction. The other rational agent will then refuse to enter into the transaction being afraid that the first agent has information advantage over him (Milgrom and Stockey, 1982). Incorporating another rational trade motivating factor, that is, the need for liquidity, does not very much improve the ability of the models to explain such high trading levels as the ones empirically observed on the market. Brunnermeier (2001) presents a comprehensive overview and discussion of investor behavior models in the context of trading volumes.

The first behavioral explanation of excessive trading volumes suggested, among others, by Black (1986), Trueman (1988), Shleifer and Summers (1990), and De Long et al. (1990a, 1991) refers in general to the presence of noise traders making frequent transactions on the basis of unconfirmed rumors and irrelevant information. A little later, Odean (1998b) points at overconfidence as the answer to why investors attach too much importance to the doubtful information they have. Odean presents a model according to which an overconfident investor decides to make the transaction believing that his analytical skills are better than those of other traders (above-average effect) and overestimates the precision of the signals he received (calibration bias). Glaser and Weber (2007) confirm empirically that investors trade with excessive frequency most of all because they are convinced of their superiority and advantage over other players. However, they do not find that excessive traders are also miscalibrated.

Excessive trading motivated by the erroneous conviction of having superior analytical skills leads in practice to worse investment results. Odean (1999) and Barber and Odean (2000, 2002) show that investors who speculate most actively have the worst average performance. This is caused mainly by transaction costs, although Odean (1999) also points out systematically wrong decisions of active investors who decide to buy or sell securities at the wrong moment. In other words, investors only think they have exceptional investment skills falling victim to overconfidence and the tendency to trade too often. They thus incur costs that they cannot compensate for by higher returns.

Barber and Odean (2001) demonstrate that, on average, men make more transactions than women. This observation echoes previous psychological studies which showed that men are generally more confident, especially in areas traditionally considered masculine. The level of self-confidence also depends on the results of previous decisions. It will be especially high in bullish periods as good investment performance will only strengthen investors' conviction of their own extraordinary skills. Bearish markets may slightly disrupt this feeling but not destroy it as it will be immediately compensated by the so-called selective attribution. Investors usually attribute positive results to their own skills and prefer to explain failures by factors beyond their control such as random events. Statman, Thorley, and Vorkink (2006) confirm empirically that a rise in prices boosts the trading volume in the US market. Kim and Nofsinger (2005) document a similar relation on the Japanese market showing additionally that previous good results have a stronger influence on the increase of activity among individual investors.

Overconfidence pushing people to invest aggressively may strengthen periodical price deviations from fundamentals, which could account not only for the high level of trading, but also for overreaction to information signals.

3.3. Myopia in Asset Allocation

According to the neoclassical theory of finance, in the long term, investment in stocks should on average generate higher returns than investment in risk-free instruments. There are many publications demonstrating that historical risk premium is actually too high than what might have been expected theoretically (see chapter 5). It is commonly claimed that the longer the investment perspective is, the larger is the part of the portfolio that should be invested in well-diversified stocks. Nevertheless, investors still prefer to be conservative allocating a relatively small part of their funds in equity even when their savings are long term.

Benartzi and Thaler (1995) suggested that the relative reluctance to invest in stocks is the result of two simultaneous psychological phenomena. First, investors get less satisfaction from making a profit than they feel pain for suffering a loss of the same magnitude. In other words, they display loss aversion assumed, among others, by the utility function described in the prospect theory. Second, most investors, even those with a very long investment perspective, evaluate their portfolios relatively often assessing the results of the evaluation separately for each short period. This is related to the psychological phenomenon of mental accounting. Benartzi and Thaler (1995) coined a name for the combination of these two factors—myopic loss aversion.

It is obvious that stock prices may fluctuate radically in short periods of time. Due to the habit of mental accounting, investors register achieved results separately for each of the short periods that they evaluate. It is harder for them to perceive cumulative returns or average values in the long-term perspective. At the same time, they are very much affected by losses even if these are short term in nature. Consequently, trying to avoid negative feelings related to potential losses in any of the observation periods, they limit the level of investment in stocks.

Benartzi and Thaler (1995) checked how often an average investor would have to evaluate his portfolio to justify the observed risk premium on the stock market. Using data from the US market for the years 1926–1990, they showed that the average portfolio evaluation period should amount to about one year.[3] Given this time frame of investment evaluation as well as average historical returns on shares and risk-free assets, an optimal portfolio maximizing Tversky and Kahneman's utility function should contain from 30 to 55 percent of stocks. Results obtained by Benarzti and Thaler (1995), both as it concerns evaluation periods and the average portfolio structure, seem to fit observed investment practice.

Myopic allocation of funds in investment portfolios is undoubtedly aggravated by institutional factors. The basic reporting period for most financial institutions is one year. This is also true for pension funds or passive index funds that should, by their very nature, have long investment perspectives as well as, for example, active management funds, for which short-term speculation and market timing are normal elements of the strategy. Managers of all types of funds and asset managers are also typically evaluated and rewarded annually. It is only natural, therefore, that they will try to optimize their portfolios and limit the level of risk within the same time frame so that, in this relatively short period of time, they do not come out badly against the benchmark.

Yet another factor exacerbating investors' myopia in the capital market is the tax system forcing individual and institutional investors to account for profits and losses annually.

Myopic loss aversion is often considered to be the main reason behind the high-risk premium in the stock market. High average returns in the long term are a necessary compensation for those investors who decide to accept strong short-term fluctuations of their investments.

3.4. Disposition Effect

Investors are more ready to keep in their portfolio assets whose prices fell from the time of purchase rather than the stocks that might be sold with profit. Shefrin and Statman (1985) give this practice the name of disposition effect.

The effect was further confirmed by Odean (1998a), Barber and Odean (2000), and Dhar and Zhu (2006), who studied a sample of individual American investors. Next, Grinblatt and Keloharju (2001) document a similar phenomenon in Finland, Shapira and Venezia (2001) doing the same in Israel. Ranguelova (2001) demonstrates that the effect is especially strong in the case of small capitalization companies. In most of the studies mentioned, analyzed data are taken straight from brokerage accounts of individual investors, which allows the researchers to follow changes in investment portfolios directly. Kaustia (2004) and Szyszka and Zielonka (2007) document the disposition effect in aggregated market data. Weber and Cramerer (1998) additionally confirm the phenomenon in controlled experiments simulating the market situation. The disposition effect is less prominent in the group of professional investors, although Garvey and Murphy (2004) point out that it can be observed among active professional market players.

It is difficult to explain such behavior rationally. Potential tax reasons would rather suggest that losing assets will be sold faster while capital profits are postponed. Odean (1998a) shows that investors do the very thing in December, but in 11 other months, they display a distinct propensity to postpone loss realization. Neither can we rationally argue that securities whose price has fallen previously are currently underpriced and investors are right to expect a return to fundamental values. As Odean (1998a) demonstrates, losing shares that investors decide to keep perform worse on average than the ones they sell in the meantime. Garvey and Murphy (2004) provide similar findings with respect to professional traders. On average, they would achieve higher profits if they kept winning stocks for a bit longer and closed the losing positions faster.

From the perspective of behavioral finance, the phenomenon can be explained in two different ways. First, investors may fall victim to the anchoring bias becoming too much attached to the price at which they bought stocks. They underestimate the possibility of new important information emerging in the meantime to lower the company's fundamental value. This attitude may be related to overconfidence and unrealistic optimism. Investors are reluctant to admit that they have made a mistake preferring to persist in their belief that it is the market that prices the asset unfavorably and this "temporary" situation will "soon" be corrected to their satisfaction. They often even decide to buy more of the same shares at the currently lower price, which they might consider attractive compared to their initial anchor. In addition, doing so will decrease the average purchase price that investors will automatically interpret to mean that the loss per individual share is lower.

The other behavioral explanation of the disposition effect refers to the prospect theory that assumes that decision makers' utility function is concave in the area of profits and convex in the area of losses. This means that when investors have shares whose current price is higher than the purchase price, that is, they may be sure of making a profit, they will display risk aversion. But if they have shares whose price has recently dropped so that they are faced with suffering a loss, they are prone to take more risks. If the probability of prices rising or falling in the following period is the same and the expected share value is equal to its current price, investors will maximize expected utility provided they decide to realize profit at once and postpone realization of losses.

Grinblatt and Han (2005) argue convincingly that the disposition effect may contribute to the efficiency of the so-called momentum strategy whereby market players consistently invest in shares that have recently gained most in value, simultaneously selling assets whose price has had the most serious fall. Due to risk aversion in the area of profits, investors will gladly sell shares that have just brought about positive returns. Increased supply of these assets may mean that the current price will be temporarily below the current fundamental value even though it is higher than the purchase price. When the supply side gets weaker, prices will get gradually back to the real value, generating positive abnormal returns in the short term. The opposite thing will happen in the case of shares that would entail a loss if sold. Unwillingness to sell at the current price, which is lower than the price of purchase, will temporarily result in a relative drop in supply making prices slightly higher than what might be expected from the current real value of shares. Consequently, future short-term returns will be lower than the ones typical for a given level of risk. Systematic short-period purchase of shares whose price has performed best recently combined with selling (or short-selling) those that have brought the greatest loss will allow investors to achieve abnormal returns. This is exactly what the momentum strategy is about.

It is rarely easy to empirically isolate the disposition effect from aggregated activities taking place on the entire market. In standard market practice, investors buy shares at different times and prices. Hence, when individual players consider whether to sell or continue investing, they have various reference points. Nevertheless, Szyszka and Zielonka (2007) point out one specific market situation that makes it possible to verify the disposition effect empirically not only at the level of decisions made by individual investors, but also in aggregated market data. This special market situation is initial public offering (IPO). As investors who participated in a public offering decide whether to sell or not on the first listing day, all of them will have the same reference point, because all typically purchased shares at the same price. They will be more willing to sell on the first listing day when stock price is above the offering price and less willing to do so if the company makes its debut at below the offering price. This should result in significant differences in trading volume, which should generally be higher for companies making their debut with a profit than for those who were first listed with a loss. Szyszka and Zielonka (2007) employ three different measures of trading volume on the first listing day. The number of shares traded during the first session was compared to the total number of shares allowed for trading, the total number offered in IPO, and the number of shares traded in an average session without IPO influence, that is, between the thirty-first and two hundred and seventieth sessions after the first listing. Analyzed companies were then divided into two groups depending on whether the first listing closed with a profit or loss for investors. Regardless of the relative trading measure applied, if the listing was profitable, the number of shares changing owners in the first session was relatively higher than if the debut price was lower than the offering price.

3.5. Practices of Institutional Investors

All the aspects of portfolio management presented so far were documented mainly for individual investors. While we cannot exclude that some observations are common for both small players and professionals, we must say that institutional investors do manage portfolios in a specific way that may influence prices on the capital market.

The types of behavior one could identify as common for the way individual and institutional investors manage portfolios are myopic loss aversion and excessive trading. In the context of the previously mentioned aspects such as the fact that the basic evaluation and reporting period for most institutions is one year, it seems justified to assume that professionals will also structure their portfolios adopting too short investment perspectives. Also, worse average long-term performance of active management funds as compared to passive index funds (after transaction costs), suggest excessive, economically unjustified, frequency of changes in actively managed portfolios (Elton et al., 1993).

Professionally managed portfolios are usually highly diversified although some specialized funds (e.g., those focusing only on specific sectors or company categories) may diversify badly constructing suboptimal portfolios. Such portfolios may be oversensitive to sector-specific risk or linked to certain characteristics of companies (e.g., small capitalization). Garvey and Murphy (2004) also demonstrated that the most active professional players, the so-called day-traders, focus on just a few companies speculating on short-term price fluctuations, disregarding the portfolio theory.

When it comes to funds, the disposition effect may be curbed as a result of two quite common practices. First, many managers need to implement a stop-loss strategy either because of administrative requirements or their own conscious decision. The strategy consists in automatically closing a position if the amount of loss exceeds the assumed acceptable threshold. Whether managers subjectively believe that the company is underestimated at the moment or not is of no importance, the very fact of exceeding the acceptable limit being enough to set off the transaction. If more funds set a similar threshold triggering a stop-loss strategy, supply may rise sharply, which will only deflate the price further. As a result, short-term negative returns will be continued.

The other practice among fund managers limiting the disposition effect is so-called window dressing. Managers avoid situations where they would have to report that the fund made major investments in companies that have recently lost in value. Analyzing a sample of 769 American pension funds, Lakonishok, Shleifer, Thaler, and Vishny (1991) document that the funds were keen to get rid of investment they were most disappointed in before the end of each quarter. At the same time, they postponed selling assets that have recently generated the highest profit. The tendency was especially strong in the last quarter, possibly because investors attach more importance to the more detailed annual reports. When such practices are common, they may result in short-term continuation of returns, increase price volatility, and be partly responsible for the so-called month-in-the-year effect as suggested by inter alia, Haugen and Lakonishok (1988).

In general, asset managers are evaluated by comparing their performance to a benchmark. Most often, generated returns are compared to changes of a relevant market index or to the average return obtained at the same time in the same category of investment funds. This may significantly influence the way portfolios are managed. First, managers are encouraged to imitate one another when allocating funds. Making investments in a way that resembles the composition of a specific index or the structure of investment portfolios run by other funds, individual managers reduce risk so that their results do not fall short of the benchmark. Sharfstein and Stein (1990) presented a formal model explaining the possibility of herd behavior among rational professionals who decide to copy decisions taken by others for fear of losing reputation. One way in which herd behavior motivated by a desire to pursue the benchmark is empirically manifested is the presence of abnormal positive returns observed at the moment of announcing that a specific asset will be included in the index (Harris and Gurel, 1986; Shleifer, 1986; Lynch and Mendelhall, 1997; Kaul, Mehrotra, and Morck, 2000). Within one to two weeks from including the company in the index, the abnormal returns are on average negative. This means that increased demand on the part of the funds leads to temporary overvaluation of the assets, such mispricing being adjusted in a relatively short period when the extra demand disappears. Wurgler and Zhuravskaya (2002) argue that the effect is especially strong in the case of companies offering little opportunity for perfect arbitrage. Index inclusion may also be a source of more permanent value due to increased stock liquidity.

In addition, the awareness of being evaluated and rewarded against a specific benchmark may make managers more willing to manage portfolio risk in response to previous performance. If during current evaluation the manager realizes that his portfolio performed much better than the benchmark, he will want to see this situation continue until the end of the period in which he is assessed. He will therefore make such changes in portfolio structure that will reduce risk and correlate future returns with the benchmark to the greatest extent possible. Doing so, managers hope that the surplus they have managed to achieve over the benchmark will still be there at the moment of assessment. On the other hand, when a manager realizes that his performance is below the benchmark, the behavior will be reversed. Wanting to catch up on lost percentage points, he may change portfolio structure to increase risk exposure. He hopes that more risk will be compensated by higher returns allowing him to meet the benchmark. However, the manager overlooks that the risk–return relationship is meant to hold only in a sufficiently long period. Changing the portfolio risk exposure based on past performance is in line with the prospect theory that says exactly the same thing—above the reference point (benchmark) people will display risk aversion; below it, they will be willing to take risks. Brown, Van Harlow, and Starks (1996) confirm empirically that managers who performed below the group average in the first half year become significantly more risk-seeking with their portfolios in the second half of the year.

To conclude—on the one hand, professional investors should potentially be more rational; on the other, the decisions they make may be influenced by specific institutional determinants as well as the entire architecture of the professional assets management system. As a result, professional market players are just as likely to cause anomalies on the capital market by their behavior as individual noise traders, the usual prime suspects. What may be especially important for price destabilization is herd behavior observed among funds, particularly those with a speculative attitude. Crucially, we do not have to dismiss the assumption of managers' rationality to assume that actions taken by others are copied in the process of portfolio management. For example, Banerjee (1992) and Bikhchandani, Hirshleifer, and Welch (1992) present models of the so-called information cascades in which rational decision makers attach more importance to information inferred from the behavior of other players than they do to signals deriving from their own analyses. The already mentioned model of Sharfstein and Stein (1990) explaining herd behavior by the fear of losing reputation also assumed that professional investors are rational. Empirical studies do in fact confirm herd behavior among funds in the process of investment selection.

CHAPTER 4

Asset-Pricing Anomalies and Investment Strategies

This chapter systematizes and thoroughly discusses a number of phenomena observed on the capital market that the classical theory of finance considers abnormal.

The following overview, systematization, and the more detailed presentation of specific anomalies later on in the chapter all show which examples of irrational investor behavior may be responsible for specific irregularities as well as what psychological factors may determine irrational attitudes among stock market players. Investment strategies based on observed anomalies are also discussed.

1. Classification of Anomalies

The aim of this chapter is not only to systematize and discuss the wide range of publications on anomalies in asset pricing, but also to show which types of behavior of individual investors may trigger specific anomalous phenomena at the aggregated level and what determines such behavior from the psychological point of view. In other words, the objective is to present a three-fold relation continuity linking psychological factors, irrational behavior of investors, and peculiar market phenomena confounding the neoclassical theory of finance.

According to the law of one price, under perfect market conditions, identical assets should have the same price. What we can observe in stock markets, however, are three major groups of phenomena where the law of one price is violated. These are close-end funds puzzle, quotations of the so-called twin stocks, and the simultaneous listing of mother- and daughter-company shares. The main reason for which the law of one price is broken is the reduced effectiveness of arbitrage when it comes to redressing incorrect stock valuation. Among the many limits that rational arbitrageurs have to face, the most important one has to do with the noise-trader risk, that is, the difficulty in predicting changes in investment sentiment and mood displayed by irrational investors (see chapter 1).

Calendar anomalies involve regular patterns in returns occurring over time. A number of studies have shown that returns may be influenced by the month of the year or the day of the week on which they occur. Among the many hypotheses that seek to explain the month-of-the-year effect, behavioral finance points mainly to the disposition effect observed in individual investors, which, during a given year, keeps them from disposing of losing shares. Its root psychological cause is loss aversion as well as irrational optimism and wishful thinking that make investors believe that prices are only down temporarily and will soon recover to previously anticipated levels. It is only when faced with an imminent year end and influenced by strong tax incentives that investors choose to take a loss. Institutional investors engage in yet another practice referred to as window dressing. The practice entails clearing security portfolios before year end of any spectacular losers and selling off stocks of small-capitalization companies so that their reported portfolio structure can be benchmarked to S&P 500, an index preferred as a benchmark by most mutual funds in the United States.

The majority of explanations of the weekend effect point to the fact that investors, particularly individual, slow their trading on Fridays in anticipation of the weekend only to accelerate it on Mondays. At the same time, companies tend to defer reporting bad news till just after the Friday closing bell; it is not until the Monday opening that such news translates into lower prices.

Extensive research has been dedicated to market reacting to information imprecisely. Whether overreaction is more common than underreaction remains debatable. Positive autocorrelation of indexes and portfolio returns (but generally no autocorrelation of returns on individual stocks) may suggest that new information spreads slowly in the market (e.g., Lo and MacKinlay, 1988, 1990). Similar conclusions are suggested by the profitability of momentum strategies relying on short-term market trends (Jegadeesh and Titman, 1993, 2001, 2002) as well as evidence of post-announcement drift in some event studies. Examples of market underreactions include corporate earnings announcements (Ball and Brown, 1968; Foster et al., 1984; Bernard and Thomas, 1989, 1990), stock splits (Ikenberry et al., 1996; Desai and Jain, 1997), changes in dividend policies (Michaely et al., 1995), and stock repurchases (Lakonishok and Vermaelen, 1990). While long-term post-announcement drifts are seen mainly as an expression of insufficient initial market response, what begins as an overly weak reaction may in time turn into an overreaction if investors who notice a steady rise in returns develop unreasonable trust in trend continuation and yield to the extrapolation bias. Note that continuing trends in returns may generally result from market underreactions or overreactions to information. Some trends remain fully uninfluenced by any substantial news, driven solely by the periodic mood swings of irrational investors.

The main underlying reason why investors underreact to information may be their cognitive conservatism to clear signals. Adverse news also evokes loss aversion triggering the disposition effect. Due to investor reluctance to sell losing stocks, it takes time for negative information to impact stock prices. The popular market saying is: "Bad news travels slowly." Reactions may also be weakened by the illusion of falsehood as true information may be considered false if reported in a convoluted manner, which requires an extra mental effort to interpret.

Ample direct evidence also exists to demonstrate market overreactions. Such evidence includes initial public offerings (IPOs) and secondary equity offerings (SEOs) (Ritter, 1991; Loughran and Ritter, 1995; Spiess and Affleck-Graves, 1995; Lee, 1997). The persistently negative abnormal returns that usually follow are deemed to constitute gradual market adjustments of initial overvaluations. A long-term reversal of market trends may also be revealed by negative correlations across long-term returns (Fama and French, 1988; Poterba and Summers, 1988) and the effectiveness of long-term contrarian strategies (De Bondt and Thaler, 1985, 1987).

Overreaction may result from the extrapolation bias, belief in trends, or herd behavior. This ties to representativeness biases, overconfidence, and excessive trust in unconfirmed rumors or noisy information.

Another group of studies that provoked many debates analyzed to what extent returns may be predicted based on certain characteristics of companies. Fama and French (1996) showed that a number of anomalies in this category overlap and may in fact be reduced to just two major phenomena: company-size effect and book-to-market effect. Financial behaviorists argue that higher returns on small firm stocks are the result of extra risk stemming from unpredictable behavior of small investors who dominate in the shareholder structure of small-cap companies. The book-to-market equity effect, on the other hand, is explained by the fact that investors overvalue the companies that have had good financial results so far, underestimating those whose performance has been comparatively poor. This is caused by the so-called extrapolation bias and a naive belief in trend continuation. Psychologically, such attitudes are driven by problems with correct perception of representativeness and the principle of regression toward the mean.

Anomalies in asset pricing have direct consequences for investors. Exhibit 4.1 presents the three-stage relation among anomalies, investor behavior, and the psychological background. Additionally, practical implications for investment strategies are outlined.

Concluding the classification of abnormal phenomena outlined earlier, we must say that the behavioral explanations are often not the only possible way to account for observed peculiarities in asset pricing. Neither are they definitive. Later on, when the chapter discusses specific anomalies, some more alternative hypotheses will also be mentioned. It must be stressed, however, that behavioral finance can comprehensively explain a wide range of anomalies. Deviations from the classical theory of finance are caused by irrational investor behavior motivated by psychological factors. In general, such behavior may be classified into three major groups—errors in the perception and processing of information, representativeness errors, and unstable preferences. This thinking lay at the origin of a Generalized Behavioral Model presented later on in chapter 5, a model that can very roughly explain most of the phenomena that the classical theory deems abnormal.

Exhibit 4.1 The relation among asset-pricing anomalies, investor behavior and its psychological background, and implications for investment strategy

Market anomaly	Investor behavior	Psychological background	Investment strategy
Violating the law of one price: • Closed-end funds puzzle • Mispricing of dual-listed stocks • Mispricing of mother- and daughter-company stocks	• Difficult to predict changes of investment sentiment among noise traders • Limited arbitrage	• Fear among rational players about changes in investment sentiment among noise traders • Treating changeability of noise-trader sentiment as an extra risk factor • Fear of losing reputation by playing alone against the market	• If you want to invest in closed-end funds, buy on secondary market and not in primary offering; be prepared for swings in the amount of *NAV* discount • If you see clear mispricing, buy cheap and sell expensive at the same time; however, be prepared that it may take some time before the mispricing will be corrected, and it may also increase in the meantime; you may expect difficulties in shorting the overpriced asset
Seasonal anomalies: • Month-of-the-year effect	• Disposition effect among individual investors • Window dressing and other practices of institutional investors	• Loss aversion • Unrealistic optimism and wishful thinking • Mental accounting based on annual periods • Asset managers' biased incentives resulting from rules of evaluating and compensation schemes	• Best time (on average) to buy stocks is end of December and the best time to sell is mid-January; particularly applicable to small-cap stocks
• Weekend effect	• Less activity from investors who begin their weekend on Fridays • More activity from small investors on Mondays • Firms prone to announce negative information right before market closes on Friday • Limited arbitrage	• Cognitive conservatism • Costs of maintaining short positions over the weekend	• Be prepared for more negative corporate announcements on Fridays afternoons

Incorrect market reaction to information: • Autocorrelation and cross-correlation of returns • Profitability of contrarian investing in the long term • Profitability of momentum strategies in the short term • Post-announcement drift	• Under- or overreaction to information • Extrapolation bias • Belief in trends • Disposition effect • Herd behavior in individual and institutional investors	• Illusion of truth • Underestimating the principle of regression toward the mean • Noticing patterns in random data • Loss aversion • Predicting behavior of other market players • Inferring information from the way others behave • Overconfidence in the case of uncertain or descriptive information • Cognitive conservatism toward confirmed information and numerical data • Asset managers' biased incentives resulting from rules of evaluating and compensation schemes	• In a short-term strategy: Buy those stocks that recently have been rising the most, and sell the biggest losers, revise your positions for up to one year • In a long-term strategy: Buy those stocks with lowest returns in last three years and sell the ones the highest returns over last three years, revise your portfolio for up to three years • Overcome your loss aversion, apply stop-loss approach, remember: If a stock price has just been hit by negative news, on average, it is more likely that it will continue to fall than it will rebounce
Possibility to predict returns based on company profile: • Small-size effect	• Fads to invest in certain categories of assets • Difficult to predict instability of small investor sentiment	• Fear among rational players about changes in investment sentiment among noise traders • Treating changeability of noise-trader sentiment as an extra risk factor	• Small-cap stocks on average in a long term are likely to yield higher returns; however, this is highly variable in particular years • Small-cap firms' valuation is highly sensitive to swings in investor sentiment; small caps are likely to be overvalued when the investor sentiment is high and undervalued when it is depressed
• Book-to-market equity effect	• Extrapolation bias • Belief in trends	• Underestimating the principle of regression toward the mean • Representativeness bias	• In the long term, invest in value rather than growth

2. Violation of the Law of One Price

The law of one price is one of the basic economic principles saying that, in a perfect market, the same assets should have the same price. Identical pricing is made possible by arbitrage. Purchasing an asset where it is cheaper while simultaneously selling it on the market offering a higher price would make it possible to reap risk-free profits. However, increased demand on the cheaper market and larger supply on the more expensive one quickly level out the prices. This, at least, is the theory of economics. But when we look at capital market practice, we can distinguish three major categories of events where the law of one price is violated. These are pricing shares in closed-end funds, listing of the so-called twin stocks and the situation where shares of mother and daughter companies are simultaneously listed on the market.

2.1. Closed-End Funds Puzzle

Closed-end funds are a special variety of mutual funds in which the number of shares is fixed over the entire life of the fund. After acquiring a specified amount of capital, such funds neither accept new contributions nor redeem their shares. The fund will invest the obtained resources on the capital market creating its portfolio in accordance with the adopted strategy. Share value will depend on profitability of the investment, that is the current net asset value (NAV). The only way to withdraw from the investment or join the fund after it has been closed is to trade shares on the secondary market. It would seem that the price of a closed-end fund share on the exchange market should be as close as possible to NAV per one share. In practice, however, share prices deviate significantly from NAV.

Anomalies related to closed-end funds are expressed in three general ways. First, shares of the new funds are issued at a premium to a NAV of up to 10 percent in the United States (Weiss, 1989) and over 5 percent in the United Kingdom (Levis and Thomas, 1995). This premium represents the underwriting fees and start-up costs associated with the floatation. The first question to ask is why would investors want to buy new shares with a premium. Second, this is all the more surprising given the fact that within three to six months after the first listing, share value falls much below NAV and trade on average with a discount. Third, discount value is highly variable both in the short and the long term. In the years 1973–1998, the average discount value among all closed-end funds fluctuated from 50 percent in the United Kingdom and 43 percent in the United States in some periods in the 1970s, to a few percent in the United Kingdom in the mid-1990s, or even turned into a meager premium in some periods during the mid-1980s' boom in the United States (Dimson and Minio-Kozerski, 1999).

Market pricing of shares finally gets close to NAV when the fund is about to be liquidated or transformed into an open-ended fund. This seems understandable as the amount shareholders will get will in fact correspond to NAV per share at the moment the fund is terminated. But then why do share prices fluctuate so much over the entire life cycle of the fund and deviate so far from NAV? Are there any rational reasons behind this phenomenon or are investors irrational and unable to establish their prices correctly? If this is the case, why is the behavior of noise traders not compensated by actions taken by rational arbitrageurs?

Attempts to provide rational explanations point at deferred tax liabilities or limited liquidity. Agency costs, understood here as the uncertainty as to future actions of fund managers, are also considered. Nonetheless, the aforementioned explanations, even though partially justified, cannot fully account for all observations related to the pricing of closed-end fund shares. One of the questions not answered by the "rational school" is why fund shares are initially listed with a premium. Neither can its proponents explain the high volatility of the discount over the fund's life cycle.

Lee, Shleifer, and Thaler (1990, 1991) offer a behavioral explanation of the closed-end fund puzzle referring to the concept of noise-trader risk (see chapter 1). Initial listings above the NAV stem from the advantage of rational professionals who benefit from the ignorance of noise traders to organize new funds in the periods of increased market optimism and take actions with the aim to sustain the high initial price. Lee, Shleifer, and Thaler (1991), and Levis and Thomas (1995) document that public offerings of closed-end funds are particularly abundant on the market when the discount on the closed-end funds is especially low or there is even a premium to NAV. Weiss, Lee, and Seguin (1996) also point out that over the first 30 sessions after new shares are placed on the stock market, the average value of one sell order is much higher than the average value of the buy order. This suggests that bigger players, probably underwriters in the offering process, sell to small individual investors just after the fund gets listed. After a time, the ownership structure of the new fund shares is dominated by small investors. Analyzing the American market, Weiss (1989) documents that as early as three quarters after the first listing, the individual investors amount to 95 percent of a fund's shareholders, on average. Because of the high percentage of small players, irrational factors are more likely to have influence on prices. Lee, Shleifer, and Thaler (1990, 1991) suggest that discount fluctuations are the result of changes in investor sentiment. Optimistic attitudes decrease the amount of discount whereas pessimism will widen the gap between current market price of a share and NAV per share.

At the same time, unpredictability of small investor sentiment constitutes extra systemic risk for which rational investors require higher returns. This is why the price of shares stays generally below their underlying NAV. Lower prices of shares in relation to their NAV do not attract arbitrageurs as they notice the extra risk involved.

If the additional risk related to noise traders is to be systematic, it should be common among all classes of instruments dominated by individual investors. Consequently, we should be able to observe correlation between the discount values for different funds as well as between funds' prices and prices of other assets that are typically popular with small investors. Indeed, the amount of discount is correlated among various funds. There is also correlation between the level of discount or premium on the closed-end fund market and prices of small-cap companies. The shareholder structure in small companies is usually dominated by small investors as big institutional players are much more reluctant to buy such shares because of, inter alia, relatively high fixed costs of carrying out relevant analyses and poor liquidity. Lee et al. (1991) and Chopra, Lee, Shleifer, and Thaler (1993) suggest that both the amount of discount on the funds market as well as returns on small-cap stocks share the same common risk factor stemming from the noise-trader sentiment.

The hypothesis that the pricing of fund shares is influenced by an additional risk factor that is not directly related to their NAV is also confirmed by Bodurtha, Kim, and Lee (1993). They find that the discount of closed-end funds specializing in investing in only one country abroad (so-called country funds) is correlated not because such funds share prospects and receive similar information from the countries in which they invest, but because they are correlated with a common factor related to the American market. In other words, prices of fund shares whose asset value depends on the situation on non-US markets are very much contingent on how the local, American market develops or what kind of sentiment it exhibits.

Another argument that could support the noise trader risk hypothesis is the fact that when the date of termination of a closed-end fund approaches, the current share price gets gradually close to NAV. The reason is that the shorter the period until the actual value of the funds' assets is calculated onto its shares, the lesser the risk that noise traders will contribute to a significant deviation of the shares' prices in the meantime. Also, rational arbitrageurs become ready to take appropriate positions in a relatively short period of time because they know that at the termination date, the value of a share must correspond to the NAV per share.

2.2. *Twin Stocks*

A twin company's charter fixes the division of current and future equity cash flows to each twin. This implies a specific ratio for the market prices of their securities. Examples of these kinds of twin companies are Royal Dutch Petroleum—a company registered in the Netherlands whose shares are primarily listed on the Dutch and American markets—and Shell Transport and Trading, PLC, which is registered in the United Kingdom with assets traded mostly on the London Stock Exchange. Years ago, shareholders of these companies decided to join up forces on a global scale and divide the net profit they generated in the following proportion: 60 percent for owners of Royal Dutch shares and 40 percent for owners of Shell shares. Similarly, dually listed are Unilever N.V.—registered in the Netherlands—and Unilever PLC—registered in the United Kingdom. Shareholders of those two entities are to be paid dividends in equal amounts on the basis of totaled net results.

Bearing in mind the agreements mentioned earlier, which are publicly available and widely explained in different publications for investors, as well as the fact that the pairs of companies have high capitalization and good liquidity, we should assume that share prices of Royal Dutch and Shell will hover around the 60:40 proportion and prices for Unilever N.V. and Unilever PLC should stay more or less on the same level. In practice, relative prices of twin shares in the 1980s and 1990s were markedly different from the theoretical assumptions (Rosenthal and Young, 1990; Froot and Dabora, 1999). Generally, until mid-1980s, both Royal Dutch and Unilever N.V. were significantly underpriced. The situation changed over the following ten years when Royal Dutch remained slightly overvalued compared to Shell whereas Unilever N.V. fluctuated between being over- and underpriced in relation to Unilever PLC with surprisingly big changes of relative prices.

Froot and Dabora (1999) have demonstrated that deviations from the theoretical parity of listings cannot be explained neither by differences in voting rights and control over dual listed companies nor by fluctuations of exchange rates or other international transaction costs. The only factor able to explain, but only just, such deviations are different tax regimes for investors located in various countries. Particularly, it is difficult to justify why in some periods there is relative overvaluation while others experience relative underpricing between twin companies.

This phenomenon presents a challenge to the self-correction ability of the arbitrage mechanism. There is no fundamental risk as such shares represent dividend rights based on the same cash flows and these are large and liquid firms that should be easy to short. The biggest risk factors, however, remain unpredictability of noise traders and the lack of synchronization among arbitrageurs (see chapter 1). Once noise traders have made the parity of twin shares deviate significantly from theoretical values, there is a danger that the growing "sentiment" on a given local market will only get aggravated increasing the deviation and exposing the arbitrageur to the risk of losses even though these might be short term in nature. Rosenthal and Young (1990) show that an investor who decided to buy Royal Dutch or Unilever N.V. shares in 1979 when they were underpriced by about 15–20 percent in relation to the prices of their counterparts listed on American and British markets would have to wait almost five years before prices got close to the theoretical level of parity. In the meantime, however, he would have to endure increasing underpricing amounting in 1981 to over 25 percent for Royal Dutch and over 23 percent for Unilever N.V.

2.3. Pricing of Mother- and Daughter-Company Shares

It is sometimes the case that shares of mother and daughter companies are listed on the market. An especially interesting situation takes place when the mother company decides to carve out a part of its business and float a daughter company on the market offering part of its shares for cash in an IPO while allocating the remaining part to shareholders of the mother company. The IPO usually happens in advance of allocating the remaining shares to mother-company shareholders. However, the intention to do so and the conditions of allocation are publicly communicated already at the moment when the company is placed on the market. Therefore, investors who are interested in purchasing daughter-company shares can do it in two ways. First, they may buy shares directly participating in the IPO or on the secondary market after listing. Or, they may buy mother company shares and wait for the allocation of daughter-company shares, which usually happens in the near future.

For example, in March 2000, the American IT company 3Com sold in an IPO 5 percent of shares of Palm Inc., a producer of electronic personal organizers extremely popular at the time. It announced publicly that it intends to allocate the remaining 95 percent of shares to shareholders of 3Com over the following nine months in the proportion of 1.5 Palm share per 3Com share. Theoretically, the price of 3Com should amount to at least 1.5 the price of Palm or should even be higher given all the assets and profits generated by 3Com from its other lines of business. In reality, at market close after the first listing day, the price of Palm Inc. shares amounted to 95 dollars while the price for 3Com was only 81 dollars. In other words, daughter-company shares were worth more than mother-company shares giving the right to purchase 1.5 of the former. By the same token, the remaining activity of the mother company was priced by the market at about minus 60 dollars per share. The situation continued for several weeks even though it was a glaring example of incorrect pricing, which, theoretically, offered an opportunity for arbitrage.

A rational arbitrageur should try to short sell Palm shares, simultaneously buying 3Com shares in the proportion of 3:2 respectively. Within a period not longer than nine months, he would realize a theoretically risk-free profit. There is no fundamental risk as exactly the same asset, Palm Inc. shares, would be settled on both sides at the moment of closing arbitrage positions. Noise-trader risk and the risk of synchronization are also reduced because the allocation of Palm Inc. shares and, consequently, the final closing of positions is supposed to take place not later than within nine months. Since the period is relatively short and defined in advance, possible further deviations from the minimal parity should not be very dangerous for arbitrageurs. So why don't large numbers of rational investors take action to benefit from such an obvious opportunity allowing the anomaly to persist for at least several weeks?

It turns out that in this case, like in five other similar situations that were thoroughly analyzed by Lamont and Thaler (2003), what was most important was the practical impossibility of short selling. Investors who want to take a short position on overpriced shares of a daughter company were either not able to borrow these shares at all or they would have to pay very high fees for borrowing the assets from their owners. Mitchell, Pulvino, and Stafford (2002) make similar observations about a much larger number of instances when the relation between the price of mother and daughter shares is wrong.

3. Calendar Anomalies

3.1. Month-of-the-Year Effect

The month-of-the-year effect, also called the January effect, is one of the best described anomalies of the seasonal distribution of returns. The phenomenon was already noticed by Wachtel (1942), but it started to be discussed more thoroughly almost 40 years later. Many publications (see, inter alia, Rozeff and Kinney, 1976; Branch, 1977; Dyl, 1977; Dimson, 1988; Haugen and Lakonishok, 1988; Lakonishok and Smidt, 1988) demonstrated that average returns are much higher in the first month of the year compared to other months. Furthermore, Roll (1981), Keim (1983), and Reinganum (1983) documented that in the United States the phenomenon is typical for small-cap companies. Hence, the January effect is often related to the company-size effect (Banz, 1981). However, later studies by Gu (2003) suggest that the January effect might just as well affect big companies. At the same time, Gu (2003) and Schwert (2003) point out that the phenomenon was much weaker over the last two decades of the twentieth century, which might have suggested that the fact it had been discovered and publicized made the market more efficient. However, the effect seems to be back in a few recent years.

The most widely known explanation of the January effect is the tax-loss selling hypothesis. At year end, investors sell stocks whose prices fell over the last 12 months in order to deduct the realized loss from their tax base. Supply pressure deflate prices in late December. Early January, investors start buying stocks that are now underpriced due to the December sellout. This activity generates high returns. Keim (1983) and Roll (1983) find that the market is most active during the first five sessions of the new year. Studies conducted by Dyl (1977), Tkac (1999), and Chen and Singal (2000) also confirm the hypothesis of the tax-motivated January effect. They find that shares whose prices fell in the previous year are traded much more often in December (tax pressure) and January (demand pressure). Reinganum (1983) documents that the great majority of the total number of stocks sold in order to settle losses are small company shares. Supply pressure has more impact on prices of small company stocks that are not usually traded intensively. Reinganum (1983) nevertheless makes the reservation that the tax sale hypothesis is most probably not the full and only explanation of the January effect as it is also observed, even though it is less intense, in the case of small companies whose shares generated profit in the previous year. Ritter (1988) answers Reinganum's doubts saying that the fall in prices resulting from the December sale can explain only a small portion of the January effect. What seems to be more important are high returns in the first days of January caused not only by repurchasing the previously sold shares, but also by investing free cash in other securities that did not necessarily bring a loss in the previous year.

Gultekin and Gultekin (1983) documented that the month-of-the-year effect was present in 16 other countries. These markets did not, however, display a relationship between the seasonality of returns and company size that would be as strong as the one observed in the United States. This was also confirmed by more recent studies by Arshanapalli, Coggin, and Nelson (2002). It is worth mentioning that the January effect was also present in countries where there capital profits are not taxed (e.g., Japan—Kiyoshi, 1985) as well as those where the end of the tax year does not correspond to the end of the calendar year (e.g., the United Kingdom—Reinganum and Shapiro, 1987; Hillier and Marshall, 2002; Zhang and Jacobsen, 2013; Australia—Brown et al., 1983).

On the face of it, these observations might seem to contradict the tax-loss selling hypothesis. Let us remember, however, that they might result from extensive connections between global capital markets. On the other hand, a fact supporting the tax-loss selling hypothesis is that higher-than-average returns in the United Kingdom and Australia were not only present in January, but also in the first month of the tax year (April in the United Kingdom, July in Australia). Menyah (1999) also demonstrated that higher January returns on the British market can be observed primarily in the case of big capitalization companies, whereas higher April returns are typical for companies with small capitalization. This may also confirm the hypothesis. In the United Kingdom and Australia, the tax year must start in April and July, respectively, but the obligation concerns natural persons only. Legal persons are free to determine their financial and tax years as they wish. Most financial institutions choose December as the last month of the tax year. We may therefore assume that higher January rates on big company assets in these countries are caused by actions taken by institutional investors who invest in big capitalization companies much more often. On the other hand, abnormal returns on small company shares in April (United Kingdom) and July (Australia) may be interpreted as a result of individual investor activity, such investors accounting for a large percentage of shareholders in small companies.

While the tax-loss selling hypothesis seems to play the most important role, it is definitely not the only explanation behind the month-in-the-year effect, nor can it be considered to be fully rational. It may be understandable that investors want to sell shares in order to offset their taxes, but it is harder to explain why they would wait to realize losses right up to the last moment in December. Investor psychology offers potential answers to these questions. It may be assumed that keeping open positions for assets whose price was systematically falling over the year is related to strong loss aversion and the disposition effect. Investors wait until the last moment hoping that the trend will turn allowing them to avoid losses. This attitude may be related to overconfidence and unrealistic optimism. Investors are reluctant to admit that they have made a mistake preferring to persist in their belief that it is the market which prices the asset unfavorably and this "temporary" situation will "soon" be corrected to their satisfaction. They also anchor to the purchase price, equating it with the fair value while disregarding events which have taken place in the meantime and might have significantly and permanently changed the value of the company. It is only the approaching year end and strong tax incentives that motivate them to close their positions at a loss that, offset on their taxes, is probably less painful. As psychologically driven biases are more typical for individual investors who usually dominate small companies, supply pressure at year end will mostly affect small-cap stocks.

Postponing investment decisions until the beginning of January is in turn caused by the psychological phenomenon of mental accounting. In December, people do not think of new investments but examine last year's profits and losses. It is the new calendar year that is traditionally associated with a new investment period bringing fresh expectations that are usually built up ignoring last year's results. Ciccone (2011) finds that investor sentiment, as measured by the University of Michigan's Index of Consumer Confidence, peaks in January.

The behavior of individual investors is additionally enhanced by actions of institutional investors who also usually reallocate their portfolios at the turn of the year (Haugen and Lakonishok, 1988; Lakonishok et al., 1991; Shefrin, 2000). Most asset managers are obliged to submit annual reports to their customers in which they also need to describe their portfolio structure. Wanting to include a portfolio where most shares are blue-chip and have recently performed well, many managers sell blocks of less-well-known shares, that is, small-company assets, especially if they have generated losses lately (window dressing). Small-cap companies are sold also because of the need to bring the reported portfolio structure closer to the benchmark, which, for most US share funds, is S&P500. The ensuing supply pressure will decrease prices at year end, but mostly in the case of small company shares. This is only natural, as trading volume in such stocks is usually poor. In the new year, managers open their positions again, purchasing shares that they consider to be most underpriced. Again, the impulse they thus generate will affect prices of small and not very liquid companies to a larger extent.

3.2. Weekend Effect

A number of independent studies have demonstrated that average returns between session close on Friday and Monday were much lower than the average rates on other weekdays, their typical values being even negative (see, inter alia, Cross, 1973; French, 1980; Gibbons and Hess, 1981; Keim and Stambaugh, 1984; Lakonishok and Maberly, 1990). However, Schwert (2003) argues that the discovery of the weekend effect and its subsequent dissemination in the literature made it disappear. He confirms the presence of the weekend effect in the years 1885–1977, and especially in 1928–1977. Nevertheless, he also documents that it is difficult to notice the anomaly in the data for 1978–2002.

The discovery of the weekend effect raised the question of when exactly observed negative returns are realized. Does it happen between session close on Friday and the Monday opening or perhaps during the Monday session? Studies into the matter have not given a clear answer. Rogalski (1984a, 1984b), using the Dow Jones Industrial Average and S&P500 indexes from 1974 to 1983, shows that negative returns on Mondays may in practice be attributed almost exclusively to declines between session's close on Friday and session's opening on Monday. Smirlock and Starks (1986) broaden the time horizon of Rogalski's studies for the period 1963–1983. Their results for the 1974–1983 subperiod confirm those obtained by Rogalski. In the case of the earlier subperiod, however, they discovered a relation that was exactly opposite. The entire weekend effect took place during Monday's session. Harris (1986) finds that the Monday negative returns are distributed in such a way that roughly half of it could be attributed to the period between sessions, that is, after Friday close but before Monday opening. The other half is realized within the first 45 minutes of the Monday session.

Jaffe and Westerfield (1985) and Chang, Pinegar, and Ravichandran (1993) discovered the weekend effect in the United Kingdom, Canada, Australia, and Japan with the difference that in the two last countries, on average, lower returns appeared on Tuesdays rather than Mondays. Bildik (2004) noticed lower Monday returns on the Turkish market, whereas Kanaryan, Lyroudi, and Patev (2004) did the same for the Czech Republic and Romania and Szyszka (2003) for the Polish market.

Damodaran (1989) put forward a hypothesis that low Monday returns may be rationally explained by information-related factors, the usual time when companies announce negative news being Friday afternoon. DellaVigna and Pollet (2005) have partially confirmed Damodaran's intuitions documenting that the Friday announcements of financial results are 25 percent more likely to contain a negative surprise. But they also argue that investors attach less importance to the information announced on Fridays even if it is made public when trading is not finished yet. The Friday trading volume for shares covered by announcement on this day is lower by 20 percent on average than the trading volume on other weekdays. They have also observed a strong post-announcement drift after Friday announcements. Insufficient market reaction to information announced during Friday's trading is also evident in studies carried out by Bagnoli, Clement, and Watt (2004).

It could therefore be argued that investors are much less concerned by news they receive on Fridays as they are anxious to begin their rest at the weekend. Corporate managers exploit this habit selecting Fridays as the days of announcing bad news. Lakonishok and Maberly (1990) find in session statistics that small market players are usually more active after weekends than they are on other days of the week, especially as it concerns supply. Monday activity of institutional investors, on the other hand, is less intense. So it might be possible that low Monday returns are the product of small investors reacting too nervously and slightly too late to negative information published much more often on Fridays than other weekdays. Irrational behavior of small investors cannot be totally compensated for by rational arbitrageurs as, in addition to standard arbitrage limitations, keeping short positions over the weekend involves extra transaction costs (Chen and Singal, 2003).

4. Incorrect Market Reaction to Information

There are many publications documenting the way markets react incorrectly to incoming information. Such reactions are visible in autocorrelation and cross-correlation across portfolio returns, the profitability of contrarian or momentum strategies, and the presence of abnormal returns persisting long after their triggering event took place on the market.

In general, it is often hard to distinguish if particular cases of return predictability are a product of overreaction or underreaction to fundamental information. Return correlation may even happen without being justified by any information, simply as a result of changing investor sentiment (see section 2.1 in chapter 5).

4.1. Returns Correlation

Lo and MacKinlay (1988, 1990) document autocorrelation of portfolio returns and index changes, but not for individual securities. This immediately raises two questions. What is the reason for this situation and how can the observation be used in the context of obtaining higher-than-average returns?

Significant positive correlation coefficients for short-term returns may suggest that the market is too slow reflecting incoming information. Information that is crucial for whole segments or groups of companies is reflected in share prices gradually. This causes positive correlation across returns on investment portfolios but not necessarily individual assets. Lo and MacKinlay (1988, 1990) document that autocorrelation is greater in the case of small-cap portfolios. Hence, it might be argued that potential anomalies related to incorrect market reaction to information affect mostly small companies that are not usually in the sight line of professional market players. Furthermore, it is more difficult to short-sell them, which seriously limits the possibility of arbitrage. As a result, shares of small companies are much more susceptible to incorrect pricing caused by noise traders. Moreover, Lo and MacKinlay find that returns of small-cap portfolios may be predicted on the basis of returns from large-cap portfolios. Information that is important for the entire market gets first reflected in the pricing of big companies. Small-cap stocks usually lag behind.

Although slow reaction to information seems to be the obvious cause, it is not the only possible explanation for positive correlation of portfolio returns. Similarly, we may observe autocorrelation of returns as a product of overreaction to information. Finally, portfolio return correlation might even be totally independent of fundamental news, being linked to changes in investment sentiment among noise traders. Positive correlations across returns are observed following such examples of irrational investor behavior as: beauty contest effect, extrapolation bias, and the self-fulfilling belief in trends. In the long term, market overreaction will be eventually adjusted, triggering long-term negative correlations across returns (Poterba and Summers, 1988; Fama and French, 1988). Again, these phenomena will be especially evident in the case of small companies where the activity of small investors is relatively high and there is little opportunity for arbitrage.

Finally, we cannot exclude that short-term continuations and long-term reversals of the returns are caused by the behavior of professional players (Lakonishok et al., 1992). Even though they are generally believed to make decisions rationally, the specific rules of evaluation and compensation may provide incentives to attach more weight to investment decisions made by their counterparts in other funds than to their own analyses. As they become involved in herd behavior, prices get destabilized, whereas severe fluctuations in demand for selected groups of assets trigger short-term continuations of the returns. These will affect shares of big companies first as this is where professional players are most active. The observed correlation will, in turn, be a signal for noise traders to take action and to follow trend. Small investors will contribute to further continuation of the returns that will now be especially visible in small-cap portfolios.

Behavioral finance does not give a straightforward answer as to which of the three scenarios outlined earlier is more responsible for the observed autocorrelation and cross-correlation of returns. Most probably, the market under- and overreacts in different situations. The two tendencies do not have to be mutually exclusive and might even reinforce each other in certain situations. First, investor reaction may depend on the type of information. It is a well-known fact that people react to information of a descriptive nature stronger, having more trouble to register statistical data (Kahneman and Tversky, 1973; Tversky and Kahneman, 1982; Griffin and Tversky, 1992). Also, decision makers are usually conservative about precise signals and overreact to unconfirmed information (Bloomfield et al., 2000). Second, it may be a case of the so-called feedback trading. In feedback trading, the correlation between returns initially triggered by weak market reaction or herd behavior of professional traders may be a signal for more intensive activity of those investors who follow trends or fall victim to the extrapolation bias. This may turn into market overreaction. Actions taken by more noise traders will detach prices from fundamentals, a deviation that will only be adjusted in the long term, resulting in negative correlation across long-term returns.

4.2. Contrarian Investing

In the strategy of contrarian investing, it is generally recommended to purchase assets that have recently lost a lot of value and sell those whose price has increased. It comes in two basic varieties: short and long term.

Lehmann (1990) suggested constructing portfolios on the basis of asset prices observed in the first four days of the previous week.[1] His simulation consisted in purchasing securities that performed worse than the market in the previous week while selling those that have recently brought higher returns than the market average. The analysis was carried out for all assets listed in the years 1962–1986 on NYSE and AMEX/ASE. The weekly return on the portfolio thus created amounted to the average of 1.21 percent and was positive in about 90 percent of weeks in the period studied. Lehmann interpreted the results as a product of the market reacting too violently to information. He argues that investors react too emotionally in a short period of time to both good and bad news while the relevant adjustment only takes place in the following week, on average. However, Lo and MacKinlay (1990) demonstrate that the profitability of Lehmann's strategy was not so much the result of overreaction as delayed reaction of some groups of shares to systemic information, that is, the kind of information that was common for the entire market. This led to cross-correlation between returns on one group of assets in week t and other assets in week $t+1$.

Jegadeesh (1990) tested the contrarian strategy over one month. The simulation was carried out for the shares traded on NYSE and AMEX/ASE in the years 1934–1987. The portfolio made up of 10 percent of shares that brought the lowest returns in the previous month performed on average 1.99 percent better (1.75% excluding January) in the following month than the portfolio containing 10 percent of companies whose results were previously the best.

In later studies, Jegadeesh and Titman (1995) confirm the profitability of the short-term contrarian strategy both for the monthly and weekly time horizons. They also demonstrate that it works best for small-cap companies. At the same time, they suggest a more precise way to decompose abnormal returns compared to the one proposed by Lo and MacKinlay (1990). They claim that investors overreact to information related to individual companies, but are too slow to process information that is common for the entire market.

The profitability of short-term contrarian strategies was also confirmed on other global markets including in France (Bacmann and Dubois, 1998), the United Kingdom (Antoniou et al., 2003), Greece (Antoniou et al., 2005), and Australia (Chan et al., 2003). The studies mentioned also demonstrated investor tendency to overreact to information that is company specific and underreact to systemic information.

In practical terms, however, the importance of the strategy of short-term contrarian investing is very limited. Given the high frequency of transactions, the amount of transaction costs remains the key. For example, Lehmann (1990) demonstrated that the critical cost threshold at which extra profit disappears amounts to about 0.2 percent of each transaction's value. This probably explains why short-term contrarian strategies do not raise so much controversy as the much more widely discussed long-term strategies related to returns over several years.

De Bondt and Thaler (1985) carried out the following simulation. In the period from January 1933 to December 1980, every three years, there was one portfolio constructed with 35 stocks that performed worst over the previous three years and another with the best performing stocks. Next, a cumulative abnormal return was calculated for each portfolio for the following 36 months.[2] It turned out that portfolios made up of companies whose value increased the fastest in the previous three years, performed 5 percent worse than the market in the following period. On the other hand, portfolios of former losers brought results that were on average 19.6 percent above the market in the following 36 months. What is interesting, almost all cumulative growth of the former losers took place in each of the three consecutive Januaries. On the face of it, this observation might suggest that the phenomenon is largely due to the January effect, the tax-loss selling hypothesis being a potential reason behind the anomaly. Nevertheless, such explanations are only relevant for the January of the first year after the portfolio was constructed. There is still no rational way to explain why portfolios with losing companies generated positive abnormal returns in the two remaining consecutive Januaries as well.

The efficiency of long-term contrarian strategies was also demonstrated on markets in such countries as Belgium (Vermaelen and Verstringe, 1986), Spain (Alonso and Rubio, 1990), and the United Kingdom (Clare and Thomas, 1995; Levis and Liodakis, 2001). It was not confirmed in Canada (Kryzanowski and Zhang, 1992), Hong Kong (Kwok-Wah Fung, 1999), and Australia (Brailsford, 1992; Allen and Prince, 1995). On the other hand, Scowcroft and Sefton (2005) documented the winner–loser effect in the global context analyzing returns on shares making up the MSCI Global Equity Index covering the total of 22 capital markets in developed countries.

Those who try to explain the winner–loser effect are traditionally divided into efficient market proponents and financial behaviorists. The former group is represented by, inter alia, Chan (1988) and Ball et al. (1995), who raise the problem of beta coefficient changeability in time. They argue that a series of falls in stock value usually takes place in response to lower company profitability and disrupts relations between the market value of equity and the amount of indebtedness. With debt staying at the same level, this induces increased financial leverage and, by the same token, higher risk. Chopra et al. (1992) find, however, that differences in betas are not enough to explain the winner–loser effect. Fama and French (1992, 1993, 1996) insist that reversals in long-term returns may be caused by additional risk factors going beyond the traditional beta measure. It must be noted that, even though the three-factor pricing model they suggested goes a long way to explain the profitability of contrarian investing, it does not have to mean that the alleged extra risk premium is indeed rational.

Proponents of behavioral finance explain the winner–loser effect by citing market overreaction (De Bondt and Thaler [1985, 1987]; Lakonishok et al. [1994]). Its primary reason is that investors fall victim to the extrapolation bias, which is, in turn, related to psychologically documented problems with the representativeness and accounting for the principle of regression toward the mean. Noise traders attach too much importance to historical performance of companies. They are too optimistic extrapolating prospects of those companies that have so far been successful on the market, underestimating the potential of weaker companies. It takes relatively long for the market to verify the pricing. When that happens, the companies investors were too optimistic about will give worse returns, whereas those which were underestimated will surprise them with good results.

Daniel, Hirshleifer, and Subrahmanyam (1998) suggested further that market overreaction may be related to overconfidence. They claim that investors overestimate the value of the information they have, which makes them react too strongly. Overreaction is, in turn, aggravated by selective attribution, which prevents it from being adjusted straight away. Having made their decisions, investors will be focused on signals confirming the position they took, downplaying the importance of information to the contrary. Even if totally random in character, observations backing up previous assumptions may only reassure investors that they are right and cause further overreaction. It is only when a lot of important contradictory signals are accumulated, which usually happens over a longer time period, that the initial decision loses its grip and investors change their minds.

Results generated by winner and loser portfolios are not symmetrical with respect to the returns on the market portfolio. Excess returns on the loser portfolios are much higher than the absolute returns on winner portfolios. We may therefore assume that pricing is adjusted much slower for overpriced companies. Because of overconfidence and selective attribution, investors take more time to perceive negative information about companies that they had a good opinion of. In addition, reluctance to realize losses, that is, the disposition effect, may postpone the adjustment of market prices.

4.3. Momentum Strategy

Momentum strategy recommends to buy shares of companies whose value has recently increased significantly and to sell those that have lost the most. Even though the principle seems to be the exact opposite of contrarian investing, the two are distinctive but not contradictory. The key difference is the time frame in which companies are assessed before portfolios are constructed as well as the length of the holding period. While contrarian strategies were concerned with very short (weeks) or very long periods (three to five years in general), the momentum strategy falls somewhere in between.

Jegadeesh and Titman (1993) carried out simulations of 32 different strategies in which the periods of evaluating assets and holding portfolios varied between 3 and 12 months. The data used came from NYSE and AMEX records for the years 1965–1989. Each time, they purchased an equal-weighted portfolio made up of a decile of stocks that were most successful in the previous period and sold an equal-weighted portfolio made up of a decile of stocks with the lowest returns. All strategies generated positive returns. This means that, on average, the shares that brought the highest (lowest) returns over the previous 3–12 months continued their good (bad) performance also in the following 3–12 months. The best results were achieved for the strategy where assets were selected on the basis of their returns over the last 12 months and the portfolios thus constructed (made up of appropriately long and short positions) were held for the following 3 months. On average, the difference between the portfolio with best and worst companies amounted to 1.49 percent per month. The strategy of choosing assets on the basis of their returns over the last half-year period and keeping them for the following six months would bring about 1 percent monthly.

Jegadeesh and Titman (1993) demonstrated that differences in profit from individual portfolios cannot be explained by beta coefficients, while Fama and French (1996) showed that taking account of potential positive premium for company size or book-to-market equity ratio does not help either. Conrad and Kaul (1998) suggested that the profitability of the momentum strategy is not determined by market predictability but by the dispersion between expected returns. They argued that multiple investments in companies that have recently brought the highest profit means more frequent purchases of assets with higher expected returns and, consequently, higher degree of risk. Nonetheless, Jegadeesh and Titman (2002) demonstrated that the dispersion in the level of expected returns may justify only a very small portion of profit generated in the strategy they suggested, if at all.

In later studies covering a larger sample (all companies listed on NYSE, AMEX, and NASDAQ, excluding those with low liquidity, in the period of 1965–1998), Jegadeesh and Titman (2001) further confirmed the importance of the momentum effect. Importantly, the phenomenon was equally strong in the 1990s, that is, after the first reports of the anomaly were published.

The momentum effect was also observed outside the American market. Rouwenhorst (1999) documented its presence in 12 developed European countries, most notably in Spain, the Netherlands, Belgium, and Denmark, while Chui, Titman, and Wei (2001) showed a similar tendency on Asiatic markets except for Japan and South Korea. In later studies, Rouwenhorst (1999) and Szyszka (2006) also confirmed the presence of the momentum effect in emerging markets. Moreover, the strategy also proved efficient when used for internationally diversified portfolios. (Rouwenhorst, 1998; Scowcroft and Sefton, 2005).

We may imagine several scenarios of price formation that could be responsible for the momentum effect. First, there is the slow market reaction to incoming information. Nonetheless, if it was the only systematic irregularity in information processing, the long-term winner–loser effect would be difficult to explain. The other possibility is that the momentum effect takes place only as a result of market overreaction. According to this line of thinking, prices deviate gradually from fundamental values over several to dozen or so months triggering returns continuation. The market would adjust pricing only later on, resulting in the long-term negative correlation. Admittedly, transitory, small adjustments could take place in the meantime, but their scope would be limited and they would not bring assets back to fundamentals. These small adjustments would also explain the results of short-term contrarian investing. Finally, we might also imagine a situation where the market both underreacts and overreacts to information depending on the time horizon or the type of information signals. We may assume that, at the outset, prices reflect incoming information only partially, gradually getting closer to fundamental values. As a result, returns will continue, a tendency that naive investors will extrapolate into the future even when asset prices have already been brought back to fundamental values. Further actions of noise traders will make asset prices deviate in the other direction causing market overreaction, which will only be adjusted in the long term. This scenario also allows for transitory fluctuations that could influence the efficiency of short-term contrarian investing without eliminating the momentum strategy in the medium term and the winner–loser effect in the long perspective.

Jegadeesh and Titman (2001) showed that the portfolios they constructed based on the momentum strategy bring average negative returns starting from 13 to 60 months from the moment of their construction. The observation confirms earlier studies on long-term contrarian investing. This leads Jegadeesh and Titman (2001) to believe that at least part of the momentum effect may be attributed to market overreaction. At the same time, they allow for the possibility that the market might underreact, which they think could contribute to the momentum effect, especially in the initial phase.

Chan, Jegadeesh, and Lakonishok (1996) link the momentum effect with the delayed investor response to reported unexpected earnings. They demonstrated that over half of the profit from a six-month-long momentum strategy is realized over several sessions around the days when successive quarterly reports are published. In other words, if the market was surprised by recent results achieved by a company, it will also be surprised, on average, by the results to come in at least two following quarters. This means that investors display cognitive conservatism, that is, they are first wary of unexpectedly good or bad results achieved by a company and are not able to immediately estimate the probability of the company continuing the good or bad trend. In time, however, their optimism or pessimism gets gradually stronger (in the case of the latter, the process is slower) until eventually the extrapolation bias makes it irrationally powerful. Soffer and Walther (2000) and Chordia and Shivakumar (2006) demonstrate the link between the momentum effect and inadequate earnings forecast.

Hong, Lim, and Stein (2000) provided another argument to back up the thesis that the momentum effect is at least partially caused by delayed processing of information. They noticed that the effect is more evident in the case of companies that attract less attention from professional analysts. This means less access to information and, consequently, slower market reaction.

It is also worth noting that most of the previously mentioned publications document asymmetrical behavior of momentum portfolios. Returns on short positions are higher than those from long positions. This is yet another evidence that the market reacts slower to bad news. Again, the phenomenon could be explained by investor psychology. We know that overconfidence, selective attribution, and cognitive conservatism make it difficult for investors to take in negative information if these contradict their preconceived ideas. Additionally, Grinblatt and Han (2005) present a model in which the disposition effect comes in as an explanation for the momentum effect. As investors are risk averse in the area of profits, they are more willing to sell shares that have just yielded positive returns. Increased supply triggers temporary underpricing, which will be adjusted when the supply pressure subsides. The opposite situation will take place in the case of shares whose sale would entail a loss. Reluctance to sell at a lower price will freeze supply for some time resulting in periodical asset overpricing. Because loss aversion in the domain of losses is higher than risk aversion in the area of profits, deviations from fundamental values and, consequently, future adjustment will be greater in the case of losing assets.

Trying to explain the momentum effect, we have so far tried to determine if it is caused by under- or overreaction to information. Another question is whether the effect is the result of a wrong reaction to company-specific or systemic information. Jegadeesh and Titman (1993, 2001) practically excluded the possibility of general market factors, while Moskowitz and Grinblatt (1999), O'Neal (2000), as well as Swinkels (2002) document industry momentum, the former for the American market, the latter using global portfolio data. A portfolio made up of industries that have grown most over the previous six months gained in value also in the following half year. By the same token, a portfolio containing companies from the sectors that have performed worst recently will continue the bad trend. Moskowitz and Grinblatt (1999) argued that the industry momentum effect could almost entirely explain the profitability of momentum strategies using individual assets.[3] Studies by Grundy and Martin (2001) gave different results. They showed that even though industry factors may play a role, it is only a small part of the momentum effect that is generated by incorrect reaction to company-specific information.

It is worth remembering in this context that the weights of individual assets in portfolios created by Moskowitz and Grinblatt (1999) and Swinkels (2002) were capitalization-weighted portfolios. On the other hand, Grundy and Martin (2001), just like Jegadeesh and Titman (1993, 2001) earlier, created equal-weighted portfolios. This discrepancy in methodology may lead to different results because part of the information specific for big companies is often interpreted as information important for the sector. For example, if a big company publishes better-than-expected financial results, it is more likely that the information will be interpreted as a sign of an improved situation in the entire sector than if similarly surprising results were published by a small company from the same sector. As a consequence, the momentum among big companies will create the impression of being caused by sectoral factors. Decomposition of momentum in a group of small companies will be more probably construed as triggered by specific factors. These assumptions are confirmed by Scowcroft and Sefton (2005).

It may be assumed that investors have problems determining correctly to what degree changes in a company's financial standing are caused by specific factors and what should be attributed to events affecting the entire industry. This is why the market reacts slowly not only to company-specific signals, but also to the gradual diffusion and delayed influence of the information on the pricing of other companies from the same sector. Prices of big companies seem to "lead" share prices of smaller companies operating in the same sector.

The momentum effect may be also potentially triggered or at the very least strengthened by activities of professional market players, at least to a certain extent. Womack (1996) documents that analysts give average better recommendation for companies whose prices have previously had a series of rises. Such information may make investors believe that the growth is likely to continue. Grinblatt, Titman, and Wermers (1995) and Chen, Jegadeesh, and Wermers (2002) also demonstrate that investment funds are more likely to buy previously rising shares, selling those that lost value. The tendency of funds to destabilize prices rather than contribute to reflecting fundamental values (at least in the short term) is confirmed by Burch and Swaminathan (2001) who show that decisions managers make to buy or sell assets depend more on the returns these assets have recently generated than on financial results reported by the companies. At the same time, managers are reluctant to react to important specific information coming from the companies if such reaction would require a major deviation of portfolio structure from the benchmark. Sias (2004) and Fong, Gallagher, Gardner, and Swan (2005) point out that there is a strong tendency for herd behavior among fund managers, but it is directed not so much at the same assets as companies from the same industry.

4.4. Market Reaction to Events

Event studies with a relatively short observation window around the announcement date usually show an immediate market reaction to important news. However, the initial reaction often seems to be too weak, generating post-announcement drift in abnormal returns. If the observation window is extended into the long term, however, results are even more controversial.[4] Many studies document the presence of abnormal returns long after an event took place. Long-term analyses give results that may suggest both under- and overreaction to specific types of information.

What seems to be particularly embarrassing for market efficiency is the presence of the post-announcement drift after announcements of unexpected earnings. Reported earnings are one of the basic pieces of financial information about a company and one should expect that investors will pay enough attention to earnings announcements and will be able to evaluate them correctly. However, this is not the case. Even though there is a clear reaction at the moment of announcement, abnormal returns persist as long as from three up to nine months (Ball and Brown, 1968; Foster et al., 1984; Bernard and Thomas, 1989, 1990; Chan et al., 1996). Delayed market reaction is especially visible in the case of unexpectedly bad reported earnings, which confirms earlier observations that bad news travels slowly into market prices.

Other examples of insufficient market reaction include announcements of forecasts and analysts' recommendations (Chan et al., 1996; Womack, 1996; Barber et al., 2001), share splits (Ikenberry et al., 1996; Desai and Jain, 1997; Ikenberry and Ramnath, 2002), changes in dividend policy (Michaely et al., 1995; Boehme and Sorescu, 2002), and stock repurchases (Lakonishok and Vermaelen, 1990; Ikenberry et al., 1995; Mitchell and Stafford, 2000).

Nevertheless, there is also vast evidence suggesting market overreaction. This includes such events as IPOs and SEOs (Ritter, 1991; Loughran and Ritter, 1995; Spiess and Affleck-Graves, 1995; Lee, 1997; Brav et al., 2000). It is argued that corporate managers decide to issue new equity when they consider the firm to be overvalued (see chapter 7). Moreover, companies usually present more optimistic forecasts and development plans shortly before they offer their equity. Also, both the company and the financial agents cooperating with it (issuer or underwriter) work intensively in the area of public relations and marketing to encourage investors to buy shares. Long-term negative abnormal returns that usually follow IPOs and SEOs are interpreted as a reflection of the market gradually adjusting the initial overvaluation.

Asquith (1983) and Agrawal, Jaffe, and Mandelker (1992) point out long-term negative abnormal returns following mergers and acquisitions. Loughran and Vijh (1997) and Mitchell and Stafford (2000) find that the effect is stronger when the acquisition is not cash-financed but done through share exchange. Rau and Vermaelen (1998) document that negative abnormal returns in the period after acquisition are observed mostly in the group of companies with a low book-to-market equity ratio. All these observations suggest that, at the moment of merger, the bidding firm is likely to be overvalued. The acquisition may actually be motivated by the very fact that the acquirer is relatively priced higher than the target firm. We may also assume that wishful thinking and excessive optimism on the part of the acquirer's management combined with agency costs may lead to overestimating possible synergies resulting from the merger (see chapter 8). The bidder might fall victim to so-called winner's curse.

As a result, the acquirer is likely to overpay for the target firm. Even if there is often an initial negative market reaction to the bidding firm's price, it turns out to be insufficient. Acquirer's valuation gets adjusted in the long term, generating a negative postacquisition drift.

5. Forecasting Returns on the Basis of a Firm's Characteristics

There are many studies demonstrating that there is a significant relationship between specific company features and returns on their stock. Banz (1981) and Reinganum (1981) documented that stocks of small-cap companies yield higher returns than one might expect judging from the level of systemic risk measured by beta. Basu (1983) pointed out that stocks with a low price-to-earnings ratio offer higher returns compared to stocks for which the ratio is high. Jaffe, Keim, and Wasterfield (1989) and Fama and French (1992) confirmed these interdependencies although they noted the paradox that firms currently reporting losses also, on average, offer abnormal returns in the future. Lanstein, Reid, and Rosenberg (1985) as well as Lakonishok, Shleifer, and Vishny (1994) pointed out that it is possible to predict abnormal returns also on the basis of such parameters as cash flow to market equity ratio and historic sales growth rate. Finally, Fama and French (1992) highlighted the important role of the book-to-market equity ratio.

Fama and French (1992, 1996) demonstrated that a lot of previously observed phenomena overlap. In reality, the wide range of identified anomalies may be reduced to two important interdependencies: the size effect as well as the book-to-market equity effect. They believe that these effects are not irrational at all but are caused by the presence of extra nondiversified risk factors not taken into account by the traditional beta coefficient. In line with this reasoning, Fama and French (1993) suggested the following three-factor asset-pricing model:

$$E(R_i) - R_f = b_i \left[E(R_M) - R_f \right] + s_i E(SMB) + h_i E(HML) \qquad (4.1)$$

where $E(R_j) - R_f$ is the expected return on asset i over the return on risk-free investment, $E(R_M) - R_f$ is the expected value of market risk premium, $E(SMB)$ is the size premium, that is, expected difference between the returns on small-cap portfolios and large-cap portfolios and $E(HML)$ is the value premium, that is, the expected difference between the return on portfolios with the highest and the lowest book-to-market equity ratios. Coefficients b_i, s_i and h_i determine sensitivity o of asset i to individual risk factors and are estimated with the use of the following time series regression equation:

$$R_i - R_f = \alpha_i + b_i \left(R_M - R_f \right) + s_i SMB + h_i HML + \varepsilon_i, \qquad (4.2)$$

where regression error ε_i is random with the expected value of 0. In addition, Fama and French (1993) developed a special method of calculating SMB and HML in such a way as to ensure their statistical independence. Fama and French (1996) demonstrated that the aforementioned model offers a good approximation of the way returns on American stocks changed in the years 1963–1993. Davis, Fama, and French (2000) confirmed the same for a longer period of 1929–1997. Griffin (2002) showed that the Fama and French factors are country specific and concluded that the local factors provide a better explanation of time-series variation in stock returns than the global factors. Fama and French (2012) analyzed models with local and global risk factors for four regions (North America, Europe, Japan, and Asia Pacific) and also admitted that local factors work better than global factors for regional portfolios. The model seems to describe returns quite well in most of developed markets.

Proponents of behavioral finance do not negate the empirical observations made by Fama and French, but they reject their interpretation. The only thing the three-factor model demonstrates is that some anomalies overlap, capitalization and the book-to-market equity ratio being the most effective in explaining returns. However, there are no grounds for saying that the small size premium and the value premium are the result of a totally rational premium for unspecified extra risk related to variability of fundamental factors. From the perspective of behavioral finance, observed tendencies have their root cause in irrational behavior of investors who are susceptible to different psychological biases. Another reason is potential limitations stemming from market architecture and the way institutional investors function, which makes it impossible to eliminate instances of incorrect asset pricing.

5.1. Small-Size Effect

Banz (1981) analyzed returns on shares listed on NYSE in the years 1936–1977 dividing the population of companies by size into five portfolios. The difference between the average annual returns on portfolios containing the smallest and biggest stocks amounted to 20 percent. In spite of the fact that small companies usually have high beta coefficients, the CAPM model is not capable of explaining the difference of this magnitude.

Fama and French (1992) analyzed returns on all shares listed on NYSE, AMEX, and NASDAQ in 1963–1990, segregating them each year into deciles by capitalization and dividing extreme deciles in half. The difference they demonstrated between portfolios covering 5 percent of the smallest and biggest companies was much lower that the one initially observed by Banz (1981) amounting, on average, to just over 9 percent annually. Nonetheless, it was still too high to be explained by higher beta coefficients for small caps.

The small-size effect was also documented internationally. Hawawini and Keim (1995) and Heston, Rouwenhorst, and Wessels (1995) report it in Germany and the United Kingdom. Chan, Hamao, and Lakonishok (1991) find the small-cap effect in Asia, and Liew and Vassalou (2000) in Canada and Australia. However, outside the United States, abnormal returns on small-size companies seem to be significantly lower.

Supporters of the traditional theory of finance tried to explain the small-size effect primarily by identifying additional risks and microstructural factors typical of this market segment. Amihud and Mendelson (1986) point out that higher returns may compensate for low liquidity of small companies and a high bid-ask spread, which entails high transaction costs. The spread could also contribute to distortions in the calculation of returns. Barry and Braun (1984) suggest that the company-size effect may be caused by information being less available. The costs related to analyzing and monitoring a company's situation are largely fixed; so small companies require higher returns in order that a relatively small investment can compensate for research expenditure.

Chan and Chen (1991) find that the group of the smallest companies listed on NYSE is mostly made up of firms that lost a lot of value in the past because of poor performance. Such companies are usually characterized by low production efficiency and are often much in debt. They also have problems with financial liquidity and access to new sources of funding. It might be expected that they will be more exposed to potential changes in the economic situation and are likely to go bust sooner than others in the event of an economic downturn. Liew and Vassalou (2000) find that the amount of the size premium predicts to some extent future growth of the gross domestic product (GDP). Huberman and Kandel (1987) point out additional cross-correlation across returns on small stocks, which was not related to the entire market. This may suggest that returns in this asset segment are sensitive to certain common factors, which do not, however, pertain to the way the entire market portfolio behaves. Fama and French (1992, 1993, 1996) argue that these factors are rational being the effect of additional, albeit unspecified, elements of risk.

Financial behaviorists interpret the phenomenon differently. They relate higher small-cap returns to the presence of noise traders whose actions are motivated more by speculation and emotions than rational information analysis. Individual investors account for a major portion of shareholders in small-cap firms. This is why such companies will be more often affected by all kinds of irrationality that may persist for relatively long periods given practical limitations to arbitrage. Such limitations are not only due to less opportunity for short-selling small-cap stocks, a fact related to limited institutional shareholding structure (Nagel, 2005), but also due to the risk of further intensification of noise-trader activity (see chapter 1).

Lee, Shleifer, and Thaler (1991) and Chopra et al. (1993) suggest that the risk related to the presence of noise traders is systematic and has similar consequences also for other categories of assets dominated by small investors. They make two observations in this context. First, the amounts of discount in the market pricing of various closed-end funds are cross-correlated, a fact difficult to explain by fundamental factors. Second, there is a relation between the amount of average discount in the group of closed-end funds and the returns obtained from small-cap portfolios in the same period. Since shares of closed-end funds and small company shares are both most often purchased by small players, the aforementioned observations may confirm the hypothesis that these categories of instruments share a common risk factor deriving from the unpredictability of sentiment among individual investors. The same interpretation may be applied to additional covariance of the returns in the segment of small companies discovered by Huberman and Kandel (1987) even though the argument has been used before to prove the presence of an additional risk factor of a fundamental nature.

Since the risk related to the sentiment of noise traders is systematic, it should be compensated for by an adequate premium. Hence, just like proponents of the efficient market hypothesis, behavioral finance justifies higher small-cap returns by the higher level of risk common for this group of assets. However, while the former saw fundamental factors at the root of extra risk, the latter relate risk to the behavior of small investors, which is irrational and difficult to predict.

Dimson and Marsh (1999), Horowitz, Loughran, and Savin (2000), and Schwert (2003) argue that the company size effect disappeared on the American market since 1984, that is, almost immediately after the famous publication by Banz (1981). Could it be that the discovery and public exposure of the company-size effect contributed to its elimination? Undoubtedly, there was a growing interest in the small-cap segment since mid-1980s, a fact made evident only by looking at the great number of funds specializing in small-cap stocks created at the time. More attention paid to this market segment and the larger number of investors who wanted to reap extraordinary profit on small companies could make extra returns simply disappear or even turn into negative ones. While this line of thinking may support the view about improving market efficiency, it nonetheless contradicts the argument that previously observed higher returns on small-cap companies were a premium for extra fundamental risk.

On the other hand, supporters of behavioral finance could argue that the change in shareholder structure in small companies, as new specialized small-cap and micro-cap funds are set up, diminishes the influence of small investors, hence lowers the noise-trader risk in that segment of the market. Yet another explanation that is slightly tongue-in-cheek, which does not make it less probable, is that it was more difficult to notice the size premium in the 1990s as the entire market behaved irrationally especially in the second half of the decade.

Finally, we must also allow for the possibility that the company-size effect decreased only temporarily, reports about the disappearance of the anomaly and self-correcting market forces being rather premature. Analyzing historical changes in the size premium, we may observe periods when small-cap shares performed worse than big company assets in the past as well, for example, in the 1950s (Figure 4.1). According to the most recent data from the years 2001–2012, small companies have again started to offer higher returns, on average.

5.2. Book to Market Equity

Book value of equity is based on historical data and does not factor in the current earnings nor the company's prospects. Market equity, on the other hand, represents the total pricing of all shares on the basis of demand and supply the assets elicit on the market at the moment. It reflects both company's asset value and the way in which investors perceive risk, current profitability, and future prospects. In general, if the market believes that the company's prospects are good, the market value should be above the book value. Companies that are

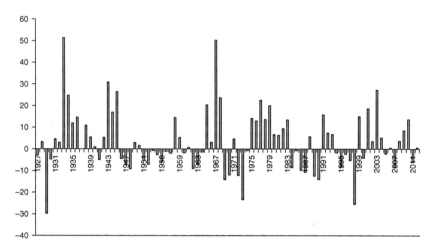

Figure 4.1 Size premium (*SMB*) in the US market in the period 1927–2012. I appreciate K. French's permission to use his data on *SMB* premium.

Source: See http://mba.tuck.dartmouth.edu/pages/faculty/ken.french/data_library.html for detail description.

valued by investors mainly for growth potential (growth stocks) will therefore have relatively low book-to-market equity ratios. On the other hand, more stable and mature firms perceived as having less chance for a spectacular growth will be priced more for the value of their assets (value stocks), exhibiting higher book-to-market equity ratios.

Fama and French (1992) documented that the book-to-market equity ratio could better explain returns on stocks on the American market in the years 1963–1990 than the beta coefficient or capitalization. The difference between returns on portfolios with the highest and lowest book-to-market ratios amounted to almost 20 percent on average annually. Interestingly, portfolios of the highest and lowest book-to-market ratios had similar beta coefficients. It follows that the observed differences between returns can by no means be explained by the traditional CAPM model.

Long-term overperformance of value stocks is also evident in other countries. Chan, Hamao, and Lakonishok (1991), Fama and French (1998, 2012), and Liew and Vassalou (2000) find higher average returns on value firms on the total of 12 global markets. The phenomenon seems to be stronger in Japan, Australia, and Singapore than in the United States, whereas in Europe, it was slightly weaker. Capaul, Rowley, and Sharpe (1993) Brouwer and Van Der Put (1997), and Fama and French (2012) confirm the phenomenon in relation to internationally diversified portfolios containing shares from many global markets simultaneously.

Similar to their discussion of the small-size effect, Fama and French (1992, 1993, 1995, 1996) claim that higher returns on companies with high book-to-market ratios constitute a rational premium for extra risk. They argue that value firms are often the "fallen stars," that is, former growth companies that got into some trouble. As their economic condition is likely to be poor, it may

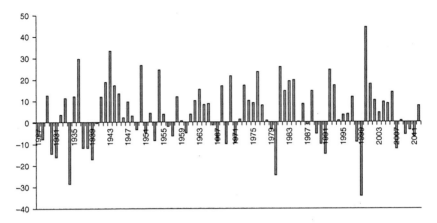

Figure 4.2 Book-to-market premium (*HML*) in the US market in the period 1927–2012. I appreciate K. French's permission to use his data on *HML* premium.

Source: See http://mba.tuck.dartmouth.edu/pages/faculty/ken.french/data_library.html for detail description.

be expected that they will be exposed to additional risks common for this segment of the market. To confirm the hypothesis, Fama and French (1996) point out the cross-correlation across returns on value stocks, such correlation exceeding their covariance with the market portfolio. Just as in the case of small capitalization companies, they suggest that this additional risk may be related to economic cycles. Liew and Vassalou (2000) find that book-to-market premium actually has some power to predict future economic growth although the relation seems to be generally much weaker than in the case of the size premium (Figure 4.2).

Proponents of behavioral finance contest this explanation. Lakonishok et al. (1994), Daniel and Titman (1997), Barberis et al. (1998), and Hong and Stein (1999) are of the opinion that higher returns on value stocks as compared with growth stocks are the result of market overreaction. Investors overestimate companies that have recently had good financial results, underestimating those whose performance was relatively weak. This is due to the extrapolation bias and a naive belief in trends. Both biases are psychologically motivated by the problems decision makers have to correctly interpret representativeness and the principle of the regression toward the mean. The difficulties are aggravated by overconfidence and selective attribution that make overreaction persist or even intensify (Daniel et al., 1998).

La Porta, Lakonishok, Shleifer, and Vishny (1997) find that in the three-day periods around the earnings announcement, date portfolios made up of growth stocks brought negative returns more often, whereas for those containing companies with value potential, the returns were more likely to be positive. This observation confirms the hypothesis that growth companies often do not live up to overoptimistic expectations extrapolated by investors, while companies that were priced relatively low by the market achieve positively surprising results in later periods. Skinner and Sloan (2002) also find that the negative reaction of investors to unexpectedly bad financial results of growth firms is much stronger than the reaction observed when poorer than expected results are published by a company with value potential.

It is worth noting that behavioral explanations of the book-to-market premium are the same as the ones offered for the winner–loser effect. The efficiency of long-term contrarian investing and the book-to-market effect are driven by the same irrational behavior of investors.

PART III

Aggregate Market Behavior

CHAPTER 5

Market-wide Consequences of Behavioral Biases

This chapter focuses on the consequences of behavioral biases to the capital market as a whole. Two major anomalies in the aggregate market-wide data, that is, the equity premium puzzle and the excessive volatility puzzle, are discussed in the first instance. Later, we move on to attempts of market modeling within the behavioral framework. Early models based on beliefs and preferences of investors do well with explaining some aspects, but lack power to describe other peculiarities of market behavior. Hence, the Generalized Behavioral Model is developed that aims to explain the whole range of market anomalies described in this book.

1. Puzzles in the Aggregate Market-wide Data

The equity premium puzzle and excessive volatility are the two phenomena observed in the aggregate market data that seem to be direct consequences of behavioral biases to the capital market as a whole. While mispricing in individual securities or in particular classes of assets or other anomalies presented in the earlier chapter may result in practical implications to investment strategies and corporate finance policies, the evidence on anomalous market behavior on the aggregated level constitutes a challenge to the general economic framework.

1.1. Equity Premium Puzzle

It is one of the fundamental rules of finance that investment in risky instruments should offer higher returns compared to risk-free investing. Stocks generally carry more risk than sovereign bonds and treasury bills; so the fact that they offer higher average returns should come as no surprise. Nevertheless, the amount of the equity risk premium, that the difference between real returns on stock market portfolio and real returns on risk-free asset, has caused a lot of controversy in economic literature for almost three decades.

The discussion was initiated by Mehra and Prescott (1985) who claimed that the average historical amount of premium on the US stock market, which stood at 6.2 percent in 1889–1978, was much too high given what had been theoretically predicted based on changes in aggregated consumption. The influence of fluctuations on the stock market on changes in aggregated consumption is not strong enough to justify such high levels of the risk premium. The model used by Mehra and Prescott was based on standard axioms behind the utility function developed by Von Neumann and Morgenstern (1944). Additionally, it assumed agent representativeness, stable level of risk aversion, market completeness, and the lack of transaction costs. It turned out that in order to account for the high-risk premium observed historically, investors would have to display unrealistically high coefficients of relative risk aversion.[1] At the same time, the relative risk-aversion coefficient in Mehra and Prescott's model is the opposite of intertemporal substitution flexibility. It follows that very high risk-aversion coefficients would mean that investors should try to even out the level of consumption in different periods. As it is the general rule that the economy keeps developing and societies get richer in time, people should increase present consumption borrowing from the richer future. If common, this attitude should result in high real interest rates. In practice, however, real historical returns on risk-free assets are surprisingly low (Weil, 1989).

Researchers tried to explain the equity premium puzzle by further empirical and theoretical studies. Siegel (1992) wondered if the phenomenon was equally strong during the entire period studied by Mehra and Prescott and beyond it. He not only broadened the scope of his research, but also divided the observation period into subperiods. These were the early phase of the American market in 1802–1871; the years 1872–1925 where the quality of available data is much better; and the period of 1926–1990. Siegel observed that average real interest rates on risk-free instruments fell drastically in consecutive periods: from 5.4 percent in the first period, to 3.3 percent in the second, to only 0.7 percent starting from 1926. At the same time, real returns on the equity market were more or less stable over the entire period. As a result, the equity premium rose significantly in the entire time-span—from 2.9 percent in the first period, to 4.7 percent in the second one, to 8.1 percent in the last. For the entire 193-year-long period, the premium observed by Siegel amounted to 5.3 percent. Fama and French (2002a) arrived at similar conclusions analyzing the period of 1872–2000 together with subperiods 1872–1950 and 1951–2000. The equity premium was 5.6 percent over the entire period, standing at 4.4 percent and 7.4 percent for the two subperiods, respectively. The high premium in the second subperiod was caused both by very high stock returns in the last decade of the twentieth century and the significantly lower real returns on safe instruments due to, inter alia, high inflation in the United States in the 1970s.

Numerous theoretical attempts to explain the equity premium puzzle questioned the assumptions adopted by Mehra and Prescott and put forward modifications of their model, which was a reference point for estimating the "normal" size of equity premium. The discussion focused on the following major areas: models accounting for additional risk; models assuming market segmentation;

arguments of market incompleteness, transaction costs, and other market imperfections; as well as behavioral models based on modified utility functions and referring to investor psychology. Additionally, Damodaran (2012) points out a number of purely methodological issues related to the calculation of the equity premium.

Reitz (1988) suggested that the high equity premium may be explained if we assume that, over the studied period, investors were afraid of the slightly probable severe economic crash that could have happened but did not. That is why the ex post premium for shares seems so high. Challenging Reitz's article, Mehra and Prescott (1988) claimed, however, that the amount of premium they calculated did account for the major crash on the stock market in 1929 and the ensuing period of the Great Depression all the way until 1933. However, disasters of this sort do not have to happen too often to impact the long-term average. In fact, the 2008 market turbulences lowered the long-term 1900–2008 average equity premium to only 3.9 percent. However, as the market bounced back in the following four years and risk-free rates stayed close to nil, the average equity premium came back to 5.3 percent for the US market (Dimson et al., 2009; Dimson et al., 2013).

Brown, Goetzmann, and Ross (1995) support the position of Reitz (1988) saying that out of 36 stock markets operating all over the world in the early twentieth century, over half experienced serious disruptions of activity or were even closed down in the 100-year-long period. In the United States, on the other hand, stock markets have practically always stayed the course. Hence, they believe that US data do not reflect the whole spectrum of risk and are burdened with the survivorship bias. However, Li and Xu (2002) argue that the severity of the survivorship bias would have to be very high indeed to explain the equity premium of this size on the American stock market. This means that the ex ante probability of an economic disaster would have to be unrealistically strong. Empirically, Dimson et al. (2013) document the average world equity premium at 4.1 percent, and the average world equity premium excluding the United States at 3.5 percent, much below the reported figure for the American market alone, which was 5.3 percent in the period 1900–2012. On the other hand, Japanese and German markets, which went through a period of significant disruptions caused by the Second World War, showed even higher equity premiums than the one present in the US market. This was, however, mainly due to negative real risk-free rates in periods of high inflation.

Mankiw and Zeldes (1991) and Haliassos and Bertaut (1995) suggest that the reason the equity premium might seem too high compared to fluctuations of consumption is because market segmentation has not been factored in. Mehra and Prescott (1985) used aggregated data on American consumption forgetting that almost three quarters of Americans do not invest in shares at all (except for pension schemes). It turns out that the level of consumption of those who do invest in the stock market is three times as sensitive to market fluctuations as the same level aggregated for the entire population. Having said that, such caveats solve the problem only partially. Even with market segmentation taken into account, equity premium still seems too elevated.[2]

When the market is incomplete, that is not all assets may be traded and it is not possible to fully hedge against fluctuations in consumption, people will be more willing to invest their savings in safe instruments. After all, such savings are a natural safety net if the situation on the market unexpectedly turns bad. As more people save, real risk-free returns will fall (Lucas, 1994; Constantinides and Duffie, 1996; Heaton and Lucas, 1996; Constantinides, 2002). Kocherlakota (1996) attempts to explain low real returns on risk-free assets by pointing out that such instruments offer limited opportunities for falling in debt and short-selling. However, such arguments are only good enough to explain low real profitability of safe instruments. They do not help to understand why real returns on shares are so high. Other attempts to explain the equity premium by significant differences in transaction costs between trading in safe instruments and shares were also far from successful (Fisher, 1994; Kocherlakota, 1996; Heaton and Lucas, 1997).

A large part of discussion in the literature focuses on ways to modify the utility function used to evaluate changes in the consumption level. Epstein and Zin (1989, 1991) suggest using a generalized utility hypothesis (running against the axioms of classical utility hypothesis), according to which current utility is a function of stable flexibility depending on the current level of consumption and future utility. The model breaks the strict inverse relation between the coefficient of relative risk aversion and the flexibility of intertemporal substitution. So it is theoretically possible that high equity premiums will coincide with low real returns on safe instruments. Even so, this approach will only explain one-third of the observed equity premium.

Constantinides (1990) suggests another modification of the utility function based on habit formation. When past consumption is taken on board to evaluate the utility of current consumption, decision makers are more sensitive to short-term limits in consumption displaying less long-term risk aversion at the same time. Nonetheless, empirical tests using this model were unsuccessful (Ferson and Constantinides, 1991; Chapman, 2002). All they could do was shed some light on low real returns on risk-free instruments.

Abel (1990) and Campbell and Cochrane (1999) claim that current consumption should be evaluated not against its past levels but rather the present consumption of other market players with whom the decision maker compares his own situation. In the model, the marginal utility of future consumption rises as it is assumed that others will also consume more in the future. This is why investors are less likely to borrow from future consumption to the benefit of the current one, which can explain low real returns on safe instruments even though it does not change much as far as the degree of risk aversion is concerned.[3]

Fama and French (2002a) tried to explain the puzzle looking at changes in fundamental values—the rate of dividend and the price-to-earnings ratio. In other words, they verified whether the historically observed equity premium is justified by a relevant increase in dividends or profits. It turned out that the equity premium stemming from an increase in fundamental factors in the second half of the twentieth century should stand at 2.6 percent for the dividend-based model and 4.3 percent for the one based on the price-to-earnings ratio, significantly below the actual empirical values in the same period.

Behavioral finance offers its own explanation of the equity puzzle. Benartzi and Thaler (1995) point out that mental accounting coexists with strong loss aversion. It is a well-known fact that stock prices may undergo severe fluctuations in relatively short periods of time. Being myopic in their attitude, investors frame and mentally account returns of each period separately. They find it more difficult to notice cumulative returns or average values in the long-term perspective. At the same time, they are very much affected by losses even if these are short term in nature. Hence, the high equity premium is a reward for taking the risk of short-term fluctuations and, as such, is necessary to overcome short-term loss aversion investors commonly experience.

Barberis, Huang, and Santos (2001) propose a formal model to explain the equity puzzle by myopic loss aversion. Drawing on the prospect theory, they assume that investors evaluate utility not only on the basis of the total level of consumption, but also changes in wealth, and that they are more sensitive to losses than gains. It is additionally assumed that the degree of risk aversion depends on previous investor's experience, as earlier noticed by Thaler and Johnson (1990). Having made profits before, investors will be more ready to take risks than they would be following a loss. The model developed by Barberis et al. (2001) predicts that the equity premium in 1926–1995 should theoretically amount to 4.1 percent annually in real terms. In other words, it can explain a major part of the actually observed real premium, which, at the time, stood at about 6 percent per annum.

Yet another psychological phenomenon that may make investors expect higher equity premiums is ambiguity aversion whereby people are reluctant to take part in lotteries with undefined probability distribution (Olsen and Troughton, 2000). Most capital market models assume that the probability distribution of future returns is known, while in real life usually, this is not the case. The best approximation available to investors is the historical distribution of returns, but history does not have to repeat itself. While forecasting future returns, investors typically face ambiguity rather than parameterized risk. Therefore, the equity premium might be seen to be a compensation not only for the risk itself, but also for the lack of precise knowledge of the exact level of risk.

1.2. Excessive Volatility

Another phenomenon affecting the aggregated stock market that the classical theory of finance struggles to explain is excessive volatility of prices compared to observed fluctuations of fundamental values, such as earnings or dividends, or changes in expected consumption. LeRoy and Porter (1981) and Shiller (1981) find that price variance is much higher than what might have been justified by changes in dividend levels. Kleidon (1986) and Marsh and Merton (1986) did raise a number of methodological problems that could overestimate the results obtained by LeRoy and Porter (1981) and Shiller (1981), but the phenomenon was generally confirmed also in later studies based on different assumptions and econometric models (West, 1988).

If the variance of the returns is higher than the variance of dividends, it is obvious that there must be fluctuations of the price-to-dividend ratio (P/D). Theoretically, the fluctuations might be explained either by changing expectations of future dividends or changes in discount rates applied when pricing streams of these dividends. Changes in discount rates, in turn, might stem from changing expectations related to returns on risk-free assets, changes in the expected level of risk, or changing risk aversion. So the potential list of factors impacting changes in the P/D ratio is relatively long. Nevertheless, Campbell and Shiller (1988), Campbell (1991), and Fama and French (2002a) document that historical P/D levels do not translate into real dividend growth rates. Neither does the P/D ratio explain changes in the risk-free rate or fluctuations of risk levels in historical time series. Therefore, the only factor that potentially can influence fluctuations of the P/D ratio and, consequently, explain higher variance for prices compared to dividends is the changing degree of risk aversion.

Following this line of thinking, Campbell and Cochrane (1999) propose a model in which people are relatively slow to get used to a specific level of consumption. Fluctuations in the level of consumption clash with what people are used to; so their attitude to risk changes. If current consumption is higher than what they are accustomed to, risk aversion will decrease even though with time they slowly get used to the higher level of consumption. Conversely, when current consumption is likely to fall below the habit level, risk aversion will increase. Changes in the attitude to risk are reflected in the level of discount rates and, as a consequence, cause fluctuations in the P/D ratio. It is assumed that habits are formed based on the observation of the general external level of consumption instead of individual experience of the decision maker. In this respect, the model of Campbell and Cochrane (1999) is close to Abel's (1990) proposal. Nevertheless, such changes would have to be irrationally high to account for the empirically observed volatility of stock prices.

Ackert (1994), Brennan and Xia (2001), and Lewellen and Shanken (2002) propose models that attempt to explain the volatility puzzle assuming that rational agents are not aware of all parameters generating the process of dividend growth, but only learn about them gradually as time goes by. In these models, fluctuations of the P/D ratio are the result of changing forecasts of future flows, which are constantly updated as more information about the earnings (dividends) generating process is known. Even if the forecasts are not confirmed by later actual data, investors are not considered irrational. It is assumed, rather, that their knowledge was not thorough enough and the ensuing uncertainty prevented them from estimating the level of future dividends correctly.

In terms of their mathematical nature, models assuming gradual acquisition of information by rational decision makers are very much alike, offering similar prediction as the models based on totally different behavioral assumptions. It is difficult to differentiate between these contradictory approaches. It is not easy to state ex post whether investors did not have relevant knowledge at the moment of making a decision or whether they did not know how to use it rationally.

Behavioral finance offers a number of potential explanations that could be roughly divided into two groups: those related to irrational investor beliefs and those based on instability of preferences. The first group includes a representativeness bias in the form of the short-series error, which leads to the extrapolation bias and a belief in trends. Having observed a firm with a consecutive series of higher-than-expected earnings, investors underestimate the probability that the situation might be random and become mistakenly convinced that a permanent change has taken place thanks to which the observed growth will continue in the future. These expectations are reflected in current prices causing irrational fluctuations in the P/D ratio.

Another mistake that may contribute to high price volatility is overconfidence combined with selective attribution. Attaching too much importance to privately acquired knowledge to the detriment of public information triggers price fluctuations that are not justified by real changes in earnings or dividends. Odean (1998b) and Daniel, Hirshleifer, and Subrahmanyam (1998, 2001) provide formal models based on the assumption of investor overconfidence, which seem very good at explaining the volatility puzzle.

The excessive volatility may also result, at least partially, from a mixture of money illusion and extrapolation bias. Investors are inconsistent about their dealings with inflation. They use historical growth rates in earnings, which reflect past inflation, to forecast future earnings. But they use current interest rate, which reflects expectations of future inflation, to estimate discount rates. When inflation increases, this will lead to a mismatch, with high discount rates and low cash flow forecasts resulting in asset valuations that are too low (subsequent returns are too high). On the other hand, when inflation decreases, the discount rates at use will be low but cash flows will be extrapolated at too high a growth rate, resulting in asset overvaluation. Shifts between under- and overvaluation will contribute to excessive returns volatility. Similar reasoning was proposed already by Modigliani and Cohn (1979) who explained in this way low equity values in the period of high inflation in the late 1970s. Ritter and Warr (2002) apply the same reasoning to explain the bull market in the period of 1982–1999 when inflation was declining. Campbell and Voulteenaho (2004) relate changes in the P/D ratio to changes in the inflation rate over time and find strong support for the hypothesis of money illusion–driven excessive volatility.

Swings between under- and overvaluation may result also from irrational instability of investor preferences and shifts in the degree of risk aversion. The model by Barberis et al. (2001), which has already been mentioned when discussing the high equity premium, assumes, inter alia, that investors will change their preferences depending on the results of their former choices. Following previous positive experiences, we should observe falling risk aversion and vice versa—after adverse events, investors will be more sensitive to risk. Shifts in the degree of risk aversion will result in applying different discount rates to forecasted cash flows resulting in periodical under- and overvaluation. We discuss the model of shifting risk attitude in more detail in the next section.

2. Behavioral Modeling

Issues related to investors' behavior and the way it affects valuation of assets are complex. Thus, researchers face much difficulty in specifying all the factors and relationships that could explain all the phenomena taking place in the capital market. This section is intended to address those issues and fill in existing gaps. First, it presents early attempts of behavioral modeling based on beliefs and preferences of market participants. Some models cannot describe all phenomena observed empirically on the market. Each model does well with explaining some aspects, but lacks power to describe other peculiarities of market behavior. Next, the Generalized Behavioral Model (GBM) of asset pricing is presented. The model develops a generalized approach that can be applied to a broad array of phenomena observed in the market. The GBM identifies key categories of psychologically driven factors and describes how these factors might determine investor behavior and how this behavior impacts asset pricing and returns.[4]

2.1. Model of Investor Sentiment

Barberis, Shleifer, and Vishny (1998) suggest a model where attitudes of investors correspond to two behavioral patterns found in the literature. According to the first pattern, investors are convinced that the profitability of each corporation has a tendency to fluctuate around a specific mean value. Hence, if the company reported a recent high profitability, deterioration of results should be expected during the coming period. In turn, the second pattern assumes the opposite—that there is a continuing trend with regard to the profitability of corporations.

An investor convinced of the validity of the first pattern will react unfavorably to financial reports in fear that a good/bad outcome for the last period is incidental and it may be eliminated during the subsequent period. Consequently, price adjustment to the new information is delayed and returns may periodically continue to follow a trend. Barberis et al. (1998) associate such investor behaviors with cognitive conservatism documented by Edwards (1968) and others. People change their previous convictions in view of new information slowly and carefully. For any opinion to completely change, the original signal needs to be confirmed by consecutive observations, which usually takes time.

On the other hand, investors who follow the second pattern attach great importance to the latest results and excessively extrapolate them into the future. In this case, Barberis et al. (1998) associate this attitude with the phenomenon generally referred to by psychologists as the representativeness heuristic (Kahneman and Tversky, 1973; Tversky and Kahneman, 1974; Grether, 1980). Under the representativeness heuristic, the probability of a specific event is judged based on how closely it resembles the explicit characteristics of the sample, subjectively distinguished from the general population. As a result of representativeness heuristic error, the weight of individual characteristics that comply with a specific pattern will be overstated and the significance of the actual statistical breakdown will be understated. Problems associated with the perception of representativeness of information signals result in premature conclusions based on too little observation (the short-series error) and in seeking regularities in completely random data sets.

Imagine a corporation that reported systematically growing profits over recent reporting periods. Perceiving this situation from the angle of the representativeness heuristic, investors may overstate the importance of the latest positive results. They may rashly conclude that the positive dynamics of the company's latest results reflect a permanent change in its condition and justify high future growth potential. Meanwhile, good financial results during the last several periods may be nothing more than coincidence. As a result, the stock of that corporation may be overvalued and may correct when the expected future profit growth does not occur.

Investors in the Barberis et al. (1998) model are homogeneous, that is, the model assumes that at a given time, all investors think alike. They either perceive financial results of companies in line with the first pattern, or are convinced that the second pattern is right. The authors suggest that investors are slightly more often convinced of the correctness of the first pattern, which usually results in underreaction to new information. However, a series of observations that indicate trend continuation will result in investor belief in the second pattern. That, in turn, will be valid until the traders realize that their trend extrapolation reached too far into the future. However, the change in investor belief will only happen as the result of several observations that differ from expectations. In other words, investors are "sentimental" about the pattern that they previously adopted as valid. Hence, they prolong the process of transition to the other pattern.

According to Barberis et al. (1998), the aforementioned mechanism, which is based on delayed changes in prevalence between the two alternative patterns of financial results perception, may explain the simultaneous occurrence of market underreaction in the short term and overreaction in the long term. Hence, the Model of Investor Sentiment suggests that trend reversals should always be observed in a long-term perspective.

Yet, the literature shows examples of both long-term reversals and long-term abnormal return continuations, that is, stock splits (Ikenberry et al., 1996), changes in dividend policy (Michaely et al., 1995), or cases of share repurchases (Ikenberry et al., 1995; Mitchell and Stafford, 2000). The investors' behavior pattern suggested by Barberis et al. (1998) is unable to explain such phenomena.

2.2. Daniel, Hirshleifer, and Subrahmanyam Model

Daniel, Hirshleifer, and Subrahmanyam (1998) assume that investors can be divided into two categories: the informed and the under-informed. Actions of under-informed traders have no significant impact on the market. Informed traders, however, may influence the market through their overconfidence. They overestimate their analytical abilities and understate their potential errors. Usually, their perceived margin of error is too narrow. In other words, investors often fall victim to the so-called calibration bias. That is, the more a person contributes personally to the analysis, the greater the error. People overestimate the precision and overstate the importance of private information as compared to the weight of the information available publicly. The results of one's own analyses are usually considered more reliable than the commonly available market information.

Investors often emphasize their contribution in achievement of a positive outcome even if it has only been achieved by accident. On the other hand, they underestimate events that do not agree with their previous conjectures and fail to notice their own mistakes. People try to attribute these failures to other factors.

If an investor assesses perspectives of a given company as positive and the assessment is subsequently confirmed by good financial results or higher stock quotes, the investor's confidence in his own skills will usually be reinforced. This happens regardless of whether the predictions are shown to be correct as a result of substantial analysis or simply by chance (e.g., as the result of other positive factors of which the investor could not have been previously aware).

In a reverse situation (i.e., if a given corporation does not measure up to expectations), investors will usually seek explanations other than self error. The investor will usually point to independent factors or third parties that are either at fault or were misleading. Investors frequently fail to notice or underestimate the unfavorable signals that contradict the earlier private diagnosis. For example, the investor will think that he or she is experiencing a temporary turbulence that will soon pass and previous expectations will be restored. Only a compilation of multiple public contradictory signals, usually received over an extended period of time, may prevail over the original private signal and change the opinion of the investor.

Daniel et al. (1998) propose a model in which investor overconfidence results in overreaction to private information, whereas distortions related to incorrect attribution of events are responsible for underreaction to public signals. They show that such investor behavior may cause short-term continuations and long-term reversals in stock returns.

In this respect, the Daniel et al. (1998) model is similar to the Barberis et al. (1998) proposal. Contrary to the investor sentiment model that assumes that investors overreact to a sequence of information signals of similar significance and underreact to new information contradicting the previous perception of reality, the Daniel et al. model differentiates between the overreaction and underreaction depending on whether information is private or public. In this way, Daniel et al. are not only able to explain short-term continuations and long-term reversals, but also the long-term continuations observed in some cases. Under this model, investors' reactions are incomplete when new information is first published because they attach more importance to their own previous assessment than to an individual public signal contradicting their private opinion. Their view changes only after receiving further public information.

The duration of the continuation period depends on the pace of the buildup and the significance of the new public information

Daniel et al.'s (1998) model anticipates that the continuation effect will occur as a consequence of all "selective events," that is, events temporarily motivated by incorrect valuation of the company. Meanwhile, the literature also contains examples of cases where the original reaction to the announced information is contrary to the later observed post-announcement long-term returns. One example concerns IPOs, as discussed in section 4.1 in chapter 4 and section 1.1 in chapter 6. The Daniel et al. model has difficulties explaining this type of observation.

2.3. Hong and Stein's Model

Hong and Stein (1999) formulate a hypothesis that the market is composed of two categories of investors: (1) the supporters of fundamental analysis, who carefully follow the incoming information affecting the value of companies ("news watchers"); and (2) the momentum traders, who primarily attach importance to the development of short-term price trends. Each group of investors is characterized by limited rationality, which, even though their average assessment of signals is correct, allows them to analyze only a specific subset of all information publicly available. The limitation of the news watchers results from the fact that they only focus on the information related to future perspectives and to the value of a given company, while completely ignoring the signals arising from historic price movements. Additionally, Hong and Stein assume that fundamental information is distributed among these investors gradually, which causes a certain delay in the reaction of the entire market. Momentum traders, in turn, only observe price movements and do not pay any attention to fundamental information.

Based on the aforementioned assumptions, Hong and Stein (1999) show that when the market is dominated by news watchers, prices adjust to the new information gradually and the market reaction is usually slightly delayed. Gradual inclusion of fundamental information results in continuation of returns and the occurrence of a trend. This, in turn, is a signal to the momentum traders, who quickly eliminate the possible absence of adjustment to the fundamental news. They also bring the prices of assets to the proximity of their intrinsic values. Momentum traders are unaware of fundamentally justified levels as their knowledge comes only from observing stock prices and searching for trends. Hence, reaching the limits set by the fundamental signals will not constitute any barrier for the activity of the momentum traders. On the contrary, their actions are stimulated by increasingly clear price changes and will trigger overreaction of the market. The more stock prices diverge from their intrinsic value, the more the news watchers come into prominence. The growing mispricing will motivate news watchers to take action. At some point, activities of the news watchers will become so significant that the critical mass will be exceeded and they will prevail over the activities of the momentum traders. A correction will occur and the general direction of market price changes will reverse.

Similarly to the Barberis et al. (1998) and Daniel et al. (1998) models discussed earlier, the model proposed by Hong and Stein (1999) appropriately handles the explanation of short-term continuations and long-term reversals. As in the case of the other models, long-term post-announcement drift after selective events is a source of certain difficulty for this model. For example, return patterns after stock splits or changes in dividend policy contradict the model expectations. This is because such events are usually accompanied by price changes of the same direction long before the news announcement, upon the announcement, and during the post-announcement period.

2.4. Model of Shifting Risk Attitude

Barberis, Huang, and Santos (2001) propose a model drawn on three main ideas. First, investors care about fluctuations in the value of their financial wealth and not simply about the total level of consumption. Second, they are much more sensitive to reductions in their wealth than to increases (Kahneman and Tversky, 1979). Third, people are less risk averse after prior gains and more risk averse after prior losses (Thaler and Johnson, 1990).

A positive fundamental signal will generate a high stock return. This event lowers investors' risk aversion because any future losses may be cushioned by the prior gains. Therefore, investors apply a lower discount rate to the future dividend stream, giving stock prices an extra push upward. A similar mechanism holds for a bad fundamental signal. It generates a negative stock return, reducing prior gains or increasing prior losses. Investors become more risk averse than before and apply a higher discount rate, pushing prices still lower. One result of this effect is that stock returns are much more volatile than dividend changes. Normally, this pattern could be viewed as exhibiting market overreaction to initial good/bad news. In this case, stock returns are made up of two "justified" components: one due to fundamental signals and the other to a change in risk aversion.

Barberis et al. (2001) demonstrate that their model fits well with several empirical observations. Price-to-dividend ratios are inversely related to future stock returns. The returns are predictable in time series, weakly correlated with consumption, and have a high mean. The equity premium is justified because loss-averse investors require a high reward for holding a risky or excessively volatile asset.

Barberis et al. (2001) study an economy with a single risky asset. Their work is applicable to the capital market on the aggregated level. Barberis and Huang (2001) further elaborate the model and focus on firm-level returns. In a similar framework of loss aversion and shifting risk attitude depending on prior outcomes, they compare two economies that differ by a degree of narrow framing exhibited by investors: one in which investors are loss averse over the fluctuations of their overall stock portfolio (portfolio mental accounting), and another in which investors are loss averse over the fluctuations of individual stocks that they own (individual stock mental accounting). Returns in both views of narrow framing have a high mean, are excessively volatile, and are predictable in the time series using lagged variables. However, as an investor's decision frame broadens from stock to portfolio accounting, the behavior of individual stock returns changes considerably. The mean value falls, returns become less volatile and more correlated with each other, and the cross-section predictability disappears. Overall, the model assuming narrow framing at the level of individual stocks is more successful in explaining the actual data.

Although the Barberis et al. (2001) and Barberis and Huang (2001) models shed light on many empirical phenomena, they do not directly address cases of market underreaction. The additional return component resulting from a change in the applied discount rate may be associated with overreaction, leading to excess volatility. However, short-term underreaction could be incorporated into these models assuming that shifts in attitude toward risk are delayed and the discount rate applied by investors changes only after considerable price movements. Under such circumstances, underreaction to fundamental signals may persist in short periods due, for example, to the disposition effect.

2.5. Generalized Behavioral Model

The starting point of the GBM proposed by Szyszka (2007, 2010) is the assumption that fundamental value follows a random walk:

$$\tilde{F}_t = \tilde{F}_{t-1} + \tilde{v}_t, \qquad (5.1)$$

where v_t is an independent random variable of zero average, related to an inflow of new information affecting the fundamental value. The randomness of the fundamental value arises from the nature of this process. The company's value changes as a consequence of the inflow of new information where the new information signal is one that cannot be predicted and is therefore random. An assumption is that fundamental value can be estimated, although only as an approximation. Even the efficient market price does not have to exactly reflect the fundamental value because as Fama (1965, p. 36) notes "in a world of uncertainty intrinsic values are not known exactly." Nonetheless, the efficient market price serves as the best approximation of fundamental values:

$$\tilde{P}_t = \tilde{F}_t + \tilde{\xi}_t, \qquad (5.2)$$

where P_t stands for the market price of an asset at the moment t and ξ_t is an independent zero-mean random variable.

Up to this point, the model is in unison with the neoclassical theory but the fundamental value and the price established in such a manner serve merely as a benchmark. Next, asset prices can at least temporarily be systematically detached from the fundamental values as a result of irrational investors' behavior. The model focuses on the deviations from the fundamental values and links them to psychological factors. Therefore, this behavioral model supplements rather than replaces the neoclassical asset-pricing models. In line with such an understanding, security prices develop as follows:

$$\tilde{P}_t = \tilde{F}_t + \tilde{B}_t + \tilde{\xi}_t, \tag{5.3}$$

where B_2 stands for a mispricing caused by factors of behavioral origin. As by definition, $\tilde{P}_t > 0$, the maximum value of asset underpricing $\tilde{B} < 0$, can be no higher than the fundamental value minus the residual component:

$$-\tilde{B}_t < \tilde{F}_t + \tilde{\xi}_t, \tag{5.4}$$

The maximum value of asset overpricing is theoretically $(\tilde{B}_t > 0)$ unlimited.

Two categories of investors are assumed to be present in the market: (1) rational traders in the sense of the neoclassical theory and (2) irrational ones who are subject to psychologically driven heuristics and biases. These two investor categories coexist in the market at all times. Despite the errors made, irrational investors are not eliminated from the market over time. They do not tend to steadily lose capital to the benefit of rational investors. This is because a behavioral mispricing is another random variable that is not taken into account by the neoclassical theory, which rational investors use. Furthermore, rational investors only have at their disposal imperfect tools that are incongruent with actual market conditions. Hence, such investors make decisions that are, at best, suboptimal. Errors made by irrational investors do not necessarily imply that they should generate worse investment results than rational traders.

What elements make up the behavioral mispricing? An in-depth analysis of the literature on cognitive psychology as well as the existing body of work on behavioral finance, summarized in earlier parts of this book, provides a basis for distinguishing among the three crucial categories of errors made by irrational investors. The combined impact of these errors is partially alleviated by the activities of rational arbitrageurs. For this reason, the model contains a measure to account for the market's ability to self-correct.

Therefore, the deviations from the fundamental value occurring in the market at any moment t are a random variable, which can be described with the following equation:

$$\tilde{B}_t = \left(\tilde{\varepsilon}_1(x_t) + \tilde{\varepsilon}_2(x_t) + \tilde{\varepsilon}_3(x_t) \right) \cdot (1 - A), \tag{5.5}$$

where in reaction to a random event x_t at a moment t:

$\tilde{\varepsilon}_1$ is a random variable resulting from aggregate errors in the processing of information,

$\tilde{\varepsilon}_2$ is a random variable resulting from aggregate representativeness errors,

$\tilde{\varepsilon}_3$ is a random variable resulting from the biases in investor preferences, and

$A \in [0,1]$ is a measure of the market's ability to self-correct.

The process of asset pricing can be thus described in the form of the following GBM originating from equations (5.3) and (5.5):

$$\tilde{P}_t = \tilde{F}_t + \left(\tilde{\varepsilon}_1(x_t) + \tilde{\varepsilon}_2(x_t) + \tilde{\varepsilon}_3(x_t)\right) \cdot (1 - A) + \tilde{\xi}_t \qquad (5.6)$$

At any moment t, there are N investors active on the market. The $\tilde{\varepsilon}_1$, $\tilde{\varepsilon}_2$ and $\tilde{\varepsilon}_3$ values depend on the value and direction of individual errors committed at a given moment by market participants and also on the relative wealth held by them. If w_n stands for the share of the value of the W_n portfolio held by an n investor in the total value of the market portfolio $W_m = \Sigma_n W_n$, that is,

$$w_n = \frac{W_n}{\sum_n W_n}, \text{ then:}$$

$$\tilde{\varepsilon}_1(x_t) = \sum_n w_n \tilde{\varepsilon}_{1_n}(x_t), \qquad (5.7)$$

$$\tilde{\varepsilon}_2(x_t) = \sum_n w_n \tilde{\varepsilon}_{2_n}(x_t), \qquad (5.8)$$

$$\tilde{\varepsilon}_3(x_t) = \sum_n' w_n \tilde{\varepsilon}_{3_n}(x_t), \qquad (5.9)$$

If all investors were rational, the $\tilde{\varepsilon}_1$, $\tilde{\varepsilon}_2$ and $\tilde{\varepsilon}_3$ values would be zero. A similar result would be attained if investors committed errors only at an individual level, which, on an aggregate basis would be mutually neutralized given the opposite directions of the errors. In such cases, the market would be efficient inw the informational sense. Remember, though, that one of the central themes of behavioral finance is the assumption that investors are not rational and that the errors they commit are systematic in nature and are not mutually neutralized. Hence, the probability that at a given moment t, individual investor errors do not occur or are mutually neutralized should be deemed close to zero:

$$P\left(\tilde{\varepsilon}_1(x_t) = \sum_n w_n \varepsilon_{1_n}(x_t) = 0\right) \approx 0, \qquad (5.10)$$

$$P\left(\tilde{\varepsilon}_2(x_t) = \sum_n w_n \varepsilon_{2_n}(x_t) = 0\right) \approx 0, \qquad (5.11)$$

$$P\left(\tilde{\varepsilon}_3(x_t) = \sum_n w_n \varepsilon_{3_n}(x_t) = 0\right) \approx 0. \qquad (5.12)$$

The more homogeneous the behavior of irrational investors (by cognitive error), the larger is their share in the total market portfolio and the more prominent a role they play. Stated differently, herding based on a cognitive error can drive the process from the fundamental value.

The aggregated $\tilde{\varepsilon}_1$, $\tilde{\varepsilon}_2$, and $\tilde{\varepsilon}_3$ values may exert a concurrent impact in the same or opposite directions. The ultimate value of mispricing is the result of the intensity and direction of the impact of the individual components at a given moment t. In addition, the ultimate scale of the mispricing depends on the market's ability to immediately self-correct, which is measured with the A measure.

Factors affecting the value of the $\tilde{\varepsilon}_1$, $\tilde{\varepsilon}_2$, and $\tilde{\varepsilon}_3$ errors are discussed in the following section. This discussion demonstrates the situations in which psychological biases are prominent and the way in which they can distort correct asset pricing. The factors influencing the market's ability to self-correct are also discussed.

2.5.1. Errors in Information Processing

Errors in the processing of information (the impact of which is measured with the $\tilde{\varepsilon}_1$ value) sometimes lead to underreaction and at other times contribute to market overreaction. Insufficient response to new positive information or overreaction to bad news results in asset underpricing ($\tilde{\varepsilon}_1 < 0$). Conversely, overreaction to positive signals or underreaction to bad news contributes to asset overpricing ($\tilde{\varepsilon}_1 > 0$). Possible underreaction and overreaction are not mutually exclusive. Investors can underreact to a given type of information while at the same time overreacting to other news. The value is a result of both underreaction and overreaction to the news of fundamental nature.

Among the key psychological phenomena that may cause market underreaction are anchoring to the existing price levels (Tversky and Kahneman, 1974), cognitive conservatism toward new explicit information signals (Edwards, 1968), and a confirmation effect. The confirmation effect is a subconscious search for information to confirm the hypothesis previously assumed while at the same time avoiding any confrontation of facts that could be contrary to the opinion so far expressed (Wason, 1966; Lord et al., 1979). The more contrary the new information is to earlier expectations and beliefs of investors, the greater is the market underreaction.

Investors tend to display unrealistic optimism (Olsen, 1997; Montgomery, 1997; Barberis and Thaler, 2003) and wishful thinking (Buehler et al., 2002). Additionally, there is a strong loss aversion among investors resulting in reluctance to close out positions at a loss (Kahneman and Tversky, 1979). These behavioral heuristics suggest that market underreaction may occur particularly in the face of negative information.

The accuracy, quality, and manner of presentation of information are also of considerable importance for the $\tilde{\varepsilon}_1$ value. Precise signals of a high degree of reliability, yet not presented in a clear or comprehensive way (e.g., numerically) requiring additional interpretation usually induce a delayed market response.

On the other hand, market overreaction can stem from such behavioral heuristics as the availability bias (Tversky and Kahneman, 1973; Taylor, 1982), overconfidence accompanied with the calibration effect (Lichtenstein et al.,

1982; Yates, 1990; De Bondt, 1998), and also the illusion of truth (Reber and Schwarz, 1999). When judging the probability of an event, people often search their memories for relevant information. However, not all memories are equally "available." More recent and salient events will weigh most heavily and can produce biased estimates. Through overconfidence and calibration bias, people underestimate the probability of being wrong and assign too narrow confidence intervals. Events they think are certain sometimes do not occur and things they deem impossible may actually happen. Illusion of truth is another bias that distorts the cognitive process in such a way that the human mind more often accepts information presented in a simple manner and rejects information that is harder to interpret, disregarding if the actual content of information is actually true or false.

Unrealistic optimism and wishful thinking lead to a situation where market overreaction is more frequently seen in the case of positive signals. Investors also usually overreact to news presented in a descriptive manner and widely publicized in mass media, even if such information has not been fully verified and confirmed (e.g., rumor, discussions in the media, and comments by analysts). Problems with a verification of the actual quality of such communication tend to make people overrate its accuracy and attach excessive importance thereto.

2.5.2. Representativeness Errors

Among representativeness errors, two phenomena—the short-series problem and the so-called gamblers' fallacy—exert the largest impact on asset pricing. Each phenomenon has the opposite impact on the stock market.

The short-series effect takes place when an investor draws premature conclusions based on limited observations and thus establishes ill-founded rules or regularities. Psychological surveys show that such situations take place when decision makers do not know the rules that underpin the generation of successive observations (Bar-Hillel, 1982; Gilovich et al., 1985; Shefrin, 2000). On the other hand, if the distribution of a random process is well known, underestimation of the importance of the sample size may lead to the so-called gambler's fallacy: an unjustified belief that even in small samples the number of outcomes should be in line with the probability distribution.

In the capital market, a short-series effect leads to attempts to discover any regularity in random sequences of price changes. Some traders may interpret a totally random, relatively short series of rises and falls in price as initiating a new and continuing trend. As surveys carried out by Shefrin (2000) and Szyszka (2007) show, the expectation that a trend should continue is stronger among individual investors. An excessive extrapolation of the growth trend will result in the overpricing of assets ($\tilde{\varepsilon}_2 > 0$), whereas a persistent downturn may lead to asset underpricing ($\tilde{\varepsilon}_2 < 0$). Because people tend to be excessively optimistic, the deviation from the fundamental value will presumably be stronger in the growth trend.

The survey by Shefrin (2000) also points to a different behavior of professional market participants. Because professionals are better acquainted with the actual rules affecting asset pricing, such investors often fall victim to the so-called gambler's fallacy. These traders underestimate the possibility of a periodical continuation of returns on a random basis, for example, in response to sequentially occurring fundamental news of similar impact on prices. As a result, they too quickly consider such a situation to be a manifestation of market overreaction and expect a price correction too early. If such expectations translate into the corresponding activity of professional traders, it would contribute to an incomplete reflection of the news in the prices. Underreaction to good news reduces the $\tilde{\varepsilon}_2$ value, whereas insufficient response to unfavorable signals makes this variable increase.

The ultimate impact of representativeness errors on asset pricing, measured with the $\tilde{\varepsilon}_2$ value at any t moment, is therefore a result of the activities of traders expecting a continuation and of traders betting on the trend reversal. Shefrin's (2000) observations suggest that the $\tilde{\varepsilon}_2$ value may be linked to the measure of impact of irrational individual investors relative to the activity of professional investors at a particular moment t.

2.5.3. Preferences

Among symptoms of irrational development of preferences, one that is central to the possible mispricing of securities is investor behavior as outlined in Kahneman and Tversky's (1979) prospect theory. While evaluating investment alternatives, traders often focus not on the aggregate final values but primarily on changes in the value of their investment from a particular reference point. These reference points are, for example, the asset purchase price, comparison with the investment performance of other traders, or a particular market benchmark. If a comparison of their situation with the chosen reference point is favorable, a trader tends to display aversion to risk. Conversely, if the investor sees his or her position as worse than the reference point, the investor becomes strongly motivated to change this situation. An option may be to take more risk provided the investor believes that the final loss could ultimately be avoided, limited, or at least delayed. Satisfaction with potential gains and the pain of losses are not symmetrical. Finding oneself below the reference point is, as a rule, more painful than a possible satisfaction with being above it. In other words, investors dislike losses much more than they desire gains.

The higher the degree of risk aversion, the more valuable an investment is above the reference point. Therefore, a common presumption about assets that have recently increased by a substantial amount in price (e.g., as a result of new positive fundamental information) is that investors will try to secure the gains and begin closing out the positions. Any additional supply generated by the investors who decided to sell at a profit will lead to an underreaction to the good fundamental news and temporary underpricing ($\tilde{\varepsilon}_3 < 0$).

However, from the point of view of the investors who find themselves above the reference point, a weaker-than-expected price reaction to the good news does not necessarily imply underpricing. Alternatively, the degree of risk aversion in this group of investors increased and now they demand higher expected returns (risk premium). Consequently, these investors discount with a higher discount rate that reduces the stock's appreciation despite the incoming good news.

In the case of assets whose prices declined, for example, as a result of new bad fundamental information coming to the market, the situation is different. The investors who held such assets would have to incur a definitive loss when selling. A strong dislike for selling at a loss, accompanied by a hope that the losses are only temporary and will be recouped soon, encourages traders to take further risk and to hold the positions. This results in a limited supply of stock. This situation leads to a weaker-than-expected price reaction to the initially unfavorable fundamental news. As a result, a temporary overpricing of assets ($\tilde{\varepsilon}_3 > 0$) takes place in the market.

In the group of investors who find themselves below the reference point, the degree of risk aversion declines and can even transform into an inclination to take risk. In such a case, one often speaks about loss aversion rather than risk aversion. Those investors who want to avoid selling at a definitive loss now demand lower expected returns. Hence, they apply lower discount rates in company valuation. From their point of view, the objectively too weak market reaction to unfavorable news does not have to imply that the current asset prices are overestimates.

The scale of temporary overpricing of assets in decline is much larger than that of underpricing of assets whose prices have gone up. This stems from the fact that investors dislike losses much more than they desire gains. Reduction of the risk aversion as a consequence of finding oneself below the reference point will be stronger than the increase of risk aversion when one considers oneself to be above the reference point. This is corroborated by empirical findings demonstrating a more prominent post-announcement drift in response to adverse events (Szyszka, 2002) or a higher profitability of short positions in investment portfolios created according to the momentum strategy (Jegadeesh and Titman, 2002).

2.5.4. Market Ability to Self-Correct

A key premise underlying the market efficiency hypothesis is that investors who behave irrationally and affect prices will still be confronted with rational investors who use arbitrage to wipe out the mispricing effect almost immediately. Behavioral finance does not call into question the arbitrage mechanism itself or its favorable impact on the correct pricing of assets. Yet, it points out various limitations that may stop rational arbitrageurs from taking immediate actions to correct prices.

The most important limits to arbitrage include fundamental risk, noise-trader risk (De Long et al., 1990a, 1991; Shleifer and Summers, 1990), synchronization risk (Abreu and Brunnermeier, 2002), as well as implementation costs and institutional or regulatory barriers (Shleifer and Vishny, 1997).

The larger the mispricing at a given moment t, representing the total of $\tilde{\varepsilon}_1$, $\tilde{\varepsilon}_2$, and $\tilde{\varepsilon}_3$, the larger is the potential tendency on the part of rational arbitrageurs to engage in activities that bring prices to fundamental values. However, the limits of arbitrage mentioned earlier inhibit such a tendency. Therefore, the value A

in equations (5.8) and (5.9) is the result of the value of mispricing (the total of the $\tilde{\varepsilon}_1$, $\tilde{\varepsilon}_2$, and $\tilde{\varepsilon}_3$ values) and the obstacles faced by rational traders who do not exploit or do not fully exploit the opportunities offered by the mispricing.

Thus, the A value is a measure of the market's ability to self-correct and can even be treated as a measure of the market efficiency. $A = 0$ means that at a particular moment t, the self-regulation mechanism is not working and the price deviates from the fundamentals by a value resulting from behavioral errors B. In turn, $A = 1$ reflects the market's full ability to immediately eliminate the impact of irrational factors. This relationship suggests that the larger the market's self-regulation ability $(A \rightarrow 1)$, the lesser is the impact of behavior-driven errors $(B_t \rightarrow 0)$ on asset pricing.

Self-correction is possible mostly when the arbitrage mechanism works efficiently. This is fostered by a well-developed capital market where numerous companies from each sector of the economy are listed and short-selling is easy. In addition, the development of derivatives markets is important so as to enable the creation of adequate structures that can serve as a substitute for the underlying instrument. Furthermore, the market needs a large number of professional traders who are financially strong and not bound by too many restrictions in applying arbitrage strategies. Using a longer time horizon to evaluate asset managers should encourage them to exploit the opportunities offered by mispricing. They will have more time to wait for the prices to return to the fundamental values should the activities of irrational noise traders intensify. The reduction of transaction costs, especially the costs of holding short positions, should also foster increased informational efficiency of the market.

2.5.5. Mispricing and Returns from Investment

The return R_i on investment i over the period $(t - 1, t)$ results from the change of the price P of the asset and from possible payments to the holder D (e.g., of dividends) in the period concerned. The logarithmic return is thus defined as follows:

$$R_i = \ln\left(\frac{P_t + D_t}{P_{t-1}}\right), \qquad (5.13)$$

whereas the arithmetic return is:

$$R_i = \frac{P_t - P_{t-1} + D_t}{P_{t-1}} . \qquad (5.14)$$

For this discussion, assume that the investment does not generate any periodic payments, meaning $D = 0$.

In an efficient market, the return results from the change in the fundamental value F of the asset. A change in the residual component ξ, which is random in nature with an expected value of zero, can also affect the return. However, given the negligible importance of the ξ parameter, it will be disregarded further in this discussion. Behavioral finance argues that asset prices may deviate from fundamental values as a consequence of systematic cognitive errors of some market participants. In such a case, the return on the investment i in the period $(t - 1, t)$ depends not only on the change in the fundamental value F, but also on the change in the value of the mispricing, B. Substituting equation (5.3) into equations (5.13) and (5.14) results in the following:

$$R_i = \ln\left(\frac{F_t + B_t}{F_{t-1} + B_{t-1}}\right) \qquad (5.15)$$

or using the definition of the arithmetic return:

$$R_i = \frac{F_t + B_t - F_{t-1} + B_{t-1}}{F_{t-1} + B_{t-1}} \qquad (5.16)$$

Define b as a relative measure of the mispricing:

$$b_t = \frac{B_t}{F_t} \qquad (5.17)$$

The higher the absolute value of b, the larger is the importance of behavioral errors relative to the fundamental value in a development of the current market price. A change in the relative value of b should be interpreted in various ways depending on whether there is overpricing or underpricing. In the event that $B > 0$, an increase in the value of measure b on a period-to-period basis will mean that the asset is increasingly overpriced. In the case of underpricing, meaning $B < 0$, the increase in the relative value of b (namely in this case a decline in the absolute value) can be interpreted as an improvement in the quality of pricing.

Using the measure b introduced here, convert equation (5.15) as follows:

$$R_i = \ln\left(\frac{F_t + b_t F_t}{F_{t-1} + b_{t-1} F_{t-1}}\right) = \ln\left(\frac{F_t \cdot (1 + b_t)}{F_{t-1} \cdot (1 + b_{t-1})}\right) \qquad (5.18)$$

Using the properties of the logarithmic function, it follows that:

$$R_i = \ln\left(\frac{F_t}{F_{t-1}}\right) + \ln\left(\frac{1 + b_t}{1 + b_{t-1}}\right). \qquad (5.19)$$

The first element of the aforementioned equation represents the return in the efficient market:

$$R_{i,\text{efficient}} = \ln\left(\frac{F_t}{F_{t-1}}\right). \qquad (5.20)$$

The second element relates to a possible change in the relative value of the mispricing in the period $(t - 1, t)$.

$$R_{i,\text{behavioral}} = \ln\left(\frac{1+b_t}{1+b_{t-1}}\right)$$

(5.21)

It follows from condition (5.4) and definition (5.17) that $b_t > -1$ for each t. Hence, the argument of the logarithmic function (5.21) will always be positive.

Using definition (5.17), the components of the return in arithmetical terms can be found:

$$R_i = \frac{F_t + b_t F_t - F_{t-1} + b_{t-1} F_{t-1}}{F_{t-1} + b_{t-1} F_{t-1}} = \frac{F_t(1+b_t) - F_{t-1}(1+b_{t-1})}{F_{t-1}(1+b_{t-1})} = \frac{F_t}{F_{t-1}} \cdot \frac{(1+b_t)}{(1+b_{t-1})} - 1$$

(5.22)

It follows from the definition of the arithmetic return that in the efficient market conditions:

$$R_{i,\text{efficient}} = \frac{F_t}{F_{t-1}} - 1$$

(5.23)

Hence, substituting equation (5.23) into (5.22) results in:

$$R_i = \left(1 + R_{i,\text{efficient}}\right)\frac{(1+b_t)}{(1+b_{t-1})} - 1$$

$$= \left(1 + R_{i,\text{efficient}}\right)\frac{1+b_{t-1}+b_t-b_{t-1}}{1+b_{t-1}} - 1$$

$$= \left(1 + R_{i,\text{efficient}}\right)\left(1 + \frac{b_t - b_{t-1}}{1+b_{t-1}}\right) - 1$$

(5.24)

Thus, the behavioral component of the arithmetic return is:

$$R_{i,\text{behavioral}} = \frac{b_t - b_{t-1}}{1+b_{t-1}}$$

(5.25)

$$R_i = \left(1 + R_{i,\text{efficient}}\right)\left(1 + R_{i,\text{behavioral}}\right) - 1$$

(5.26)

Irrespective of using logarithmic or arithmetic return definitions, both make common observations on the impact of behavioral factors on those returns. First, if the market is efficient and behavioral elements do not affect asset prices at all, meaning that at the beginning of the period (i.e., at the $t-1$ moment) and at the end of the period (i.e., at the t moment), the assets are priced correctly ($B_{t-1} = B_t = 0$), then also $b_{t-1} - b_t = 0$. As a result, the value of equations (5.21) and (5.25) is zero. Second, if the value of the mispricing is other than zero ($B_t \# 0$), but the mispricing value B changes proportionately to changes in the fundamental value F (the relative mispricing as compared with the fundamental value is constant), the returns observed will be the same as in the case when the market is efficient. The value $R_{i,\text{behavioral}}$ is in such a situation zero both for the logarithmic and the algorithmic definitions of the return and $R_i = R_{i,\text{efficient}}$. If the value of measure b increases ($\Delta b > 0$), then $R_{i,\text{behavioral}} > 0$ and then the return R_i on the asset is higher than one that would result merely from the change in the fundamental value of the underlying instrument. Such a situation may take place where the overpricing trend increases or possibly when the previous underpricing decreases. An opposite situation occurs when the value of measure b declines ($\Delta b < 0$). Then, the return will be lower than the change in the fundamental value. This is possible when the scale of the previous overpricing relatively decreases or when the instrument becomes increasingly underpriced.

2.5.6. Summary of the GBM Predictions

The GBM assumes that the level of asset prices is affected by fundamental value and three behavioral variables resulting from errors in the processing of informational signals, representativeness errors, and unstable preferences. Errors made by investors may result in considerable deviations from the fundamental value, thus leading to a temporary overpricing or underpricing of assets. The ultimate scale of mispricing depends on the market's ability to self-correct. This ability is measured by the measure A introduced to the model. The model presents factors influencing the value of random variables representing these error categories.

The psychological factors specified in the GBM can induce distortion in asset pricing and influence returns, the latter being made up of two elements: the rational ($R_{i,\text{efficient}}$) and the behavioral ($R_{i,\text{behavioral}}$). Gradual escalation or reduction of the behavioral error B may result in continuations or reversals of returns. A continuation of gains does not necessarily follow from the initial market underreaction. Likewise, any reversal does not necessarily result from the previous market overreaction. In addition, the positive (negative) value of the behavioral element ($R_{i,\text{behavioral}}$) does not have to explicitly mean that the asset is overpriced (underpriced).

The GBM is capable of describing not only continuations and reversals of returns but also other market anomalies. Fluctuations in the intensity of the behavioral error B may be responsible for an excessive volatility of asset prices. Temporary intensification of behavioral factors can explain calendar anomalies. Dispersion in the intensity of errors among different markets or assets can be responsible for the manifestations of a violation of the law of one price and the existence of potential unexploited arbitrage opportunities. Finally, varied intensity of behavioral factors with respect to various asset classes results in different levels of returns for the particular categories of companies (e.g., the firm size effect and the book-to-market value effect).

Fluctuations of the behavioral error B may be seen as an additional factor of systematic risk. In this context, rational investors should demand an increased risk premium on investment in certain classes of assets, which are particularly susceptible to irrational traders. A gradual escalation of behavioral errors may lead to an increase in returns expected by rational investors as compensation for the growing unpredictability of the market and may thus reduce the asset's fundamental value. The discrepancy between the behavioral and the rational valuation will escalate until the impact of irrational factors lessens or is outweighed by the market's ability to self-correct. In this way, the GBM explains various market manias and temporary investment fads as well as their subsequent corrections.

CHAPTER 6

Behavioral Insights into Financial Crisis

In a few recent years, we experienced market turbulences on the scale and scope not seen since the Great Depression in the 1930s. First, the problems started in the United States with the burst of the real estate bubble and the credit crunch. Soon the crisis spread globally. Its spin-off effects revealed major weaknesses of the Eurozone, particularly unbearable levels of public and private indebtness in a few member states.

This chapter presents first of all a time line of key events both in the United States and Europe. It aims to offer a perspective into the sequence of events and to the exacerbation of the symptoms of crisis. Subsequently, it briefly discusses the genesis of the problems, particularly in the macroeconomic and political context. Last but not the least, attention is focused on behavioral aspects of the turbulences. Even if behavioral biases were not the unique root of the crisis, they greatly contributed to the development of the problems at first, and also demonstrated themselves later, when the crisis became already apparent.

1. Credit Crunch in the United States

1.1. Time Line of Events

The long-term growth trend in the real estate prices in the United States has been slowing down since the beginning of 2006. Simultaneously, more and more borrowers, particularly from the higher-risk segment, euphemistically referred to as *subprime*, have faced difficulties related to repayment of the mortgages. Banks begin to foreclose the property of insoluble debtors and offer it for sale, all the while generating additional supply at relatively lower prices, due to the enforced nature of the sale. This causes further breakdown of the market and by the end of 2006, the property prices in selected regions of the United States drop by as much as 30 percent.

In the beginning of January 2007, the first financial institution lending in the subprime sector—Ownit Mortgage Solutions, part-owned by Merrill Lynch—goes under. Since the scale of its operations is minor, the incident goes practically unnoticed by the market.

In August 2007, the first major wave of difficulties related to financial liquidity affects the financial institutions operating in the mortgage market. The American Federal Reserve (Fed), the European Central Bank (ECB), and the Bank of Japan pump significant funds into the banking system.

At the end of August 2007, G. W. Bush announces a relief plan for Americans struggling with mortgage repayment, subsidized with federal funds. The plan temporarily placates the market, as it gives hope to stop the process of foreclosures of indebted properties by banks and their mass resale leading to a further drop in prices. For banks, it is significant that credits are paid off timely without the need to create the respective reserves.

In mid-2007, it turns out that mortgage-related problems are not specific to the United States. The Bank of England grants financial aid to the Northern Rock bank that specialized in extending credits for purchase of real estate in the United Kingdom and that additionally invested significantly in American mortgage-based securities.

All these warning signs and the preliminary symptoms of crisis seem to not yet appeal to stock exchange investors. Stock exchanges are at the height of the frenzy. On October 9, 2007, the Dow Jones Industrial Average (DJIA) sets the historic high at 14,164 points (whereas a little over a year later on November 20, 2008, it falls to a daily low of 7,552 points, which means a drop by almost 50 percent!).

However, soon enough, the American banking sector must face the increasing lack of current liquidity. As mutual trust is lost, banks do not want to lend to one another in the interbank market. On November 1, 2007, the Fed intervenes again, granting direct loans to the total amount of 41 billion dollars to various entities. Simultaneously, an increasing number of financial institutions are forced to write off reserves in view of the drop in the value of mortgage-based assets. This affects the current bottom lines and equities in the financial sector and undermines the credibility of the most prestigious institutions. The problem concerns both American banks and European entities, which, as a part of their operations, invested in mortgage-based financial instruments. The capital market reacts with a rapid price drop in the stocks of the financial sector. Despite a relatively low valuation, many entities are forced to authorize new share issues, as they need additional equity to improve their balance-sheet structure disturbed by vast losses.

In February 2008, it turns out that despite the previously granted aid of the Bank of England, the Northern Rock is again on the verge of bankruptcy. Fearing the ripple effect and negative consequences for the entire UK financial system, the British government decides in favor of an unprecedented increase in the national debt by an additional 100 billion British Pounds (GBP), an equivalent of nearly 200 billion US dollars at that time. The government allocates acquired funds to capitalize Northern Rock by purchasing shares of the bank and hence causing its actual nationalization.

The nationalization of Northern Rock gave the market a clear signal that authorities were determined to defend the stability of the financial system at all cost, which temporarily appeased the situation. However, simultaneously, a discussion flared up in the United Kingdom concerning the limits of state interventionism in a liberal economy and the legitimacy of allocating public funds to save private institutions that run into trouble as the result of their own risk mismanagement.

Soon afterward, the American Federal Reserve (Fed) was to face similar dilemmas. In March 2008, a renowned American investment bank, Bear Stearns, found itself insolvent. The only way to save the falling bank was its purchase by another institution, but there was no one willing to take over the company in its current state. This was because the value of potential liabilities was difficult to determine as it was related, among others, to the unverified quality of financial assets and collaterals held by the bank, as well as to difficulties with assessing the scale of losses from transactions on derivatives, including, in particular, credit risk swap (CRS) transactions. Under such circumstances, for the acquisition by JP Morgan Chase to actually happen the Fed issues a guarantee for potential liabilities of Bear Stearns up to 30 billion dollars. JP Morgan Chase pays 10 dollars for each Bear Stearns share (prior to the guarantee that it was only offering 2 dollars a share and that offer was rejected by the Bear Stearns shareholders), whereas only a year earlier the shares were listed at about 170 dollars a share. In total, JP Morgan Chase invests a little over a billion dollars in the transaction, which may seem a moderate amount taking into consideration the potential involvement of the Fed of 30 billion dollars. It should also be noted that JP Morgan Chase was particularly interested in rescuing Bear Stearns from collapsing, as JP Morgan Chase itself was involved in derivatives transactions where the counterparty on the liabilities side was none other but Bear Stearns. The collapse of Bear Stearns would therefore result in severe losses incurred directly by JP Morgan Chase. Hence, the Fed, risking public funds in the form of guarantees, de facto, supported two private investment banks in this transaction.

The scale of involvement of the Fed in the Bear Stearns acquisition would soon seem less significant. In the beginning of September 2008, the situation becomes particularly dramatic. The two largest mortgage market institutions Fannie Mae and Freddie Mac, with the total of about 5 billion dollars invested in real estate–based instruments, also face the risk of a collapse. These institutions dealt, among others, with securitizing mortgage claims and extending mortgage guarantees for subprime borrowers. Historically, they were established by the US government to increase the availability of financing for Americans with a view to promoting the ownership of houses in the society. The roots of Fannie Mae go back to 1938 when it was established during Franklin Roosevelt's presidency as a part of the New Deal plan aimed at coming out of the Great Depression. Freddie Mac was established in 1970 as a competitive entity, which was to prevent market monopolization by Fannie Mae. With time, both companies were privatized and started operating as commercial financial institutions focused on servicing the mortgage market, although they still enjoyed various forms of support from the federal government (e.g., availability of a special credit line directly from the Treasury Department, state and federal tax exemptions). Once again, they had to be nationalized by the federal government to be saved from collapse. Their bankruptcy would send a ripple effect across the entire financial system, making the situation difficult for other institutions for which Fannie Mae or Freddie Mac were a party to mortgage contracts (e.g., by selling securitized bonds, CRS, or guarantees issued by Fannie or Freddie).

In September 2008, substantial state funds of 85 billion dollars were also pumped into the largest American insurance company—American International Group (AIG). AIG found itself in trouble even though only a portion of its business activity was associated with insuring the mortgage insolvency risk. At the same time, AIG was strongly involved in insuring trade contracts and servicing large American industrial corporations. Hence, its possible bankruptcy would be detrimental not only to the financial sector but would also be reflected in other sectors of the economy.

A renowned investment bank Lehman Brothers collapses almost at the same time. In that case, the US federal government decided against rescuing that respectable institution with almost 160 years of history. It may seem strange why between two institutions facing bankruptcy at the same time, one, AIG, is saved at the expense of the taxpayers' money and the other, Lehman Brothers, is doomed to fail. Perhaps, the answer lies in the fact that the bankruptcy of AIG would affect both the American financial system and American corporations in other sectors of the economy. Meanwhile, Lehman Brothers, even though it was an American bank, had strong relations with foreign entities, particularly Asian and European banks, where it acted as the counterparty to transactions with exposure to the American mortgage market. The collapse of Lehman Brothers, although still not without influence on the American financial system, seems to have affected to a greater degree the foreign institutions cooperating with Lehman Brothers. Perhaps, the Fed deliberately decided that it was not worthwhile to involve the American taxpayers' money in the operations that would significantly benefit foreign banks.

During the first half of September 2008, another renowned investment bank with a long tradition is also subject to acquisition. Merrill Lynch is purchased by the formerly second-tier Bank of America, for about 50 billion dollars, that is 29 dollars per share. On the one hand, it means a 70 percent premium in relation to the last share price listed before the acquisition was announced, but on the other, it only corresponds to a fraction of the value from a year ago when the Merill Lynch was quoted above 98 dollars per share.

All the events that happened until that time result in a very high uncertainty in the market. Financial institutions do not trust one another and fear that consecutive banks will declare losses that may contribute to a significant drop in their capitals and to the deterioration in their credit standing or even to subsequent bankruptcies. No one is willing to lend money in the interbank market. The difference between the official Fed interest rate and the interest rate in the interbank market on the day of the collapse of Lehman Brothers amounts to almost 5 percentage points. Trading on the secondary money market among financial institutions is practically frozen. Every entity tries to accumulate cash in its own assets.

Under those circumstances, on September 19, 2008, Henry Paulson, the American Treasury Secretary announces a 700 billion dollars bailout plan, which assumes, among others, the buyout of the so-called toxic assets, that is nonliquid assets related to the mortgage and derivatives markets, the value of which is at risk or presently difficult to assess. Paulson's plan is based on the conviction that if the state buys out the problematic assets, it will provide a one-off cleansing of bad components that are the source of uncertainty off the balance sheets of financial institutions. Simultaneously, bailing out the toxic assets will pump a significant amount of money into the bloodstream of the financial system, which should assure liquidity and reinstate the normal functioning of the entire financial system. Financing of Paulson's plan required the US debt to go up to an astronomical amount of 13.1 trillion dollars and the plan itself had yet to be approved by the Congress. Nevertheless, the very presentation of such a broad plan of action by the Treasury Secretary arouses hope that the situation may be brought under control, at least in the American market. On the day when Paulson's plan is announced, the DJIA goes up by 3.3 percent.

Governments of European countries will soon have to face problems similar to those from across the Ocean. In the last week of September 2008, France saves Dexia Bank from collapse, Germany organizes a multi-billion rescue package for Hypo Real Estate and—most of all—the governments of the Benelux countries take over the control of the Fortis Bank in an unprecedented manner. Simultaneously, instead of buying out any toxic assets, as assumed by the Paulson's plan in the United States, individual governments of the European Union (EU) states attempt primarily to restore calmness and confidence by increasing guarantees for bank deposits for citizens and/or by guaranteeing transactions in the interbank market with a view to avoiding losing liquidity in the financial system.

On September 29, 2008, the financial market goes into a shock resulting from the fact that Paulson's plan is rejected by the House of Representatives of the American Congress. On that day the DJIA records the largest drop in history—by over 777 points, that is, almost 7 percent in one day.[1]

The American administration makes urgent arrangements with the Congress with a view to developing a modified version of Paulson's plan. According to the modification, the planned bailout amount of 700 billion dollars is to be divided into tranches: The first 350 billion dollars is to reach the market immediately. Hundred billion dollars is to be left at the disposal of the president and the expenditure from the last tranche will require further consent of Congress. The modified version of Paulson's plan is finally adopted on October 3, 2008, by both Houses of Congress and immediately signed by the US president. Nevertheless, this time, market participants do not show the same enthusiasm as when Paulson's bailout plan was initially announced. The DJIA drops by 1.5 percent that day. Investors still display high uncertainty and high degree of risk aversion.

On October 7 and 8, 2008, the world is shocked by revelations regarding the insolvency of the three largest Icelandic banks whose indebtedness exceeded nine times the GDP of this relatively small country. Iceland as a state is not able to aid its financial system and it de facto finds itself on the verge of bankruptcy. Assistance comes from Russia who offers Iceland a special anti-crisis loan of 4 billion Euro.

On October 8 and 9, 2008, six central banks—the American Federal Reserve, the ECB, the Bank of England, the Bank of Canada, the Swiss National Bank, and the Riksbank of Sweden—perform a co-coordinated global reduction of interest rates. The banks simultaneously reduce the interest rates by 50 basis points. Additionally, the reduction of interest rates is supported by the Central Bank of China, which decreases its financing costs by an untypical 27 basis points. In the short term, stock exchanges worldwide react with a rise in indexes and the foreign exchange market reacts with an increase in the EUR/dollar and GBP/dollar rates and with a reduction of the price of yen to the leading currencies. The coordinated action of interest rate cuts is received by the investors as a positive signal that the central banks of various countries can cooperate with a view to overcome the crisis. It seems that the actual reduction of the financing cost was of lesser importance, to the extent that the effect was limited due to the still relatively high spreads and remaining low liquidity in the interbank market, which was still related to a high uncertainty in the financial market.

On November 4, 2008, the Democratic Party candidate senator Barack Obama wins the presidential election in the United States under the slogan "Time for change." Economic commentators point out the high hopes entrusted to the new administration on the one hand and, on the other hand, they voice concerns with regard to the extensive social components of Obama's electoral campaign.

On November 14 and 15, 2008, a G20 summit is held in Washington, gathering the representatives of the 20 top industrialized countries of the world who meet to discuss preventive measures in view of the global crisis. The meeting is hosted by the outgoing US President George W. Bush, and the president elect, but the probable representatives of his future administration are practically not involved in the sessions. The summit does not result in any specific solutions, except for general declarations about the need to coordinate international activities and the need of another meeting in the beginning of 2009.

Simultaneously, more and more macroeconomic signals indicate that the crisis has spread from the financial markets onto the real economy on a global scale. For two consecutive quarters, the economies of the United States, Great Britain, Germany, Japan, Italy, and Spain showed negative dynamic of the GDP; so it can be officially confirmed that they had entered the stage of recession. Economies of other countries also suffer from the effects of the global crisis, which is reflected if not by recession then at least by an economic growth slowdown.

1.2. Background of the US Problems

1.2.1. US Economy in the Global Context

In 1991–2005, the US economy was developing faster than the entire worldwide economy collectively and, on average per annum, about three times faster than the economies of the 15 states of the so-called old EU (EU-15). However, the highest pace of GDP growth among the key economies of the world during that period was recorded by China. On average per annum, it amounted to almost 9.6 percent.

The US growth was driven by the household demand (current consumption and housing), whereas the demand of the business sector and that of governmental agencies ranked much lower.

One of the material ways in which the US economy influenced the world economy was its high import demand. It led to an increasingly unfavorable external imbalance in trade relations, additionally fostered by the long-term policy of China aimed at artificially maintaining the undervalued exchange rate of the Chinese currency (RMB/yuan). The Chinese interventions in the foreign exchange market, aimed at preventing the RMB appreciation, resulted in significant foreign exchange reserves accumulated in China, denominated mainly in US dollars. According to the data of the International Monetary Fund, since 2006, China has outrun Japan and has become the largest holder of foreign exchange reserves in the world.

1.2.2. Twin Deficit and Dollars Exchange Rate

Apart from the increasing external account deficit resulting from the foreign trade imbalance, the US economy was also threatened by an internal budget deficit. Although the United States still recorded a budget surplus of over 1 percent in 2000, after the first term of office of G. W. Bush, the deficit already amounted to 4.3 percent GDP and it indicated a further decline tendency. A growing budget deficit was caused not only by relatively lower revenues resulting from a temporary economic slowdown directly after the dotcom bubble burst and after the terrorist attacks of 9/11, but also from tax cuts introduced by G. W. Bush on two separate occasions. On the other hand, budget expenses were on a significant rise, due to, among others, financing the war in Iraq and the war on terror (Chinn, 2005).

The phenomenon of a simultaneous existence of a negative balance in the current account and a governmental expense surplus over budget revenues is referred to as the twin deficit. The literature had warned against the impossibility of maintaining such a situation for a long term long before the crisis occurred (e.g., Lewis, 2004; Chinn, 2005).

Financing the American budget deficit required vast sales of treasury bills. Still, investors accepted the low yields on American debt because of the credibility of the US Treasury Department. Warnock and Warnock (2005) estimated that the inflow of the official foreign capital to the United States affected the decrease in profitability of ten-year treasury bills by about 150 basis points.

However, the long-lasting foreign trade imbalance and the combination of the expansive fiscal policy and low interest rates led in the end to a material depreciation of the US dollar against other leading world currencies, in particular against the EUR. Asian and Arab countries became virtual hostages of their own foreign exchange reserves denominated in US dollars. On the one hand, they suffered increasingly from the dropping dollar—on the other, even announcements of possible corrections in the foreign exchange reserve structures were causing nervous reactions of the market.

1.2.3. Cheap Money Policy

The expansive fiscal policy of the US government has been accompanied for a long time by the Fed policy of low interest rates. The interest rates in the United States were significantly reduced after the dotcom bubble burst in 2000/2001 and additionally after the 9/11 attacks in 2001 to ensure the economy's soft landing. Only in mid-2004 did the Federal Reserve decide to gradually raise them.

Combining the aforementioned relaxed fiscal policy and low interest rates, the United States created a boom in the economy. However, the boom was mainly based on the consumer demand and on the expenditures on housing. American society, with its traditionally low saving tendencies, took advantage of the benefits of cheap money and continued to go deeper and deeper in debt.

When the interest rates started growing again and peaked in 2006, many households faced problems with debt servicing. First of all, the problem affected Americans with the lowest credit status that had nevertheless been granted risky mortgages. Financial institutions were even willing to lend to people who could not demonstrate permanent employment, regular income, or any material assets. Such persons were referred to as NINJA (*No Income No Job or Assets*). All this was based on securing the extended loans on properties the prices of which were expected to continue to grow.

However, the real estate bubble burst. Price drops were additionally intensified by the supply of properties seized by banks from borrowers and sold below value at foreclosure auctions. The falling prices of real estate also meant that the value of bank collateral was also decreasing. Banks could not fully recover the extended loans and were forced to write off reserves for uncollectible debt. Earlier, to gain capital required to increase the lending operations, banks borrowed money from other institutions or issued special securities collateralized on the portfolio of the previously extended mortgages. Now banks got into trouble with servicing their own indebtedness, which, to a large extent, was to be synchronized with the payments received from borrowers.

1.2.4. Development of Derivatives Market and Financialization

The turn of the twenty-first century also witnessed a dynamic development of the derivatives market. Gradually, derivatives have been more and more frequently used for speculative purposes rather than risk hedging, which was their primary purpose. In the end, the value of turnover in the derivatives markets exceeded several times the markets for underlying assets. According to the data of the Futures Industry Association (FIA), in 2007, the total trade volume of derivatives in 54 stock exchanges worldwide amounted to 15.2 billion pieces of Futures contracts and options, whereas in 1999, that volume only amounted to 2.4 billion pieces. The Bank for International Settlement (BIS) estimated that in 2007 the value of the stock exchange trading in derivatives amounted to almost 2.3 trillion US dollars. This value should also be increased by the value of derivatives transactions entered into on the over-the-counter (OTC) market. Statistics concerning the total volume of transactions in the global OTC market are not available but its size is reflected by the actual value of outstanding contracts that the data of BIS valued at 595.3 billion dollars at the end of 2007. A vast majority of derivatives transactions concerned financial underlying assets. According to FIA, the share of derivatives transactions associated with nonfinancial assets (e.g., agricultural produce, energy, precious metals, raw materials) did not exceed 10 percent at the end of 2007.

The dynamic development of the derivatives markets led to abandoning the typical function of money in the economy, that is, its traditional currency function. In the beginning, money followed merchandise. When specific goods were purchased, money was used to pay for them. Now, the cash and goods circulations are largely separated. Money and monetary products became merchandise themselves.

There were two primary reasons underlying this effect. First of all, development of the derivatives market was driven by a chase after profits accompanied by a simultaneous growing tolerance for risk. Various derivatives with built-in leverage mechanism were able to generate high returns to satisfy investor greed. Second, supply of cheap money facilitated asset financialization. Creating new derivative products enabled offering new categories of assets, which under normal circumstances could not be traded at all or which would be characterized by low liquidity. Derivatives with values associated with particular sector-specific indexes were rapidly gaining popularity. For example, it was possible to invest in water by purchasing derivative products based on the index of water treatment companies or wind by investing in index of companies operating in the wind power sector.

Actually the most spectacular and, as it later turned out, the most fateful type of asset financialization was the creation of derivatives with the value associated with mortgage portfolio. Two kinds of financial products are of particular interest here: collateralized debt obligations (CDOs) and the so-called CRS.

Issuing CDOs helped credit institutions acquire new lending funds from the market on the basis of their previous lending portfolio. At the same time, it was assumed that the funds to service CDOs, that is, to cover current coupon payments and to buy out the bonds in the future would come from the cash flowing from the already acquired borrowers. The claims were secured by mortgages on credited properties and grouped into specific portfolios. The bonds based on such secured and respectively diversified claim portfolios were placed in the market as relatively safe instruments. They constituted a source of cheap capital for lenders and encouraged them to continue credit expansion. Funds obtained in return for the bonds were involved in extending new credits and such credits were immediately securitized and used as the basis for the issue of yet another block of mortgage securities. The cycle was repeated multiple times, which contributed to a substantial creation of money in the economy.

CRS made it possible to transfer the risk of borrowers' insolvency within a given claim portfolio from a borrower onto another entity. Thus, the lending institution gained some sort of insurance in the event of insolvency of a particular group of its customers. The ease with which new lending funds could be obtained and the possibility to transfer the risk onto another entity prompted lending institutions to accept applications from clients with increasingly low credit scores. Lenders were interested in maximizing their credit sales, as they earned profits primarily on credit service commissions and on the differences between the credit cost and their own financing cost. With the CRS they did not have to consider any potential losses that could occur in the future as the result of insolvency of some of their clients.

Development of the global derivatives market, and in particular development of CDO and CRS contracts, did not cause the crisis directly but determined its scale. These two transaction types were among the factors contributing to the fact that mortgage-related risk became widely spread throughout the entire financial sector both in the United States and globally, even among financial institutions that did not have operations in the United States at all or which did not offer financing directly in the mortgage market. Mortgage-based derivatives became the main cause of the strong domino effect that we have observed during this crisis.

1.2.5. Rally on Commodity Prices

Since the beginning of 2002, we have witnessed dynamic price growth in commodity markets, which continued and only reached its peak in mid-2008. Initially, it could seem that the growth was justified in the context of an intensified demand for commodities from fast-developing economies, particularly China. However, the growth dynamics of commodity prices was much higher than the accompanying increase in global demand. A significant portion of raw material appreciation was caused by investors' speculations. They started treating commodities as ordinary financial assets they could invest in with their surpluses of cheap money and they expected further growth in prices.

In 2006, oil-exporting countries became the biggest source of capital in the world. The capital originated primarily from the Middle East, Nigeria, Norway, Indonesia, Russia, and Venezuela. An inflow of petrodollars resulted both from a rapid increase in oil prices and from the rising volumes of oil export. Contrary to classic foreign exchange reserves of central banks, which are usually conservatively invested in safe governmental debt securities, petrodollars also funded higher-risk investment in various segments of the capital market. A significant portion of that capital found its way into the world markets through governmental agencies and sovereign funds, independent investment funds, and individual wealthy investors. The McKinsey Global Institute (2008) estimated that, in 2006, only 200 billion petrodollars went toward global stock markets, 100 billion dollars were invested in debt securities, and around 40 billion dollars were fed into high-risk funds (venture capital and private equity, hedge, property funds, etc.). These funds greatly contributed not only to the drop in profitability of debt securities but also to high valuations on the stock market, hence lower cost of equity.

2. Euro Crisis

2.1. *Time Line of Events*

From the second half of 2009, fears of a sovereign debt crisis developed among investors and politicians as a result of the rising private and government debt levels in some European states. On October 18, 2009, the new Greek prime minister, George Papandreu, revealed a black hole in Greek official accounts and admitted that the budget deficit will be double the previous government's estimate, reaching as much as 12 percent of the Greek GDP. The FTSE100 dropped by 200 points, that is, by nearly by 4 percent, following that announcement.

On December 8, 2009, Fitch was the first rating agency to downgrade Greece's rating, but only from A– to BBB+. It is not until April 27, 2010, when Standard and Poor and Moody's downgraded Greek bonds to junk status, and Fitch joined them as late as in January 2011. Much before that, the market was pricing Greek debt already as junk, offering high yields on Greek bonds and high premiums on credit default swaps (CDS) against Greece's bankruptcy. In the meantime, European politicians worked hard to set the first bailout plan for Greece, conditional on severe budgetary savings.

In spring 2010, it became evident that the European debt crisis was spreading. Lenders demanded ever higher interest rates not only from Greece, but also from Spain, Portugal, and Ireland. This in turn made it difficult for some governments to finance further budget deficits and service existing debt, particularly when the economic growth was weak. To fight the crisis, some governments introduced austerity measures, such as higher taxes and cuts in expenses, which contributed to social unrest, but also deepened the slowdown of the economy. On April 27, 2010, Standard and Poor lowered its view on Portugal and a day later downgraded the rating of Spain from AA to AA–. Fitch followed with Spain's downgrade a month later. Ireland faced the first downgrade by Moody in July 2010.

For the whole year 2010, markets remained very nervous with the volatility of bond and stock prices greatly increased. For example, on May 6, 2010, concerns about the ability of the *Eurozone* to deal with the spreading crisis caused a severe market sell-off, particularly in the United States where the DJIA had a nearly 1,000 point intraday drop, to recover somewhat the same day and close 347 points down. This was just after the Eurozone countries and the International Monetary Fund agreed to a 110 billion euro (then almost a 150 billion US dollars) loan for Greece on May 2, 2010.

A week later, Europe's Finance Ministers approved a comprehensive rescue package aimed at ensuring financial stability across Europe by creating the European Financial Stability Facility (EFSF). This was a temporary rescue mechanism to be later supplemented by the permanent European Stability Mechanism (ESM) with effective lending capacity up to 500 billion euro. These measures were also accompanied by the so-called sixpack, a legislation initiative aimed to strengthen economic integration and budgetary discipline within the Eurozone. However, it took over a year of negotiations before all six acts were eventually approved by the European Parliament in September 2011, and the ESM came into operation not earlier than in September 2012 after the Federal Constitutional Court of Germany had confirmed its legality.

In the meantime, Ireland received an 85 billion euro (then 110 billion US dollars) rescue package in the end of 2010. Portugal was next with 78 billion euro (then below 110 billion US dollars) bailout in May 2011.

Aside from all the political measures and bailout programs being implemented to combat the European sovereign debt crisis, the ECB also did its part by lowering interest rates, reactivating the dollar swap lines, buying up Spanish and Italian bonds, and providing cheap loans of more than one trillion euros to maintain money flows between European banks.

The whole 2011 remained volatile with hopes and fears mixing. Rating agencies continued to downgrade not only troubled peripheral countries, but also cut ratings of Italy, France, and Belgium. There were serious worries particularly about financial situation in Spain and Italy, as these two economies are much bigger than Greece, Portugal, or Ireland. The initial aid program for Greece turned out to be insufficient and the problem of the country's insolvency was back in the second half of 2011. Tensions increased and resulted in changes of the governments in Greece, Spain, and Italy before the end of 2011.

Concurrently, there was a lot of speculation activity on the market. In August 2011, Spain introduced a ban on shorting stock of financial institutions. In December 2011, the European Parliament attempted to stop speculation in the CDS market forbidding so-called naked transactions, that is, engaging in CDS contracts without having the underlying securities. These restrictions had a rather limited effect on the market.

2012 started with the continuation of the Greek drama that had its final in February when a second bailout worth 130 billion euro was agreed, conditional on the implementation of another harsh austerity package. For the first time, the bailout deal also included a debt restructure agreement with the private holders of Greek government bonds (banks, insurers, and investment funds), to "voluntarily" accept a bond swap with a 53.5 percent nominal write-off, partly in short-term EFSF notes, partly in new Greek bonds with lower interest rates and the maturity prolonged to 11–30 years (independently of the previous maturity). "Voluntarily" was the keyword as such a swap formally was not considered as a default event and did not trigger activation of CDS on the debt under the program. It was the world's biggest debt restructuring deal ever done, affecting some 206 billion euro (then 275 billion US dollars) of Greek government bonds. The debt write-off had a size of almost 110 billion euro (150 billion US dollars) that constituted nearly one-third of the total debt of Greece in March 2012.

When the "Greek tragedy" seemed to be eventually over, attention focused on mounting problems in Spain whose economy is twice the size of the Greek, Portuguese, and Irish combined. The country was facing unemployment rate above 25 percent and recession. Over 2012, Spain experienced a series of downgrades by major agencies with the last cut rate to BBB– and a "negative outlook" attached by the Standard and Poor in October. The Spanish banking sector lacked liquidity, starting with Bankia, the fourth biggest Spanish bank, that needed to be recapitalized and practically nationalized in May 2012. In June, Spain secured a 100 billion euro (125 billion US dollars) package from the ESM for bank recapitalization. Despite that, the yield on Spanish ten-year governmental bonds peaked above 7.5 percent in July, and the country faced difficulty accessing bonds markets. Only when the ECB announced on September 6 the unlimited purchases of sovereign debt, the yield started to decline and fell to about 5.5 percent by the end of 2012.

On the other hand, there were also first signs of recovery. On July 26, 2012, for the first time since September 2010, Ireland was able to return to the financial markets selling over 5 billion euro in long-term government debt, with an interest rate of 5.9 percent for the 5-year bonds and 6.1 percent for the 8-year bonds at sale. Still, the budgetary situation was far from comfortable in that country as of the end of 2012.

2.2. Background of the Euro Problem

2.2.1. A Monetary Union of Dissimilar Economies

The European Monetary Union (EMU) was principally a political project aimed to irrevocably join the French, German, and other European economies and cement European unity. Since the end of World War II, generations of political leaders and policy makers chose economic integration as an instrument to prevent any future wars on the Old Continent. This process was gradual over decades, but eventually, German reunification in October 1990 provided the political impetus for the creation of the Maastricht Treaty, which in 1992 laid the legal foundation and detailed design for today's Eurozone.

As a result of primacy of politics over economics, the EMU was launched in 1999 comprising of a set of countries that were far more diverse in their economic fundamentals and far less economically integrated than what economic theory would have predicted feasible. At least two major clusters of the Eurozone countries may be distinguished—*the Core*, consisting of Austria, Finland, France, Germany, and the Benelux and the *Peripheries* represented by Greece,[2] Italy, Ireland, Portugal, and Spain. *The Core* can be characterized as efficient and highly productive, prudent net savers, consuming moderately and providing for their future. This is reflected in stable and high private saving rates and persistent current account surpluses. The net foreign asset positions of these countries are almost balanced on average. On the other hand, *Peripheries* are less efficient, consume in excess of their resources, and consequently these countries have low savings and current account deficit that is financed by foreign capital inflows (Figure 6.1). Moreover, the servicing of high net foreign debt positions constitutes a considerable burden for these countries, especially since investors finally realized the differences among the Eurozone issuers, and yields on the *Peripheries'* bonds spiked. Thus, we observe growing external and internal imbalances across the Euro-area and an increasing indebtedness of the *Peripheries* to the *Core*.

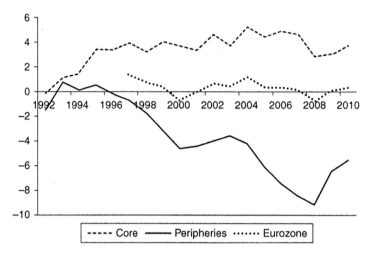

Figure 6.1 Current account deficit, 1992–2010 (as percent GDP).
Source: Own computation based on public data from the Eurostat.

Nevertheless, this should not lead to a premature and naive conclusion that the *Core* is generously subsidizing the *Peripheries* because of solidarity and purely for the sake of European unity and safety. The *Core* countries, and Germany in particular, also have an overwhelming economic interest in the survival, and indeed strengthening, of the Eurozone. Their entire economic model is based on export-led growth and world-class international competitiveness. Before the euro, however, large trade surpluses would often lead to sharp appreciation in the exchange rate of their national currencies, which would dampen their international competitiveness, harm export, and thus limit their growth. The *Core* countries may enjoy preferable economic situation of trade surpluses and relatively weak currency, as the euro averages out also much weaker economies of the *Peripheries*. Recently, this unusual combination has been an important handicap particularly to the German economy that has remained in a relatively good shape during the global slowdown.

It is not the case that the disparity between the *Core* and the *Peripheries* was unnoticed prior to the crisis. Until recently, however, the observed pattern in current accounts was mainly attributed to the European convergence process (Blanchard and Giavazzi, 2002; Arghyrou and Chortareas, 2008). The theory of intertemporal maximization suggests that diverging current accounts are the natural consequence of a convergence process among countries with different levels of economic development. Countries with a lower per-capita income attract foreign investment as expected higher productivity and economic growth rates promise superior returns. At the same time, these countries consume more and save less in anticipation of higher growth in the future. In the same convergence process, inflation is likely to rise in the catching-up economies. Given a fixed nominal exchange rate within the Eurozone, relatively higher inflation rates means an immediate real exchange rate appreciation and thus a loss in international competitiveness of the *Peripheries* and worse trade balances. As a result of the whole process, the peripheral countries register high current account deficits that are financed by inflows of capital investment from the *Core*. On the other hand, the *Core* enjoys current account surpluses while financing the *Peripheries*.

The convergence process is enhanced in the presence of integrated real and financial markets. Therefore, one could put forward a controversial statement that those cross-country imbalances may well be perceived as a success of and not a threat to the euro. The question, however, is how long such a situation can be sustained. Current account deficits in the past lead unavoidably to the accumulation of net foreign debt positions that need to be serviced out of current income. Persistent trade deficits, declining net current transfers, and increasing net factor income payments lead to a spiral of foreign indebtedness.

The high productivity of the invested capital is crucial to the assumption that the accumulated foreign debt can be serviced regularly and repaid ultimately by the *Peripheries*. Therefore, the growth needs to be real, sustainable, and actually should lead to the convergence with the *Core*.

Yet, Holinski, Kool, and Muysken (2010) demonstrate that the economic convergence hypothesis does not stand up to the empirical facts. They document that real income differentials are persistent, total factor productivity remains low in the *Peripheries* (with the exception to Ireland), and the terms of trade data surprisingly do not confirm a substantial loss in international competitiveness as inflation differentials could initially suggest—at least not to the degree that would justify the magnitude of current accounts deficits in the peripheral economies. They argue that the main drivers of the current account dispersion are the private sectors—households and firms in the *Peripheries*—for which they find a tremendous decrease in savings from about 24 percent of GDP in the beginning of the1990s to about 14 percent of GDP in 2007. This was reflected in a corresponding increase in consumption and, to a lesser extent, investment.

Consumption and savings patterns in peripheral countries did not adjust to higher burdens resulting from net factor income payments (mainly due to the increasing cost of servicing of accumulating debt) and declining current transfers (partly due to the enlargement of the EU and redirection of the EU funds toward the new member states). The imported capital was wasted in the public administration, misallocated in overinflated property sectors, or spent on other poor investments.

The necessary high productivity growth generally was never achieved. Over the period 1997–2007, labor productivity per employee grew on average by 1.3 percent per year in the *Peripheries*, compared to 1.2 percent annual growth in the *Core*. Over the same period, per capita employee compensation rose by an average annual rate of 5.9 percent in the *Peripheries*, considerably faster than the *Core*'s average of 3.2 percent. As a result, unit labor costs rose by 32 percent in the *Peripheries* from 1997 to 2007, compared to a 12 percent increase in the *Core* (Dadush and Stancil, 2010).

When relatively inefficient economies were faced with the global slowdown and, concurrently, international investors started to demand higher yields on bonds, it turned out to be too much to uphold by the *Peripheries*. Ireland, which was an exception in terms of high productivity, and where the problems originated mainly in the banking sector and the housing bubble, is already able to provide first signs of recovery. Other peripheral economies seem to have bigger structural problems. It remains an open issue, if the currency union with its fixed nominal exchange rates and common monetary policy is best suited to all member countries of the Eurozone.

2.2.2. Monetary Policy Inflexibility

Before the monetary union was created, imbalances between various economies of the EU could have been corrected by nominal exchange rates and interest rate adjustments. Market forces as well as the monetary policy of a country with permanent current account deficits and growing indebtedness would eventually lead to currency devaluation. By depreciating its own currency, the country would increase its international competitiveness and improve its trade balance. At the same time, it would also decrease the real value of its debt denominated in the national currency.[3] However, in the case of a monetary union, such adjustments are simply not feasible. Thus, if there are no valuation gains, persistent current account deficits lead inevitably to the accumulation of net foreign debt. Higher indebtedness means higher costs of servicing that translate into higher net factor income payments and still poorer current account balance. This devil's loop may end up by default in the longer term, unless the situation is healed by structural reforms that guarantee high productivity and better international competitiveness of the infected country.

Since the EMU establishes a single monetary policy, no individual member state can act individually in this respect. Paradoxically, this creates a higher default risk of a euro-country than in a case of a non-euro-country. A state that has its own national currency and is able to perform sovereign monetary policy can always increase the supply of money to repay its debt, at least as long as the debt is denominated in its national currency. As mentioned earlier, such an operation would depreciate the local currency to the benefit of the trade balance, but unfortunately also could result in high inflation.

The EMU implies also the same nominal interest rate in all member states. However, countries within the Eurozone vary in terms of the level of inflation and dynamics of development. Thus, they should optimally differ also in the levels of interest rates. Generally, prior to the crisis, the peripheral economies exhibited inflation rates 1 to 2 percent points higher (Figure 6.2) and were growing slightly faster than the *Core* (with the exception of Italy and Portugal).

The single monetary policy of the euro was too loose for these peripheral countries that enjoyed the biggest boom (Spain, Ireland, and Greece). It emphasized their inflation, put pressure on growth of wages relative to productivity, and therefore finally contributed to competitiveness loss. At the same time, it might have been too tight for larger economies like Germany or France, depressing domestic demand and contributing to higher unemployment.

Under the common monetary policy this was of course impossible do differentiate interest rates. The same nominal interest rate in the whole Eurozone

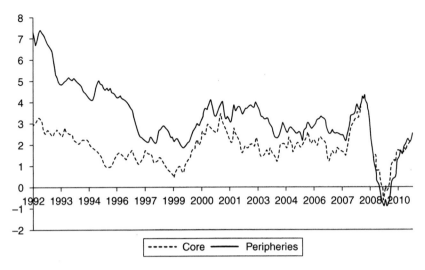

Figure 6.2   Consumer prices (year to year percent change), 1992–2010.
Source: Own computation based on public data from Eurostat.

implied that the real interest rates were actually lower in the *Peripheries* due to higher inflation there. This constituted an additional stimulus both for consumption and investment and might have contributed to bubbles, mainly in the real estate and construction sectors. From 1997 to 2007, housing prices rose at an average annual rate of 12.5 percent in Ireland and 8 percent in Spain, compared to 4.6 percent in the United States during its bubble. Over the same period, construction as a share of gross output rose from 9.8 percent to 13.8 percent in Spain and from 7.9 percent to 10.4 percent in Ireland. In the United States, the same figure only increased from 4.6 percent to 4.9 percent (Dadush and Stancil, 2010). Easy access to cheap financing encouraged indebtedness and led to waste and inefficiencies in public as well as in private sectors.

2.2.3. Lack of Fiscal Discipline and Mounting Public Debt
The Maastricht Treaty, signed in 1992, imposes four main macroeconomic criteria on the EU countries wishing to enter the EMU and to adopt the single currency. Besides the fixed exchange rate period, low inflation, and long-term interest rates, there are also important fiscal criteria. The ratio of annual government deficit to GDP theoretically must not exceed 3 percent and the ratio of gross government debt to GDP must stay below 60 percent. However, in reality, these threshold values have been anything but fixed as there were some gaps in the treaty that allowed exceptions. The decision if a country could become a member of the Eurozone or not was more political than objectively determined by the fundamental economic conditions. And, as it was politically unimaginable to launch the EMU without Italy, the third largest economy in continental Europe, or Belgium, home of the European capital Brussels—both countries became members despite having gross debt levels vastly exceeding

the Maastricht Treaty reference value of 60 percent. Moreover, shortly after the introduction of the euro, European policy makers further undermined discipline and coordination of national fiscal policies within the Eurozone. Already in March 2005, France and Germany pushed through a relaxation of the Stability and Growth Pact that earlier had been meant as the safeguard of public finances. As a result, over the years, a growing number of the Eurozone countries were in breach of the initial Maastricht criteria that remained mainly only as reference values. As of the end of 2011, Luxemburg and Finland were the only two countries out of 11 initial EMU members still meeting the Maastricht criteria. The average budget deficit in the Eurozone was 4.1 percent and the average debt-to-GDP ratio amounted to 87.3 percent.

The *Core* was not dealing better with public finance than the *Peripheries*. Germany and France had similar scale problems as Italy and Portugal. Greece was constantly registering the highest budget deficit in the whole EMU, but Spain and Ireland were having fiscal surpluses for many years until the end of 2007.

However, it is not only the net balance of public finance that matters, but also its flexibility and ability to adapt in the case of changing macroeconomic situation. In this context, the structure and dynamics of governmental spending are important. In the *Peripheries*, lower borrowing costs and the expansion of domestic demand boosted tax revenues. Rather than recognize that the revenue increases from the boom might be temporary gains that should be saved, the peripheral governments accelerated expenditure with approximately double dynamics than in the *Core*. From 1997 to 2007, public spending per person in peripheral economies rose by an average of 76 percent and government's contribution to GDP rose by 3.5 percentage points. Over the same period, average per capita spending increased in the *Core* by 34 percent and the government's contribution to GDP stayed unvarying (Dadush and Stancil, 2010). It is easy and tempting to increase spending when revenues are growing. However, it is much more difficult to cut expenditures, especially when the economy slows down.

The problems of public finance have increased dramatically since 2008 as the spin-off effect of the credit crunch in the United States and also a bubble burst in property and construction markets locally, mainly in Spain and Ireland. European banks that held US toxic assets or were involved in financing the overpriced real estate market, registered significant losses. Several European governments were forced to run huge deficits and to issue additional debt in order to provide large bailout packages to the financial sector. At the same time, European economies were faced with the global slowdown. As a result, most of the Eurozone countries registered record high budget deficits and levels of indebtedness in the years 2009–2011.

In the extreme case of Greece, total mismanagement of public finance led to such a high amount of debt that the country was not only unable to repay, but it could not even service ongoing interest payments. Ireland and Portugal avoided insolvency thanks to rescue packages from the ECB and the IMF. Spain also received a rescue package, although relatively small in relation to the size of the economy and the scale of their problems. Italy is still watched anxiously as it is the third biggest economy of the Eurozone and its bailout would constitute a true challenge.

However, speaking more generally, the large public debt is not as such the root of the crisis in Europe. It is more the effect of earlier lack of fiscal discipline and the result of external factors added on top. Historically accumulated indebtedness makes it difficult for governments to navigate public finances in the current period of the slowdown and decreasing tax revenues. High cost of servicing the debt consumes funds that might have been otherwise used for fiscal stimulus.

2.2.4. The Eurozone Banking Crisis

The first symptoms of a banking crisis in Europe appeared in 2008 when the sector was contaminated with toxic assets linked to the US credit crunch. Major European financial institutions suffered severe losses and needed recapitalization, state guarantees, or other forms of public aid. At that time, Ireland was the only Eurozone country where the banking crisis emerged due to domestic factors, namely the property bubble burst and a high leverage in the private sector. By the end of 2009, the situation seemed to be under control and already on the way to recovery, when the new wave of the crisis came. In 2010 and 2011, Eurozone's financial sector suffered further record high losses resulting from writedowns of Greek debt and revaluation of bonds of other peripheral governments for which market yields jumped up.

There are several systematic characteristics of the Eurozone's banking system that make it far more exposed and sensitive to the sovereign debt crisis and problems in peripheral economies, and make consequences of trouble in the banking sector difficult to manage. First of all, the Eurozone's banking system is very large relative to the size of the overall domestic economies, with the average financial institution's gross debt equal to 143 percent of GDP (the US average is equal to 94 percent). Second, bank leverage in the euro area is very high at tangible assets 26 times common equity (the US level is 12 times).[4] Third, and most importantly in the context of the sovereign debt crisis, European banks tend to own a lot of the debt issued by their own governments. Finally, they have been also actively involved in financing poor investments in the *Peripheries*. Via cheap financing and relatively high-risk appetite, the banking system was fueling the economic boom, and also led to dynamically growing indebtedness of private sectors in peripheral countries. It was an important channel of capital flows from the *Core* to the *Peripheries*.

The large scale of the euro area banking system makes it problematic for already indebted European governments to credibly issue new guarantees or use public funds for yet another wave of recapitalization. At the same time, high leverage of the European banking system actually increases the risk that this need may actually materialize, as only a thin layer of common equity capital is available as first-loss risk capital (tier 1). The large bank ownership of government debt in the Eurozone presents a particularly obstinate worry. Under the Basel Agreements, banks are not required to set aside any risk capital to offset any future losses on government bond holdings. Sovereign bonds have by definition been considered risk free, including Greek bonds until recently. Consequently, when government debt must be restructured, it imposes upon banks credit losses for which they have previously not set aside capital. There is consequently a large degree of interdependence between the financial solidity of the banking system and government solvency across the Eurozone. Moreover, losses in banks may come also from the private sector, particularly in the *Peripheries*, where the high leverage has been confronted with structural problems and inefficiency exposed in the slowdown. As the banking system was one of the channels of capital flows within the Eurozone, there is also a high risk of contagion among the EMU states.

3. Behavioral Contribution

3.1. Greed of Investors and Managers

According to Shefrin and Statman (2000), investors are guided by two kinds of emotions when investing: fear and greed. During a long-lasting prosperity period, the fear of a drop in consumption weakens and hence an increasingly small portion of investment is mentally accounted as security for incidental needs. Greed comes to the fore and motivates people to make increasingly risky investment. It seems that greed has been the main driving factor of investors' behaviors at least several years before the financial crisis occurred. Encouraged by the long-lasting market boom, investors required higher and higher returns, oblivious to the risk. At the same time, they exerted pressure on both corporate managers and on investment fund managers demanding high profits from them. In turn, both corporate and asset managers adopted more and more risky business and financial strategies to meet expectations of the investors.

The main instrument to ensure returns on investors' money at the level significantly exceeding the natural pace of economic development was to apply the financial leverage to a greater and greater extent. In the case of corporations, this was most frequently reflected in an increased share of debt in capital structure, whereas financial asset managers increasingly often used derivatives along with traditional credit lines. Of course, financial risk increases as a result of the leverage, but in the times of hot markets, people seemed not to notice that risk.

Greed that pushed investors and managers toward risky investment strategies did not as such directly contribute to the financial crisis whose sources should be sought in the global macroeconomic imbalance, but it rather determined its scale, arising from material leveraging of business operations and involvement in derivatives.

3.2. Underestimation of Risk

It can be said that greed blinded consumers, businesses, and politicians. Risk was often forgotten in the midst of the chase after consumption, higher returns, or more popularity among voters. Several strong behavioral inclinations, mostly related to overconfidence, were conducive to the underestimation of risk. The confirmation bias blocked certain warning signals that could have eroded investors' faith in the never-ending bull market. During the relatively long period of market prosperity, citizens got used to high consumption and investors got used to easy and high profits. As the result of the self-attribution effect, many market players attributed the profits primarily to their own skills rather than to the general market situation. Previous growth intensified their confidence and encouraged them to take even higher risks.

Underestimation of risk was also fostered by people's tendency to treat unlikely things as if they were completely impossible and, on the other hand to treat highly probable, events as if they were to certainly occur. Hence, it was not accepted that an unfortunate coincidence of several macroeconomic factors may ultimately lead to a sequence of negative events that individually seemed very unlikely. Similarly, the risk of failure of positive developments that were assessed as highly probable and treated almost as a certainty was played down. Reality showed that the coincidence of such almost impossible situations not only came true but also proved to have colossal impact on the entire global economy.

3.3. Extrapolation Bias and the Time Horizon Issue

Extrapolation error consists in attaching too much weight to past trends, particularly those observed during a relatively short period of time and in inadequately extending them onto subsequent future periods. Another problem is the inadequate time perspective. Behavioral finance provides evidence that decision makers are usually short sighted. Humans focus mostly on the nearest future and fear an immediate loss most, but highly discount more remote outcomes (Kahneman and Tversky, 1979; Benartzi and Thaler, 1995, 1999). The evaluation period for ordinary consumers equals most often the interval between their salary payments, that is, one month. The evaluation period for investors and businesses is usually one year. Politicians pay a lot of attention to the direct political impact and media coverage following their decisions. Their evaluation period rarely exceeds the time till the next elections. Yet, the laws of macroeconomics often demonstrate themselves in a long-term horizon. Thus, there is a danger that, due to human myopia, the rules of macroeconomics may be overlooked and forgotten, at least temporarily until their consequences are revealed in their full power.

During the last economic boom, consumers, investors, and politicians in some of the Eurozone peripheral countries (Ireland, Spain, Greece) commonly committed the extrapolation error that additionally was enhanced by myopia. Creation of the EMU and introduction of the common currency gave a strong initial growth impulse. People, so much focused on the present, extrapolated the good situation into the future, failing to see the long-term consequences of the EMU and associated risks. Current prosperity built up confidence and created expectations for more growth. Based on that conjecture, individuals consumed too much, businesses invested far beyond their capacities, and politicians spent irresponsibly. On the one hand, it created a bubble—on the other, high consumption and high investment led to low saving rate and over-leveraging of the peripheral economies.

3.4. Bounded Rationality and Mistakes of Rating Agencies

During the last several-year period of worldwide economic prosperity, we witnessed a spectacular development of the derivatives, not only with regard to the increasing volume but also the degree of their complexity. Frequently, they constituted a complex and less obvious combination of many classic derivatives. At the same time, the underlying assets were not always clearly understood. Often, the value of the derivative depended on a specific industry index with a complicated structure and ambiguous rules of inclusion or exclusion of individual components and their weight changes. Derivatives for which other derivatives acted as underlying assets were also often created. Securitized mortgage portfolios increasingly often constituted a mixture of different quality debts, difficult to evaluate by an external investor.

All this led to the situation in which it was not ultimately clear what the potential payoff structure was and what factors actually affected the real value of a given security. The human brain's perception and the ability to process numerous variables is limited (see chapter 2). Therefore, even professional investors were forced to apply specific heuristics and simplifications in evaluation of individual financial products. Many of them unquestioningly accepted evaluations by rating agencies. It was also common to rely on the institutions that construed and defined parameters for yet newer base indexes that provided a basis for evaluating derivatives.

Rating agencies came under a lot of criticism both during the US credit crunch and later during the euro crisis. First, they had failed to recognize systematic risk associated with mortgage-backed securities. They had granted favorable ratings to instruments that soon after were worthless and toxic to the whole financial system. In the Eurozone initially, they failed to recognize the vast differences and the risk disparity among the EMU debt issuers. Until 2009/2010, Ireland's and Spain's ratings were equal to Germany's highest possible rating at triple A level. Agencies were also very late with the decision to downgrade Greek bonds to the non-investment level. Greek bonds had been already trading at yields adequate for junk bonds much before the actual downgrade came. On the other hand, agencies overreacted in the case of Portugal and Ireland, downgrading them to the non-investment status similar to Greece despite much better fundamentals of those economies and disregarding the fact that both countries complied with the restructuring programs.

Many of the mistakes made by rating agencies might be explained on behavioral grounds. Let us start with myopia and problems with representativeness. By nature, loans drawn to purchase property are long-term liabilities. Meanwhile, to evaluate the worthiness of mortgage debt portfolios, rating agencies applied statistical data based on a relatively short historical sample, often going back only several or a dozen or so months. While assessing the risk, it was wrongly concluded that since a small percentage of cases of failure to meet obligations was recently observed in a given category of borrowers, the situation was going to be similar during the entire lending period. It could be said that in that case, rating agencies committed a type of the short-series error.

Rating agencies also believed that major diversification of debt within a given portfolio could practically eliminate the insolvency risk of an individual borrower. A certain analogy to the Markowitz portfolio theory could be found here. Just like in a well-diversified portfolio of stocks, it is possible to eliminate the unique nonsystematic risk of an individual asset; also in the case of debt portfolio, it was assumed that the possible insolvency of one of several hundred borrowers will not have any material impact on the total value of the specific group of mortgages. Hence, CDOs issued on the basis of securitized debt portfolios were assessed as safe and rated high. Rating agencies committed a mistake of underestimating the systematic risk. It was reflected in the fact that a major number of borrowers could simultaneously, as the result of the same external factors, find themselves in financial trouble and stop paying off their liabilities. When the unexpected factors affected a relatively numerous group of borrowers, it certainly had an impact on the total value of an even well-diversified mortgage portfolio.

A coincidence of negative events that could materially affect the condition of numerous borrowers and shake the entire system was assessed as very unlikely or simply impossible. In that case, rating agencies fell victim to a psychological inclination consisting in treating events that are very unlikely as if they were not to take place at all. Such an approach directly results from the discontinuity of the weighting function for low probabilities in the prospect theory of Kahneman and Tversky (1979), as discussed in section 2.1 in chapter 2.

3.5. Euro Heuristic

It looks like market participants were subject to the "Euro heuristic," sticking the same "Euro-label" to all countries of the EMU. It led to a situation where financial markets underestimated the risk disparity among members of the Eurozone and treated them too homogeneously. As a result, the nominal cost of financing was very similar in all economies of the EMU, and taking into account the higher inflation, the effective real cost of financing was even lower in the *Peripheries* despite higher risk. For example, in 2007, the average annual spread between ten-year government bonds of Greece and Germany was only 0.27 percentage point.[5]

There are at least two psychological effects that might have supported the Euro heuristic. The halo effect causes someone who likes one outstanding characteristic of an object to extend this positive evaluation also on other features of that object. People notice predominantly the most visible characteristic and base on it their entire opinion about something or somebody without taking into account other details (Thorndike, 1920; Nisbett and Wilson, 1977a; Rosenzweig, 2007). The halo effect is related to the availability bias (Kahneman and Tversky, 1974). When judging the probability of an event, people often search in their memories for relevant information. But it turns out that not all information is equally available to human minds. More recent events, more salient or those from personal experience, are easier recalled and weigh more heavily. As a result, our estimations of probability are often distorted.

Since it was launched, the euro received a lot of positive publicity. It was praised as Europe's great unifying achievement and treated as a synonym of economic strength and solidness. Until mid-2008, the euro was in a long-term appreciation trend against the US dollar. Such a situation was sufficient ground for the halo effect and the availability bias. Financial market participants automatically extended their favorable opinion about the euro to actually all countries that had adopted the common currency. Other characteristics of particular euro-economies, which might have shed different light on risk assessment and valuation of debt, were disregarded.

3.6. Bad News Travels Slowly

The first financial institution lending in the subprime sector—Ownit Mortgage Solutions—went under at the beginning of 2007. Since the scale of its operations was minor, the incident went practically unnoticed by the market. However, in August 2007, the first major wave of difficulties related to financial liquidity affected the financial institutions operating in the mortgage market. Around the same time, the Bank of England granted financial aid to the Northern Rock bank that specialized in extending credits for purchase of real estate in the United Kingdom. All these warning signs and the preliminary symptoms of crisis seemed to not yet appeal to investors. Stock exchanges were at the height of the frenzy. On October 9, 2007, the DJIA set the historic high at 14,164 points. The market needed much more time to fully realize the scale of the problems.

The truth about Greek budget deficit and the level of indebtedness has been known at least since late 2009. Practically, since then Greece has been bankrupt, but no one wished to admit it. Despite the bad news getting public, we saw relatively small impact on the financial statements of European banks through the whole of 2010. Much more write-offs happened as late as in 2011. Concurrently, we observed the whole high-tension drama to avoid declaration of Greek insolvency, which eventually was declared formally only with the respect to a small portion of Greek debt that was not a part of the second bailout deal in March 2011. Someone may ask why it took so much time to face the truth.

Behavioral biases come in again with helpful explanation. There are at least three strong human inclinations that may explain the reluctance to accept bad news (see chapter 2). Excessive optimism or wishful thinking make us believe that positive outcomes are still possible even if realistically the situation is hopeless. Cognitive conservatism is responsible for the underweighting of new evidence contradictive to earlier perception. People unconsciously undermine the meaning of new contra-facts and stick to their earlier conviction. However, most importantly, loss aversion is a very strong inclination that discourages admittance of the definite failure.

3.7. Herding, Hedge Funds, and Self-Fulfilling Prophecies

Herding in the financial world means to make decisions based on observation of other market participants rather than based on own information and analysis. In the context of the euro crisis, herding manifested itself both during the prosperity period and when the problems already started. During the boom, herding among consumers and investors drove the prices up, particularly in the real estate. People were ready to pay high amounts of money not because of their own valuations, but because they saw other people buying and thus expected prices to reach even higher levels. There was also herding among banks and other financial institutions that hurried to finance the overinflated development projects. While competing for the market share, institutions were copying each other's actions and often disregarded risk. For example, when foreign banks from other capital-rich EU countries decided to enter the credit market in the *Peripheries*, competition increased in those local markets. This was particularly the case in Ireland where the banking sector faced strong competition with new entries from the United Kingdom.[6]

Herding has been apparent also in financial markets ever since the crisis started. In this context, it is worth mentioning the activities of hedge funds and the role of rating agencies. Statistics of open derivative positions, particularly the number of CDS on Greek bonds, short-selling of the euro, media interviews with key players, and public commentaries of respected analysts, may indicate that at least till the end of the third quarter of 2011, hedge funds bet on the default of Greece and the euro deprecation against the US dollar. There are over 2,000 hedge funds in the United States. Top 225 of them have 1.3 trillion US dollar assets under management. The largest one—Bridgewater Associates—has 58.9 billion US dollars.[7] With such a scale of operations that additionally may be enhanced by an easy access to high leverage, herding hedge funds are able to influence markets, even such a liquid and deep market as the euro–dollar exchange. Political leaders in Europe were attacking the role of hedge funds and other financial speculators, while the European Commission opened a formal investigation on speculative activities with a view to tighter regulation. On December 1, 2011, the European Parliament officially banned so called naked transactions on CDS; this means engaging in a credit default swap without actually holding the underlying bond or other instruments for which a CDS would work as an insurance. However, this ban was more a political gesture and remained rather ineffective in financial markets. European regulations are not binding for hedge funds operating outside of the EU even if those funds engage in speculation on instruments related to European debt or currency.

A more effective way of winning the game with speculators has been elaborated by managing a "controlled insolvency" of Greece and structuring a special program of "voluntary" exchange of bonds as a form of debt reduction. March 1,

2012, the International Swap and Derivatives Association (ISDA) officially confirmed that a voluntary exchange of bonds does not constitute the so-called credit event, that is, it does not activate payments for CDS holders. On March 9, the same body declared a "credit event" only with respect to those bonds issued under Greek law that had not participated in the voluntary exchange program and were forced into the reduction scheme under a special bill of the Greek Parliament. This event activated CDS in the value of approximately 3.3 billion dollars[8]—a relatively small number compared to the scale of the debt reduction program that amounted just below 140 billion dollars.

Rating agencies constitute another category of institutions that play a prominent role in enhancing herding in financial market. Market participants often pay a great deal of attention to ratings assessed by respected third parties, and take information included in a rating as granted with no need for further own analysis. A change of rating may work as a self-fulfilling prophesy. For example, as a result of a downgrade, investors consider the issuer more risky and thus require higher returns. This translates to higher cost of debt servicing and a potential problem with refinancing. If the downgrade is severe, it may end up with insolvency of the issuer, even if, prior to the downgrade, the situation was not so dramatically bad.

Gärtner, Griesbach, and Jung (2011) provide empirical evidence for agencies' overreaction. Regressing historical evaluations against fundamentals, they demonstrate that previous practices of the agencies and the later situation in some of the peripherial countries did not justify such heavy downgrades. It is also important to notice in their study that the arbitrary (i.e., not attributed to changes in fundamentals) component of the rating actually impacts the cost of debt. This observation confirms the power of rating agencies to influence the market and highlights the self-fulfilling character of the unfavorable rating.

PART IV

Behavioral Corporate Finance

CHAPTER 7

Rational Corporations in Irrational Markets

In this chapter, it is assumed that corporate managers behave in a fully rational manner and attempt to take advantage of investors' irrationality and temporary market anomalies. We investigate how investor biases and market inefficiency may impact financial and investment policy of corporations. In the area of financial decisions, we study equity offerings, stock repurchases, debt issues and asset exchange offers, and dividend policy. In regard to investment choices, we investigate real investment, mergers and acquisitions, decisions to enter a new market, and the choice between focus or diversity in business operations. We also look at earnings management, adjusting nominal share price, changing firm names, and other managerial practices targeted at market timing, catering to investor tastes, and exploiting market inefficiencies.

1. Financial Decisions

In an effective equity market, the cost of raising capital by a company through an equity issue is evaluated adequately both in bull and bear markets. But if we reject this hypothesis and assume that the valuation may be inadequate, then it may impact the capital structure policy. It should be remembered, however, that such mispricing must be present on the market for some time, long enough for the management to base their decisions upon it and take action.

In the case of stock overvaluation, the cost of equity decreases encouraging issuers to generate new shares supply. On the other hand, when stock seems to be undervalued, corporations will tend to postpone new equity issues and rely more on debt financing. Believing in stock undervaluation, they may feel encouraged to announce a repurchase program and buy back own shares (under the condition, of course, that they have financing available for that purpose). The decision of whether to pay out dividends and how much to distribute might be influenced by signaling efforts, smoothing and avoidance of future negative dividend announcements, the effect of clientele, as well as catering to temporary fads and shifting preferences of investors.

Altogether, financial decisions of rational managers in the irrational world are about catering to investor taste and market timing, that is, supplying the market with instruments that investors are particularly fond of at a given moment in time and taking advantage of temporary mispricing.

1.1. Equity Offerings

Clustering of IPOs has been relatively well documented in capital markets worldwide. Starting with Ibbotson and Jaffe (1975), a number of studies have demonstrated that IPOs tend to cluster both in time and in sectors (Ritter, 1984; Ibbotson et al., 1988, 1994; Derrien, 2010).

Theoretically, there might be a rational explanation to this phenomenon—IPO clustering could be potentially due to the clustering of real investment opportunities, which prompt companies to seek capital with a view to use these opportunities in similar periods of time. However, empirical evidence suggests that the connection to real investment is weak. Rather, decisions on equity issue seem to be driven mainly by temporary overvaluation and market timing attempts. Lerner (1994) and similarly Pagano, Panetta, and Zingales (1998) argue that private firms decide to go public when listed companies from the same sector are valued favorably in terms of market comparable ratios. Loughran, Ritter, and Rydqvist (1994) find that aggregate IPO volume and stock market valuations are highly correlated in major stock exchanges worldwide. Plotnicki and Szyszka (2013) find that current market situation may also impact the speed of the IPO process. In hot markets, the average time between the formal decision to go public and the IPO day is significantly shorter than in periods when markets are cooler. Firms tend to hurry to list their stock when the market situation is favorable (possibly fearing that the good valuation may soon vanish) and take more time if they get listed in a relatively worse period (they might wait for the market to go up a bit before the public offer is made or simply have trouble placing the offer).

The IPO market timing hypothesis is also supported by the evidence of poor post-IPO performance both in terms of operational results (Jain and Kini, 1994; Mikkelson et al., 1997; Pagano et al., 1998), as well as negative abnormal long-term post-IPO stock returns (Ritter, 1991; Loughran and Ritter, 1995). However, post-IPO long-term abnormal returns have been widely debated with some results questioned due to measurement issues. For example, Brav and Gompers (1997) argue that when the Three Factor Fama and French model is used to account for size and book-to-market effect, most of the abnormal negative post-IPO returns documented earlier actually disappear.[1]

Similar to first equity offerings, seasoned (secondary) equity offerings (SEOs) also tend to be driven by temporary market valuation. Marsh (1982) examines the choices UK listed firms made between equity and long-term debt in the years 1959–1974, and finds that firms are inclined to issue equity following recent stock appreciation. Jung, Kim, and Stulz (1996) and Erel, Julio, Kim, and Weisbach (2010) find a strong relationship between stock prices and SEOs in the US market. The market timing and overvaluation hypothesis for

SEOs are also supported by poor post-SEO returns (Loughran and Ritter, 1995; Spiess and Affleck-Graves, 1995; Lee, 1997; Ritter, 2003). Opportunistic corporate behavior is illustrated particularly well by the research of Burch, Christie, and Nanda (2004). They examine subsequent performance of seasoned equity issued via rights offers targeted at current shareholders, and compare it to the performance of seasoned equity issued via commitment offers aimed at new shareholders. According to their findings, underperformance is concentrated entirely in the latter group of equity sold to new investors.[2]

Post-SEO returns have also been the subject of many discussions raising similar methodological issues as in the case of post-IPO underperformance. Some authors highlight the usual joint hypothesis problem, arguing that low post-equity issue returns are justified because those firms have more equity and are therefore less risky and/or more liquid (Eckbo et al., 2000). Other debated topics are related to measurement and statistical problems (Brav and Gompers, 1997; Schultz, 2003).

In any case, even if the post-event long-term returns should be interpreted with caution as having low power, they should not be considered in isolation. The hypothesis of market overvaluation as one of the key drivers of equity issuance is strongly supported by survey evidence. In anonymous interviews conducted by Graham and Harvey (2001) and Brau and Fawcett (2006), chief financial officers (CFOs) who went public directly admitted that overvaluation and general market conditions were important choice determinants in their timing of equity offerings. Similar findings are reported in the original survey presented in chapter 9.

1.2. Buybacks

A buyback is a transaction in which a company repurchases its own stock either on open market or in a fixed-price tender offer. Out of the many possible reasons behind this kind of operation (e.g., takeover defense, stock-based bonus plans, substitute to dividend payments, capital structure changes, earnings-per-share [EPS] enhancement), temporary undervaluation seems to be a particularly strong motive. Rational managers who believe that their firm is undervalued and therefore decide to repurchase stock achieve two or even three objectives. First, if the firm is really undervalued, such an operation is in the best interest of long-term shareholders who do not answer to the repurchase program and, consequently, take advantage of those who decide to sell below value. Second, the buyback may send a strong signal to the market community that the management is deeply convinced about the stock being traded below its true value (Dann, 1981; Vermaelen, 1981, 1984). The initial increase in demand for stock resulting from the buyback program might be supported by an additional hike in demand from investors encouraged by the positive signal. Both may eventually lead to better pricing. Finally, if the company decides to redeem shares purchased from the market, the number of shares outstanding will decline. This should improve financial ratios such as EPS or dividend per share (DivPS) simply by lowering the denominator.

Empirical evidence supports the view that undervaluation is an important motive for buybacks. 86.6 percent out of 384 CFOs surveyed by Brav, Graham, Harvey, and Michaely (2005) replied that corporations repurchase their stock when it is below its true value. Hong, Wang, and Yu (2008) argue that buybacks cluster after market crashes and point out repurchase waves that followed crashes in October 1987 and September 2001. A number of studies carried out on the US data found positive long-term excess returns following buybacks (Dann, 1981; Lakonishok and Vermaelen, 1990; Ikenberry et al., 1995). In their extensive study, Peyer and Vermaelen (2009) reconfirmed the persistence of the buyback anomaly on the US market. Applying their results in practice, they set up a fund that follows investment criteria based on the research. The PV Buyback USA Fund made a return of nearly 21 percent in 2012 beating the Russell 2000 Index—the benchmark for the fund—by 7 percent.[3] Positive abnormal returns following buybacks may suggest that managers are on average right about stock undervaluation and successful in the timing of repurchases.[4]

Peyer and Varmaelen (2009) observe that stocks experience the most significant positive long-run excess returns if the repurchase is triggered by a severe stock-price decline during the previous six months. They argue that the buyback anomaly is driven mainly by the market overreacting to bad news publicly available prior to the repurchase, rather than being a result of positive insider information held by the management. This is somehow contradictory to the results of Babenko, Tserlukevich, and Vedrashko (2012) who find a positive relation between insider purchases prior to buyback announcements and post-announcement short-term and long-term returns. Their findings suggest that management's private information may at least partly explain the buyback anomaly.

Gong, Louis, and Sun (2008) provide some evidence on managerial manipulation prior to repurchases that might be responsible, at least to some extent, for the abnormal returns after buybacks. They argue that both post-repurchase abnormal returns and reported improvements in operating performance are driven, in some measure, by the management of pre-repurchase downward earnings rather than genuine growth in profitability. Gong et al. (2008) note that downward earnings management increases in proportion to both the percentage of the company that managers repurchase and managerial ownership.

Supporters of market efficiency argue that the buyback anomaly is not really anomalous. There are various methodological issues that bias long-term abnormal returns and provide illusory results (Fama, 1998; Mitchell and Stafford, 2000). There might be a problem with the survivorship bias—companies that conducted a buyback and later went bankrupt are naturally not included in the long-term sample collected from ex post data series. As the sample misses out cases of extreme negative returns, the average return calculated for the sample is overstated. There is also the risk-change hypothesis whereby a buyback changes the capital structure of a company. After a buyback, a portion of shares might be redeemed. There is less equity and less cash in the company, some firms even raising additional debt in order to finance the operation. In other words, companies after the buyback are exposed to more financial risk. In the light of the efficient market theory, higher returns are simply a justified premium for higher risks. The liquidity hypothesis argues that a repurchase reduces liquidity and the abnormal returns are due to this omitted liquidity factor that ought to be priced (Pastor and Stambaugh, 2003).

1.3. Debt Issues

Market timing of debt issuances is related to two general aspects—a decision to issue new debt when its cost is unusually low and a choice between issuing short- and long-term debts. In a way, the first problem derives from the market timing hypothesis of equity issuances as the willingness to issue debt depends also on company valuation. If the stock is highly overvalued, the firm may decide to finance with equity rather than debt even if the cost of debt is low. On the other hand, when the firm perceives itself to be strongly undervalued, it is more likely to use debt to a greater extent regardless of its cost.

Survey evidence offers support for market timing being a factor in debt issuance decisions in both situations mentioned earlier. CFOs interviewed by Graham and Harvey (2001) admitted that they issue debt when they think "rates are particularly low." Their answers also indicate that the yield curve influences the maturity of new debt. Managers pick short-term debt "when short-term rates are low compared to long-term rates" and when "waiting for long-term market interest rates to decline." These answers show that CFOs clearly do not believe in the expectation hypothesis (Fisher, 1930), according to which the cost of the long-term debt is essentially the average of the expected short-term interest rates. In other words, the expectation hypothesis implies that the slope of the yield curve reflects the market expectation of the future change in interest rates.[5] If the hypothesis holds and the market is correct, the overall financial cost should be the same in the case of issuing short-term debt and subsequently rolling it over the next periods or issuing long-term debt at once. The answers given by corporate managers in the survey better fit the segmented market hypothesis, according to which financial instruments of different terms are not substitutable. As a result, the supply and demand in the markets for short- and long-term instruments are determined in a largely independent manner. Under such conditions, market timing for bond issues may actually make sense.

Using real data, Marsh (1982) shows that the cost of borrowing tends to be one of considerable factors in the sample of the UK listed firms who choose to issue either new long-term debt or new equity. Guedes and Opler (1996) confirm the survey responses with respect to maturity timing. In their sample consisting of 7,369 debt issues in the United States between 1982 and 1993, debt maturity shows a strong negative relation to the difference between long- and short-term bond yields (term spread). Similar results in aggregate data are documented by Baker, Greenwood, and Wurgler (2003). In US Flow of Funds data for the period between 1953 and 2000, they find a negative relation between the cumulative share of long-term debt issues in total (long and short) debt issues and the term spread.

Liu, Ning, Davidson (2010) find evidence of income-increasing earnings management prior to new bond offerings. Bondholders fail to see through the inflated earnings numbers in pricing new debt. Liu et al. document that firms that manage earnings upward issue debt at a lower cost after controlling for various bond issuer and issue characteristics.

1.4. Exchange Offers

An exchange offer is a tender made by a company to give one security in return for another. Most commonly, exchange offers are used in mergers and acquisitions (M&A) when one stock is exchanged for a stock of another firm, an aspect we are going to discuss in section 2.3 of this chapter. Here, we are interested in another kind of exchange offer that is part of the corporate financial policy and results in a change of the capital structure. In other words, we investigate situations when a firm offers its own security of one type in exchange for another type (e.g., bonds for equity).

Masulis (1980) studied various exchange offers including conversion of debt into equity, common bonds to convertible bonds, and preferred stock to ordinary shares. The last type of exchange offers was also analyzed by Pinegar and Lease (1986). Cornett and Travlos (1989) looked at debt-for-equity and equity-for-debt exchange offers. All these studies suggest that, on average, the market reacts positively to announcements of exchange offers that result in an increase of the financial leverage, being negative about announcements after which the financial leverage decreases. This is in line with Myers and Majluf's (1984) pecking order theory. Under information asymmetry, rational managers might use exchange offers to signal the overall condition of the firm—an increase in the financial leverage signals optimism, and vice versa.

However, managers might also use exchange offers to cater to temporary investor preferences related to the capital structure. There is not much evidence on the timing of exchange offers, but there are some hints that it could be an effective way to swap one kind of instrument for another in order to exploit potential mispricing at a given moment of time. For example, De Jong, Duca, and Dutordoir (2013) suggest that convertible bond issuers act opportunistically by pricing their offerings more favorably following increases in investor preferences for convertibles, and by adjusting the design of their offerings toward changes in investor tastes.

1.5. Dividend Policy

There is common agreement on some empirical facts about dividends.[6] Fama and French (2001) document that the proportion of dividend-paying firms has been declining since 1960s. They associate the decline in part with changing characteristics of the population of publicly traded firms, which tilts toward small firms with low profitability and strong growth potential that typically do not pay out cash. Konieczka and Szyszka (2013) focus on a sample of firms over 100 million US dollar market capitalization and over 10 million US dollar

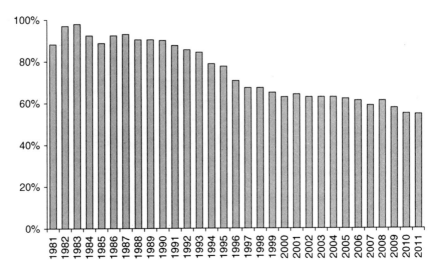

Figure 7.1 The percentage of dividend-paying firms from the NYSE, AMEX, and NASDAQ sample between 1981 and 2011. The sample includes 2,226 firms above 100 million US dollar market capitalization and minimum 10 million US dollar net profit.
Source: Konieczka and Szyszka (2013).

net profit. They review the dividend policy of 2,226 firms from the NYSE, AMEX, and NASDAQ between 1981 and 2011, and confirm that the declining payout trend generally persists also when extremely small and low-profit firms are excluded from observations (Figure 7.1).

Dividends are primarily paid by large and well-established firms with low idiosyncratic risk and relatively lower market risk. In 2011, dividend payers constituted only 55 percent of their sample, but contributed to over 74 percent of market capitalization. The highest share of dividend-paying firms was among utilities (95 percent), which had the lowest average beta of only 0.54 (Exhibit 7.1). The lowest proportions of payers were in the health care and IT sectors where betas stood at 0.97 and 1.34, respectively.

Dividends are often taxed disadvantageously compared to capital gains.[7] In many tax regimes, stock repurchase is a more efficient way of distribution to shareholders. Still, despite the fact that it might be harmful to their wealth, investors consider dividend initiation (omissions) as a good (bad) signal. Stock prices react positively to dividend initiation and negatively to announcements of dividend omissions. The market reaction is, however, asymmetric, negative reaction to omissions being much stronger (Michaely et al., 1995).

Because of the strong adverse market reaction to dividend omissions or declines, managers consider dividend payout as a sticky decision, which might be costly to reverse. They are cautious about initiating or increasing dividend payments unless they are convinced that the firm will be able to maintain the payout policy. As the market reaction to dividend announcements is asymmetric, firms also tend to smooth the payments over time. They pay out less

Exhibit 7.1   The share of dividend-paying firms by industry in the sample of NYSE, AMEX, and NASDAQ stocks in 2011

Industry	Percentage of dividend-paying firms	Average beta
Consumer discretionary	42	1.48
Consumer staples	58	0.82
Energy	60	1.15
Financials	83	1.11
Health care	28	0.97
Industrials	55	1.37
Information technology	27	1.34
Materials	65	1.52
Telecommunication services	50	0.97
Utilities	95	0.54

Source: Konieczka and Szyszka (2013).

than they could in good times in order to "save" for worse periods and to avoid market disappointment (Michaely and Roberts, 2012). In the result, dividend volatility is far lower than the volatility of earnings and of course lower than the volatility of stock prices (LeRoy and Porter, 1981; Shiller, 1981; Campbell and Shiller, 1988).

Baker and Wurgler (2013), using core features of the prospect theory, propose a model in which past dividends are reference points against which future dividends are judged. The model fits well with empirical observations about the asymmetric market reaction to dividend announcements and smoothing practices of managers. Baker and Wurgler also document that dividend levels are established and changed typically in round numbers, for example, multiples of five or ten cents. Managers who raise dividends strive to exceed round number thresholds. Market reaction to dividend changes is stronger when they cross a round number, and also when the same DivPS has been paid for several consecutive periods.

In the survey by Brav, Graham, Harvey, and Michaely (2005), managers directly (albeit anonymously) admit to the aforementioned practices in their dividend policy. They attempt to avoid reducing dividends per share (of the 384 managers surveyed, 93.8% agreed); they try to maintain a smooth dividend stream (89.6%); and they are reluctant to make changes that might have to be reversed (77.9%). Managers follow such policies because they believe that there are negative consequences to reducing dividends (88.1%), in the sense that it conveys information to investors (80%).

Brav et al. (2005) also find that managers consider their investor preferences toward dividends, focusing in particular on the likings of institutional investors. This is in line with the well-known clientele theory, which suggests that investors may have different reasons for favoring dividends such as institutional requirements, tax differentials, or behavioral aspects and personal preferences. Brav and Heaton (1998) identify a preference to dividend payouts using the "prudent man" rule that requires certain types of institutional investors to hold dividend-paying firms. Grinstein and Michaely (2005) find that institutional investors avoid investing in non-paying firms, but, surprisingly, when it comes to payers, they favor those who pay low rather than high dividends. It might be that those investors want to comply with the requirement to hold dividend-paying stock, but focus more on growth opportunities than the value of the dividend stream. Dhaliwal, Erickson, and Trezevant (1999) and Seida (2001) support the existence of tax-based clientele. Perez-Gonzales (2002) provides evidence that, in their dividend policy, firms actually respond to the tax preferences of large shareholders.

According to the Behavioral Life-Cycle (BLC) hypothesis by Shefrin and Statman (1988), personal life-cycle considerations may also determine dividend preferences of individual investors. In this way of thinking, Graham and Kumar (2006) find that older and low-income retail investors tend to hold a larger fraction of dividend-paying stocks than other investors. They argue that older investors' preference for dividends is the result of their desire for income, and that low-income investors have an advantageous tax status. Another way of interpreting these results, however, might be that these groups of investors are particularly risk/loss averse and consider dividend-paying firms to be safer.

The catering theory of dividend proposed by Baker and Wurgler (2004a), and motivated initially by Long (1978), might be seen as a special case of managers adapting their policy to the clientele, where the "clientele" is changing due to its own dynamic preferences. In other words, investor sentiment and demand for dividend stocks vary over time causing differences in relative valuation of payers and non-payers. Trying to exploit this mispricing, managers respond with shifts in their dividend policy. To determine the relative valuation of payers and non-payers, Baker and Wurgler use an ex ante measure called the dividend premium, which is the difference between the average market-to-book ratios of payers and non-payers. They argue that firms initiate dividends when the existing payers are trading at a premium to non-payers. On the other hand, dividends are more likely to be omitted when payers are traded at a discount. They also use ex post returns, and find that when the rate of dividend initiation increases, the future stock returns from the portfolio of payers are lower than those from the portfolio of non-payers. Li and Lie (2006) report similar empirical findings.

Baker and Wurgler see the dividend premium as a reflection of investor sentiment for "risky" non-paying growth firms versus "safe" dividend payers, since it falls in growth stock bubbles and rises in crashes. Fuller and Goldstein (2011) show explicitly that payers outperform in market downturns.

There might be a behavioral explanation to this phenomenon based on mental accounting and the prospect theory, particularly given the specific feature of the value function, which is concave in the domain of gains and convex in losses. Dividends allow investors to flexibly repackage what would otherwise be a large capital loss into a slightly larger capital loss and a dividend. If the capital loss is large, then a slightly larger loss causes little extra pain, while the dividend can be accounted for as a gain relative to a reference point of no dividend and thus a return to the value function where marginal utility is higher.

This notion is partially in line with the proposition of Shefrin and Statman (1984), even though they extend their reasoning to explain why investors may like dividends in good times.

2. Investment Decisions

In the domain of investment decisions, managers, in a sense, become investors themselves and so are likely to be subject to behavioral biases. However, in this chapter, we continue with the assumption that managers are rational agents. In this framework, let us see how firms might attempt to benefit from market inefficiency, fads, and investor sentiment by adapting their investment decisions in order to boost the stock price, at least in the short term.

Similar to financing decisions, it is once again about managerial market timing and catering, that is, delivering to investors what they like at a given moment of time. If the market is in favor of growth stock, the scale of investment (both in real assets, R&D, as well as in M&A) should tend to be higher. On the other hand, if investors are skeptical about growth prospects and prefer to have cash in hand, the level of investment will be lower. Higher stock prices will also enhance investment, as better firm valuation lowers the cost of equity and hence improves the NPV of a potential new project. Likewise, the unusually low cost of debt should also boost investment. If there is a fashion among investors for a particular industry or segment of the market, firms may decide to invest in this new opportunity, despite the fact that it might be sometimes quite remote from what they have been doing so far. Similarly, the history of financial markets knows of shifts in investor preferences toward conglomerates or companies focused on a core business. These changing fashions sparked waves of takeovers or disinvestments, respectively.

The link between capital market inefficiency and investment decisions is particularly important for the economy. It is one thing to say that investor irrationality and resulting misevaluation of assets lead to the transfer of wealth among investors. But it is much more important to understand that mispricing may lead to underinvestment, overinvestment, or the general misallocation of capital, which may potentially cause heavy losses in the economy as the whole.

2.1. Real Investment

There are many ways in which irrational investor sentiment may influence decisions of rational managers about real investment. First, which is perhaps the most common view of the financial market's influence, stock and debt markets affect investment through their influence on the cost of funds. Second, when managers make their investment decisions, they often cater to investors' beliefs and temporary preferences. Generally, catering may take the form of increasing the scale of investment when investors favor growth, and underinvesting when investors are more skeptical. The full effect of an investment project on a firm's fundamentals may be usually observed only in a longer period of time.

However, if biased investors attach too much weight to current information about new investment, managers may use investment decisions also for short-term purposes. This is especially true if managers are motivated by the short-term stock performance, for example, through option plans.

The empirical evidence on the direct link between stock prices and investment is mixed. Barro (1990) advocates for a substantial independent effect of stock returns over the level of investment. Morck, Shleifer, and Vishny (1990) find a similar relation, but only when constant fundamentals are assumed. After taking into consideration changes in firms' fundamentals, such as the growth rate in cash flow and sales, the explanatory power of returns on investment is weak compared to what could have been expected. Blanchard, Rhee, and Summers (1993) also find that non-fundamental residuals of stock price changes have little predictive power when it comes to the level of investment. On the other hand, Galeotti and Schiantarelli (1994) document that both fundamental and non-fundamental parts of stock price changes have significant effects on firms' level of investment. Similar conclusions are reached by Chirinko and Schaller (2011).

Another approach to establish the relation between stock mispricing and real investment has been more successful. Rather than controlling for fundamentals and looking for a residual effect of stock prices, various proxies for mispricing are used and then the relations between these proxies and investment are examined. Gilchrist, Himmelberg, and Huberman (2005) developed a model in which increases in dispersion of investor opinion cause stock prices to rise above their fundamental values. They demonstrate that rational managers should increase real investment in response to such mispricing. By using the variance earnings forecasts made by analysts as a proxy for the dispersion of investor beliefs, they verify the model empirically. Polk and Sapienza (2009) use discretionary accruals, a measure of the extent to which the firm has abnormal noncash earnings, to identify mispricing. Firms with high discretionary accruals have subsequently relatively low stock returns, suggesting that they are overpriced. Polk and Sapienza regress firm-level investment on discretionary accruals and find a significant positive relation between the two variables. Baker and Wurgler (2007) propose the sentiment index as a proxy for misvaluation. McLean and Zhao (2013) use that measure and show that investor sentiment has a significant impact on firms' investment decisions. The relation between internal cash flow and investment declines with the growth of sentiment. The hotter the market, the easier it is to obtain funding and the less managers care about internal cash flow in order to finance new investment. When firms invest during periods of low sentiment, operational efficiency improves, but when they do so in high sentiment periods, operational efficiency declines. When the sentiment is low, more projects are forgone due to financing constraints. If managers are careful to select the few most profitable projects, then the average return on investment is high. Furthermore, firms tend to overinvest in high sentiment states, either because they cater to investors' expectations, or because easy and cheap access to funding encourages acceptance of projects of lower quality. As a result, stock returns following investment made in high sentiment states are significantly lower than stock returns on investment made in low sentiment periods. Albagli, Hellwig, and Tsyvinsky (2011) propose a model that captures the aforementioned observations. They argue that explicitly linking managerial compensation to stock prices gives managers an incentive to manipulate the firm's investment decisions to their own benefit. The managers take advantage of shareholders by taking excessive investment risks when the market is optimistic, and investing too little when the market is pessimistic.

Stein (1996) and Baker, Stein, and Wurgler (2003) show that mispricing-driven investment is most sensitive in equity-dependant firms, that is, firms with no option but to issue equity to finance new investment. Particularly, if stock of such firms is undervalued, managers are likely to underinvest rather than issue equity below its fair value.

2.2. Entering New Markets

Firms tend to invest in projects that are currently in fashion, and to which investors are likely to assign high values. This is yet another manifestation of catering to investor preferences. It also shows managerial short termism, that is, the efforts managers take to boost short-term stock prices even if the decisions taken have potentially long-term consequences.[8]

In the history of capital markets, there have been many cases when firms decided to enter new fashionable markets, sometimes quite remote from what they had been doing earlier. For example, ARIEL, a footwear producer listed on the Warsaw Stock Exchange, announced in 1999 that it was entering the hot Internet market—besides its traditional core business (i.e., shoe making), it was going to act as an Internet provider. In the response, the stock price rose by 600 percent within three weeks after the announcement was made. Similarly, the stock price of Active Apparel—a swimming costume producer listed in New York—rose from 50 cents to 25 dollars a share after the firm announced its intention to create an online shop.

Earlier evidence of firms entering into fashionable industries in order to take advantage of a bubble include cases from the period of the electronic boom of the late 1950s and the early 1960s, gambling stocks in the late 1970s, and biotechnology and high-tech sectors in the 1980s. The bubbles did not usually last for more than two to three years in a given industry, but the consequences of a firm's engagement in a new sector often persisted much longer.

Hirshleifer (1993) suggests that decisions to take up investment projects, particularly in new areas, may also be driven by reputation concerns. The incentives of managers to use *investment* choices as a tool for building their reputations or the reputations of their firms come in three main forms. The first one is visibility bias, which encourages a manager to make an investment as a short-term indicator of success. In other words, managers want to show off with their new investment project. The second form of reputation-driven investment incentive is resolution reference, which encourages managers to try to advance the arrival of good news and delay bad news. By taking up new investment, particularly in a novel and fashionable area, managers want investors to focus on the positive signal and divert their attention from potential negative news about other aspects of their firm. Finally, investment policy may be motivated by mimicry, which encourages managers to take the actions that the best executives are seen to do.

2.3. Mergers and Acquisitions

There are many theories attempting to explain forces driving M&A. The traditional approach is the one adopted in the Brainard and Tobin's (1968) Q theory of investment with its extensions along the lines of the agency theory. In this view, markets are efficient and the main sources of M&A activities are potential synergy effects and the disparity in the quality of management between the bidder and target firms. In other words, firms merge in order to share synergies or the bidder takes over the target in order to redeploy its poorly managed assets in a more efficient way.

Behavioral finance framework offers two general concepts here. First, it is assumed that managers are fully rational and the source of M&A activity lays in the inefficient market that allows relative mispricing between the bidder and/or target firms. The second concept, which we are going to investigate in the next chapter, points to irrationality and biases among managers as other potential drivers of M&A activities.

Shleifer and Vishny (2003) propose a model in which fully rational managers take advantage of market inefficiencies through M&A. They argue that if acquirers are overpriced, their motive for acquisition is not to gain synergies, but to preserve some of the temporary overvaluation for long-term shareholders. Although the total lack of synergies seems to be a strong assumption, the model offers a rich set of interesting implications and predictions that are close to the empirical evidence. First, by acquiring less-overvalued targets and paying with overvalued equity, acquirers can cushion the future fall of their stock price by "diluting" the temporary overvaluation among shareholders of the target firm. The target firm is likely to accept the overvalued stock because of the premium paid over its own shares, particularly when short horizons of target managers and shareholders are assumed. The greater the relative overvaluation of the bidder above the target, the higher premium might be paid in the form of the bidder's equity, and therefore, the higher positive return on the target stock directly after the announcement of the bid. However, the target shareholders might gain in the short term, but they lose in the long run, as the premium usually does not fully compensate the relative undervaluation of the target. The long-run post-merger abnormal returns in this scenario are likely to be negative.

As we know well, acquisitions can also be financed by cash. According to Shleifer and Vishny's model, the only way the bidder can profit in such a scenario is when the target is underpriced. The greater the undervaluation of the target, the higher the potential premium in the cash offer. However, if the bidder is to profit, the premium cannot compensate the total target's undervaluation.

Therefore, rational target's managers acting in the best interest of their irrational shareholders should be more resistant to such takeover bids. As a result, there will be more hostile takeovers among purely cash-financed transactions compared to stock- or mixed-financed acquisitions. The model also predicts that, in the long term, cash acquirers earn positive abnormal returns that result directly from the undervaluation of the target rather than from any synergy effects.

Rhodes-Kropf and Viswanathan (2004) propose a different model of M&A that is also based on the assumption of market mispricing, but additionally allows for the existence of synergies. In their model, misvaluation has a market or at least sectoral component in addition to a firm-specific component. Target managers are rational, but less than fully informed. They cannot identify the source of the mispricing between the two components. They rationally accept merger offers in times of high valuations, because of the positive correlation between pricing and estimates of the synergy. Unlike the Shleifer and Vishny (2003) model, the Rhodes-Kropf and Viswanathan (2004) model does not require the assumption that target managers have short horizons. Otherwise, both models give similar predictions that fit well with the empirical evidence.

First, it is a well-known fact that the bidder valuation is, on average, relatively higher than the target valuation at the time of the offer. Gort (1969) finds that acquirers on average have higher price-to-earnings (P/E) ratios than their targets in his relatively small sample of takeovers completed in the 1950s. Andrade, Mitchell, and Stafford (2001) find that two-thirds of bidders had higher Tobin's Q ratios than their targets in the sample covering the period from 1973 to 1998. In more recent studies, Rhodes-Kropf, Robinson, and Viswanathan (2005), Dong, Hirshleifer, Richardson, and Teoh (2006), and Ang and Cheng (2006) all find that market-level mispricing proxies correlate positively with merger activity, and that acquirers tend to be more overpriced than targets. All three papers also indicate that equity offers are associated with higher bidder and target valuations than cash offers. Additionally, Dong et al. (2006) document that the disparity between bidder and target valuation is greater among equity than among cash offers. They also find that offers for undervalued targets are more likely to be hostile with a lower probability of success. More overpriced acquirers are prepared to pay higher takeover premiums, particularly if they bid equity. Similarly, the more undervalued the targets, the higher premiums are offered. Quite understandably, the positive announcement effect on targets' returns increases in proportion to the amount of the takeover premium. On the other hand, the higher the takeover premium, and the higher the bidder valuation, the larger is the negative announcement effect on the bidder's returns. In this case, investors either think that the bidder is paying too much (failing to recognize the bidder initial overpricing), or the announcement actually triggers a more careful analysis following which a bidder's valuation is corrected downward.[9]

The long-term effect of acquisitions on bidding firms is sensitive to the method of payment and the sample period. It also runs into statistical problems of measuring abnormal returns in a long period. Early studies by Agrawal, Jaffe, and Mandelker (1992), Loughran and Vijh (1997), Rau and Vermaelen (1998), and Agrawal and Jaffe (2000) look at stock returns three or five years after acquisition and find negative abnormal returns following stock mergers, especially for low book-to-market glamor bidders, and positive abnormal stock returns following cash tender offers, based on sample periods prior to 1993. However, Mitchell and Stafford (2000) argue that this conclusion is sensitive to the treatment of cross-event return correlations. To address the problem, Bouwman, Fuller, and Nain (2009) use the event-time buy-and-hold approach. They document that cash bidders outperform in the 1980s, but underperform in the later period, which suggests that cash bidders were also overpriced in the late 1990s. Not surprisingly, there is convincing evidence of underperformance following stock mergers carried out in that period (Moeller et al., 2005; Bouwman et al., 2009; Savor and Lu, 2009). Friedman (2006) uses a large sample covering the period from 1962 till 2000 and documents poor post-merger performance of stock bidders contrasted to outperformance following cash acquisitions.

Verter (2002) documents that merger volume increases with the aggregate market valuation as well as the dispersion in valuation. Looking at aggregate data, he also finds that periods of high levels of stock acquisitions are followed by low market returns.

Overall, the empirical findings dovetail with the models proposed by Shleifer and Vishny (2003), and by Rhodes-Kropf and Viswanathan (2004). There is a strong possibility that market misvaluation might be the primary reason for M&As, though other economic forces are also likely drivers of M&A waves on the aggregated level. For example, Harford (2005) provides evidence that industry merger waves are driven by economic, regulatory, and technological shocks, provided there is enough overall capital liquidity.

One question that remains unresolved in the Shleifer–Vishny misvaluation framework is why managers prefer a stock merger to issuing new equity and using the raised cash to pay for the takeover. If bidding managers are driven by market timing attempts, they should be indifferent to both means of financing the acquisition. To explain this, Baker and Wurgler (2013) suggest that a merger actually hides the underlying market timing motive from investors, as the equity issue and investment decision are bundled. Rational managers take advantage of biased investors who frame and perceive the stock-financed transaction differently to a pure SEO. Baker, Coval, and Stein (2007) consider another mechanism that can also explain the generic preference for equity issues via mergers. The first point is that the bidder faces a downward sloping demand curve for its stock. Second, a large portion of the target's shareholders follow "the path of least resistance," passively accepting the bidder's shares even if, under normal circumstances, they would not have participated in a stand-alone equity issue of the acquirer. Such a behavior might be attributed to the psychological phenomena of the status quo effect and the endowment effect (see section 2.3 in chapter 2). Given these two assumptions, the impact of a stock merger on the current price may be much smaller than that of an SEO.

2.4. Conglomerate or Core Business

Typically, companies either merge horizontally with firms involved in the related business or vertically with suppliers or customers. However, conglomerates combine companies operating in completely unrelated industries. Cross-industrial M&A may lead to very complex organizations, and their economic efficiency is discussible. Traditional explanations for entering unrelated lines of business point at agency problems or try to look for synergies justifying the existence of unrelated businesses under one organization. The synergies may for example result from tax shields or better access to financing via internal capital markets (Hubbard and Palia, 1999). The other line of reasoning is that business diversification lowers the overall risk of the conglomerate, and thus increases the value to shareholders. This way of thinking, however, should be rejected in the presence of well-developed capital markets. Instead of being forced to hold a bundle of various businesses in one conglomerate stock, investors can easily diversify according to their own tastes and risk appetites by selecting stocks of different firms that focus on a core business and are thus more transparent and understandable. Conglomerates could make sense if they operated in poorly developed capital markets where particular sectors of the economy might not be represented by publicly listed firms. In such a case, conglomerate stocks would provide investors with at least partial exposure to industries otherwise not available on the public market. Similarly, multinationals might open the door to some foreign markets that normally would be difficult to access for investors.

Having said that, it is hard to explain rationally the huge conglomerate wave in the well-developed capital market in the United States in the 1960s. Over the whole decade, almost 25,000 firms disappeared through mergers, and these were predominately conglomerate transactions (Brooks, 1987).

Early concerns were that rational managers use unrelated business acquisitions to mislead investors and to dress up (increase) their EPS. Bidders who acquire targets with relatively low P/E ratio automatically increase the EPS of the combined firm. Of course, there may be a rational reason why the unrelated business has a lower P/E ratio, for example, when the target has a different risk profile or growth prospects than the bidder. As the result of the merger, the risk/growth profile of the target contributes to the overall characteristics of the conglomerate and the combined profile of the corporation changes. Thus, the mathematically higher EPS of the combined firms does not necessarily mean value creation. However, irrational investors tend to overlook that. Concerns regarding potential window-dressing motivation of conglomerate mergers were so high that they actually inspired regulatory reforms. In July 1968, The Federal Trade Commission announced that it would make an in-depth investigation of conglomerate mergers. The Security and Exchange Commission (SEC) and the auditing firms responded by making attempts to set accounting principles and to clarify reporting standards for M&A (Malkiel, 2007). Barber, Palmer, and Wallace (1995) find evidence that window-dressing might have been a particularly strong motivation in the case of friendly conglomerate acquisitions, but less so when it comes to hostile takeovers.

Baker and Wurgler (2013) propose that the conglomerate wave of the 1960s might be explained by the catering theory. They argue that rational managers responded to temporary investor preferences and simply exploited the fad to boost the short-term value of their stock. Investor demand for conglomerates appears to have reached its peak in 1968. Ravenscraft and Scherer (1987) find that the average return on 13 top conglomerates was 385 percent from July 1965 to June 1968, while the S&P 425 gained only 34 percent. But high valuations did not last long and started to fall in mid-1968. Between July 1968 and June 1970, their sample portfolio lost 68 percent, roughly three times more than the S&P 425 index in the same period. Perhaps responding to valuation incentives, conglomerate mergers accelerated particularly in 1967 and peaked in 1968, although the merger wave continued for a few years yet. At that time, investors seemed to welcome M&A announcements of unrelated businesses and actually dislike acquisitions of related firms. Schipper and Thompson (1983) report short-term positive abnormal returns for firms announcing acquisition programs (predominantly unrelated acquisitions) during the 1960s. Matsusaka (1993) finds positive abnormal announcement returns for friendly unrelated acquisitions, and negative abnormal announcement returns for hostile related takeovers. Later on, however, the announcement effect of diversification acquisitions has turned around. Morck, Shleifer, and Vishny document a flat market reaction from mid- to late-1970s and a negative effect in the period from 1980 till 1987. Klein (2001) finds that the market rewarded conglomerates with "a diversification premium" of 36 percent in the period from 1966 till 1968. Subsequently, the premium turned into a discount of 1 percent in years 1969–1971, and increased to 17 percent in the period 1972–1974.[10] Clearly, the market lost its appetite for conglomerates, but it remains unclear why.

The aforementioned evidence conforms to the Baker and Wurgler's (2013) catering hypothesis that the conglomerate wave in the 1960s might have been just a fad to which rational managers responded accordingly. However, it might also have been the case that irrational investors were initially fooled by window-dressing and EPS manipulation techniques, and only learned to recognize the trick later when the problem was brought up to regulators and widely discussed by accounting and auditing professionals.

The shift in investor taste launched the divestment era, particularly strong in the 1980s, when firms began to sell their unrelated operations and to focus on the core business. There is vast evidence of positive market reaction to divestment announcements. Breakups or spin-offs may actually release value tied up in complex structures of combined unrelated businesses (Markides, 1992; Lang and Stulz, 1994; Comment and Jarrell, 1995; Berger and Ofek, 1995, 1996, 1999). Current market consensus seems to be that conglomerates are generally less efficient than stand-alone firms. Moves toward greater focus are often interpreted as a triumph of corporate governance.

3. Other Managerial Practices

3.1. Earnings Management

Earnings management is the process by which management can potentially manipulate financial statements to represent what they wish to have happened during the period rather than what actually happened. The reasons why management may want to manage earnings include pressures that are both internal (the board of directors) and external (shareholders' thresholds and analysts' expectations, rating agencies, potential debt covenants on profitability), as well as managers' own incentives (reputation, option plans, or other compensation schemes). There is a spectrum of ways in which a company can manage earnings, but generally they can be split into two categories: related to cash flow management and to noncash accruals. There are also different degrees to which earnings management is discretionary, when it becomes unethical, and when it is clearly illegal and fraudulent.

A firm may engage in timing activities related to its expenses and revenues, at least to some extent (e.g., increasing/decreasing maintenance expenditures, doing a restructuring in a given period that it may not otherwise have done, or selling a valuable asset when it needs to recognize higher incomes). Other examples of cash flow manipulation practices include recognizing revenues from transactions that have delayed reversal options and are not definite sales (e.g., sell-and-buy-back-later operations). However, there might also be transactions with related companies that do not fall under the requirements on financial statement consolidation. Cash flow manipulation is generally more difficult, more serious, and likely to be illegal.

The reported net income for a given period differs from the actual cash flow by various noncash accruals that are to some extent discretionary. There is a common opinion that investors care more about earnings than about cash flows (Easton et al., 1992; Kothari and Sloan, 1992), and managers tend to believe so (Graham et al., 2005). This gives stimulus for managers to manipulate the reported net income via accruals. Examples may include recognizing gains (losses) on assets that have a fair market value above (below) the current book value, manipulation of expenses based on estimates in a given period, the choice of inventory methods, estimation of pension liabilities, capitalization of leases and marketing expenses, allowances for bad debt, and so on. If a company is having a particularly good year and next year's results are uncertain, they can over-accrue some reserves and provisions in the current year and then have the ability to under-accrue them in the next year if needed. By doing so, they effectively inflate the following year's income at the expense of the current one. Thus, income appears smoother, and the company may be able to publicly forecast higher profits for the following year even if their business is not actually going to do any better.

Other ways to manipulate reported earnings include creative acquisition accounting or playing with the materiality thresholds. As discussed in the earlier sections of this chapter related to M&A (2.3) and conglomerates (2.4), the acquirer might impact its own, post-merger results by buying a relatively cheaper or more profitable target. With the advent of accounting principles regulating this area (SFAS Nos. 141 and 142), this does not seem to be as much of a problem as it was prior to these regulations. Materiality thresholds do not leave much room in the case of small firms, as nearly everything is material for them. However, for large, publicly traded companies with revenues and assets in billions of dollars, materiality thresholds may potentially let them get away with millions of dollars worth of misstatements. Materiality has the potential to allow these companies to slightly cook their numbers, especially if very little is necessary to meet the analysts' earnings consensus.

Degeorge, Patel, and Zeckhauser (1999) develop a model and also provide the empirical evidence on earnings management. They identify three prominent reference points for managers who want to manage earnings. The strongest motivation is to achieve earnings that are positive. Past reported earnings constitute the next threshold, and the last aim is to meet analysts' expectations. Earnings falling just short of thresholds are managed upward. Earnings far from thresholds, whether below or above, are reined in, in order to make future thresholds more achievable in the next reporting period. Burgstahler and Dichev (1997) examine earnings management to meet only the first two thresholds, that is, to avoid earnings decreases or losses. They point at two components of earnings, operational cash flows and changes in working capital, which are used to improve reported figures. Matsumoto (2002) and Burgstahler and Eames (2006) show that managers also avoid reporting earnings below analysts' forecasts. They provide empirical evidence of upward management of earnings, as well as downward management of analysts' forecasts. By increasing reported figures and decreasing analysts' expectations, managers aim to achieve zero and small positive earnings surprises.

The aforementioned evidence may suggest that rational managers manipulate earnings to cater to shareholder preferences as described in the prospect theory of Kahneman and Tversky (1979). If investors anchor to salient earning reference points (loss/gain, past earnings, or analysts' forecasts), managers attempt to be above those points to save investors from the unpleasant sensation of a relative "loss."[11]

Earnings manipulation is generally condemned. The requirement of quality and transparency in financial reports is based on the assumption that investors can correctly read financial statements and make rational decisions on the basis of information provided. However, if we dismiss the notion of investor rationality, it is possible that some degree of consistent earnings management might be actually beneficial for the firm and its shareholders. This is not of course to advocate fraudulent manipulation on a scale that led to accounting scandals such as Enron or WorldCom cases. But some reasonable earnings smoothing, that is, slightly lowering reported earnings in good periods to stretch them upward when times are bad, might be good when investor preferences are shaped according to the prospect theory. The absolute utility of a positive earnings surprise is smaller than that of a negative surprise. In other words, people do not like decreases in reported earnings more than they like increases. Additionally, a positive surprise in one period builds up expectations for further growth in the future. However, if earnings are volatile, the subsequent period may bring a negative surprise. Lower reported earnings will be perceived as a double loss, because not only are the growth expectations disappointed, but also the figures are below the results from the previous period. Market reaction to positive earnings surprises is weaker than to negative ones

(Foster et al., 1984; Szyszka, 2002). Loss aversion may induce investors to require higher rates of return to compensate for the unpleasant feeling. As a result, the firm's cost of equity will be higher and its market valuation will be lower. Through earnings smoothing, rational managers can limit the buildup of expectations in good periods and avoid subsequent disappointments. A firm with less volatility in reported figures and smaller but steady earnings growth will appear safer in investors' eyes. It should also lower the volatility of the stock prices. The required risk premium will be lower; hence the market valuation is higher. If earnings smoothing is responsible and consistent over time, and does not go beyond legal methods and discretionary rules of accounting, it might in fact be good for the firm and its less-than-rational shareholders. Jiraporn, Miller, Yoon, and Kim (2008) find a positive relation between firm value and the extent of earnings management, although their reasoning is set in the agency theory framework.

However, it is also possible that managers engage in earnings management not because they want to cater to investor preferences, but because they act opportunistically in their own interest being motivated by short-term considerations. Cheng and Warfield (2005) point at the link between managers' equity incentives—arising from stock-based compensation or stock ownership—and earnings management. Bergstresser and Philippon (2006) find that the use of discretionary accruals to manipulate reported earnings is more pronounced in firms where the CEO's potential total compensation is more closely tied to the value of stock and option holdings. In addition, they document that during the years of high accruals, managers exercise unusually large amounts of options and sell large quantities of shares. This might be interpreted as managers using accruals to boost the stock price and then to exploit the temporary overvaluation. The interpretation is consistent with an earlier finding by Sloan (1996) who documents subsequent underperformance of firms with exceptionally high accruals. In a similar line of reasoning, Teoh, Welch, and Wong (1998a, 1998b) argue that earnings management might be responsible for overvaluation of firms issuing equity. They find that post-offer underperformance is greatest for firms that manage pre-issue earnings most aggressively. On the other hand, Gong, Louis, and Sun (2008) document downward earnings management prior to open-market repurchases, a phenomenon particularly strong in firms with CEO ownership. Post-buyback abnormal returns and reported improvement in operating performance are driven, at least partially, by pre-repurchase downward earnings management rather than genuine growth in profitability. Erickson and Wang (1999) find that acquiring firms exhibit income increasing accruals prior to stock-based acquisitions. Bergstresser, Desai, and Rauh (2006) also find evidence of earnings manipulation prior to merger activities, when managers exercise stock options, or when they are near critical earnings thresholds.

Overall, there is clear evidence of earnings management. Earnings smoothing and catering to investor preferences by avoiding negative surprises is one thing that, under certain circumstances, can be even beneficial to the firm in the long run. Unfortunately, there are more signs indicating opportunistic managerial behavior driven simply by a desire to boost the stock price in the short-term perspective.

3.2. Splits and Reverse Splits

It appears that managers engage not only in earnings management, but also in active management of nominal share prices. A split is a corporate action in which a company's existing shares are divided into multiple shares. Although the number of shares outstanding increases by a specific multiple, the total dollar value of the shares should remain the same compared to presplit amounts, as the operation itself creates no real value. Nevertheless, many studies document abnormal positive returns around stock split announcements, starting with early work by Fama, Fisher, Jensen, and Roll (1969) to the recent work by Kalay and Kronlund (2012). The reason why we observe positive abnormal returns is a puzzle that remains unsolved. Different theories have emerged in the literature to explain the abnormal returns around split announcements.

The early theories hypothesize that markets learn about firms' fundamentals from stock splits. Fama et al. (1969) argue that splits are a good signal of dividend growth as about 75 percent out of 940 firms in their sample from the years 1929–1959 actually increased payments to shareholders in the post-split period. Asquith, Healy, and Palepu (1989) find some evidence supporting the connection between stock splits and earnings. However, their paper mainly identifies a pattern of strong earnings growth prior to splits, followed by modest growth afterward. Pilotte (1997) associates the weak link between splits and future earnings growth in the Asquith et al. (1989) sample with poor economic conditions in the 1970s. He argues that in his later sample for the period between 1982 and 1989, splits were in fact a signal of future earnings increases. Analyzing the large sample of 2,097 firms splitting shares between 1988 and 2007, Kalay and Kronlund (2012) reconfirm that splits carry information indicating subsequent earnings growth.

According to later, alternative theories, it is not the information, but rather increased marketability that stocks achieve via splits that cause the abnormal returns. A lower share price increases the pool of potential investors in the company. Consequently, the demand for the stock should increase as well pushing the overall firm's valuation upward. Surveys by Baker and Gallagher (1980) and Baker and Powell (1993) show that managers seem to share this way of thinking. However, direct tests of the increased marketability for stocks following a stock split suggest that there is no long-term improvement (Lakonishok and Lev, 1987), and if there are any short-term effects, they are negligent (Byun and Rozeff, 2003).

Splits are also said to increase liquidity, although this seems to be associated with higher trading costs. First, the relative bid-ask spread increases after splits (Copeland, 1979; Conroy et al., 1990; Kadapakkam et al., 2005). Angel (1997) develops a theory of "relative tick size," according to which a higher relative tick size after a split is an economic incentive for more dealers to make markets for the stock and to provide additional liquidity. However, this reasoning could apply only to relatively illiquid stocks, whereas splits are also undertaken by firms with typically high trading volumes. It is also worth to mention that institutional investors tend to pay a fixed brokerage commission per share regardless of share price. Pricing of brokerage for retail investors has also changed in recent years—investors are often charged a flat fee up to a certain fixed number of shares traded. Higher bid-ask spreads combined with the structure of brokerage fees mean that, in terms of trading costs, both individual and institutional investors are likely be worse-off after splits.

The hypothesis that adjusting the share price to an optimal trading range might be a source of value does not stand up to the fact that the market reacts on average adversely to announcements of reverse splits (Woolridge and Chambers, 1983; Lamoureux and Poon, 1987; Desai and Jain, 1997; Kim et al., 2008). Most reverse splits are declared by relatively small firms whose shares have been trading at unusually low levels. Penny stocks have high relative ticks, thus high relative bid-ask spreads, and appear to be highly volatile, as a change in price by one tick automatically triggers relatively large percentage change in valuation. Han (1995) documents that reverse splits actually increase the liquidity, while Dravid (1987) and Koski (2007) demonstrate that the post-reverse-split volatility decreases. Still, the market does not reward bringing nominal prices back to "optimal trading levels." On the contrary, even though they underreact, investors perceive a reverse split as a negative signal of future poor performance. Martell and Webb (2008) and Vafeas (2001) confirm that firms engaging in reverse splits report subsequently disappointing results. Investors seem not to be fully aware of how bad the firm's situation is at the time of the reverse split announcement. There is evidence of negative abnormal returns for up to three years following reverse splits (Desai and Jain, 1997; Kim et al., 2008; Martell and Webb, 2008).

Benartzi, Michaely, Thaler, and Weld (2009) document that the average US share prices have remained constant at around 35 dollars in nominal terms since the Great Depression, while the general price level in the US economy has risen more than tenfold over the period of 80 years. This is mainly the result of splits, but also the fact that IPO prices have remained relatively constant. Generally, managers appear to choose stock splits in an attempt to bring share prices back in line with their size and industry peers. Benartzi et al. (2009) argue that neither signaling nor optimal trading range hypothesis are able to fully explain the constancy of nominal prices. In their opinion, managers are simply following norms, adhering to an arbitrary historical convention from which there is no particular reason to deviate from given investor expectations. However, Benartzi et al. (2009) do not address the question why managerial actions taken to keep share prices in the traditional range are rewarded by investors with positive returns in the case of splits, and penalized in the case of reverse splits.

Market reaction to splits and reverse splits, at least to some extent, may also result from irrational anchoring to presplit prices. Although splits are rather transparent and mathematically simple operations, market participants may still subconsciously attach too much weight to prices at their presplit level.

Nominal post-split price may look very cheap and so may induce, at least in the short term, additional demand pushing the firm valuation upward. In the same line of reasoning, the post-reverse-split price may seem horrendously expensive causing negative market reaction. The literature on the psychology of finance cites many examples when people have problems distinguishing real and nominal values even in simple tasks (e.g., Shafir et al., 1997). In addition, experiments run by Kahneman and Tversky (1974) showed that people may anchor to completely unrelated and arbitrary values suggested subconsciously to them (see section 1.1 in chapter 2).

Baker, Greenwood, and Wurgler (2009) propose that nominal share prices are used as another tool to cater to time-varying investor preferences. In analogy to the dividend premium proposed in Baker and Wurgler (2004b), they postulate a "low-price premium" as the average market-to-book ratio of stocks whose prices fall in the bottom three deciles minus the average of those with prices in the top three deciles. They find that as existing low-price firms are valued relatively high by the market, more and more firms split, and those who decide to do so use higher split ratios, that is, they split to lower prices. They also document that average IPO prices vary closely with the low-price premium. In other words, when investors place higher valuations on low-price firms, managers respond by supplying shares at lower price levels—either via splits or by setting lower IPO prices in the case of firms getting listed.

3.3. Changing the Firm's Name

Managers sometimes attempt to boost the stock price by changing the company's name to create a salient association with a temporarily fashionable category of stocks. This is one of the most evident examples of direct catering to investor taste. And, surprisingly, it is often a successful way to increase the company value and improve stock liquidity, at least in the short term.

Malkiel (2007) provides an example of the "tronics boom" in years 1959–1962 when company names often included some mangled version of the word "electronics" even if the firm had nothing to do with the electronic industry. A similar situation took place later during the Internet bubble. Cooper, Dimitrov, and Rau (2001) document that in a period of only one year between June 1998 and July 1999, nearly 150 firms changed their names to *Company.com* style. The announcement about the name being changed in such a way that it was associated with the Internet caused a sharp increase in the company's stock price. This "dotcom" effect produced cumulative abnormal returns as high as of 74 percent for the 10 days surrounding the announcement day! The market reaction was equally strong in the group of companies that did operate in the Internet sector as in the group of those whose activities were merely involved in it.

The effect seems to work also the other way around. Cooper, Khorana, Osobov, Patel, and Rau (2005) document that name changes were later used to dissociate companies from the Internet sector after the prices crashed in mid-2000. The "dotcom" deletion effect produced cumulative abnormal returns on the order of 64 percent for the 60 days surrounding the announcement day.

Again, the effect was almost as large for firms that dropped the dotcom name but stayed in the Internet business, as for those that changed not only the name but also their business focus. Hence, the name change does not appear to signal a change in growth opportunities for the firm.

3.4. Communication with the Market

Quality reporting, proper disclosure policy, and good investor relations are said to reduce information asymmetry, increase liquidity, and reduce volatility of stock prices. Through all these, they contribute to lower cost of equity, hence higher firm valuation. Less information asymmetry should also foster lower cost of debt. This follows from the assumption that investors rationally perceive, absorb, and properly use all information that firms try to communicate to them. However, we already know that market participants are often subject to various biases and limitations in information processing. Firms may attempt to exploit this weakness and influence investors by the way in which corporate news is presented.

Perception of a press release depends on its content and wording. As we explained in chapter 2 of this book, due to representativeness errors, people tend to overestimate descriptive information and underestimate numerical and statistical data. Thus, good news should be presented in a descriptive manner, whereas worse information should come in numerical form. Consider, for example, a company choosing to report in the headline that the "Company Achieves Record Quarterly Revenues; Balance Sheet boasts nearly $1.1 billion in cash and marketable securities," while the accompanying tabular income statement shows a loss per share of 3.54 dollars compared to the previous year EPS of 2.70 dollars (*Business Wire* 2001).[12] Investors are likely to focus on good descriptive news rather than much worse numerical data.

From the prospect theory, we also know that people are sensitive to framing and they do not like losses more than they desire gains. Hence, it is important to set the reference points for the release right. A firm should select a benchmark that allows to describe its performance as improved compared to that benchmark. For example, a firm that reports earnings higher than last period but below analysts' expectations should concentrate its release on the favorable period-to-period comparison. Experimental research demonstrates that two press releases presenting identical financial statements but accompanied by different textual explanations, for example, selectively emphasizing favorable comparisons, have a different impact on investors (Krische, 2005; Brooke, 2006). The empirical evidence from the field also confirms that strategically selected reference points do in fact influence investors (Lougee and Marquardt, 2004; Schrand and Walther, 2000; Bowen et al., 2005).

Positive framing also requires the use of affirmative wording, for example, "increase," "higher," "better," and so on. There are several studies confirming that language of communication impacts market reaction (Henry, 2008; Sadique et al., 2008; Davis et al., 2011; Demers and Vega, 2011). Hales, Kuang, and Venkataraman (2011) demonstrate experimentally that vivid and emotional tone of expression significantly influences the judgment of investors, but only when they hold contrarian positions. Interestingly, vivid language has limited influence on the judgment of investors who hold positions consistent with the general sentiment of the market.

The psychological effect of the "illusion of truth" suggests that we should communicate good news in simple manner and in plain words, whereas unfavorable information should be passed through sentences where the logic is convoluted and the structure obscure. Henry (2008) finds that earning releases containing negative surprises are longer and more complex textually.

Finally, the timing of releasing information is important, too. If we have good news to communicate, we should aim to issue the release at the time when investors will pay most heed. Particularly, our announcement should not coincide with other events that might compete for investor attention. However, if we have to announce bad news—weekend effect is the order of the day.

Overall, a large part of information releases is discretional in the United States. Managers have relatively much room for presenting information to investors in whatever manner they want. Nonetheless, it is worth remembering that too much of a short-term game with news releases may impact the long-term credibility of a firm.

CHAPTER 8

Managerial Biases in Corporate Policy

In the previous chapter it was taken for granted that corporate managers act fully rationally and adopt their decisions to temporary market inefficiencies and investor biases. In this chapter we take a different approach and assume that managers, similar to investors, may behave in less than fully rational ways.

We look at how psychological biases among managers may impact corporate policy. In the area of financing decisions, we study equity issuances and the IPO process, raising debt, buybacks, and financial risk management. In the field of investment decisions, we investigate evaluation of startup projects, real investment in mature firms, as well as mergers and acquisitions.

1. General Framework

The psychology literature provides vast evidence on biases and nonstandard preferences of decision makers (chapter 2). Behavioral finance applied these findings first to the behavior of investors (chapter 3). However, the other group of market participants—corporate managers—also comprises human beings. Despite being generally well educated in economics and finance, managers may still sometimes depart from axioms of full rationality. This chapter will argue that managers are subject to various biases that make their decisions diverge from rational expectations and traditional expected utility maximization and become replaced by nonstandard preferences. Hence, imperfect managerial decisions and inappropriate corporate policies that managers make might be the result of their psychological background. The potential impact of rational moral hazard and standard problems resulting from the agency theory are not taken into account in this framework.

Perhaps the simplest case of deviating from fully rational behavior is the concept of bounded rationality, introduced by Simon (1955). Bounded rationality assumes that some type of cognitive barriers or information-gathering costs prevent decision makers from making fully optimal decisions. This is particularly likely to happen in a world where tasks are complex and decision makers are flooded with a large number of information signals of varying relevance. Less-than-fully rational managers cope with such complexity and the ensuing problems with information processing by using heuristics and the rule of thumb. By simplifying reality, they hope to ensure acceptable, suboptimal levels of performance. Unfortunately, bounded rationality and adherence to the financial rule of thumb may sometimes lead to serious distortions.

When, instead of diligent analysis, judgment is based on mental shortcuts and stereotypes, it may be fraught with errors of representativeness. In case of aspects they are familiar with, professionals are likely to fall victim to gambler's fallacy and wrongly interpret the regression to the mean. For example, experts tend to expect reversals more often than trend continuations in forecasted sequences of data (Shefrin, 2010).

The psychology literature also provides evidence that experts with know-how in a given field may fall into the trap of overconfidence to a much higher degree than nonexperts. Professionals are particularly exposed to overconfidence if a specific task is vague and does not explicitly suggest the right solution. Overconfidence often leads to excessive optimism and unrealistic wishful thinking.

Overconfidence and ungrounded optimism are aggravated by selective-attribution bias, which consists in people attributing successes to themselves while blaming failures on independent external factors, such as bad luck or mistakes made by others. Lack of objectivity in the assessment of successes and failures limits people's ability to learn from their own mistakes contributing to the persistence of overconfidence and optimism.[1]

The corporate world, where decisions are highly complex and idiosyncratic, and where a large number of information signals is in constant flow, provides a conducive setting for bounded rationality, representativeness biases, overconfidence, and problems with debiasing through learning. Other compellingly documented psychological determinants of managerial behavior include narrow framing and anchoring to reference points.

For managerial biases to have an impact on a firm's policy, corporate governance must be limited in its ability to constrain managers into making only rational decisions. Efficient corporate governance potentially offers a protection against managerial biases, just as arbitrage theoretically serves as a mechanism to correct irrationality of some investors. Hence, inefficient corporate governance is analogous to limited arbitrage in that failures in both mechanisms expose psychological biases in real-life situations.

While reading the sections to follow, please keep in mind that the behavioral approach often competes with more established theories of corporate finance: the misalignment of managerial and shareholder interests, known as the "agency theory" (Jensen and Meckling, 1976; Jensen, 1986), or the theory of information asymmetry between corporate insiders and the capital market (Myers and Majluf, 1984). These theories frequently share similar predictions and offer alternative explanations of many empirically well-documented facts. It might be difficult to distinguish if a manager acts nonoptimally because of psychological biases or because she rationally maximizes her private goals at the expense of shareholders. She might also rationally attempt to exploit the typical information advantage of an insider being at the same time bounded by costly external finance due to information asymmetry. For example, the fact that managers are more prone to overinvest than pay out cash windfalls (Blanchard, Lopez de Silanes, and Shleifer, 1994) may look like a moral hazard problem or the result of managerial overconfidence and excessive optimism that funds create more value when invested further rather than when kept by shareholders. Similarly, the pecking order of the preferred sources of financing may result either from information asymmetry that makes external sources costlier or from overconfidence and excessive optimism leading managers to a mistaken belief that external finance costs too much.

We argue here that the behavioral approach, even if it is not the only possible explanation, fits better with empirical findings and provides a better understanding of many stylized facts.

2. Financial Decisions

2.1. Capital Structure

Generally, overconfidence and excessive optimism lead to underestimation of risk. Following the traditional theory of the trade-off between bankruptcy costs and tax shield benefits, one may say that biased managers believe they are less likely to experience financial distress and overestimate the use of tax shields. Hence, to finance their firms, they tend to use more debt than equity. Undertaking too much financial risk might turn out to be detrimental to shareholder wealth.

Specifically, when considering financing a new investment project, an overconfident manager underestimates the risk of failure while excessive optimism leads her to overestimate potential revenues the investment may bring. Both biases jointly contribute to a higher-than-justified expected value of the project that needs to be financed. The manager, being convinced that she acts in the best interest of current shareholders, does not want to dilute their shares in the project that she considers to be very good. Thus, she is strongly averse to the idea of issuing new equity. Due to overconfidence and excessive optimism, she is also likely to see available debt financing as offered at too high a cost and to overweigh internal cash flows. As a result, the manager exhibits a standard pecking-order preference. That is, she prefers internal financing to risky debt and risky debt to equity.

The above reasoning is in line with a formal model developed by Heaton (2002). The model is consistent with much of the existing evidence of pecking-order polices (e.g., Fama and French, 2002b), while the notion of managerial optimism receives support from psychology literature and, directly, from surveys of executives.

Gider and Hackbarth (2010) extended Heaton's approach to the analysis of managerial overconfidence. However, they defined overconfidence specifically as a bias in beliefs about the value of the project in good and bad scenarios, but with the expected value being unbiased (hence no excessive optimism). In other words, in their approach, managers tend to overestimate the value of the project in the negative scenario and underestimate it in the case of good development. They demonstrate that in such a setting, the overconfident manager would exhibit a reverse pecking-order preference. That is, she would prefer internal financing over risky debt, but equity to internal financing. These findings seem to be counterintuitive and are sensitive to the specific modeling framework proposed by Gider and Hackbarth (2010).

Past negative experience may strongly influence the willingness to take up financial risk and sometimes override the general overconfidence and excessive optimism. For example, Donaldson (1961) claims that managers who experienced the Great Depression as youngsters seemed to be particularly unwilling to use debt financing for many years to come. They exhibited high sensitivity to the availability of internal funding. On the other hand, Malmendier, Tate, and Yan (2011) find that executives with military experience pursue more aggressive policies, including heightened leverage.

Malmendier et al. (2011) provide empirical evidence that managers who believe their firm is undervalued view external financing as overpriced, which is particularly true for equity. Such overconfident and overoptimistic managers use less external finance and, provided they access external capital, issue less equity than their peers. Oliver (2005) finds that managerial confidence, as proxied by the University of Michigan Consumer Sentiment Index, is highly significant in explaining corporate financing policy. More confident managers tend to use higher level of debt in their firms. Ben-David, Graham, and Harvey (2007) show that narrowly calibrated managers use more debt, particularly long-term debt, are less likely to pay dividends, and more likely to repurchase shares. Finally, Graham and Harvey (2001), in their survey of 392 CFOs, and Shefrin (2005), who cites the Financial Executive International survey, argue that there is little support for the information asymmetry hypothesis of the pecking order. Instead, standard pecking-order preference seems to be driven by managerial overconfidence and excessive optimism.

Bounded rationality is also present in capital structure policy in the form of various rules of thumb and targets (Graham and Harvey, 2001). These are often set on the basis of book values of equity and debt rather than on market values (see sections 2.2–2.4 in chapter 10). Welch (2004) confirms that market leverage is allowed to float with stock prices to a large extent. This indicates that managers focus more on slower moving book values rather than on volatile market values when deciding about the degree of financial leverage.

2.2. Equity Issues

As explained in the previous section, overconfident and excessively optimistic managers generally use new equity only as a last resort. When they eventually decide to do so, reference dependence plays a prominent role in their decisions about the timing and pricing of equity issue.

Baker and Xuan (2011) find evidence that equity issuance is responsive to recent stock returns, considerably more so when the stock price has highly increased during the current manager's tenure. When the stock price exceeds the level that prevailed when the manager took the helm, the probability of equity issuance rises sharply. Managers anchor to historical levels of stock prices and are more likely to issue new equity if they consider it temporarily overvalued compared to the reference level. This may explain clustering patters in IPO activities that tend to coincide with a good situation on the market or in the industry (Ritter, 1984; Ibbotson, Sindelar, and Ritter, 1988, 1994; Derrien, 2010).

Loughran and Ritter (2002) point at reference dependence combined with mental accounting to explain the well-documented IPO underpricing. They argue that managers of IPO firms mentally account for two quantities: (1) the perceived gain between the first trading day closing price and the midpoint of the filing range in the book-building process, and (2) the real loss in the amount of money left on the table. Due to framing, these two aspects are mentally accounted for in isolation. The gain must be much higher to outweigh the loss, and it usually is, as the number of offered shares is typically much smaller than the number of shares retained by pre-IPO shareholders.[2]

In a test of Loughran and Ritter's proposition, Ljungqvist and Wilhelm (2005) construct a proxy for pre-IPO shareholder satisfaction equal to the sum of underpricing losses and perceived gains arising from differences between the midpoint of the filing price range and the first-day closing price. They find that the managers who are more satisfied with their IPOs, as measured by this proxy, are likely to use the same underwriter for follow-on season offerings, and pay higher fees for underwriting services. Thus, the executives are clearly not upset with underwriters leaving large amounts of money on the table.

Hanley (1993) documents that the first-day return is significantly higher, hence more money is left on the table for firms that eventually had the issue price above the midpoint of the filing range. Similarly, Loughran and Ritter (2002) find that offers priced above the maximum of the filing range enjoy particularly high returns on the first day. Both findings suggest that, when making the final decision about the offer pricing, managers anchored to the midpoint of the filing range in the book-building process and did not adjust the issue price sufficiently to the indications of strong demand for the stock.

In a similar line of reasoning, anchoring to the reference points may also explain why there is generally more money left on the table when the market is particularly hot and has been going up for already some time. Intuitively it should be the other way around—in the bull market underpricing should be lower, because it is in fact easier to allocate the new equity. The actual explanation might be based on managerial anchoring to the earlier valuation of the firm. The issue price they eventually decide to set does not fully account for the fact that the market has been rising a lot since they started considering the IPO.

Plotnicki and Szyszka (2013) investigate the differences in the speed of IPO process in bull and bear markets and argue that there is some evidence of the disposition effect among managers. When managers start considering a public offer, they usually have some initial valuation of their company in mind, mainly based on comparisons to market ratios of similar companies already listed in the market. Managers anchor to this initial valuation, and their preferences are driven by a utility function similar to the value function in the prospect theory, which is concave in the domain of gains and convex in the domain of losses. When the market is hot, ratios of comparable companies are getting more and more favorable, and a potential valuation of the IPO firm turns out to be even better than the initial anchor. A manager of the IPO firm considers it to be a "gain." Similarly, to an investor who sees her stock growing, the concave utility function makes the manager keen on capitalizing "gains" quickly. On the other hand, if the initial valuation of the IPO company is high (e.g., made at the top of the market boom), and the market then starts falling, a manager who did not conduct the IPO on time considers the declining valuation of the firm as a "loss." Similarly, to an investor who keeps the losing position opened for too long, the manager postpones the process of getting listed (the convex utility function). She hopes that the bullish market might come back and the firm's initial valuation will be available after all. When this expectation does not materialize, some managers give up the idea of the IPO while others eventually decide to get listed, but with a lower valuation than what could have been achieved if the IPO process had not been slowed down in the hope for a market rebound.

Plotnicki and Szyszka (2013) find a statistically significant negative correlation between the market return and the speed of the IPO process. They provide evidence suggesting that the speed of the IPO process depends to a greater extent on managerial decisions influenced by observation of the market rather than on independent external factors, such as difficulties in placing the offer. They also document that for firms debuting faster than the median of the sample, the average market return in the period between the IPO date and the median is positive. On the other hand, in the group of slower firms, the average market return in the period between the median and the IPO date is negative. There is an analogy between firms debuting too fast in bullish markets and too slow in bearish markets on the one hand, and investors selling winning stocks too quickly and keeping falling stocks for too long in their portfolios on the other.

2.3. Buybacks

In chapter 7 we suggested that managers tend to time the market when they decide to carry out a buyback. Repurchasing is particularly likely to happen after the stock has been severely downpriced and might look undervalued. Under such assumptions, buyback is a rational response of a manager acting in the best interests of long-term shareholders.

Szyszka and Zaremba (2011) propose a different hypothesis, which is also in line with behavioral reasoning, but assumes that managers might be subject to psychological traps that may distort their perception of the company's value. These managerial biases include anchoring to historical high price levels after the stock has dropped down, strong loss aversion if management compensation is based on stock performance, overconfidence about one's own management skills, and excessive optimism with regard to future development. It cannot be ruled out that stocks are in fact correctly priced at the time of the repurchase, but become overvaluated after the announcement. Dann (1981) and Vermaelen (1981, 1984) argue that stock repurchases send a positive signal to the market, which may be used by managers to influence the price. If the market overreacts to this signal, abnormal returns occur.

The hypothesis of post-repurchase positive market overreaction is supported by a number of potential reasons. First, stocks may be overvalued after a buy-back as a result of manipulative actions taken by the management trying to prove that its earlier decision was right (EPS management). This will be par-ticularly the case when the management is strongly motivated by a compensa-tion scheme or worried about losing reputation or the job.

Second, positive feedback trading may take place (Cutler, et al., 1990; De Long, et al., 1990b). Tender offer repurchases are usually done with a premium. Open market repurchases create additional demand that may push prices upward, particularly in the case of less liquid stocks. In both situations the initial positive impact on the stock price may attract more investors. Individual investors are usually trend followers, have shorter horizons, and focus on the recent history of the stock (De Bondt, 1993). In this particular context, as recent growth after the buyback grabs investors' attention, more demand is created and the price continues to rise steadily. On the other hand, institu-tional investors and analysts have longer horizons and usually bet on reversals (Shefrin, 2000). They still remember the time when the company was down-graded and/or the price was going down, so even though they can see the stock going up, they react with a delay due to cognitive conservatism (Edwards, 1968). Only after some time do they start to think that a reversal may be about to happen. And so institutions finally come into the picture creating yet more demand that contributes to further price growth.

If the post-buyback overreaction hypothesis is true, we should observe a reversal of excess returns over a longer term. Peyer and Vermaelen (2009) do not report any turnaround evidence in abnormal stock returns for up to three years after the buyback date (looking further ahead might produce statistically doubtful results). Using the standard event study methodology and the cumu-lative abnormal return approach (ACAR) to analyze the sample of European repurchases from 1998 to 2008, Szyszka and Zaremba (2011) find that buyback stocks outperform the market mostly in the first year after the operation. Next, after reaching their climax in the second year, stocks on average lose their excess returns, to eventually underperform by the end of the third year. Szyszka and Zaremba (2011) also used the calendar-time portfolio method,[3] which is believed to be more appropriate for long-horizon event studies. Their results consistently documented that the best performing buyback portfolio was the one with a single-year holding period. However, their study might be sensitive to a relatively small sample size of European stocks.

2.4. Debt Issues

Overconfidence and excessive optimism may influence debt maturity struc-ture in inducing more short-term financing. Overconfident and optimistic managers allow for more risk and tend to believe that it will be possible to repay the debt faster or obtain easy refinancing. The latter belief also leads to the construction of loan plans that assume the so-called balloon repayment, that is, the unusually large payment made at the end of the loan. This practice is not only related to overconfidence and excessive optimism, but also results from irrational preferences over time.[4] Decision makers mentally underweigh the meaning of the large balloon payment in the future, focusing more on current financial liquidity.

Similar to balloon repayment, refinancing of large amounts of maturity bonds clustering around the same date is often based on the assumption of rolling over, which consists in substituting old series of bonds with new issues. Particularly, replacement of a long-term debt with a subsequent issuance of short-term bonds, which might look cheaper, might turn out to be very risky. As the credit crunch of 2008 showed, such practice, based on the optimistic assumption that the firm will always have easy access to refinancing, might be potentially very harmful to the company and to the whole financial system. Graham, Harvey, and Puri (2013) provide empirical evidence showing that optimistic CEOs in fact use more short-term debt than their less optimistic colleagues.

The second category of biases related to debt issues has to do with anchoring. Borrowers and lenders use past financial terms as reference points for current terms. Dougal, Engelberg, Parsons, and Van Wesep (2012) find that current cost of borrowing is strongly influenced by the nominal level of historical borrowing costs, controlling for a variety of the firm's fundamental characteristics and market conditions that typically might impact financing costs. For example, companies that took out credit from a bank in the period 2005–2007, that is, in the pre-credit-crunch era, saw a smaller impact on their borrowing costs in the following year despite the drastic change in market conditions. Surprisingly, nearly one-third of the firms whose credit rating remained constant over this period received exactly the same borrowing rates as prior to the crisis, even if the market price of risk had changed a lot. Fundamentally similar firms that had not established such anchor terms before had to face much higher borrowing costs.

Anchoring to historical debt cost is a puzzling finding, because nearly all theories of corporate finance require that a firm's cost of capital be forward looking. Interest rates on new loans should depend upon the risk the firm runs and the market price of that risk. Because risk by definition is determined by future outcomes, theoretically there is no role for historical variables. Yet, historical interest rates do matter for current pricing of debt.

Dougal et al. (2012) show that the effect is strongest when the historical reference deal is more recent and when the firm borrows again from the same bank. However, when a firm changes its CEO or CFO, the effect of anchoring to past terms is diminished. This suggests that some kind of personal relationship is built between managers and bankers. When this link is broken, anchoring is not so much in evidence.

2.5. Risk (Mis)Management

Rational theories of corporate risk management have established conditions under which hedging financial risks adds value to the company because it reduces the effects of market frictions, such as taxes, bankruptcy costs, agency costs, information asymmetries, and undiversified stakeholders of the firm (see, inter alia, Stultz, 1984, 1996; Mello and Parsons, 2000). Traditional theories also assume that derivative contracts are fairly priced and that managers are rational and act in the best interests of shareholders. However, attempts to test the predictions of these theories empirically have met with only limited success (Tuffano, 1996; Mian, 1996; Geczy, et al., 1997).

There is growing evidence that many managers systematically incorporate their market views into corporate risk management programs. Stulz (1996) argues that this practice of selective hedging may be economically justified if the firm has private market information. But he also highlights the danger when some firms may engage in selective hedging by overestimating the superiority of their information relative to the market. Indeed, recent empirical evidence that, on average, firms fail to generate positive cash flows from selective hedging is consistent with the theory that managerial overconfidence may distort corporate decisions in the area of risk management.

Beber and Fabrii (2012) show that firms where the manager holds an MBA degree, is younger, and has less previous working experience, engage in more speculation. Adam, Fernando, and Golubeva (2009) demonstrate that managers increase their speculative activity when their derivatives portfolios yield positive cash flows, but do not reduce such activity when the portfolios yield losses. This behavior might be related to the selective attribution bias, on the one hand, and loss aversion, on the other. When derivative positions are generating gains, the manager attributes this to her superior knowledge, even if this is simply a matter of good luck. In the result, selective attribution induces higher confidence and inclines the manager to engage in more speculation in derivatives. Overconfidence also leads to excessive shifting of derivative positions, higher turnover, and higher transaction costs. Managers trade more aggressively based on the mistaken belief that they have a relative information advantage. On the other hand, when derivative positions are generating losses, managers attribute the situation to bad luck. Still, because of loss aversion, managers do not reduce their exposure to speculative positions and hope that the situation will change favorably in the future.

Brown, Crabb, and Haushalter (2006) and Adam et al. (2009) find that those managers who have hedged their underlying operations tend to systematically reduce their hedging positions when the market moves against them, even though the underlying net position remains unchanged. The reaction is asymmetric—when the market moves in favor of derivative positions, managers do not increase them. Again, such practices might be explained by behavioral biases, namely, mental accounting and loss aversion, status quo bias, and the theory of regret.[5]

Managers account losses from the derivative positions and gains from the underlying positions separately. They are more sensitive to losses on derivative positions than they are to gains. When it comes to traditional hedging rather than speculation, however, the status quo bias and the theory of regret become apparent and additionally impact managerial attitudes. The underlying position is typically related to the normal business operation of the firm. Generally speaking, the status quo bias inclines the manager not to take actions that depart from a given initial position. To have engaged in hedging in the first place, the manager must have overcome the status quo bias. When she discovers later that hedging was not beneficial in a given market situation, an unpleasant feeling of regret sets in. Wishing to avoid the feeling in the future, she decides to reduce the degree of hedging, that is, apply a lower hedge ratio in the following periods.

Overall, risk mismanagement and insufficient hedging due to behavioral biases are potentially dangerous and might be harmful to the wealth of shareholders.

3. Investment Decisions

In the area of investment decisions, managers become, in a sense, investors themselves, so it is justified to assume that they are prone to exhibit biases and inclinations similar to those typical for individual investors in the capital market.

Evidence is accumulating that overconfidence and excessive optimism do affect business investment, generally leading to overinvestment and a waste of resources. However, under special circumstances, overconfidence might be also considered beneficial as it allows to overcome risk aversion and to take up some valuable projects that otherwise would be rejected (startups, innovative R&D). What is more, the overall tendency to overinvest might be bounded by the amount of internal funds and the upper limit of debt available at a reasonable cost. On the one hand, overconfidence and optimism breed overinvestment—on the other, as explained in the earlier section, it causes aversion to external financing, which is particularly true for equity. Overconfident managers might sometimes prefer to resign from a project or even underinvest than issue new equity subjectively considered to be undervalued (Heaton, 2002; Malmendier and Tate, 2005a; Baker and Wurgler, 2013).

There are also other managerial biases that distort corporate investment decisions. Narrow framing might be responsible for evaluating investment projects in isolation while overlooking the bigger picture. This may lead to bottlenecks in supply channels or between different parts of production process. Loss aversion manifests itself in the form of sunk costs, that is, the inclination to continue investment projects that turn out to be unprofitable and should be canceled.

Managerial biases affecting financial policy, as described in the previous section, most often result in inappropriate exposure to financial risk, a situation that could potentially be detrimental to shareholders. It also results in direct waste of resources, albeit to a lesser extent. In the case of investment decisions, distortion impact of psychological traps is usually more evident in specific examples as it usually leads to misallocation of assets where losses are more apparent and measureable.

3.1. Startup Projects

Startup investment is typically very risky, as it often involves entering novel markets with innovative, unproved concepts or the use of pioneering technology. Seed financing funds apply the rule of thumb according to which one in ten projects at the early stage of development will turn out profitable. Scarpetta, Hemmings, Tressel, and Woo (2002) find that only half of startups survive for more than three years. Van Gelderen, Thurik, and Bosma (2005) follow a sample of 517 nascent entrepreneurs over the same period and find that only 195 ventures achieve any measure of success after three years.

Despite common agreement on the great amount of risk involved in startups and the evidence of many failures, managers running such projects tend to display a lot of confidence and optimism. In fact, Busenitz and Barney (1997) document that an exceptionally high level of overconfidence is a key trait that differentiates small entrepreneurs from managers in large corporations. Cooper, Woo, and Dunkelberg (1998) find that 68 percent of entrepreneurs think that their startup is more likely to succeed than comparable enterprises, while only 5 percent believe that their odds are worse, and over a third of entrepreneurs view their success as all but guaranteed. Likewise, the majority of managers in young high-tech firms surveyed by Corman, Perles, and Vancini (1988) perceive no risk in their prospect of success. In a multinational survey of entrepreneurs, Koellinger, Minniti, and Schade (2007) find that countries in which entrepreneurs display a high degree of overconfidence enjoy more startup activity, but also have higher failure rates.

Of course, high failure rates for startups do not result purely from overconfidence, but are predominantly driven by the nature of risk and uncertainty in this kind of ventures. One can say that reducing overconfidence would lead to fewer startups with higher survival and success rates, hence less resources wasted. However, many startups pave the way for some great innovations in everyday life. In this context, overconfidence and excessive optimism may actually play a positive role, as they push entrepreneurs to take action despite the overwhelming shadow of cases where others have failures. It may be that many sparking ideas would have never materialized if their chances of success had been diligently and rationally scrutinized. Typically, startup ventures have a high probability of failure or, at best, mediocre performance, and only little chance for an exceptional success.. The underdiversified nature of entrepreneurial engagement, both financial and personal (time, effort, reputation, opportunity costs), might have not been offset by the vision of potential high rewards in the positive scenario, if the probability of this scenario had not been biased upward by overconfidence and optimism.

3.2. Real Investment

Overconfidence and excessive optimism also may influence real investment in more mature corporations. Merrow, Phillips, and Myer (1981) compare forecast and actual construction cost for investment projects in the energy sector.

Statman and Tyebjee (1985) survey several other studies of this sort in the design of military hardware, drugs research, chemicals, and other development projects. Buehler, Griffin, and Ross (2002) provide numerous examples of incorrect estimation of the time required to complete planned large-scale public infrastructure investment. Lovallo and Kahneman (2003) provide more anecdotal evidence on delusions of success. They all conclude that optimistic biases in cost estimation and sales forecast are fairly widespread. Overconfident and optimistic managers initially evaluate investment projects too favorably, hence they tend to invest more than would be plausible under rational expectations. In many cases, this may lead to nonoptimal allocation of assets and a waste of resources.

Malmendier and Tate (2005a) perform cross-sectional tests of the effect of optimism on corporate investment. They use a proxy for managerial optimism based on executives' predisposition to voluntarily hold in-the-money stock options of their firm. The reasoning for such a proxy is that since the managers' professional life is already so much exposed to firm-specific risk, they should not increase their exposure additionally by holding in-the-money stock options. If managers do so, it may be interpreted as a strong sign of insider optimism. Using this proxy, Malmendier and Tate find that the sensitivity of investment to cash flow is higher in the case of more optimistic managers. It turns out to be highest in equity-dependent firms, that is, those which are constrained in new debt rising. In other words, more optimistic executives generally tend to invest more conditional, however, on available cash flows. Rational financiers may curb to some extent the managerial desire to overinvest by refusing to provide external financing, at least not at the price the overconfident manager expects. When internal funds are not enough and there is no debt available, overoptimistic managers refrain from issuing new equity, which they subjectively see as undervalued. This is consistent with optimism-driven pecking order of capital structure, as discussed in section 2.1 earlier in this chapter.

Similar findings are confirmed in Malmendier and Tate (2005b) with the use of a different proxy of overconfidence based on managers' press portrayals. This alternative approach to measuring overconfidence relies on the perception of outsiders rather than on the managers' own actions or self-perception.

Ben-David et al. (2007) use survey-based measures of overconfidence. Over six years, they collect a panel of nearly seven thousand observations of probability estimations made by top financial executives regarding the stock market. The striking result is that managers are, in fact, extremely miscalibrated: realized market returns fall within the executives' 80 percent subjective confidence intervals only 38 percent of the time. Using their survey-based measure of overconfidence, Bed-David et al. show that companies with overconfident CFOs use lower discount rates to value cash flows, and that they invest more.

Hirshleifer, Low, and Teoh (2012) investigate the relationship between managerial optimism and the level of research and development (R&D) spending. They use two proxies for overconfidence and optimism: one related to the amount of in-the-money stock options in the hands of managers, as in Malmendier and Tate (2005a), and the other one related to the way managers are described in the press, as in Malmendier and Tate (2005b). They find that managerial overconfidence is associated with riskier projects, higher volatility of stock prices, greater investment in innovation, and greater total quantity of innovation as measured by patent applications and patent citations even after controlling for the amount of R&D expenditure. In other words, the R&D investments of overconfident managers are more efficient in generating innovation. However, greater innovative output of overconfident managers is achieved only in innovative industries. The important question is, however, whether greater innovation translates into firm value creation. Hirshleifer et al. (2012) find some evidence that higher engagement of overconfident managers in R&D investment may actually result in higher firm value, again only in those industries where innovation is an important source of competitive advantage. Perhaps, in the case of R&D investment, overconfidence plays the same positive role as in startup projects. It biases upward the subjective probability of success and pushes managers to take up ventures that would be difficult to accept if diligently and rationally scrutinized. It also allows firms to exploit growth opportunities in innovative industries, albeit with remarkably higher risk (higher volatility of stock returns).

Overconfidence might turn out to be particularly dangerous if combined with loss aversion. Overconfident and optimistic managers initially evaluate investment opportunities too favorably and decide to invest in projects that, under rational expectations, should not have been taken up. When their estimates get a hard reality check and it becomes apparent that the project is not financially justified, they are reluctant to admit they have made a mistake and terminate the investment. Instead, overconfidence makes them believe that it is possible to find a positive solution to the situation, while loss aversion prevents them from seeing sunk costs as definite losses. Statman and Sepe (1989) find positive market reaction to termination of historically unprofitable investment ventures. Investors seem to recognize that managers have a tendency to continue poor projects and welcome the ability to overcome this inclination with a positive stock return. Shefrin (2001, 2005) offers several anecdotes concerning major corporate investment programs indicating the presence of the sunk cost bias. Importantly, examples provided by Shefrin show that even those managers who are among the company founders and hold a large portion of shares are also reluctant to terminate poor projects and admit to making a mistake. This suggests that agency problems are clearly not the only explanation of the sunk cost phenomenon. Guedj and Scharfstein (2008), who study R&D investment in the pharmaceutical industry, show that the sunk cost bias tends to be particularly strong in young single-project companies. Managers of such firms appear to be highly reluctant to abandon their only drug candidates, even when faced with unpromising clinical tests. This corresponds to the high level of overconfidence and optimism usually present in startups and young firms. Additionally, it might also result from the fact that termination of the only project might mean the end of the firm itself.

Bounded rationality also appears to be a plausible explanation for the managerial practice of investment project evaluation. In the efficient market theory, the net present value (NPV) criterion should be the optimal decision rule. Managers should only implement projects with a positive NPV—having a choice of two competing projects, they should, of course, prefer the project with a higher NPV. Using a discounting procedure, managers should apply a project specific rate reflecting the risk and the actual cost of capital of the given venture. It is only for common projects, not much different from normal activities of the firm, that the discount rate could be the firm-wide weighted average cost of capital (WACC).

Real managerial practices often differ from what is suggested in standard text-books on corporate finance. When evaluating projects, managers tend to follow simpler rules. In their survey of 103 large corporations, Gitman and Forrester (1977) find that only 10 percent of managers use NPV as a primary tool for project evaluation, while 54 percent use the internal rate of return (IRR) that does not require to estimate the cost of capital in order to discount forecasted cash flows. Stanley and Block (1984) find that 65 percent of respondents reported IRR as their primary capital budgeting technique. Graham and Harvey (2001), in their more extensive survey, also confirm that IRR is slightly more popular than NPV. Approximately three quarters of respondents declared they use IRR and NPV "always or almost always." However, over a half of managers also admitted they commonly use the payback period rule, an even less sophisticated technique that requires neither cost of capital input nor cash flow forecasts beyond a payback moment. Graham and Harvey also find that managers with high ownership stakes in a company are more likely to use the payback rule and less likely to rely on the NPV analysis. Hence, the tendency to use simpler project evaluation methods is unlikely to be an agency problem, that is, managers are not using easier techniques opportunistically to save time and effort. The original survey presented in chapter 9 of this book also indicates the high practical importance of IRR and payback rules for project evaluation.

Graham and Harvey (2001) also document that among managers who do use NPV analysis, most tend to apply a single company-wide discount rate rather than a project-specific rate. They found that 59 percent of the respondents declared they use "always or almost always" the company-wide discount rate, even though the hypothetical project most likely had different risk characteristics. Krueger, Landier, and Thesmar (2012) suggest that this practice causes significant investment distortions in multidivisional corporations. They document that division-level investment is positively correlated to the spread between the division's beta and the firm's average beta. In other words, by applying the same overall WACC to all projects, multidivisional firms tend to overinvest in high beta divisions and underinvest in low beta divisions.

3.3. Real Options

A real option is commonly defined as any decision that creates the right, but not the obligation, to pursue a subsequent decision. The idea of viewing corporate investment opportunities as real options has been around for nearly three decades (McDonald and Siegel, 1985, 1986). This approach has emerged in industries such as natural resources (Brennan and Schwartz, 1985) or real estate developments (Titman, 1985) where large investments with uncertain returns are commonplace. It is also popular in energy, IT, and life sciences sectors, as well as in the case of any investment with highly unsure or remote positive outcomes where traditional valuation techniques based on cash flow discounting are less helpful. A real-options perspective encourages both low-cost trials, where failure is not catastrophic, as well as taking strategic positions without tying up extensive amounts of resources. Used effectively, these options can minimize losses while preserving potential gains.

The real option approach is not easy to adopt, though. In practice, most real option problems must be solved with the use of various numerical methods. Relatively simple problems, involving one or two state variables can be solved using binominal or trinominal trees in one or two dimensions (Cox, Ross, and Rubinstein, 1979). But if problems are more complex and involve more variables and/or are path-dependant, it is necessary to use of Monte Carlo simulation methods (Longstaff and Schwartz, 2001) and more advance option pricing models (Black and Scholes, 1973; Merton, 1973b). The general problem is to compare the value of immediate option exercise with the conditional expected value of continuation. It requires predicting future states and attaching probabilities to each possible outcome. Obviously, the more complex the setting is, the more possibility for potential managerial biases, such as overconfidence, optimism, loss aversion, and others.

Overconfidence, understood here mainly as too-narrow-calibration, leads managers to overestimate the precision of the information they have, underestimate the possibility of negative scenarios, and, consequently, undervalue or even neglect the importance of real options, if there are any, built in a project. As a survey by Busby and Pitts (1997) shows, managers are sometimes ready to give up options, believing they reduce organizational commitment to a project. Excessive optimism leads to overestimation of potential positive future outcomes, irrationally increasing the conditional expected value of continuation. Howell and Jägle (1997) confirm in a laboratory setting that managers, although pricing their real options quite erratically, generally tend to be optimistic. Finally, loss aversion may play a similar role as in the case of sunk cost bias. The real option premium, that is, the initial investment already made, is generally perceived as a loss and might be sometimes difficult to sacrifice, inclining managers toward continuation.

Miller and Shapira (2004) provide evidence on a whole range of behavioral biases affecting real option valuation. They studied responses by *potential* managers, that is, students of an MBA program, given to a questionnaire that included real option problems expressed in the simplest terms possible. Each task involved only two possible outcomes for the values of the underlying assets and probabilities were set at 50 percent throughout the questionnaire. Despite the fact that the tasks were much easier than real-life complex situations, the answers given by respondents indicate specific biases affecting subjective valuations of options. Buyers and sellers price options below their expected values.

This naturally results from narrow calibration and the underestimation of risk. Puts are valued relatively lower than calls. This is consistent with framing and the prospect theory. Call options are framed in the domain of gains and reflect risk aversion while put options are framed in the domain of losses and reflect risk-seeking attitude, hence lower premium is associated to puts. Discount rates vary with the option time horizon giving some indication of hyperbolic discounting. Changes in option values do not fully reflect increases in exercise prices. This might result from cognitive conservatism and anchoring to earlier values. Finally, irrelevant outcomes have impact on the perception of option values.

Tiwana, Wang, Keil, and Ahluwalia (2007) document that managers associate real options with value only when the project's easily quantifiable benefits are low, but fail to do so when they are high. This might be interpreted in two ways. First, real options are valuable when it comes to overcoming ambiguity aversion. However, when ambiguity is relatively low, their value is neglected due to managerial overconfidence. Second, the real option approach might also be used as an excuse when a manager is not even able to estimate benefits from a potential project but still wants to invest in it driven by "intuition" or other biases.

3.4. Mergers and Acquisitions

There is rich empirical evidence indicating that mergers, on average, do not create any value for the bidding firms. Studies of share price movements on major stock markets in the period around takeover announcements show that target company shareholders typically experience large gains in wealth, but acquiring company shareholders do not. If there is some synergy generated by the merger, it tends to be handed over to the target shareholders in the form of the premium above current market valuation of their stock. Jensen and Ruback (1983) review the early literature on corporate control. Subsequent studies by Bradley, Desai, and Kim (1988) and Berkovitch and Narayanan (1993), and more recent works by Andrade, Mitchell, and Stafford (2001), Goergen and Renneboog (2004), and Moeller, Schlingemann, and Stulz (2005) support this view.[6]

In an effort to explain the price patterns of bidding and target firms around takeovers, Roll (1986) outlines a hubris-based theory of acquisitions. He suggests that successful acquirers are overconfident and optimistic in their valuation of deal synergies and fall victim to the winner's curse. An exuberant CEO bids too aggressively and is likely to overpay for the target, destroying the wealth of shareholders but satisfying her pride and ego. Roll argues that, on average, a takeover is associated with little or no change in combined value for the target and bidder firms.

An early attempt to link managerial overconfidence with merger activity is the work of Rovenpor (1993) who uses a kind of linguistic proxy to measure overconfidence. She relies on independent readers to rate confidence levels of executives based on their recent speeches. She finds the confidence of managers to be positively related to the number of acquisitions they attempt, the number of transactions they complete, and the dollar value of these transactions.

Hayward and Hambrick (1997) document that, after controlling for various known determinants of the acquisition premium, the size of premiums paid is highly associated with four proxies of CEO hubris: the recent performance of the acquiring firm, the recent media praise of the CEO, the compensation of the CEO relative to that of the next highest paid executive in the firm, and a composite factor of those three variables. They also show that the relationship between managerial overconfidence and takeover premiums is stronger when corporate governance seems to be weaker, that is, when there is a high proportion of insider directors on the board and the CEO is also the board chairman. They find that in the sample of 106 large transactions between 1989 and 1992, acquirers, on average, destroyed shareholders wealth, and the greater the CEO hubris and acquisition premiums, the greater the shareholder losses.

Malmendier and Tate (2008) use two different proxies for overconfidence: one based on executives' predisposition to voluntarily hold in-the-money stock options of their firm, the other based on managers' *press portrayals*. They argue that the odds of making an acquisition are 65 percent higher if the CEO is classified as overconfident, after controlling for various determinants of mergers, including size, cash flow, and Tobin's Q of the acquiring firm. The effect is largest if the merger does not require external financing, which corresponds to earlier findings of overconfidence being associated with investment sensitivity to internal cash flow.[7] The market seems to recognize the problem of managerial overconfidence and the danger of falling prey to the winner's curse. On average, the market's negative reaction to merger announcement is significantly stronger when the CEO exhibits signs of overconfidence than for nonoverconfident CEOs.

Ben-David et al. (2007) investigate the calibration ability of CFOs and find that those who are overconfident about long-term return distributions tend to engage in more acquisitions. Again, the market seems to notice the problem of managerial overconfidence. On average, the market reaction to transaction announcement in the group of bidders with overconfident CFOs is more negative than for the median firm.

Croci, Petmezas, and Vagenas-Nanos (2010), using similar methodology on stock option to Malmendier and Tate (2008) and merger data from the United Kingdom, confirm that highly overconfident CEOs lead their firms into more value-destroying acquisitions than their less confident counterparts.

John, Liu, and Taffler (2011) explore the parallel role played by overconfident target firm CEOs in explaining the takeover premium and value destruction in such deals. Using the same two proxy variables to measure CEO overconfidence as in Malmendier and Tate (2008), they confirm that overconfident acquiring firm CEOs pay more than nonoverconfident ones. On the other hand, overconfident target firm CEOs do not, on average, appear to be able to achieve a significantly higher bid premium. However, much more interestingly, the joint effect of acquirer and target firm CEO overconfidence is to raise the bid premium greatly. John et al. (2011) also show that not only acquiring firm

CEO, but also target firm CEO overconfidence has a significant impact on merger announcement returns. The three-day market reaction is most negative when both acquiring firm and target firm CEO overconfidence exist concurrently. The above evidence may suggest that when an overconfident bidder meets with an overconfident target, both sides are likely to overestimate potential gains from the merger. Additionally, the overconfident target's manager tends to bargain hard to secure the biggest possible portion of those "virtual" synergy gains for the target shareholders, because overconfidence and excessive optimism make the CEO subjectively perceive the market price of her stock to be too low. In other words, the overconfident target's manager expects to be paid a higher premium that not only reflects a willingness to participate in potential, overestimated synergy gains, but also offers some compensation for the perceived undervaluation of the firm. The overconfident acquirer also overestimates the synergy gains or her capability to extract value from the target that the current management was not able to realize. Hence she is ready to pay a lot to the target shareholders in order to succeed with the deal. As real merger gains turn out to be much smaller or even nonexistent, the transaction is harmful to the wealth of bidder shareholders.

Narcissism is a personal trait that is related to but distinct from overconfidence. The central idea of narcissism is that individuals are not only convinced about their superiority but also have a need to maintain a positive sense of self by engaging in ego-defensive high-stake activities. Liu (2009) provides an extensive literature review of narcissism among leaders and corporate managers. It turns out that negotiations in the process of mergers and acquisitions provide excellent environment for narcissism. Liu (2009) and Aktas, de Bodt, Bollaert, and Roll (2012) measure CEOs narcissism by investigating linguistic aspects of their speeches. Narcissistic CEOs are more likely to have initiated their transactions, and are more likely to be acquirers. Unfortunately, they maintain their high ego at the expense of shareholders. The narcissism of acquiring firm CEOs has a significant negative impact on the firm's announcement returns, as well as on long-term post-acquisition buy-and-hold returns. On the other hand, targets run by narcissists secure higher bid premiums possibly because narcissistic managers demand extra compensation for the loss of ego associated with losing control. Securing higher returns for their shareholders may give them the recognition needed to feed their superior self-perception.

Reference dependence is another very important managerial bias related to mergers and acquisitions. In particular, it involves the offer price that often takes into account not only the target's current market price, but also some salient and specific historical levels at which both bidder's and target's management as well as target's shareholders are likely to anchor. Prices from historical tender offers (e.g., defensive buybacks or competing bids) or recent peaks, such as the target's 52-week high, are typical candidates for strong reference points, despite the fact that, theoretically, they are economically irrelevant.

In this case, managerial biases are likely to coexist with shareholder biases and may be difficult to distinguish empirically. Managers anchor when they subjectively valuate the target firm and when they engage in negotiations. If they want to succeed with a deal, they should also take into account potential biases among target's shareholder and adjust the offer price accordingly. Target's shareholders anchor when they consider responding to a public tender offer or voting in favor of or against the merger. Similar to the disposition effect, they may resist selling at a "loss" to a recent peak, and may be more willing to sell if the offer price exceeds their threshold.

Baker, Pan, and Wurgler (2012) document that deal participants will in fact focus on recent price peaks. They investigate over 7,000 transactions between 1984 and 2007 and observe that offer prices clearly tend to cluster around a 13-week high, 26-week high, 39-week high, 52-week high, and 104-week high. They notice that "peak" price often serves not merely as a subtle psychological anchor but as one sufficiently heavy that there is no "adjustment" from it at all." (Baker et al., 2012, p. 50). The probability of accepting a deal increases discontinuously when the offer even slightly exceeds the 52-week high. Conversely, bidding-firm shareholders react increasingly negatively as the offer price is pulled upward toward that historical peak. There is a negative relation between the bidder announcement return and the component of the offer price that is driven by the 52-week high, which suggest that the acquirer's shareholders interpret this portion of the offer price as unjustified overpayment.

Gropp (2012) investigates 1602 European takeovers, mainly from the United Kingdom, in the period 1985–2011. He reconfirms findings of Baker et al. (2012) for the impact of historic reference peaks on bid prices, but fails to affirm that offer acceptance rate is discontinuously positively influenced by exceeding the reference points. This evidence hints that reference dependence might be more a managerial bias than shareholder predisposition.

The approach based on reference dependence may also help to explain why merger activity and stock market valuations are positively correlated: higher market valuations mean that more targets are trading closer to their peak prices. Therefore, these reference points may become easier to satisfy (from the perspective of targets) and to justify (from the perspective of bidders) when valuations are high. Conversely, when market valuations have recently plunged, targets may still anchor to high prior peaks and ask for valuations that are simply implausible to bidders under the new market circumstances. As a result, higher merger and acquisition activity is observed in bullish rather than bearish markets.

However, the above line of reasoning based solely on reference points and the disposition effect should predict higher volume but lower takeover premiums in prosperity periods and lower volume but with higher premiums in bad times. This was clearly not the case in late 1990s and at the turn of the millennium when market was very hot and premiums were still at the highest in the capital market history. It is possible that at that time reference dependence was overridden by high level of optimism and irrational exuberance, to use Shiller's (2000) expression, on the side of both bidder and target.[8]

CHAPTER 9

Managerial Practice

In previous chapters, we discussed the theoretical background and empirical evidence behind the actual behavior of market participants, that is, investors and corporate managers. With respect to corporate managers, first, we showed how rational managers may attempt to exploit investor irrationality and market inefficiency (chapter 7). Later, we argued that not only investors, but also corporate managers might be subject to psychological biases and act irrationally (chapter 8).

This chapter presents the original empirical research on the real-life practice of corporate managers in the main areas discussed in the earlier part of the book. We survey CEOs and CFOs of publicly listed companies regarding their financial decisions, investment projects evaluation, earnings management, and—last, but not least—what managers perceive as important to investors.

1. Methodology

1.1. Purpose and Scope of the Study

The aim of the empirical study was to examine selected aspects of managerial practice out of the full range discussed in chapters 7 and 8. Elements to be covered by the study were selected on the basis of how important their potential influence on corporate behavior was. In the area of financial decisions, we investigate factors influencing the decision to go public, the choice between equity and debt financing, and the steadiness of the capital structure policy. In the area of investment policy, we look at project evaluation methods, seek for evidence of the sunk cost effect, and consider nonfinancial factors influencing investment decisions. Further, we investigate motives and methods of earnings management. Finally, we ask managers what they think is important for investors when they value their stock.

For each of the above elements of the study, proper research hypotheses were constructed in such a way as to either confirm or deny the presence of a given phenomenon or to check the significance of selected factors influencing managerial decisions. Detailed hypotheses are formulated in individual subsections of the study that follows.

1.2. Survey Design and Sample

In our investigation, we employed a survey methodology. The questionnaires came either in the traditional hard copy or electronic format as a specially designed webpage with multiple choice options and rankings. All the ranks used in the survey were transformed so that the greatest (lowest) value represents the most (least) important item. Preliminary analysis indicated that responses from the different forms of the survey, that is, hard copy or webpage, were not statistically different. Therefore, we present the combined results.

The research procedure was organized in such a way as to guarantee anonymity of the participants. It is obvious that revealing true corporate practices in publicly listed companies is highly sensitive, so the fact of anonymity was emphasized strongly to participants in order to encourage them to give honest answers.

Invited to participate in the survey were chief executive officers (CEOs) and chief financial officers (CFOs) of companies listed at the main market of the Warsaw Stock Exchange (WSE) and the alternative market NewConnect (NC) also run by the Warsaw Stock Exchange in Poland. Typically, the firms listed in the alternative market are younger, less mature, and smaller, but usually have a higher growth potential. We present combined results where preliminary analysis showed that responses from WSE and NC were not statistically different,. When there are differences between the two groups, we present results in subsamples and try to identify reasons for the disparity. We excluded from our sample firms from the financial sector due to their different characteristics and their specific business approach.

The invitation letter was mailed to 749 companies, and was followed by e-mails and phone calls in order to increase the number of responses.[1] Managers were also motivated to participate in the survey by the promise that each filled-in questionnaire would result in a fixed charity donation. The last question in the survey asked about the preferred charity purpose and the one with the largest number of votes was to receive the whole sum of money depending on the number of active participants. The survey was carried out between December 12, 2012 and January 11, 2013.

The response rate in our survey was 16.2 percent, which compares favorably with other surveys of financial executives. For example, Trahan and Gitman (1995) obtained a 12 percent response rate in a survey mailed to 700 CFOs, and Graham and Harvey (2001) obtained a 9 percent response rate for 4,400 faxed surveys. Graham, Harvey, and Rajgopal (2005) and Brav, Graham, Harvey, and Michaely (2005) obtained 10 and 16 percent response rates, respectively. Eventually, a total of 121 surveys were carried out. Not all questionnaires were completed in the full. Hence the number of answers is slightly different between individual questions. Our sample should be considered as a convenience sample of cases available for study rather than as representative of the entire population of corporate managers, although the relatively high response ratio could give grounds to treat it as a representative sample of managers from firms listed in the Warsaw Stock Exchange. However, as Statman (2007) shows, managerial behavior and ethical standards may vary across countries depending on different social and cultural environments.

We investigated for possible nonresponse bias and concluded that our sample was representative of the population of managers from firms listed in the Warsaw Stock Exchange, excluding the financial sector. As no nonresponse bias was identified in terms of distribution of key variables (e.g., company size, industry, etc.), we may assume a certain randomness in nonresponse to the survey invitations.

1.3. Procedures for Testing Statistical Hypotheses

In general, two types of significance tests were carried out for each type of questions (ranked or single-answer) that appear in this chapter. For ranked ones, a two-stage procedure was applied, starting from the Friedman test[2] and followed by the Wilcoxon pair-by-pair post-hoc test.[3] However, if the first test resulted in no variability between item averages, the second test was not performed. This procedure was chosen as it was necessary to compare average ranks among items, while basic assumptions for ANOVA (e.g., normal distribution, interval scale) were not held. In contrast, applied tests are nonparametric and no additional assumptions about the nature of distribution needs to be met. This two-stage procedure was carried out in R language and environment.[4]

The second test type was a chi-square test. This was applied to single-answer questions in two situations: (1) to test independence between two variables on the basis of their joint distribution; and (2) to test uniformity of the variable.

In each section, test results are preceded by the corresponding exhibits including basic sample statistics (frequencies and descriptives).

It turned out that answers to some questions in the survey lack statistical significance. Nevertheless, we attempt to draw some cautious conclusions, bearing in mind that they may sometimes be speculative. We allow this lack of scientific rigor for two reasons. First, to present some interesting hints that may give incentive for further research, which hopefully will provide clearer findings in the future. Second, in some cases, our statistically weak results get support from other empirical evidence and therefore might look a bit more justified.

2. Financial Decisions

2.1. Factors Influencing the IPO Decision

Managers were asked to rank the following factors that potentially had influenced their decision to go public :

- financing needs of the company,
- shareholders' need to divest partially or totally from their stakes,
- favorable stock market situation, thus possible higher IPO valuation,
- desire to capitalize the firm's good historical financial results, and
- intention to strengthen the image of the company (PR and marketing effect).

The results of the survey presented in Exhibits 9.1 and 9.2 indicate that the most important driver for the decision to go public was the need for capital. This factor was ranked number one by nearly 33 percent of responding managers and it also enjoyed the highest average rank. This finding is in line with the classical approach to finance. Generally, companies issue equity and go public when their financing needs exceed their internal financing means and debt-capacity levels. However, what may be astonishing is that the financing need was the least important consideration for more than 21 percent of firms in the sample.

The second most important factor by the average rank was the desire to capitalize the firm's good historical result. It was the most important reason for 25 percent of firms going public. Managers tend to time the public offer to coincide with the moment when they can boast very good reported results. They hope that analysts and investors will extrapolate the favorable past into the rosy future, hence the IPO valuation will be high. The evidence on the extrapolation bias among market participants suggests that the bet might be actually right as investors are likely to be misled by historical good performance of the firm (see section 1.1 in chapter 3).

Timing in accordance with the situation of the firm seems to be closely related to the timing of the market situation. Between these two factors, the average ranks are not statistically different at 90 percent confidence level. Similar to surveys by Graham and Harvey (2001) and Brau and Fawcett (2006), our managers also admitted that positive general market conditions, thus possible higher valuation, was an important choice determinant in their timing of the equity offering. In fact, it was the most important reason for over 18 percent of firms in our sample.

Exhibit 9.1 Rank distribution among items and rank parameters
Question: Which of these factors was responsible for the decision to go public?

Items	Percentage of answers indicating rank value					Rank statistics		
	1	2	3	4	5	N	Mean	Standard deviation
(1) Financing needs of the company	21.1	11.4	18.4	16.7	32.5	114	3.28	1.537
(2) Shareholders' need to divest partially or totally from their stakes	14.8	21.7	29.6	22.6	11.3	115	2.94	1.223
(3) Favorable stock market situation, thus possible higher IPO valuation	18.1	15.5	30.2	17.2	19.0	116	3.03	1.351
(4) Desire to capitalize on the firm's good historical financial results	14.7	25.0	14.7	20.7	25.0	116	3.16	1.426
(5) Intention to strengthen the image of the company (PR and marketing effect)	29.6	26.1	8.7	20.9	14.8	115	2.65	1.463

Note: Respondents were required to order all the above-mentioned items. The highest rank was assigned the value 5 and the lowest was assigned the value 1. No ties were accepted. Cases with missing values were excluded.

Exhibit 9.2 Results of Friedman and Wilcoxon tests
Question: Which of these factors was responsible for the decision to go public?

Friedman Test statistic value: 3.1449
p-value: 0.01446
Wilcoxon post-hoc paired test

		Item				
		1	2	3	4	5
	1	x				
	2		x			
Item	3			x		
	4				x	
	5	**			*	x

Note: The null hypothesis for the Friedman test states that the difference between the mean rank profile and the global mean rank (equal to 3) is zero. The null hypothesis for the Wilcoxon post-hoc test states that the mean difference between a given pair is zero. Item numbers correspond to the items in parenthesis in exhibit 9.1. Exhibit 9.2 presents relationships between all pairs of items in terms of statistical significance in mean rank difference: ***, **, and * indicate significance at the level of 0.01, 0.05, and 0.1, respectively. Empty cells indicate no significant difference.

Both firm-specific timing and market-specific timing are aimed at exploiting possible overvaluation of the company going public. In the result, post-IPO long-term returns should be low. If the firm-specific timing component was in place, the firm might disappoint in terms of future operational results (Jain and Kini, 1994; Mikkelson, et al., 1997; Pagano et al., 1998) and there will be abnormal negative stock returns, that is, returns lower than that from other companies comparable in terms of risk and other characteristics (Ritter, 1991, 2003; Loughran and Ritter, 1995). On the other hand, if the market-specific (or industry-specific) timing component was predominant at the IPO date, absolute stock returns are likely to be low in the future. In this scenario, firm-specific negative abnormal returns might not be significant, as the correction of mispricing occurs in the whole market or at least in a given industry. Obviously, both firm-specific and market-specific timing are no good for long-term investors participating in public offers.

The willingness to divest stock by current shareholders was fourth in the ranking of factors influencing the IPO decision. It was not the top priority (11 percent of responses), but it was not of the least importance either (15 percent). It is worth explaining that pre-IPO owners often cannot immediately capitalize on the favorable market valuation either due to selling restrictions (lock-up periods declared when going public), or because the information about a major shareholder disposing of stock just after the firm went public could harm the valuation.

Finally, a potential public relations and marketing effect related to the fact of being publicly listed appeared to carry the least weight in the eyes of managers. This factor had the worst average rank. It was below all other averages and significantly below item (1) and (4). Over 29 percent of managers indicated it as the least important and only nearly 15 percent as a top priority.

Overall, the survey documents that the most vital reason to go public is financing need. However, firm-specific and market-specific timing in order to capitalize potentially high valuation of the firm also seem to play an important role.

2.2. The Choice between Equity and Debt

The next point of the survey was to verify the importance of selected factors for the fundamental choice between issuing new equity or taking more debt in order to finance the firm's expansion. First, we investigated if managers looked back at stock pricing over the last 12 months (market-timing hypothesis), considered the direct short-term impact of their decision on current pricing (managerial short-termism), or were interested in long-term value creation. Additionally, we asked managers if they took into account the impact of their decision on corporate ratios such as earnings-per-share (EPS) or return on equity (ROE). These ratios will of course look different depending on the choice between new equity and new debt. Typically, dilution of EPS, at least in the short term, suggests that managers should refrain from new equity issues. Similarly, a higher degree of financial leverage results in higher ROE, encouraging more debt. However, increased debt financing also results in higher financial risk. Therefore, we also asked managers if they considered the aspect of risk while making the choice between equity and debt financing.

It turned out that managers, while making the choice to issue new equity or new debt, mostly considered the firm's valuation retrospectively in the last 12 months (Exhibit 9.3). This factor had the highest average rank and also the highest number of indications as number one (nearly 26 percent). It might be supposed that managers were more likely to issue new equity after the stock price had been rising, and they would prefer to issue debt after the stock had lost a lot of value in the preceding 12 months. Such reasoning is in line with earlier surveys by Graham and Harvey (2001), and Brau and Fawcett (2007). These results constitute yet another manifestation of managerial market timing, as also suggested by Baker and Wurgler (2002).

The second highest average rank was assigned to the immediate impact of the decision on current stock pricing. Even if only 17 percent of respondents indicated it as number one, it was often pointed as number two or three to be considered. Only 12 percent of managers perceived it as the least important concern. On the other hand, the long-term influence of capital structure decision on firm valuation was indicated most often as the third in the line and was also the third by the average rank. However, the long-term implication of the capital structure decision was of the least importance for nearly 24 percent of managers, a figure that seems to be quite high.

To a lesser extent, managers cared about how the choice between issuing new equity or debt was going to impact financial ratios such as EPS or ROE. The average rank placed this aspect in the fourth position, and there was almost an equal number of managers indicating this factor as the most and the least important (22 and 21 percent, respectively).

Exhibit 9.3 Rank distribution among items and rank parameters
Question: What factors would you consider most when making the choice to issue new equity or new debt?

Items	Percentage of answers indicating rank value					Rank statistics		
	1	2	3	4	5	N	Mean	Standard Deviation
(1) Your company stock pricing during the last 12 months	17.4	15.6	19.3	22.0	25.7	109	3.23	1.438
(2) Potential short-term impact of your decision on the current stock pricing	11.9	25.7	23.9	21.1	17.4	109	3.06	1.286
(3) Potential impact of your decision on company valuation within the period longer than 12 months	23.6	10.9	26.4	19.1	20.0	110	3.01	1.437
(4) Impact of your decision on such corporate ratios as earnings per share (EPS) or return on equity (ROE)	21.1	26.6	13.8	16.5	22.0	109	2.92	1.473
(5) Impact of your decision on the financial risk of the company	25.7	20.2	16.5	22.0	15.6	109	2.82	1.435

Note: Respondents were required to order all the above-mentioned items. The highest rank was assigned the value 5 and the lowest was assigned the value 1. No ties were accepted. Cases with missing values were excluded.

Exhibit 9.4 Results of Friedman test
Question: What factors would you consider most when making the choice to issue new equity or new debt?

Friedman Test statistic value: 1.9495
p-value: 0.2912

Note: The null hypothesis for the Friedman test states that the difference between the mean rank profile and the global mean rank (equal to 3) is zero. As the null hypothesis was not rejected at 0.05 significance level, further Wilcoxon post-hoc tests were not performed

Surprisingly, the least consideration was given to the level of financial risk. This factor had the lowest average rank and also the highest number of responses indicating the least importance (nearly 26 percent). According to the classical trade-off theory, firms have an incentive to increase the degree of financial leverage as long as the danger of insolvency does not offset the benefits of the tax shield. In that line of reasoning, consideration of the level of risk ought to be the essential element in the choice between new equity or debt. Still, it appears to be far down on the list of managerial considerations.

Overall, the survey gives some indication that managerial inclinations to timing and short-termism are more important in the debt/equity choice than the commonly believed trade-off between maximization of ROE and the acceptable level of financial risk. However, conclusions regarding ranks of preferences in this question should be drawn carefully due to the low statistical significance of the results (Exhibit 9.4).

2.3. The Target Capital Structure

We ask how managers perceive their capital structure policy. Do they have a fixed debt-to-equity ratio or do they act opportunistically and use more debt or more equity depending on current market conditions. If they have a target capital structure, do they think the firm has already reached the optimal level and tend to stick to it, or do they rather set the target toward which the firm moves slowly rebalancing from time to time.

Results in Exhibit 9.5 show that less than 16 percent of respondents in the overall sample indicated that the firm had already reached the optimal capital structure and tended to stick to it. However, answers in this case differed significantly between the group of firms from the main market of the Warsaw Stock Exchange (almost 24 percent) and the group from the alternative market NewConnect (only 4 percent). The difference is highly significant statistically. This should come as no surprise if one remembers that firms listed in the alternative market are typically younger and less mature. It is unlikely that such firms have already achieved the optimal ratio of debt and equity.

Most managers admitted that their firm had a target capital structure at which they aimed rebalancing from time to time. Such an answer was given in over 56 percent of cases in the overall sample and in 53 and 61 percent in the WSE and the NC subsamples, respectively. (The difference between WSE and NC is not statistically significant.) This finding is in line with the studies by Leary and Roberts (2005), Kayhan and Titman (2004), and Flannery and

Exhibit 9.5 Conditional distribution and significance tests

Question: Mark only one answer that best fits the situation of your company regarding capital structure:

	WSE		NewConnect		Total	
	Count	%	Count	%	Count	%
My company has reached optimal capital structure and generally sustains it	17	23.6	2	4.1	19	15.7
My company has a target optimal capital structure at which we are aiming, rebalancing from time to time	38	52.8	30	61.2	68	56.2
The optimal capital structure of the company is not defined; we use more equity or more debt depending on current market conditions	17	23.6	17	34.7	34	28.1
Total	72	100.0	49	100.0	121	100.0

Chi-square test of uniformity of margin distribution

Chi-square statistics 31.256

Degrees of freedom 2

Significance: 0.01

Note: The null hypothesis that margin distribution of row variable is uniform is rejected.
Note: Comparison of adjusted residuals (Z-scores test) between two columns WSE and NC indicates statistical difference on the first item only.

Rangan (2006), who also find that firms rebalance toward a target. Welch (2004) and Huang and Ritter (2009) argue that rebalancing to the target is slow, so deviations from the optimal level are long lived.

However, a relatively high portion of managers admitted to an opportunistic behavior. Over 28 percent of respondents in the overall sample (and nearly 24 and 35 percent in the WSE and the NC subsamples, respectively—the difference is not statistically significant) stated that the target capital structure is not defined, and financing with debt or equity depends on current market situation. This is yet another manifestation of managerial opportunism and market timing, as argued by Baker and Wurgler (2002).

2.4. Money Illusion in Capital Structure

Managers were also surveyed on how they understood the capital structure. They were asked to choose between the definition based on *book* values of debt and equity and the definition based on *market* values of debt and equity.

As we can see in Exhibit 9.6, most managers (almost 64 percent) correctly associated the capital structure with market values. However, a surprisingly large portion of managers (over 36 percent) answered that their understanding of capital structure is based on book values. According to the accounting standards, equity and debt are registered in books in historical values that might significantly differ from current market values. It is appalling that such a big portion of managers admitted to evaluating their capital structure on the basis of historical values rather than current market prices. This distortion may lead to potentially serious consequences and various nonoptimal corporate decisions.

This unjustified attachment to book values might be seen as another manifestation of the so-called money illusion. Earlier studies in economic psychology showed that even experienced decision makers might sometimes have problems with making the right distinction between the nominal and real value of money. People usually attach too much weight to the nominal value of money, underestimating the importance of the real value (see section 1.1. in chapter 2).

Exhibit 9.6   Distribution and significance test
Question: Which one of the below-mentioned definitions of capital structure is closer to you?

	Count	%
The capital structure is defined by relation of the equity book-value to the debt book-value	44	36.4
The capital structure is defined by relation of the equity market-value to the debt market-value	77	63.6
Total	121	100.0
Chi-square test of uniformity of the distribution		
Chi-square statistics 9.0		
Degrees of freedom: 1		
Significance: 0.01		

Note: The null hypothesis that the variable is uniformly distributed across items is rejected.

3. Investment Evaluation

3.1. Methods of Project Evaluation

Managers were asked to rank the following project evaluation methods according to the importance they assign to them in their practice:

- NPV analysis, using as a discount rate the weighted average cost of capital (WACC) of the entire company,
- NPV analysis, using as a discount rate the weighted average cost of capital (WACC) for the project considered,
- internal rate of return (IRR),
- payback period from the investment, and
- other assessment tools (in this case, respondents were asked to specify).

The evaluation method that received the highest average rank was the internal rate of return (IRR). It was closely followed by calculation of the payback period. This method was ranked on average slightly below the IRR (the difference is not statistically significant), although it was indicated more often as number one (20 and 25 percent of cases, respectively). Net present value (NPV) analysis came next in managers' responses. Managers attributed slightly higher meaning to NPV calculation based on the average weighted cost of capital (WACC) estimated separately for the considered project rather than for the entire firm. In fact, this approach is more accurate, though the use of the overall WACC of the firm is also correct as long as the considered project is not drastically different from the average firm operations in terms of risk. It is worth noting that, although it was

Exhibit 9.7 Rank value distribution among items and rank parameters
Question: Please rank the following methods of project evaluation, according to your practice

Items	Percentage of answers indicating rank value					Rank statistics		
	1	2	3	4	5	N	Mean	Standard deviation
(1) NPV analysis, using as a discount rate the weighted average cost of capital (WACC) of the entire company	12.7	30.0	15.5	12.7	29.1	110	3.15	1.447
(2) NPV analysis using as a discount rate the weighted average cost of capital (WACC) for the project considered	13.4	17.0	23.2	24.1	22.3	112	3.25	1.339
(3) Internal rate of return (IRR)	6.3	16.1	29.5	27.7	20.5	112	3.40	1.166
(4) Payback period from the investment	4.4	30.7	18.4	21.9	24.6	114	3.32	1.264
(5) Other assessment tools	60.7	4.7	12.1	13.1	9.3	107	2.06	1.453

Note: Respondents were required to put all of the above-mentioned items in the order of priority. The highest rank was assigned the value 5 and the lowest was assigned the value 1. No ties were accepted. Cases with missing values were excluded.

Exhibit 9.8 Results of Friedman and Wilcoxon tests
Question: To assess projects efficiency, I use:

Friedman test statistic value: 6.1681
p-value: 3.152e-09
Wilcoxon post-hoc paired test

		Item				
		1	2	3	4	5
	1	x				
	2		x			
Item	3			x		
	4				x	
	5	***		***	***	x

Note: The null hypothesis for the Friedman test states that the difference between the mean rank profile and the global mean rank (equal to 3) is zero. The null hypothesis for the Wilcoxon post-hoc test states that the mean difference between a given pair is zero. Item numbers correspond to items in parenthesis in exhibit 9.7. Exhibit 9.8 presents relationships between all pairs of items in terms of statistical significance in mean rank difference: ***, **, and * indicate significance at the level of 0.01, 0.05, and 0.1, respectively. Empty cells indicate no significant difference.

generally in the fourth position by the average rank, the NPV calculation based on the WACC estimated for the entire firm was viewed as the most important method by as many as over 29 percent of the respondents. Conclusions about the first four ranks should be treated with caution as the results are hardly significant statistically (Exhibits 9.7 and 9.8). Other evaluation tools seemed to play a much smaller role. Among additional techniques specified by managers, a strategic approach to project evaluation was the most represented one.

Our results are generally in line with earlier studies. For example, in the survey of 103 large firms by Gitman and Forrester (1977), 54 percent of managers indicated IRR as the primary project evaluation method. Stanley and Block (1984) found that 65 percent of respondents reported IRR as their primary capital budgeting technique. Graham and Harvey (2001) reported that 75 percent of CFOs always or almost always used NPV analysis, and 76 percent declared using IRR always or almost always. The last study also documented that most firms would use a single company-wide discount rate to evaluate the project. In addition, 59 percent of the respondents would always or almost always use the company-wide discount rate, even though the hypothetical project would most likely have different risk characteristics.

3.2. Sunk Cost Effect

The next task in the survey was aimed at identifying potential managerial biases related to the sunk cost effect. Managers were asked to imagine the following situation:

Imagine you are in charge of an investment project in which you have already invested 5 million dollars with no chance to recoup this sum. The primary budget of this project was planned at 10 million dollar. Unfortunately, in the course of project implementation you receive information that, due to unforeseen items, the project will require an additional sum of 15 million before it is finished, making the total new budget of the project reach 25 million. What steps will you undertake? Please select only one answer.

- I calculate the NPV of the project within the new budget taking into account total investment outlays, including the 5 million already spent, and decide to continue the project if the new calculated NPV is greater than zero. However, if the new calculated NPV is less than zero, I decide to stop the project and write off the 5 million.
- I calculate the NPV of the project within the new budget taking into account only investment outlays left to be completed, and decide to continue the project if the new calculated NPV is greater than zero. However, if the new calculated NPV is less than zero, I decide to stop the project and write off the 5 million.
- I skip the NPV calculation and verify whether the project will bring profits after its completion. If so, I decide to continue the project regardless of the increased budget. Otherwise I decide to stop and write off the 5 million.
- I do not want to write off the 5 million, and decide to continue the project till it is completed. Even though the project seems presently unprofitable, I expect the future market conditions to change favorably so that the project is profitable again the investment outlays and investment outlays can be recovered.

Results presented in Exhibit 9.9 show that only less than half of managers (just below 45 percent) correctly answered that they would calculate the NPV of the project within the new budget taking into account only investment outlays left to be completed, and decided to continue the project if the new calculated NPV was greater than zero.

Nearly 16 percent of managers were more restrictive. They indicated they would calculate the NPV of the project within the new budget taking into account total investment outlays, including the 5 million already spent, and decided to continue the project if the new calculated NPV was greater than zero. Otherwise they were ready to stop the project and write off 5 million of the initial outlays.

On the other hand, a relatively large group of respondents (nearly 36 percent) admitted that they would not use the NPV method at all, but would simply check if the project was likely to be profitable, and if so, they would continue it regardless of the increased budget. In this approach, managers focused on the aspect of profits, but overlooked the notion of money in time, risk, and the relation of the amount profits to the amount of investment outlays. Potential future profits were enough justification to continue the project, even if achieving the profits meant higher investment outlays. Economically, taking into account the time value of money and risk, it might not have made sense to continue the project.

Exhibit 9.9 Distribution and significance test

Question: Imagine you are in charge of an investment project in which you have already invested 5 million dollars with no chance to recoup this sum. The primary budget of this project was planned at 10 million dollar. Unfortunately, in the course of project implementation you receive information that due to unforeseen items the project will require an additional sum of 15 million before it is finished, making the total new budget of the project reach 25 million. What steps will you undertake? Please select only one answer:

	Count	%
I calculate the NPV of the project within the new budget taking into account total investment outlays, including the 5 million already spent, and decide to continue the project if the new calculated NPV is greater than zero. However, if the new calculated NPV is less than zero, I decide to stop the project and write off the 5 million.	19	15.7
I calculate the NPV of the project within the new budget taking into account only investment outlays left to be completed, and decide to continue the project if the new calculated NPV is greater than zero. However, if the new calculated NPV is less than zero, I decide to stop the project and write off the 5 million.	54	44.6
I skip the NPV calculation and verify whether the project will bring any profits after its completion. If so, I decide to continue the project regardless of the increased budget. Otherwise I decide to stop and write off the 5 million.	43	35.5
I do not want to write off the 5 million, and decide to continue the project till it is completed. Even though the project seems presently unprofitable, I expect the future market conditions to change favorably so that the project is profitable again and investment outlays can be recovered.	5	4.1
Total	121	100.0

Chi-square test of uniformity of the distribution

Chi-square statistics 31.256

Degrees of freedom: 3

Significance: 0.01

Note: The null hypothesis that the variable is uniformly distributed across items is rejected.

Few managers (4 percent) showed a very strong determination to complete the project. They were ready to spend another 20 million in order not to recognize the 5 million loss, despite the fact that, under current market conditions, the project seemed to be unprofitable. Still, they hoped the future market conditions would change favorably so that the project was profitable again and investment outlays could be recovered.

Overall, the survey showed mixed evidence regarding the treatment of the sunk costs. Only less than half of managers presented a correct approach to the problem. There was a group of overrestrictive managers who would include the sunk cost in the calculation of the new NPV, and thus possibly were ready to abandon the project too early. On the other hand, there was over twice as big a group of managers who declared they would skip the NPV calculation and focus on potential profits from the project that would justify its continuation. This could be seen as a managerial bias resulting from the reluctance to recognize losses from the sunk costs. However, very few managers admitted they were very much determined not to write off the sunk cost and were ready to continue the project even if currently it seemed to be unprofitable.

3.3. Nonfinancial Factors in Project Evaluation

Managers were also asked to rank nonfinancial factors potentially influencing them to take up a new investment project. These were:

- My competitors in the same sector have successfully carried out similar projects.
- Other companies have successfully carried out similar projects, although these projects are outside of my core business.
- Investment of the same kind as the project in question is appreciated by investors, and information about taking up such a project by other companies brought about stock price rise.
- Considered project will enjoy a positive response in the mass media and will improve the image of the company and its products within the target group.
- This project meets the expectations of an important company shareholder.

As we can see in Exhibit 9.10, managers attached highest importance to the fact that their competitors had successfully carried out similar projects. The

Exhibit 9.10 Rank distribution among items and rank parameter

Question: Apart from the positive result of the financial analysis, the following premises convince me to start a new investment project:

Items	Percentage of answers indicating rank value					Rank statistics		
	1	2	3	4	5	N	Mean	Standard deviation
(1) My competitors in the same sector have successfully carried out similar projects	20.5	11.6	14.3	23.2	30.4	112	3.31	1.519
(2) Other companies have successfully carried out similar projects, although these projects are outside of my core business	21.1	21.1	23.7	21.1	13.2	114	2.84	1.334
(3) Investment of the same kind as the project in question is appreciated by investors and information about taking up such a project by other companies brought about stock price rise	21.1	21.9	22.8	14.9	19.3	114	2.89	1.410
(4) Considered project will enjoy a positive response in mass-media and will improve recognition of the company and its products within the target group	18.3	20.9	16.5	21.7	22.6	115	3.10	1.439
(5) This project meets the expectations of an important company shareholder	18.6	23.0	20.4	17.7	20.4	113	2.98	1.408

Note: Respondents were required to put all the above-mentioned items in the order of priority. The highest rank was assigned the value 5 and the lowest was assigned the value 1. No ties were accepted. Cases with missing values were excluded.

factor received the largest number of indications as the number one consideration (over 30 percent), and it was also the most important by the average rank. There might be a strategic reason (e.g., fighting for the market share or to gain competitive advantage) why managers pay attention to what their competition does and are likely to engage in similar projects. However, there might also be an element of herding in corporate investment decisions. Observing that the competition carried out a similar project with success, a manager may deduce that such an investment is worth undertaking. This line of reasoning is not necessarily wrong, as long as it is accompanied by independent diligent analysis. However, if the manager bases his decision predominantly on observation of the actions taken by the competition rather than his own information, it may lead to inefficient investment and misallocation of resources. First, the specific situation of the firm might differ from the situation of its competitors. For example, firms may have different competences, resources, and cost structures, including the cost of capital. Further, market space might be limited so that first players in the niche are likely to have a privileged position. Therefore, a project valuable to one firm does not have to be good for another, even if both firms compete in the same industry. Managerial herding may lead to overlooking of these details.

The survey also revealed that managers took into account the media coverage related to their potential investment projects. They hoped for positive PR and marketing effects leading to greater recognition of their products in the target group. On average, this factor was ranked second.

Catering to investor sentiment and preferences seemed not to be tremendously important for project evaluation. Expectations of an important shareholder were identified as the most vital aspect by 20 percent of respondents and, on average, were ranked third. General consideration of investor inclinations and the market reaction to similar project announcements was most important only to 19 percent of managers, ranking fourth on average.

The least consideration was given to projects outside of the firm's core business that had been successfully carried out by other firms.

Overall, the survey did not allow for drawing strong conclusions regarding nonfinancial factors influencing the evaluation of an investment project. The differences between average ranks were not statistically significant (Exhibit 9.11). Only comparison to successful projects run by competitors seemed to stand out in importance among suggested factors, based on the highest number of first-rank indications.

Exhibit 9.11 Results of Friedman test

Question: Apart from the positive result of the financial analysis, the following premises convince me to start a new investment project:

Friedman Test statistic value: 2.4092

p-value: 0.1126

Note: The null hypothesis for the Friedman test states that the difference between mean rank profile and global mean rank (equal to 3) is zero. As the null hypothesis was not rejected at 0.1 significance level, further Wilcoxon post-hoc tests were not performed.

4. Earnings Management

Earnings management is a very sensitive part of corporate practice. In some cases, the line between discretional accounting measures and fraudulent illegal behavior might be very thin. Additionally, earnings management typically receives a lot of scrutiny by external auditors.

In the survey, managers were asked about their motives and the employed techniques of earnings management. The assumption of no adverse actions or reservations from the firm's auditor was clearly communicated in the questionnaire. Respondents were also assured that their answers were totally anonymous.

4.1. Motives behind Earnings Management

Managers were requested to select one answer that would best fit their practice from the following options:

- I engage in earnings management to maximize reported results.
- I try to adjust reported results to the forecasts and/or market expectations—both when the actual result is higher or lower than forecasted.
- I try "to smooth out" periodic fluctuations by slightly diminishing the results in favorable periods and increasing them slightly in poorer periods.
- I engage in earnings management when the actual result is slightly lower than forecasted and I need to meet the forecasts.
- I engage in earnings management only when the actual result is slightly negative and I want to avoid reporting a loss.
- I never engage in earnings management.

Exhibit 9.12 Distribution and significance test

Question: If I have an opportunity to influence by accounting means (assume no auditor reservations), the final level of reported results in a given period:

	Count	%
I would engage in earnings management to maximize the reported results	8	6.6
I would try to adjust the reported results to the forecasts and/or market expectations—both when the actual result is higher or lower than forecasted	5	4.1
I would try "to smooth out" periodic fluctuations by slightly lessening the results in favorable periods and slightly increasing the results in poorer periods	26	21.5
I would engage in earnings management, when the actual result was slightly lower than forecasted and I wanted to meet the forecasts	8	6.6
I would engage in earnings management only when the actual result is slightly negative and I want to avoid reporting a loss	13	10.7
I would never engage in earnings management	61	50.4
Total	121	100.0

Chi-square test of uniformity of the distribution

Chi-square statistics 115.6

Degrees of freedom: 5

Significance: 0.01

Note: The null hypothesis that the variable is uniformly distributed across items is rejected.

Only half the number of surveyed managers denied getting involved in earnings management at all (Exhibit 9.12). Nearly 22 percent declared earnings smoothing, and 11 percent confessed that they might have manipulated the results in an attempt to avoid reporting a loss. Just below 7 percent of respondents admitted to earnings management if they wanted to avoid reporting below the forecasts, and exactly the same number of managers stated they engaged in earnings management in order to maximize reported results.

Generally, the results indicate stronger motivation to manipulate earnings in order to avoid reporting a loss than to meet the forecasts. This is in line with earlier studies, for example, Degeorge, Patel, and Zeckhauser (1999). What might be a bit surprising is that managers were more likely to smooth earnings than to potentially engage in earnings management to avoid reporting a loss. However, earnings smoothing need not necessarily be harmful to shareholders as it leads to lower stock price volatility (See section 3.1. in chapter 7).

4.2. Techniques of Earnings Management

In the next section of the survey, managers were requested to assume they wanted to increase reported figures and asked to rank suggested techniques of earnings management according to what they found most adequate and preferable. The list of techniques was as follows:

- avoiding costs in a given period by shifting necessary cost-generating activities to the next period;
- avoiding costs recognition in a given period by shifting the formal delivery/invoice date to the next period, even if services or goods were mostly delivered in the reporting period;
- avoiding costs recognition in a given period by applying accruals;
- revaluation or sale of assets booked historically below their fair market value, and generation of one-time profit by this opportunity;
- recognizing in the current reporting period all revenues from transactions whose completion deadline exceeds the reporting period; and
- reversing of provisions and reserves made in previous periods, as long as some justification may be found.

Results in Exhibit 9.13 show that many managers were willing to reverse provisions and reserves from previous periods, as long as at least some justification might have been found. This method was indicated as number one in the largest number of questionnaires (almost 28 percent). Its average rank, however, came in the second place. The highest average rank was assigned to cost avoidance by postponing necessary cost-generating activities till the next period. This method was indicated as the most preferable by 26 percent of managers, and it was ranked second by the same number of respondents. The difference between the top two average ranks was not statistically significant.

Exhibit 9.13 Rank distribution among items and rank parameters
Question: If I have an opportunity to influence the final level of financial results in a given reporting period through accounting (assume no auditor reservations):

Items	Percentage of answers indicating rank value						Rank statistics		
	1	2	3	4	5	6	N	Mean	Standard deviation
(1) Avoid costs in a given period by shifting necessary cost-generating activities to the next period	8.3	13.0	12.0	14.8	25.9	25.9	108	4.15	1.640
(2) Avoid costs recognition in a given period by shifting the formal delivery/invoice date to the next period, even if services or goods were mostly delivered in the reporting period	12.1	14.0	21.5	23.4	18.7	10.3	107	3.53	1.507
(3) Avoid costs recognition in a given period by applying accruals	9.3	20.6	29.0	17.8	15.0	8.4	107	3.34	1.420
(4) Revaluation or sale of assets booked historically below their fair market value, and generation of one-time profit by this opportunity	23.4	14.0	15.9	16.8	18.7	11.2	107	3.27	1.719
(5) Recognize in the current reporting period all revenues from transaction whose completion deadline exceeds the reporting period	25.9	25.0	10.2	16.7	3.7	18.5	108	3.03	1.816
(6) Reverse of provisions and reserves made in previous periods, as long as some justification may be found	21.3	11.1	11.1	10.2	18.5	27.8	108	3.77	1.936

Note: Respondents were required to put all the above-mentioned items in the order of priority. The highest rank was assigned the value 6 and the lowest was assigned the value 1. No ties were accepted. Cases with missing values were excluded.

Manipulation to cost timing by postponing the formal acceptance of delivery or delaying the date of the invoice was ranked third on average, and it was also indicated as third in the highest number of answers (nearly 21 percent).

Avoidance of cost recognition by applying accruals came fourth by the average rank. It was also indicated as fourth in the largest number of answers (nearly 26 percent). The relatively low rank of earning management techniques related to accruals, although a bit surprising, coincided with the answers given in section 5.2 of the survey. The fact that managers were convinced that the figure of accruals was important to and hence closely monitored by investors might have stopped them from using this item to manage earnings in order not to make their intentions apparent.

Exhibit 9.14   Results of Friedman and Wilcoxon tests
Question: If I have the opportunity to influence the final level of financial results in a given reporting period through accounting (assume no auditor reservations):

Friedman test statistic value: 4.3499
p-value: 0.0002056
Wilcoxon post-hoc paired test

		Item					
		1	2	3	4	5	6
	1	x					
	2		x				
Item	3	**		x			
	4	**			x		
	5	***				x	
	6						x

Note: The null hypothesis for the Friedman test states that the difference between the mean rank profile and the global mean rank (equal to 3.5) is zero. The null hypothesis for the Wilcoxon post-hoc test states that mean difference between a given pair is zero. Item numbers correspond to the items in parenthesis in exhibit 9.13. Exhibit 9.14 presents relationships between all pairs of items in terms of statistical significance in mean rank difference: ***, **, and * indicate significance at the level of 0.01, 0.05, and 0.1, respectively. Empty cells indicate no significant difference.

Revaluation or sale of assets whose book value was below the market value allowing for the recognition of an extraordinary gain was next in manager preferences. Finally, immediate recognition of all revenues from transactions spread over time was, on average, the choice of the last resort. However, despite the lowest average rank, it was indicated as the most preferable method in as much as almost 17 percent of answers.

The differences between average ranks were statistically significant between item (1) and items (3), (4), and (5), while there was no significant difference among other pairs of items (Exhibit 9.14).

5. Managerial Beliefs about Investor Focus on Information

In this section we investigate managerial convictions about what investors look at while evaluating the stock. It is important to know what managers think investors pay attention to, because it is a good indicator of what managers are likely to care about most if they want the firm to look good in investors' eyes.

5.1. Profit and Loss Accounts or Cash Flows Statements

First, we check what managers think about the importance of different levels of profit and loss accounts and cash flows statements to investors. What ranks higher in investors' books: total sales, EBITDA, net profit, operating cash flows, or total free cash flows? Managers were requested to rank the above elements according to their subjective beliefs about what was important to investors—not necessarily what they personally perceived as fundamental.

The results in Exhibits 9.15 and 9.16 do not allow to draw clear conclusions. The average ranks for net profit, total sales, and EBITDA came very close, and the differences between the three averages were not statistically significant. Net profit was indicated as the most important element to investors in more than 27 percent of the responses. However, it was also marked as the least important in almost 22 percent of cases. The total level of sales was ranked first in 24 percent and EBITDA in 19 percent of answers. Overall, managers perceived the

Exhibit 9.15 Rank distribution among items and rank parameters.
Question: When evaluating the company, investors pay most attention to the following elements of financial statements:

Items	Percentage of answers indicating rank value					Rank statistics		
	1	2	3	4	5	N	Mean	Standard deviation
(1) Total sales	18.4	16.7	17.5	23.7	23.7	114	3.18	1.441
(2) EBITDA	14.8	18.3	24.3	23.5	19.1	115	3.14	1.330
(3) Net profit	21.9	14.0	18.4	18.4	27.2	114	3.15	1.512
(4) Operating cash flows	17.4	25.2	20.0	21.7	15.7	115	2.93	1.342
(5) Total free cash flow	27.2	25.4	18.4	13.2	15.8	114	2.65	1.414

Note: Respondents were required to put all the above-mentioned items in the order of priority. The highest rank was assigned the value 5 and the lowest was assigned the value 1. No ties were accepted. Cases with missing values were excluded.

Exhibit 9.16 Results of Friedman and Wilcoxon tests
Question: When evaluating the company, investors pay most attention to the following elements of financial statements:

Friedman Test statistic value: 2.4949
p-value: 0.09171
Wilcoxon post-hoc paired test

		Item				
		1	2	3	4	5
	1	x				
	2		x			
Item	3			x		
	4				x	
	5	*				x

Note: The null hypothesis for the Friedman test states that the difference between the mean rank profile and the global mean rank (equal to 3) is zero. The null hypothesis for the Wilcoxon post-hoc test states that mean difference between a given pair is zero. Item numbers correspond to the items in parenthesis in exhibit 9.15. Exhibit 9.16 presents relationships between all pairs of items in terms of statistical significance in mean rank difference: ***, **, and * indicate significance at the level of 0.01, 0.05, and 0.1, respectively. Empty cells indicate no significant difference.

figure of net profit to be the most important to investors, followed by the value of EBITDA and the amount of total sales. The belief that sales and EBITDA are less informative to investors may result from the fact that these figures show general business performance on operating level. Net profit is a more comprehensive measure, for example, it depends on financial costs and depreciation that are often firm-specific and relatively fixed. On the other hand, however, it might be influenced by one-off items. Net earnings are also used in common comparative valuation techniques, and the popularity of price-to-earnings ratio multiple seems to be greater than, for example, EBITDA multiple.

It is worth noting that EBITDA was perceived as more important to investors than operating cash flows. Nevertheless, the difference between the average ranks of EBITDA and operating cash flows was not statistically significant. EBITDA differs from operating cash flows mainly by the changes in working capital. Although, EBITDA is an informative measure about the company's operating profitability, it does not capture potential problems with growing levels of receivables or inventory that might be early signs of worse operating performance. These aspects are typically better visible in operating cash flows. Still, EBITDA is commonly used in simple comparative valuation methods (EBITDA multiple), and it was probably for this reason that managers perceived it as more important to investors than operating cash flows.

Total free cash flows were indicated as the weakest evaluation criterion investors look at. It received the lowest average rank and it was also ranked last in the largest number of responses (over 27 percent). On the one hand, the figure of total free cash flows is a very comprehensive measure and is likely to be influenced by many components. On the other hand, however, it indicates how much of free cash is available and might potentially be distributed to shareholders. Still, managers perceived total free cash flows to be of the least importance to investors. Statistically, there was a significant difference between average ranks of sales and total free cash flows, but only at the level of 0.01.

5.2. Balance Sheet Items

In the next step we focus on accounting measures related to the balance sheet. We wonder what is more important to investors: the value of tangible assets, the total value of assets, the amount of short-term liabilities, the total amount of liabilities, or accruals. Similar to the previous section, managers were requested to rank the above elements according to their subjective beliefs about what was important for investors, and not according to what they personally found fundamental.

The results presented in Exhibits 9.17 and 9.18 do not allow to draw clear conclusions. The average ranks for the total value of assets and the sum of accruals came very close, and the differences between the two averages were not statistically significant. Despite the slightly higher average rank assigned to the total value of assets, the amount of accruals was indicated more often as the most important feature to investors (respectively, 20 and 23 percent; the difference is not statistically significant). The high rank of accruals is a

Exhibit 9.17 Rank distribution among items and rank parameters.

Question: When evaluating the company, investors pay most attention to the following elements of financial statements:

Items	Percentage of answers indicating rank value					Rank statistics		
	1	2	3	4	5	N	Mean	Standard deviation
(1) Value of tangible assets	27.0	20.9	14.8	13.0	24.3	115	2.87	1.548
(2) Total value of assets	13.0	22.6	20.0	24.3	20.0	115	3.16	1.335
(3) Amount of short-term liabilities	16.5	21.7	20.9	23.5	17.4	115	3.03	1.350
(4) Total amount of liabilities	22.8	21.1	19.3	21.1	15.8	114	2.86	1.401
(5) Accruals	20.9	12.2	24.3	19.1	23.5	115	3.12	1.446

Note: Respondents were required to order all the above-mentioned items. The highest rank was assigned the value 5 and the lowest was assigned the value 1. No ties were accepted. Cases with missing values were excluded.

Exhibit 9.18 Results of Friedman test

Question: When evaluating the company, investors pay most attention to the following elements of financial statements:

Friedman Test statistic value: 1.3825
p-value: 0.639

Note: Null hypothesis for the Friedman test states that the difference between mean rank profile and global mean rank (equal to 3) is zero. As the null hypothesis was not rejected at 0.05 significance, further Wilcoxon post-hoc tests were not performed.

bit surprising. However, it might be the reason why managers seemed not to like accruals as a tool to manage earnings, as it was unexpectedly revealed in section 4.2 of the survey. If managers were convinced that the figure of accruals was important to and hence closely monitored by investors, then they were not likely to use this particular technique in order not to make their earnings management apparent.

The high rank of total assets might indicate that managers perceived company size to be an important feature for investors. Parallely, the bottom rank of total liabilities suggests that the amount of total assets was not associated with valuation, because total liabilities were not perceived to be very significant to investors. If the value of assets were the proxy of valuation, then of course it would have to be the net value of assets, that is, less the total amount of liabilities. As managers perceived total assets to be important and total liabilities not to be important for investors, one can suppose that total assets were rather the proxy of size. In other words, it might be concluded that managers were convinced that investors pay relatively high attention to the size of a company.

It is also worth mentioning that the amount of short-term liabilities was considered by managers to be more crucial for investors than the amount of all liabilities, yet the difference between those two average ranks was not statistically significant. This is understandable as the level of short-term liabilities is crucial to the current liquidity of the company, and hence to the likelihood of bankruptcy.

Finally, the total amount of assets was considered by managers to be much more important for investors than the amount of fixed assets. Fixed assets, as typically more durable, could potentially be seen as a driver of value by investors. However, this view was not shared by the surveyed managers.

5.3. Information Sources

In this section we investigated managerial beliefs about major sources of investors' information. Managers were requested to rank the following items, according to what they thought was important for investors in the process of firm evaluation:

- historical financial statements and reported results of the company;
- official managerial forecasts of company's future results;
- current press releases from the company;
- analysts' recommendations about the company; and
- news about general condition of the market and the economy, and other information nonspecific to the company.

Results are presented in Exhibits 9.19 and 9.20. Managers perceived the official forecasts of future results of the company, on average, as the most vital kind of

Exhibit 9.19 Rank distribution among items and rank parameters
Question: When evaluating the company, investors pay most attention to:

Items	Rank value					Rank statistics		
	1	2	3	4	5	N	Mean	Standard deviation
(1) Historical financial statements and reported results of the company	23.5	13.4	18.5	18.5	26.1	119	3.10	1.520
(2) Official managerial forecasts of company's future results	10.8	20.0	22.5	25.0	21.7	120	3.27	1.301
(3) Current press releases from the company	21.0	21.8	24.4	18.5	14.3	119	2.83	1.342
(4) Analysts' recommendations about the company	21.8	23.5	21.8	11.8	21.0	119	2.87	1.438
(5) News about general condition of the market and the economy, and other information nonspecific to the company	22.3	17.4	19.0	24.0	17.4	121	2.97	1.420

Note: Respondents were required to put all the above-mentioned items in the order of priority. The highest rank was assigned the value 5 and the lowest was assigned the value 1. No ties were accepted. Cases with missing values were excluded.

Exhibit 9.20 Results of Friedman test

Question: When evaluating the company, investors pay most attention to:

Friedman Test statistic value: 2.1261

p-value: 0.2089

Note: The null hypothesis for the Friedman test states that the difference between the mean rank profile and the global mean rank (equal to 3) is zero. As the null hypothesis was not rejected at 0.05 significance level, further Wilcoxon post-hoc tests were not performed.

information for investors. This item enjoyed the highest average rank, but was ranked first by less than 22 percent of respondents and actually received the highest number of indications as the second most important factor (25 percent of answers).

Historical financial statements and reported results were perceived to be the next important source of investors' information. This item ranked second by the average, but was indicated at the top position by the highest number of respondents (26 percent). The difference between the first and second average ranks was not statistically important.

Next, managers ranked the general condition of the market and the economy and other information nonspecific to the firm. This kind of information was seen as more important than current press releases from the company or analysts' recommendations about the firm. The difference between the third average rank and two lower ranks, however, was not statistically significant. At first glance, it might be a bit puzzling when one remembers that managers were asked about the relevance of various information sources for investors in the process of evaluating *the firm*, not the general market conditions or economic perspectives. However, information about particular stock behavior might also be deduced from news related to the general situation in the economy and in the capital market. For example, some stocks are more sensitive to the macroeconomic cycle than others or have higher covariance with the market changes (higher betas). It might also be the case that some categories of stocks are simply more in fashion than others depending on the general market sentiment, and so on.

Two bottom average ranks, that is, analysts' recommendations and current press releases by the firm, were not significantly different. Managers perceived these two kinds of information, on average, as being of less importance for investors. Analysts' recommendations were more often placed at the top of the ranking (21 percent) than press releases (only 14 percent). Nonetheless, analysts' recommendations were also quite often ranked as the least important (nearly 22 percent).

CHAPTER 10

Heuristics and Biases among Corporate Managers

In chapter 2, we presented psychological aspects of decision making as well as various heuristics and biases. Certain phenomena previously described in the psychology literature were later transposed onto economics and finance in an attempt to explain the real behavior of market participants. Typically, most of the focus on the irrational behavior of investors.

This chapter presents the original empirical evidence on the existence of selected psychological biases in the other group of market participants, that is, among corporate managers. We survey CEOs and CFOs of publicly listed companies to check for overconfidence and optimism, problems with probability estimation, and managerial approach toward risk.

1. Methodology

1.1. Purpose and Scope of the Study

The aim of the empirical study was to examine whether some of the psychological phenomena, described earlier in chapter 2, also exist among corporate managers. It is important to confirm psychological heuristics and biases in this group of decision makers, as it might be the root of irrational managerial practices, as discussed in chapter 8. Items to be covered by the study were selected on the basis of the importance of their potential influence on corporate behavior. The investigated biases belong to each of the three main groups of errors identified in the Generalized Behavioral Model (see chapter 5). Overconfidence and managerial optimism represent problems with processing of information signals, difficulties with probability estimation correspond to representativeness errors, and the variable approach toward risk relates to unstable preferences.

For each of the mentioned items of the study, proper research hypotheses were constructed in such a way as to either confirm or deny the presence of a given phenomenon in the group of surveyed managers. Formal hypotheses are presented in individual subsections of the study that follows.

1.2. Survey Design and Sample

The study on psychological phenomena in managerial behavior was a part of the same survey as the one described in chapter 9. Therefore, the general design of the research and the sample were alike. The construction of questions was slightly different. We did not use rankings, but only multiple choice options and estimation tasks. Questions were grouped in a separate section of the questionnaire. This section was preceded by clear instructions telling participants they should answer according to their best knowledge or intuition.

Similar to the earlier section of the survey, we investigated if responses were statistically different depending on the form of the questionnaire (hard copy or webpage based) or if they were different in the group of managers from the main market of the Warsaw Stock Exchange compared to the NewConnect alternative market. Preliminary analysis indicated no statistically significant differences. Therefore, we present the combined results.

1.3. Procedures for Testing Statistical Hypotheses

A variety of tests was performed in order to verify different forms of null hypotheses, depending on the testing situation. Exhibit 10.1 presents statistical

Exhibit 10.1 Statistical testing procedure

Query	Null hypothesis	Test statistic and theoretical distribution under null hypothesis
Is there any answer that stands out in the distribution of the variable?	Distribution of the variable is uniform. For discrete variables, it means equal frequencies in each distribution cell. A special case of this testing situation refers to dichotomous variables, where null hypothesis is formulated as $p_1=p_2=0.5$, where p is the frequency of an item.	Chi-square statistic with degrees of freedom equal to the number of cells minus one minus the number of estimated parameters
Does the mean of the variable differ from zero (or other fixed value)?	Mean value of the variable is equal to zero. In a general case, zero is substituted by a fixed value.	One sample t-test, where statistic has t-student distribution with degrees of freedom equal to the number of observations minus one. If the variable is non-negative, the test is one-sided.
Does the mean of the variable between two groups differ?	Difference between the two groups is equal to zero	Independent sample t-test, where statistic has t-student distribution with degrees of freedom equal to the number of observations minus two
Do the means of the two variables differ?	Difference between the means of the variables is equal to zero	Two-sided paired sample t-test, where statistic has t-student distribution with degrees of freedom equal to the number of observations minus two. Missing cases are eliminated listwise.

testing procedure employed in this chapter. The first column describes the type of research query formulated in a general form. The second column contains formal descriptions of the null hypothesis. The last column presents information about the theoretical distribution under the null hypothesis.

2. Overconfidence and Managerial Optimism

Overconfidence can be based on four possible reasons: a belief in being better than average, a calibration bias, an unrealistic optimism, and an illusion of control (see Section 1.2 in chapter 2). The study focused on the first three.

2.1. Above-Average Effect

When making assessments and constructing beliefs about reality, people often consider their knowledge and skills to be above the average. We checked if this cognitive bias was also present in the group of managers from publicly listed companies. We asked two separate sets of questions: one was related to how managers self-assess their knowledge and capabilities in more general fields; the other focused specifically on self-assessment of managerial qualifications. The two sets of questions were positioned in different parts of the questionnaire and were formulated in a slightly different manner in order to limit the impression that they might be related to each other.

At the first stage, managers were required to mark statements that reflected their own conviction about their skills and capabilities. The task was formulated in the following way:

Please, mark the statements reflecting your personal opinion:

- I am/I am not*) more competent at economy than an average top manager.
- I have better/worse*) understanding of politics than an average top manager.
- I have better/worse*) knowledge of culture than an average top manager.
- I have a better/worse*) sense of humor than an average top manager.
- I am more/less*) perceptive while watching a movie than an average spectator.
- I am more/less *) lucky at lotteries than an average player*) mark the correct answer.

The first four statements included a comparison of personal features to an average person from the same environment, that is, to an average top manager. The last two compared personal characteristics to the general population, that is, to an average spectator or an average player. The statements differed also by the scope of compared competences, starting with knowledge closely related to what managers actually do (economy), to knowledge somehow related to business (politics), to something totally nonrelated (culture). We checked also for self-perception in areas that have not so much to do with knowledge about a subject, but rather with the intellect and personal qualities (sense of humor, being perceptive). The last statement (luck) was a kind of control question, clearly indicating to respondents the randomness of the compared future.

Statements were designed so that in each of the groups there should have been more or less the same number of answers identifying respondents as above and below average for a given population ($H_0 : p = 50\%$). If the percentage of people convinced of their above-average capabilities significantly exceeded 50 percent, it showed that at least part of the respondents were overconfident and overestimated their skills in comparison with others ($H_1: p > 50\%$). On the other hand, if "below-the-average" answers prevailed significantly, it meant at least part of the respondents were underconfident and underestimated their capabilities ($H_2: p < 50\%$).

Results of the experiment presented in exhibit 10.2 give grounds for several interesting observations. First, managers demonstrated strong above-average beliefs in the domain of economy. It is worth emphasizing they were convinced their economic knowledge was above average compared to other top professionals, and not to laypeople. On the other hand, underconfidence was revealed in the area of culture. Nearly 70 percent of managers felt less competent in cultural matters than their average peers. Such findings correspond with research by Lundenberg, Fox, and Punccohar (1994) and Hayward, Shepherd, and Griffin (2006), who argue that the phenomenon of overconfidence occurs especially in those areas in which respondents specialize. On the contrary, underconfidence might appear in fields that respondents are typically weak in. This is despite the fact that comparisons are made to peers of the respondents and not to the general population.

Results regarding the area of politics or characteristics such as sense of humor and being perceptive or lucky were not statistically different from 50 percent. Hence, in those facets, no underconfidence or overconfidence was formally revealed.

Exhibit 10.2   Self-perception of corporate managers in various areas of life

Statement	Count	%	Chi-square test
I am more competent at economy than an average top manager	86	85.1	***
I have better understanding of politics than an average top manager	45	44.6	
I have better knowledge of culture than an average top manager	31	30.7	***
I have a better sense of humor than an average top manager	46	45.5	
I am more perceptive while watching a movie than an average spectator	43	42.6	
I am more lucky at lotteries than an average player	45	44.6	
Total	101		

Note: Percentages in the count column do not sum to 100 due to multiple choice type of the question. For each item the following null hypothesis was tested: mean value = 50 percent, ***, **, and * indicates significance at the level of 0.01, 0.05, and 0.1, respectively.

In another section of the questionnaire, we asked managers directly about self-evaluation of their managerial competences. The task was formulated in the following manner:

How do you assess your own competences in the field of management against other top-level managers from publicly listed companies? Please, mark one of the two statements:

- I think that my competences are *above* the average qualifications of other top executives in publicly listed companies.
- I think that my competences are *below* the average qualifications of other top executives in publicly listed companies.

Similar to the earlier experiment, the proportion of managers marking each answer should not be different from 50 percent ($H_0 : p = 50\%$). If the percentage of managers convinced of their above-average competences significantly exceeded 50 percent, it showed that at least part of them were overconfident ($H_1: p > 50\%$). On the other hand, if below-the-average answers prevailed, it meant at least part of the respondents were underconfident ($H_2: p < 50\%$).

The experiment provided direct evidence of the above-average effect in the group of managers from publicly listed companies (Exhibit 10.3). Over 69 percent of respondents claimed they had better managerial competences than the average among peer top professionals. This is in line with earlier evidence. For instance, Lichtenstein and Fischhoff (1977) provide examples of how experts are much more likely to fall into the trap of overconfidence than laypeople. Stael von Holstein (1972) documents the above-average phenomenon among stock market professionals.

Overall, the survey confirmed the above-average effect among corporate managers, but only in those areas which they are supposed to be good at. Managers indicate their superior competences even if they are clearly instructed that they should compare to the average in *their* group.

Exhibit 10.3 Self-evaluation of managerial skills

	Count	*%*
I think that my competences are *above the average* qualifications of other top executives in publicly listed companies	84	69.4
I think that my competences are *below the average* qualifications of other top executives in publicly listed companies	37	30.6
Total	121	100.0
Chi-square statistic value 18.256		
Degrees of freedom 1		
Significance: ***		

Note: Null hypothesis that distribution is uniform, that is, proportions in % column equals to 50%, was rejected at 0.01 significance level.

2.2. Calibration Bias

The calibration bias is another form in which overconfidence may be demonstrated by the managers. Generally, when asked to provide information or make a forecast within a certain confidence range, people give answers which indicate that they are overconfident about the precision of their knowledge. Forecasters assess the probability of events wrongly, usually overestimating the chances of a predicted incident.

We tested for calibration bias in the following way. We asked managers to make their best guess as to how much the price of their stock would rise or fall within the next three months and within the next twelve months. Similarly, we asked how much the market index WIG20 would change in three and twelve months. Managers were also requested to estimate the probability of each scenario.

For the time being, we skip the results regarding forecasted future prices and index levels till the next section of this chapter. At present, we will focus only on probability estimates (exhibit 10.4). If there is no calibration bias, probability estimates for the long term should be lower than that for the short term. There are more factors potentially influencing the stock price or the market index in a longer period, hence the precision of the forecast should be lower in the longer term. We checked for the differences between averages of probability estimates in short- and long-term periods for the following scenarios: rise of the market index, rise of the stock price, fall of the market index, fall of the stock price.

Let us remember that managers were asked to make their *best guess* of the market index or the stock price changes. Hence, they were asked to give forecasts to which they could assign highest probabilities in each scenario. Theoretically, they should have exhibited higher precision of forecast in the short rather than the a long term. However, it seems that respondents did not take into account that their long term forecasts were, by definition, likely to be less precise. They tended to assign slightly higher probabilities to their best guesses in the long horizon than in the short term. Statistically, however, there is no significant difference between realization probability assigned to short- and long-term forecasts. Our tests are powerful enough to discover such a difference if one existed. The lack of difference between short- and long-term forecast precision might be interpreted as a demonstration of the calibration bias. These conclusions are in line with De Bondt (1998) who found that people asked to make long-term predictions tend to show more confidence than those asked for predictions in the short term.

It is also worth noting that probability estimates were significantly higher for predictions of stock price changes than for index changes in the short term. This might have been the result of overconfidence, but not necessarily. On the one hand, it is possible that managers overestimated their influence on the future stock price of the firm they controlled and underestimated the impact of general market conditions. However, higher probability estimates might have also been a rational result of insider information that managers are likely to

Exhibit 10.4 Forecasts of market changes and stock price changes in 3 and 12 months with estimated probability of forecast realization

Direction of change	Item	Short-term prediction			Long-term prediction			p-values difference in probabilities (short vs. long)
		% of answers	Mean change in %	Mean probability	% of answers	Mean change in %	Mean probability	
Rise	market index	70.9	7.6	51.9	80.4	32.3	55.3	0.165
	stock price	90.3	15.3	58.3	90.3	25.0	55.6	0.223
Fall	market index	29.1	−7.7	60.9	19.6	−13.3	56.6	0.378
	stock price	9.7	−9.8	63.4	9.7	−15.5	65.0	0.529
Overall	market index	–	–	54.5	–	–	55.5	0.654
	stock price	–	–	58.8	–	–	56.5	0.289
Sig. of difference in absolute index change (market rise vs. fall)		–		–		***	–	
Sig. of difference in absolute stock price change (stock rise vs. fall)		–	*	–		*	–	
Sig. of difference of probabilities (market index vs. stock price)		–	–	*	–	–		

Note:

(1) Differences between mean probabilities between short and long term were tested by paired-samples *t*-test with null hypothesis stating that means between short and long term are equal.

(2) Differences between mean probabilities between WSE and stock were tested by paired-samples *t*-test with null hypothesis stating that means between WSE and stock are equal.

(3) Due to low numbers of responses predicting fall of the stock price, the power of *t*-test for differences between averages in this case was too low to draw any conclusions. To overcome this difficulty some stronger non-parametric test was needed. Whitney-Mann test was carried out to test hypothesis about means equality.

(4) Differences between mean rise/fall of market index/stock were tested by independent-samples *t*-test with null hypothesis stating that means between rise and absolute value of fall of market (stock) indices are equal
*,**,*** indicate that the difference between means deviates from zero at 0.1, 0.05, and 0.01 significance level, respectively.

have about their firm. It is impossible to clearly differentiate between those alternatives.

Another interesting observation is that probability estimates were significantly higher for forecasts of falls than those predicting rises. The tendency was similar for predictions concerning market changes as well as stock prices. In other words, pessimists, although in minority, were more confident about their predictions and assigned higher probabilities to their negative scenarios. This aspect will be elaborated further in section 2.5.

2.3. Optimism Regarding Future Market Returns

Overconfidence and, in particular, above-average beliefs may lead to ungrounded optimism. People who consider themselves to be better than average are usually also overoptimistic. Given this, we first asked managers to generally predict if the market was going to rise or fall in the next three and twelve months. Following the general answer about the future direction, they were asked to make their best guess as to how much the main market index WIG20 would rise or fall in the time horizon of three and twelve months. Managers were requested to assess the probability of each scenario which allowed us to calculate the expected value of the index change in the short- and long-term periods. The expected value of the index change was calculated in the following way: the predicted index change was multiplied by the probability assigned to a given change by each respondent; and the mean of the products constituted the expected value of the index change.

Exhibit 10.5 reveals that 71 percent of managers expected the stock market to rise in the next three months. They forecasted, on average, the return of 7.6 percent and a moderate probability of realization at approximately 52 percent. Managers who predicted the index to fall, on average by 7.7 percent, were evidently in minority. However, they assigned, on average, higher probability to their forecasts (mean of 61 percent statistically different from the mean of 52 percent). The expected return on the market was 1.5 percent for the period of the next three months and it was statistically different from zero.

The expected market return in three months seems to be relatively low. In this case, estimations might have been influenced by the market situation in the period when the survey was carried out. At that time, the market had been strongly rising for several weeks. Executives might have expected a reversal of this short-term trend. As time passed during the writing of this book, it turned out that managers were proved right. Soon after the survey was completed, the

Exhibit 10.5 Managerial predictions about market changes in short and long term

Direction of change	Short-term prediction			Long-term prediction		
	% of answers	Mean WIG20 index change in %	Mean probability	% of answers	Mean WIG20 index change in %	Mean probability
Rise	70.9	7.6	51.9	80.4	32.3	55.3
Fall	29.1	−7.7	60.9	19.6	−13.3	56.6
Expected value		1.5***			12.9***	

Note: All expected values presented above are statistically different from zero at 0.01 significance level.

WIG20 index started to fall and by the end of the third month it was approximately 10 percent down.

There was more optimism in the long term. Almost 81 percent of executives predicted the stock market to rise in the next twelve months. The mean forecasted return in the group of optimists was 32 percent and the mean probability of realization amounted to 55 percent. The mean change of the index predicted by pessimists was minus 13 percent and the average probability was estimated at nearly 57 percent. In total, the expected market return within the next year was 12.9 percent. This was statistically different from zero and considerably higher than the expected return for the first period of three months.

Overall, the population of surveyed managers were dominated by optimists. The degree of optimism seems to be higher in the longer time horizon. It is possible that the fact that the survey was carried out during a local peak in market performance cooled down managerial expectations about returns within the next three months. Professionals are generally more likely to anticipate short-term reversals of market returns, as discussed in section 3.2.

2.4. Optimism Regarding Stock Valuation

In the next step, managers were requested to share their opinion about future performance of their stock. If above-average beliefs contribute greatly to the level of optimism, it might be presumed that managers will be particularly optimistic about future performance of their firms. Likewise, in the earlier task of market index forecasting, managers were first asked to indicate if the stock price would rise or fall within the next three and twelve months, and then requested to estimate the degree of the change and assign probability to their best guesses. The results were aggregated in a similar manner as forecasted market returns in the previous section and presented in exhibit 10.6.

We see that 90 percent of managers indicated that the stock price of their firm will rise in the next quarter. The mean predicted return was 15.3 percent and the mean probability amounted to 58 percent. A small group of pessimists predicted the return on their stock to be, on average, minus 9.8 percent and the

Exhibit 10.6 Managerial predictions about their stock price in the short and the long term

Direction of change	Short-term prediction			Long-term prediction		
	% of answers	Mean stock price index change in %	Mean probability	% of answers	Mean Stock price index change in %	Mean probability
Rise	90.3	15.3	58.3	90.3	25.0	55.6
Fall	9.7	−9.8	63.4	9.7	−15.5	65.0
Expected value		7.3***			12.1***	

Note: All expected values presented above are statistically different from zero at 0.01 significance level.

mean probability to be above 63 percent. Again, pessimists seemed to assign a slightly higher probability to their judgment, hence they were likely to be more confident than optimists. Due to the low number of observations in the second group, the t-test did not prove that these differences were significant, but a nonparametric Whitney-Mann test indicated statistical difference with p-value equal to 0.07. Overall, the expected stock return was 7.3 in the period of three months. This was significantly higher (at 0.01 level) than the expected market return in the same period.

The same high proportion of optimists also predicted a favorable long-term stock return. The mean predicted return was 25.0 percent and the mean probability amounted to 55.6 percent. A small group of pessimists predicted the return on their stock to be, on average, minus 15.5 percent and the mean probability to be above 65 percent. Again, pessimists seemed to assign a slightly higher probability to their judgment, but this time the statistical significance of this finding was slightly higher (t-test indicated significance at 0.1 level and the nonparametric Whitney-Mann test, more appropriate in this case, indicated 0.05 significance). The total expected return was 12.1 percent for one year which was significantly higher than for the period of three months. There was no significant difference between the expected long-term market return and the expected long-term stock return.

Overall, the degree of managerial optimism regarding the stock seems to be higher than their optimism about market performance. There was a higher percentage of executives forecasting a rise of their stock price rather than a positive change of the market index. This might give some hint that managers perceived their stock to be undervalued relative to the market. We investigated this path further by asking the managers directly how they perceived the current market valuation of their firm.

Results in exhibit 10.7 reveal that most managers (79 percent) in fact considered their firm to be undervalued. Only 17 percent of respondents believed that their stock was correctly priced by the market, and 3 percent admitted they considered their company overvalued. These findings correspond with results

Exhibit 10.7 Distribution and significance test
Question: Please, mark one of the below statements that best fits your personal opinion regarding current market valuation of your company:

	Count	%
Our stock is adequately priced by the market at the moment	21	17.4
Our stock is undervalued at the moment	96	79.3
Our stock is overvalued at the moment	4	3.3
Total	121	100.0
Chi-square statistics 118.8		
Degrees of freedom: 2		
Significance: ***		

Note: Null hypothesis stated that distribution is uniform and was rejected at 0.01 significance level.

of the earlier task and constitute yet another evidence of strong optimism displayed by managers, particularly as regards the stock of the firms they run.

2.5. Confidence of Pessimists

Inspired by the results in exhibit 10.4 indicating that pessimists, on average, assigned higher probabilities to their predictions, we carried out additional tests to check if these initial conclusions persist. This is important, because, in the overall sample, pessimists were in evident minority in relation to optimists, hence the number of observations in the pessimistic subsamples is low.

We decided to aggregate all answers from exhibit 10.4. regardless of whether they were related to market or stock predictions, and whether they concerned short or long horizons. The only aspect that we focused on to differentiate the answers is their pessimistic or optimistic attitude. Then, we calculated the mean estimated probability of realization in the group of pessimistic forecasts and compared it to the mean probability assigned to optimistic forecasts (exhibit 10.8).

Aggregating attitudes (pessimism vs. optimism) implicates using the same respondents' answers many times (maximum four in our case), which implies transition from population of respondents to the population of respondents' answers. This has a twofold effect on testing. On the one hand, it increases its power (due to larger sample), but on the other, it violates the assumption of observations' independence. However, performed t-test allowed us to reject the null hypothesis at 0.01 significance level. The result is sufficient even after eliminating conditional dependence between observations. Probabilities of rises and falls of the market index were generally intradependent. In other words, those who predicted the market to fall in the short term were more likely to predict a decrease also in the long term. Similarly, those who bet on market increase in the short term were also likely to be optimistic about market performance in twelve months. Overall, we confirm that pessimists tend to be, on average, more confident about the precision of their estimations. At first glance, it might look puzzling, as optimism is often identified with higher confidence. Our results show something different. We confirm managerial optimism in the sense that the number of respondents indicating a rise of the market index or the stock price was much higher than the number of those predicting a fall. However, when asked to assign the probability of realization to their best guess, optimistic managers were less confident than pessimists.

Exhibit 10.8 Main descriptive statistics of the tested variables

Attitude	Number of answers	Mean probability	Std. deviation
Optimists	311	58.4	10.5
Pessimists	62	64.8	11.9

Note: Null hypothesis that the mean probability does not differ across attitudes was rejected on grounds of a t-test at the 0.01 significance level.

3. Probability Estimation

Contrary to the theoretical assumptions of the efficient market hypothesis, in practice, market participants are often convinced that changes in asset prices do not follow the random walk model[1] but are shaped by trends or reversals. Because of the problems people have in interpreting representativeness and estimating probability correctly, in some cases decision makers erroneously identify trends and expect them to continue (e.g., hot hands effect or short series mistake). At other times, they prematurely forecast that the trend will reverse (e.g., gambler's fallacy or incorrect understanding of the principle of regression toward the mean—see section 1.3 in chapter 2). We investigate if similar biases are present in the group of top managers from publicly listed firms.

3.1. Estimating the Probability of Event Sequence

The aim of the first experiment carried out in this area was to verify whether respondents were able to estimate probability of relatively short event sequences. More precisely, the question was how they interpret the randomness in a short series of stock market prices. The managers were requested to estimate the probability of the following events: occurrence of five consecutive market sessions with a rising WIG20 index, and occurrence of five consecutive market sessions with a falling WIG20 index. Later on in the survey, they were also asked to estimate the probability of getting five consecutive tails when tossing a coin. The question about tossing a coin was asked after some time. It was not posed directly after the two preceding questions about stock market prices to avoid a situation where the two questions, put together, might have suggested that the processes were somehow similar. For each question, respondents were asked to indicate a range in which they believed the correct answer to lie. Each question also came with a suggestion of the following probability ranges: less than 1 percent, between 1 percent and 5 percent, between 5 percent and 10 percent, and over 10 percent. If we were to follow the efficient market hypothesis and assume that the current level of prices at moment t is the best approximation of the real intrinsic value of assets and prices in the following period $t + 1$, prices changing at random only as a result of new information coming to the market, the probability of prices rising or falling during each of the sessions should be basically the same and would equal 50 percent. Therefore, the probability of observing five consecutive rising or falling sessions should amount to 0.5^5, that is about 3.1 percent.[2] The same applies, of course, to the probability of getting five consecutive tails when tossing a coin.

Having analyzed the results of the experiment presented in exhibit 10.9, we may make a few interesting observations. First, most of the managers (72 percent) were able to correctly estimate probability in the case of tossing a coin, that is, a relatively simple event sequence which is obviously random. The number of respondents who overestimated versus those who underestimated the chances was not significantly different. In this respect, managers seem to do

Exhibit 10.9 Distribution of answers
Task: Please estimate the probability of the following sequences of events:

Suggested answers	Five consecutive market sessions with a rising WIG20 index		Five consecutive market sessions with a falling WIG20 index		Five consecutive tails when tossing a coin	
	Count	%	Count	%	Count	%
< 1%	7	6.8	4	3.9	13	12.6
between 1 and 5%	28	27.2	19	18.4	74	71.8
between 5 and 10%	36	35.0	45	43.7	10	9.7
> 10%	32	31.1	35	34.0	6	5.8
Total	103	100.0	103	100.0	103	100.0

better than laypeople. In earlier experiments conducted among nonprofessionals (Szyszka, 2007), almost half of the respondents could not correctly identify the range of probability of tossing five consecutive tails, and there were more people who overestimated than underestimated the probability.

However, the answers given to the questions about the WIG20 index clearly show that respondents usually did not treat successive changes as probabilistically independent. The percentage of answers within the correct probability estimation range was only about 27 percent for five consecutive rising market sessions and only a little above 18 percent for five falling market sessions. Most respondents overestimated the probability of a series of five consecutive rising or falling sessions. What is especially conspicuous is the considerably high percentage of answers suggesting probabilities over 10 percent.

When we compare correct estimations made about coin tossing to biased answers given in regard to stock market changes, we can conclude that, generally, managers are able to assess the probability of a sequence of random events. However, they most likely do not perceive market changes to be completely random. The fact that their estimates are biased upward means that managers overestimate the probability of the occurrence of short-term series of changes. In other words, they believe that short-term trends are more likely to happen than what a random walk model and historical statistics would suggest.

3.2. Predicting Reversals

In the next task, we investigated how managers perceived probability of the next immediate change of the stock market or the currency market after a sequence of consecutive changes in the same direction. Their short-term judgments were compared to the correctness of probability estimation for the long period. The aim was to find out if managers believe in trends or bet on reversals in the short term, and if they correctly perceive the likelihood of market situation in a longer horizon. The task was formulated in the following way:

Please, estimate the probability of each item in the range of 0%-100%:

- The WIG20 index will rise for the fifth time in a row after it has been rising for the last four consecutive sessions.

- The WIG20 index will be higher in 12 months after it has been rising for the last four consecutive sessions.
- The Polish zloty (PLN) will decline against the Euro (EUR) for the fifth time in a row after it has been declining for the last four consecutive days.
- The Polish zloty (PLN) will be lower against the Euro (EUR) in 12 months after it has been declining for the last four consecutive days.

If consecutive changes in stock or currency markets are statistically independent, then the correct probability estimation for each of the above scenarios should be equal to 50 percent ($H_0 : p = 50\%$). Answers significantly above 50 percent mean that respondents expect trend continuation ($H_1 : p > 50\%$) in the short or long term, respectively. On the other hand, answers significantly below 50 percent indicate that respondents anticipate trend reversal ($H_1 : p < 50\%$).

Results in exhibit 10.10 show that managers assigned probability significantly below 50 percent to the scenario of a fifth successive rise in the stock market as well as to the scenario of a fifth decline in a row in the currency market. This might be interpreted as anticipation of short-term reversals in both markets. Even in a short series of observations, the expectation to see a reversal is an example of gambler's fallacy, which is more typical for professional market participants (De Bondt, 1993; Shefrin, 2000—see section 1.3 in chapter 2). Individual investors and laypeople are more likely to extrapolate short series, and thus to expect trend continuation (Szyszka, 2007).

Probability estimations for long-term scenarios are not similar. On average, managers correctly estimated that a stock market rise in twelve months is as likely as a fall. However, they considered the decline of the Polish currency

Exhibit 10.10 Distribution and significance tests
Task: Please estimate the probability of each item in the range 0%–100%

	N	Mean	Std. Deviation	t statistic value	Significance
The WIG20 index will rise for the fifth time in a row after it has been rising for the last four consecutive sessions.	103	37.4	16.5	−7.743	***
The Polish zloty (PLN) will decline against the Euro (EUR) for the fifth time in a row after it has been declining for the last four consecutive days.	103	35.6	18.0	−8.149	***
The WIG20 index will be higher in 12 months after it has been rising for the last four consecutive sessions.	103	46.3	22.0	−1.681	*
The Polish zloty (PLN) will be lower against the Euro (EUR) in 12 months after it has been declining for the last four consecutive days	103	37.6	19.7	−6.416	***

Note: For each item the following null hypothesis was tested: mean value=50. ***, **, and * indicates significance at 0.01, 0.05, and 0.1 level, respectively.

(PLN) against the Euro (EUR) less likely in the horizon of twelve months than the expected 50 percent. This answer might have been influenced by numerous analysts' forecasts and media commentaries that appeared at the turn of a calendar year when, typically, the currency exchange rate is forecasted for the next twelve months. The forecasts were predominantly favorable for the Polish currency[3]. Coincidently, our survey was carried out also around the same time.

4. Preferences Toward Risk

In the following three sections, we investigate if corporate managers exhibit similar preferences toward risk as those generally documented in the psychology literature and described in the prospect theory (see section 2.1 in chapter 2). First, we look at risk aversion in the domain of gains and loss aversion (risk seeking) in the domain of losses. Then, we check if managers demonstrate different risk attitudes when they make decisions regarding their personal or corporate wealth. Finally, we investigate if managers are likely to exhibit the disposition effect both in corporate matters and when they become private investors.

4.1. Risk Aversion versus Risk Seeking

Earlier experiments by Szyszka (2007) revealed that the approach toward risk might be influenced by the value of a potential gain or loss. Generally, people are more likely to take risk in the case of small amounts regardless of whether the potential outcome is perceived as a small gain or a small loss. However, when larger amounts are involved, people tend to behave according to the prospect theory—they are risk averse while considering decisions about smaller but more certain, or higher but more risky, gains. Conversely, they are seek risk (are loss averse) when they make a choice about suffering a loss that is either smaller but more probable, or greater but less probable.

To address these issues in the sample of corporate managers, we carried out a two-part experiment. Respondents were asked to make choices in lotteries with the same expected value. In each lottery, one variant involved risk at the level of 50 percent, the other was a sure event. Questions were divided into two pairs with respect to the value of the potential loss or gain and placed in different parts of the questionnaire. The point was to make it more difficult to notice similarities between the two lottery sets. In the first step, managers were presented with a choice in the following two lotteries involving relatively small amounts. The first lottery was focused on a possible positive outcome:

Imagine that you are visited by a friend you have not seen for a long time. Being in a good mood, he suggests you play a game: You need to choose from the following options:

a) Get US$50 as a welcome gift to celebrate the pleasure of meeting your friend.
b) Toss a coin with your friend—if it is heads, you will get US$100; if it is tails, you will not get anything.

Mark answer a) if you prefer to get US$50 as a welcome gift, or answer b) if you prefer to toss a coin.

This was directly followed by another lottery with a possible negative outcome:

Imagine now that you pay a return visit to your friend. He suggests the same game, only this time you are the payer. You need to choose from the following options:

a) Pay US$50 as a welcome gift to celebrate the pleasure of meeting your friend.
b) Toss a coin with your friend—if it is heads, you will pay US$100 to your uncle; if it is tails, you will not pay him anything.

Mark answer a) if you prefer to pay US$50 straightaway as a welcome gift or answer b) if you prefer to toss a coin.

In the later part of the questionnaire, respondents were faced with two problems that involved much higher amounts. The first problem focused on the domain of gains:

Imagine you are taking part in a two-stage radio contest in which you can make the following choice:

a) Win a prize of US$10,000 for the very fact of phoning in and pursue the game no further.
b) Play on and stand a chance of winning twice as much, i.e., US$20,000 or leave with nothing with equal probability.

Mark answer a) if you prefer to stop playing after the first stage, or answer b) if you want to continue with the second stage.

The second problem was in the domain of losses:

Imagine you have been sued personally and you face the following choice:

a) Reach the settlement by agreeing to pay US$10,000 to your opponent.
b) Continue with the trial as a consequence of which you can win or lose the case with equal probability. If you lose, you will have to pay US$20,000 to your opponent. If the case is dropped, you will pay nothing and gain nothing.

Mark answer a) if you prefer settlement, or answer b) if you want to continue with the trial. Legal costs are not important in this example and you are not obliged to appear in person in the court.

If decision makers were to behave in line with the neoclassical theory of finance, that is, display risk aversion regardless of the context in which their choice is made, they should choose risk-free options (answer a)) in all the examples above. If, however, their preferences follow the prospect theory, they should choose certain variants in the lotteries with a positive expected value (i.e., in the area of profits), and options involving risk (answers b)) in lotteries with a negative expected value (i.e., in the area of losses). Neither under the classical utility theory nor the prospect theory should there be important differences in decision makers' preferences when they choose between the first and second lottery set. In other words, the propensity to take risk should not be generally contingent on whether the decisions concern relatively small or big amounts.

Exhibit 10.11 presents results of the experiment expressed as a percentage of respondents selecting certain outcomes and those who decide to take risk. First, managers were risk averse when faced with the choice of a certain large prize or a gamble that could double the prize with 50 percent probability. In the example with the radio contest, as many as 69 percent of respondents preferred to accept the lower but certain prize and did not decide to go further into the

Exhibit 10.11   Risk aversion and risk seeking depending on decision context

Situation	N	%
Imagine that you are visited by a friend you have not seen for a long time. Being in a good mood, he suggests you play a game: You need to choose from the following options		
Get US$50 as a welcome gift to celebrate the pleasure of meeting your friend	45	43.7
Toss a coin with your friend – if it is heads, you will get US$100; if it is tails, you will not get anything	58	56.3
Imagine now that you pay a return visit to your friend. He suggests the same game, only this time you are the payer. You need to choose from the following options		
Pay US$50 as a welcome gift to celebrate the pleasure of meeting your friend	29	28.2
Toss a coin with your friend – if it is heads, you will pay US$100 to your uncle; if it is tails, you will not pay him anything	74	71.8
Imagine you are taking part in a two-stage radio contest in which you can make the following choice		
Win a prize of US$10,000 for the very fact of phoning in and pursue the game no further	71	68.9
Play on and stand a chance of winning twice as much, i.e. US$20,000 or leave with nothing with equal probability	32	31.1
Imagine you have been sued personally and you face the following choice		
Reach the settlement by agreeing to pay US$10,000 to your opponent	19	18.4
Continue with the trial as a consequence of which you can win or lose the case with equal probability. If you lose, you will have to pay US$20,000 to your opponent. If the case is dropped, you will pay nothing and gain nothing	84	81.6

Note: Total counts for each question above equal to 103 observations.

second stage of the game. This observation is in line both with the neoclassical utility theory as well as the prospect theory.

The second apparent observation is a strong loss aversion motivating people to take risks in lotteries with a negative expected value. In all cases where the choice was between accepting a lower but certain loss, or participating in a lottery in which suffering a loss twice as high or avoiding it altogether was equally probable, most respondents displayed risk propensity and decided to take a chance.

The puzzling observation is that respondents were risk seeking in the area of gains when the gamble was about relatively small amounts (50 dollars for sure vs. 100 dollars with 0.5 probability). While the observed risk seeking in the area of losses confirms the prospect theory, it is difficult to explain why it should also be present in the area of small gains. The observation that 56 percent of managers were willing to gamble rather than accept the granted US$50 undermines not only the classical utility theory, but also the proposition of Kahneman and Tversky (1979). Similar empirical findings were documented in studies carried out among nonprofessionals, including experiments in which real money was used to motivate participants (Szyszka, 2007).

Let us relate these results to the prospect theory by Kahneman and Tversky (1979). The theory assumes that decision-maker preferences are a product of two functions—the value and the weighting one. The value function is convex in the area of losses (second derivative is positive for arguments below zero) and concave in the area of profits (second derivative negative for arguments higher than zero). In general, this should result in risk propensity when decision makers are faced with an alternative of losses and risk aversion when the choice is to be made between options with positive expected value.

With very small probability values, this general rule may be reversed by the weighting function which will override the influence of the value function in this particular case. The reason is that, according to the prospect theory, one of the properties of the weighting function is that decision makers significantly overestimate the probability of unlikely events. On the one hand, overestimating the probability of events which are not likely to happen may prevail over the general risk aversion in the area of profits inducing decision makers to, for example, purchase a lottery ticket. On the other, the same phenomenon may discourage a decision maker from taking risks in the area of losses and prompt him to buy an insurance policy.

As risky events in our experiment had a probability of 50 percent, it is doubtful that the weighting function was responsible for the observed propensity to take risks in the area of relatively small profits. On the contrary, properties of the weighting function suggest that one should expect so-called subcertainty for high-probability events. As demonstrated by studies carried out by Kahneman and Tversky (1979), people often prefer to be certain of getting a specific value to participating in a lottery offering a slightly higher expected value, but at a small risk.

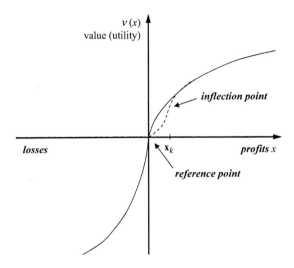

Figure 10.1 Shape of the value function suggested by Kahneman and Tversky (1979) with a dotted line marking the modification for positive arguments of small value.

Therefore, in order to explain the observed risk propensity we should rather look at the shape of the value function. It may be assumed that its properties are slightly different from the ones initially described by Kahneman and Tversky, at least where it concerns valuing positive arguments (profits) with relatively small values (see Figure 10.1). Results suggest that the inflexion of the value function from convex to concave shape does not happen precisely at the reference point, but only in the area of profits for an unspecified, positive, subjective, critical value of argument xk (formally $v''(x) < 0$ for $x > x_k$ and $v''(x) > 0$ for $x < x_k$).

The convex shape of the value function for arguments which are positive but located below critical value x_k means that the difference in wealth between zero and, for example, US$50 brings less satisfaction (utility) than the difference between getting US$50 and US$100. The outcome is that relatively small values of certain payoffs will not be enough of an incentive, and decision makers will usually decide to participate in a risky lottery even if it has the same expected value but offers the possibility of getting a potentially higher reward. It is only when decision makers are offered amounts at the level of at least critical value xk, that they will become risk averse and opt for the certain variant.

The above-mentioned specific property of the value function may potentially have serious consequences in some situations on the capital market. Risk seeking by investors in the area of small profits may reduce the supply of those financial instruments that, if sold immediately, allow investors to realize only a small return, but if kept for longer, offer a chance of making a potentially higher profit. As a result, these instruments may be periodically overpriced.

In such cases, investors require lower expected returns than the ones actually resulting from the risk associated with these assets.

Investor preferences and their propensity to take risk in the area of losses and small profits may turn out to be especially important in the case of public tender offers. When the price offered to current shareholders is only slightly higher than the present market price, the offer may fail. This is especially likely to happen if prices in the previous period were falling or have been neutral for a long time. Some shareholders will feel strong aversion to selling at a loss while others will not be interested in letting go of their assets at a price not much higher than the purchase price. Certain but small profit relative to current market pricing may turn out to be an insufficient incentive to accept the offer. We cannot exclude this from being one of the reasons why business units wanting to buy shares from the market are compelled to offer prices that are at least a dozen or so percent higher than the current market price (Dodd and Ruback, 1977; Asquith, 1983; Franks, et al., 1991).

4.2. Personal versus Corporate Loss Aversion

In the next step we go further in investigating loss aversion. We check whether managers exhibit different attitudes toward a potential loss in personal wealth as opposed to a potential loss for their company. We presume that managers are highly averse to personal loss, but might be less sensitive to a potential corporate loss. In order to verify if there is any difference in treatment of personal versus corporate losses, we modified the earlier example about a court trial in the following manner as presented in exhibit 10.12.

Results in exhibit 10.12 do not support the hypothesis that managers are less sensitive to a corporate loss. The experiment revealed no major differences in managerial approach toward a personal versus company's loss. Answers given in

Exhibit 10.12 Personal versus corporate loss aversion

Situation	N	%
Imagine you have been sued personally and you face the following choice		
Reach the settlement by agreeing to pay US$10,000 to your opponent	19	18.4
Continue with the trial as a consequence of which you can win or lose the case with equal probability. If you lose, you will have to pay US$20,000 to your opponent. If the case is dropped, you will pay nothing and gain nothing	84	81.6
Imagine your company has been sued and you face the following choice		
Reach the settlement by agreeing to pay to your opponent the amount of money representing five percent of your company net profit for the last year	15	14.6
Continue with the trial as a consequence of which you can win or lose the case with equal probability. If you lose, you will have to pay to your opponent the amount of money representing ten percent of your company net profit for the last year. If the case is dropped, you will pay nothing and gain nothing	88	85.4

Note: Chi-squared test was applied with result of 1.248 of the statistic value, which indicated no significant difference between these distributions (p-value = 0.264) of answers regarding personal versus corporate loss.

the example in which the firm was sued were similar as in the earlier example about a personal court trial. In both examples, a vast majority of managers were ready to continue the trial with an equal probability of winning the case and paying nothing or losing the case and paying double the amount of what they could have paid in the settlement.

4.3. Disposition Effect among Managers

The disposition effect is a general tendency to realize gains too quickly and to hold open positions generating losses for too long.[4] It is a direct consequence of anchoring to the purchase price and the S-shape utility valuation function as predicted by the prospect theory. The utility function is concave in the area of profits and convex in the area of losses. This means that when investors have shares whose current price is higher than the purchase price to which they anchor, they will display risk aversion. On the other hand, if they have shares whose price has recently dropped so that they are faced with a loss, they are prone to take more risks. If they perceive the probability of prices rising or falling in the following period to be the same and the expected share value to be equal to the current stock price (the situation is equivalent to our experiments with court trials), investors will maximize expected utility by deciding to realize profit at once and postpone realization of losses.

In our survey we investigated the disposition effect among corporate managers by asking them to put themselves in investors' shoes. We focused on the stronger part of the disposition effect, that is, on the tendency to hold stocks that have been losing value. Respondents were presented with the following sequence of questions:

After a long and thoroughly made analysis of a company (not yours), you decided to invest in its stock. Unfortunately, the stock you had just bought lost 10 percent in value over the following few days. What would be your reaction? Please, mark only one option.

a) I realize I made a mistake in evaluation of the company and *I decide to sell* the stock with a loss to avoid possible further price drop.

b) I think I had made no mistake in my analysis, but after I bought the stock some negative information must have come out, which I had not been able to foresee earlier, and which had an adverse effect on the firm's valuation—not sure about future developments, *I decide to sell* the stock.

c) I think I had made no mistake in my analysis, but after I bought the stock some negative information must have come out, which I had not been able to foresee earlier, and which had an adverse effect on the firm's valuation—not sure about future developments, *I decide to hold* the stock and wait.

d) I think I had made no mistake in my analysis. The stock price fell temporarily due to market mispricing and it will soon rise. Consequently, I *decide to hold* the stock.

e) I think I made no mistake in my analysis. The stock price fell temporarily due to market mispricing and it will soon rise. Therefore, not only I do not sell the stock, *but I decide to buy more*, using the opportunity of temporarily low prices.

Respondents who gave answers other than a) or b) were faced with the next question:

By how much percent must the stock price fall for you to decide to sell? Please, mark only one option:

a) at least by additional 5 percent,
b) at least by additional 10 percent,
c) at least by an additional 25 percent,
d) I am not going to sell the stock as long as the price is not at least back at the purchase level, or
e) I am not going to sell the stock as long as the price is not at the level allowing me to make profit.

Those who answered d) or e) in the second question were asked yet another:

Assuming the stock price is not coming back to the satisfying level, how long would you wait for an improvement before you consider selling shares with a lower or bigger loss?

a) a month
b) a quarter
c) half a year
d) one year
e) I will keep waiting until the price comes to the satisfying level regardless the passing time.

Results in exhibits 10.13–10.15 reveal a strong tendency to hold the stock that has been losing value. In the first question, only 2 percent of the surveyed managers admitted that they might have committed a mistake in their analysis and decided to sell the stock with a loss. Another 10 percent decided to sell the stock, but attributed the loss to circumstances that must have come out later and could not have been foreseen. The majority of respondents decided to hold the stock. Most of them (71 percent) did not even consider the possibility of new unfavorable information that had influenced the stock price, but were convinced that their initial analysis had been correct and the stock price fell only temporarily due to the market being wrong. These outcomes not only confirm a strong disposition to avoid a loss, but may also suggest overconfidence and attribution bias among managers.

Nearly half of those, who decided to hold the stock in the first question, were very persistent in the second question, and declared their intention to keep the stock regardless of further losses. They were not willing to sell as long as the price did not come back to the purchase level (34 percent) or even to the level allowing at least some profit (14 percent). In the second question, 46 percent of respondents were ready to sell only after the price dropped by another 25 percent.

Those who decided to hold the stock regardless of further losses in the second question were also patient with regard to timing in the third question. wThere

Exhibit 10.13 Distribution of answers to the question: After a long and thoroughly made analysis of a company (not yours), you decided to invest its stock. Unfortunately, the stock you had just bought lost 10 percent in value over the following few days. What would be your reaction? Please, mark only one option.

Decision	N	%
I realize I made a mistake in evaluation of the company and *I decide to sell* the stock with a loss to avoid possible further price drop	2	1.9
I think I had made no mistake in my analysis, but after I had bought the stock some negative information must have come out, which I had not been able to foresee earlier, and which had an adverse effect on the firm's valuation—not sure about future developments, *I decide to sell* the stock.	10	9.7
I think I had made no mistake in my analysis, but after I had bought the stock some negative information must have come out, which I had not been able to foresee earlier, and which had an adverse effect on the firm's valuation—not sure about future developments, *I decide to hold* the stock and wait.	18	17.5
I think I had made no mistake in my analysis. The stock price felt temporary due to market mispricing and it will soon rise. Consequently, I *decide to hold* the stock.	57	55.3
I think I made no mistake in my analysis. The stock price felt temporary due to market mispricing and it will soon rise. Therefore, not only I do not sell the stock, but *I decide to buy more*, taking opportunity of temporarily low prices.	16	15.5
Total	103	100.0

Exhibit 10.14 Distribution of answers to the question: By how much percent must the stock price fall for you to decide to sell? Please mark only one option.

Decision	N	%
At least by an additional 5 percent	2	2.2
At least by an additional 10 percent	3	3.3
At least by an additional 25 percent	42	46.2
I am not going to sell the stock as long as the price is not at least back at the purchase level	31	34.1
I am not going to sell the stock as long as the price is not at the level allowing me to make profit	13	14.3
Total	91	100.0

Exhibit 10.15 Distribution of answers to the question: Assuming the stock price is not coming back to the satisfying level, how long would you wait for improvement before you would consider selling shares with a lower or bigger loss?

Decision	N	%
A month	0	0.0
A quarter	0	0.0
Half a year	0	0.0
One year	34	77.3
I keep waiting until the price comes to the satisfying level regardless of passing time	10	22.7
Total	44	100.0

was no one willing to sell earlier than after a year. Ten managers declared their intention to keep the stock regardless of further losses and regardless of passing time.

In section 2.2 in chapter 8 we discussed some evidence suggesting the presence of the disposition effect among corporate managers of firms going public. It is worth noting that both samples from our research correspond to some extent—we studied IPOs at the Warsaw Stock Exchange and we interviewed managers from companies listed at the same exchange. It is likely that at least some of the surveyed managers were the same people who went public with the company. Results of the two studies consistently point out the existence of the disposition effect among corporate managers.

Concluding Remarks

This book was aimed to address a few aspects. First, the key elements of the traditional financial theory have been confronted with the main reservations made against them by the proponents of the behavioral school. Further on, it demonstrated the relationship among psychological factors, irrational investor behavior, and capital market anomalies. Alternative explanations for specific phenomena and discussions between the opponents and supporters of the classical theory were systematized by kind. This was accomplished by juxtaposing different points of view in a way that reflects academic discourse and highlights the most important differences between both sides. The author did not shy away from taking a stand, especially when it comes to the new interpretation of events drawing on investor psychology or regulatory and institutional factors. In this sense, the content of the first four chapters systematizes the current state of knowledge while introducing some new elements.

The book offers a comprehensive explanation for a number of anomalies observed in the capital market. It describes instances when the law of one price is violated through inadequate pricing of the same, or essentially the same assets, demonstrating potential reasons for which unused arbitrage opportunities persist on the market. It presents alternative hypotheses on the seasonality of returns, especially as it concerns the month-of-the-year effect. It also points out incorrect investor reactions to public information. Market overreaction may be inferred from such phenomena as, inter alia, negative correlation of long-term returns and the profitability of contrarian investing. However, one may also come across numerous examples of underreaction. These include the following: correlation of time series of portfolio returns and the cross-correlation between small-cap and large-cap portfolios, large capitalization companies leading small caps. What is especially striking is the profitability of the momentum strategy. Another indication of delayed market reaction is the post-announcement drift in which abnormal returns persist for a relatively long period of time after the events triggering them. Finally, there are also a lot of studies suggesting that it is possible to predict abnormal returns on the basis of certain company characteristics such as the price-to-dividend ratio, price-to-earnings ratio, or price-to-cash-flow ratio. Fama and French (1992, 1993, 1996) demonstrated that the wide range of these interdependencies may be in fact reduced to two key ones—the size effect and a book-to-market equity effect. At the aggregated market-wide level, the book also delivers explanation for the equity premium puzzle and excessive price volatility.

All the aforementioned phenomena have been thoroughly discussed, each one with alternative explanations. Characteristically, the most convincing explanations were the ones offered by behavioral finance. It was demonstrated what attitudes adopted by investors may be responsible for the occurrence of specific anomalies and what is their psychological background. Practical implications for investment strategies have also been outlined.

Thanks to exhaustive literature overview giving a good picture of the current state of knowledge about the topic, it was possible to critically evaluate the most popular and influential behavioral models of the capital market. For each of them, it was demonstrated which categories of empirically observed phenomena the model can explain and which it does not account for or is even inconsistent with. It turned out that none of the popular behavioral models put forward so far was able to explain the entire range of market peculiarities. Consequently, the GBM developed by Szyszka (2007, 2010) has been proposed. The GBM assumes that asset prices are influenced not only by fundamental values, but also by three behavioral variables resulting from psychological errors in the processing of information, representativeness, and unstable preferences. Mistakes made by investors may cause significant deviations from fundamentals leading to periodical over- or underpricing of assets. How severe the mispricing will be depends on the market's ability for self-correction, the measure A that is closely related to limits in arbitrage. The GBM explains when, how, and what psychologically driven phenomena may distort correct asset pricing. The model offers an explanation for a vast array of market anomalies. However, it is characterized by a high level of generality. This is a necessary compromise in order to arrive at a comprehensive model of complex human behaviors that influence asset pricing in a multidirectional and multilevel manner. The GBM is descriptive rather than normative in character. It systematizes the relationships among psychological factors, investor behavior, and valuation of assets. The model can be used to describe processes and to explain events *ex post*, but it is not directly applicable for pricing and precise *ex ante* predictions. This is a general ailment of behavioral models, particularly when compared to the neoclassical theory that usually offered normative predictions. In this sense, neoclassical and behavioral finance might be seen as complementing each other. The neoclassical model delivered a kind of benchmark on how markets should behave while the behavioral model explains why empirical findings differ from neoclassical predictions.

The GBM stands as another proposal in behavioral finance and, as such, may be the subject of further theoretical and empirical studies. Future research may focus on a more precise description of the functions impacting the value of the behavioral inclinations the model specifies. Volatility of the behavioral error B described by the model may be treated as an extra systemic risk factor.

In this context, rational investors should require a higher risk premium from investments in those categories of financial assets that are especially sensitive to disruptions caused by irrational traders. Considered dynamically, a gradual escalation of the variability of the behavioral error B may lead to a rise in the expected returns required by rational investors as compensation for the growing unpredictability, and so decrease the fundamental values. The discrepancy between behavioral and rational pricing will continue to widen until the force of irrational traders subsides or is outweighed by the market's ability for self-correction. This reasoning fits a whole range of periodical manias and investment fads usually followed by abrupt adjustment.

The book has also touched on other innovative areas within the behavioral framework. It offers a behavioral perspective on the 2008 credit crunch in the United States and on the later Eurozone crisis. Those two events pave the way for introducing the psychological elements into macroeconomics. Future studies in this direction may potentially seek links between changing risk aversion and economic cycles or the role of overconfidence, excessive optimism and extrapolation bias in bubble creation. Actually, the idea would not be so much new. Keynes (1936) already highlighted the role of psychology in economics long before behavioral economics and behavioral finance were formed. While studying the Great Depression, he argued that sentiment, reflecting unrealistic optimism or pessimism, leads to booms and busts. He noted that securities prices often diverge from their intrinsic values, and explored the implications of such divergence for employment, income, and money.

Finally, as many as four out of ten chapters of this book are dedicated to behavioral corporate finance. This vein of research emerged naturally within the behavioral framework only after the aspects of irrational investor behavior and asset mispricing had established their firm presence in the academic world. It is still a relatively new area, but the review of current evidence and theoretical works presented in chapters 7 and 8 already indicates that the behavioral approach offers a useful complement to other corporate finance theories. Findings in this area may have direct consequences not only for shareholders' wealth, but also for the entire economy. It is one thing to say that investor irrationality has an impact on capital market prices, which leads to transfer of wealth among investors, but quite another to suggest that mispricing leads to corporate under- or overinvestment, or the general misallocation of capital and heavy losses for the entire economy.

The last two chapters of this book present results of a survey carried out among executives from publicly listed companies. There are a number of behavioral inclinations in managerial practice documented in chapter 9. These include both rational managerial attempts to exploit market inefficiency as well as irrational biases in managerial decisions. For example, over one-fifth of surveyed managers admitted that financing needs was a factor of the least importance when deciding to go public while one quarter were driven by a desire to capitalize the firm's good historical results. It seems that the decision of the IPO was not about the market timing so much as about timing of the firm's good performance. When managers were asked about the choice between equity and debt financing, financial risk came out to be the least important factor. Over half of the respondents declared to have a target capital structure around which they rebalance. Twenty-eight percent of respondents stated that the capital structure in their firms was not defined at all and they used equity or debt opportunistically, depending on market situation. Some evidence of a kind of money illusion was also found in respect to capital structure. Over one-third of managers said they used book values rather than market values to define capital structure of their firm. There is some evidence of the sunk cost bias. As much as 36 percent of respondents were ready to abandon the NPV analysis and continue the investment whose budget had increased by two and half times, if only there was hope that the project will bring any profits in the future (risk and value of money in time being unaccounted for). A half of the surveyed managers admitted to earnings management, mostly in the form of earnings smoothing, and to a lesser extent to avoid reporting a loss or not meeting the forecast. The most common techniques were cost avoidance by postponing the necessary cost-generating activities to the next reporting period and avoiding costs recognition in a given period by applying accruals.

Chapter 10 offers some direct evidence of psychological heuristics and biases among corporate managers. We confirm the above-average bias, although managers felt more competent as compared to their peer top executives only in the domain of economic matters. On the other hand, underconfidence was revealed in the area of culture. When asked to provide short-term and long-term forecasts about the market index or their stock performance, managers on average assigned values with similar precision in both time horizons. We interpret this as a version of the calibration bias, as the long-term forecast typically should be less precise due to more possible factors influencing outcomes in the longer period. We also find that managers tend to be optimistic, particularly about future performance of their firms. Interestingly, the pessimists, who were in minority, displayed higher confidence in predictions of both the market index and their stock price changes. Executives also had problems with correct estimation of probability and made inconsistent errors. On the one hand, they overestimated the probability of occurrence of short-term series of market returns. On the other, they expected return reversals both in the short and long term, demonstrating the gambler's fallacy. Loss aversion and the disposition effect among managers is also documented. Finally, managers exhibited a risk-seeking approach not only in the domain of losses, but also in the area of small gains—a deviation from the prospect theory that was earlier found among nonprofessionals by Szyszka (2007).

Further research on behavioral finance still offers a lot of potential. On the investor side of the market, more behavioral modeling and testing is needed in order to come up with normative tools allowing not only to explain market phenomena *ex post* but also to forecast investor behavior and its impact on asset pricing *ex ante*. Also, further studies into bubble creation, financial crisis, and behavioral links to macroeconomics are likely to bring interesting and useful (preventive) results. On the corporate side, one path of research may be aimed at confirming more psychological biases in managerial attitudes directly in surveys. Another approach includes attempts to identify a link between a given managerial bias and corporate practice. Inventing and applying right proxies of managerial inclinations constitutes another challenge. More research is needed especially in areas where the behavioral approach competes with more established theories of corporate finance, mainly the agency theory and the information asymmetry theory. These theories and the behavioral approach frequently share similar predictions and offer alternative explanations of many empirically well-documented facts. More detailed investigation may help to distinguish which theory is closer to reality and should prevail.

This book hopefully can be a good starting point for anyone interested in pursuing further studies in any of the aforementioned areas of behavioral finance.

Notes

1 Behavioral Approach versus Neoclassical Finance

1. It is commonly believed that the rule was discovered by the English mathematician Thomas Bayes (1701–1761) although his writings on the topic were published posthumously. A similar rule was formulated independently by the French scholar Pierre-Simon Laplace (1749–1827).
2. Coming from the classical school of finance, Ross (1976) put forward the arbitrage pricing theory (APT) whose assumptions are less restrictive than the ones behind CAPM. The APT model provides for the simultaneous occurrence of many systemic risk factors, each one of which is appropriately priced. The drawback of this approach is that it does not offer any formal definition of those risk factors or their measures. It is also worth noting that the CAPM model equation is a special case of APT in which risk factors are reduced to just one.
3. Roll's (1976) objection was that early CAPM tests gave tautological results. He claimed that the adopted methodology based on calculating average returns for balanced stock portfolios does not in fact check whether CAPM is correct or not since it is possible to obtain similar results regardless of the relationship between returns and risk. What is more, he believed that the CAPM cannot be tested at all as we are not able to verify the efficiency of the global market portfolio encompassing all the assets.
4. The literature on dividend policy has produced a large body of theoretical and empirical research. No general consensus has yet emerged after several decades of investigation. It would be out of the scope of this book to present here all competing dividend theories. For comprehensive surveys, please see Baker, Powell, and Veit (2002), Frankfurter and Wood Jr. (2003), Al-Malkawi, Rafferty, Pillai (2010).

2 Psychological Aspects of Decision Making

1. The most important psychological papers used in behavioral finance may be found in the following compilations: Kahneman, Slovic, and Tversky (1982) (ed.), Kahneman and Tversky (2000) (ed.), and Gilovich, Griffin, and Kahneman (2002) (ed.).
2. A middle-aged gentleman wanted very much to have a son, but instead he got only daughters. After the birth of each child, he claimed that "the next one is bound to

be a boy because there needs to be balance in nature." He gave up trying when his sixth daughter was born.

3. I conducted the following experiment with my finance students: I showed two charts without legends. One of them presented actual weekly changes o the S&P500 index in the period of 52 weeks. The other presented results of multiple tosses of a coin (heads—the "index" goes up by 3%, tails—it goes down by 2.5 percent, making the expected value of "index" change stand at 0.25%; we can therefore assume that coin toss results followed a random walk with a drift). I then asked students to point out potential regularities or figures of technical analysis. I was being vigorously persuaded that there were clear, repetitive patterns visible in both charts.

4. Camerer (1998) offers a review of early criticism of Von Neuman and Morgenstern's utility theory.

3   Investor Behavior

1. Market efficiency is often equated with the fact that time series of security prices follow the random walk model or, more precisely, a slightly less restrictive martingale model. Importantly, market efficiency and the randomness of returns do not always have to be the same.

2. Data from www.nyxdata.com

3. More precisely, the average period of portfolio evaluation was 13 months in the case of using nominal returns as a reference point and 10–11 months if real returns were taken into account.

4   Asset-Pricing Anomalies and Investment Strategies

1. Lehmann assumed the first weekday to be Wednesday. Each week, portfolios were constructed based on prices from the period between previous Wednesday and Monday. One day was skipped in order to minimize disruptions resulting from the buy–sell spread. A similar method was also used in later studies simulating contrarian strategies applied over one week.

2. Abnormal returns were calculated as the difference between the return on a portfolio and the equal-weighted return on the entire market. Even though they do not present the results in the paper, De Bondt and Thaler (1985) claim that a similar tendency could be observed applying the criterion of abnormal returns calculated with the use of the classical CAPM model. Conrad and Kaul (1993), Dissanaike (1994), and Ball, Kothari, and Shanken (1995) point out potential distortions of results caused by the adopted method of calculating abnormal returns. Chopra, Lakonishok, and Ritter (1992) and Loughran and Ritter (1996) demonstrated, however, that the winner–loser effect is equally strong when alternative methods of calculating abnormal returns are used.

3. Taking this cue, some proponents of the efficient market hypothesis suggested that the momentum effect is the result of changing sectoral risk and may be related to economic cycles. Results of empirical studies are not straightforward here. For example, Bacmann, Dubois, and Isakov (2001) and Chordia and Shivakumar (2002) provided some evidence suggesting that there is a relation between income obtained by the momentum strategy and changeability of the economic cycle. On the other hand, publications such as those by Liew and Vassalou (2000) or Griffin and Martin (2003) make observations to the contrary.

4. Long-term event studies have also been controversial for the reasons of methodology related most of all to the way abnormal returns were measured. See Barber

and Lyon (1997), Kothari and Warner (1997), Fama (1998), Loughran and Ritter (2000), Mitchell and Stafford (2000).

5 Market-wide Consequences of Behavioral Biases

1. The relative risk aversion coefficient is interpreted in the following way: A coefficient of value A means that if consumption falls by 1 percent, the marginal value of a unit of income increases by A percent. Mehra and Prescott (1985) argue that most empirical studies suggest A values within the range of 1.0–2.0, whereas in order to explain the observed level of the equity premium, the coefficient would have to exceed 30. Adopting a theoretical approach, Arrow (1971, p. 98) argues that the A value should hover around 1 allowing for slightly higher values in the case of people with low consumption levels and lower values for affluent people. Poor people are usually more sensitive to the risk of their income diminishing by one unit compared to the rich.
2. Mankiw and Zeldes (1991) obtain relative risk-aversion coefficients at the level of about 10.
3. Campbell and Cochrane (1999) demonstrate that the suggested model may explain the high equity premium assuming that the relative risk aversion coefficient amounts to about 6. It is still a lot, although much less than coefficients initially obtained by Mehra and Prescott (1985) and the ones from Mankiw and Zeldes's (1991) model.
4. This section is based in part on Szyszka, A. (2010), *Belief- and Preference-Based Models* initially published in: Baker, K. and Nofsinger, J. (eds.), *Behavioral Finance. Investors, Corporations, and Markets*. This material is reproduced with permission of John Wiley & Sons, Inc.

6 Behavioral Insights into Financial Crisis

1. During the Great Depression of the 1930s, an even higher percentage drop of the DJIA index was recorded, although it was a lesser drop in terms of points, as at that time the index was dropping from a lower level.
2. Greece joined the EMU in 2001.
3. Devaluation of national currency may be indeed harmful, if a country is indebted in a foreign currency either via public or private sector. For example, this was the case of many Latin and South American economies in the previous century.
4. Source: IMF Global Financial Stability Report, September 2011, available online at www.imf.org/External/Pubs/FT/GFSR/2011/02/index.htm
5. Source: Eurostat.
6. Misjudging Risk: Causes of the Systemic Banking Crisis in Ireland. Report of the Commission of Investigation into the Banking Sector in Ireland, March 2011, available online at www.bankinginquiry.gov.ie
7. Hedge Fund Research Industry Report, www.hedgefundresearch.com
8. ISDA: Greek Debt Restructuring Triggers CDS Payouts, *The Wall Street Journal*, March 9, 2012.

7 Rational Corporations in Irrational Markets

1. See Derrien (2010) for a detailed review of the literature on IPOs.
2. Burch et al. (2004) analyzed a relatively old sample of SEO between 1933 and 1949, a period when rights offers were more common than at present.

3. Lee A. (2013), "INSEAD Professors' Fund Ranked Number One," *Forbes, 2/07/2013*.
4. See section 2.3 in chapter 8 for an alternative explanation assuming biased value perception among corporate managers.
5. This is the so-called pure (unbiased) version of the expectation theory. There are also various adaptations of the expectation theory with risk/liquidity premium, according to which long-term interest rates are determined by expectations of future interest rates and the risk premium that is either constant or may change over time. See Shikano (1985) for detailed classification.
6. See Allen and Michaely (2003), DeAngelo, DeAngelo, and Skiner (2009), and Ben-David (2010) for a comprehensive summary on dividend policy theories and empirical evidence.
7. Dividend income for individuals had been taxed more heavily than capital gains in the United States, until the passage of the Jobs and Growth Relief Reconciliation Act of 2003.
8. It is also possible that managers are not actually responding to fads and preferences of investors, but are rather influenced by investor sentiment and share similar biases. For example, they hold exceptionally optimistic views about investment opportunities in a particularly fashionable industry.
9. Lang, Stulz, and Walkling (1989) and Servaes (1991) document the opposite effect in their samples prior to 1990. They find that higher bidder valuations are associated with higher positive announcement returns. This evidence contradicts the misvaluation hypothesis. Instead, it supports the view that market was appreciating management skills of the bidding firms, hoping for synergies and a more efficient use of targets' assets.
10. Klein (2001) results are partially inconsistent with Servaes (1996) who finds that conglomerates were traded at a discount in the 1960s, although the discount was gradually disappearing by the end of the decade.
11. There is also a nonbehavioral explanation to this pattern. Stein (1989) argues that earnings management can be a Nash equilibrium result under asymmetric information. His model assumes irrational, myopic managers and the efficient market.
12. This example is taken from Henry (2008).

8 Managerial Biases in Corporate Policy

1. See section 1.2 in chapter 2 for more literature review on overconfidence, excessive optimism, and selective-attribution biases. Section 2 in chapter 10 provides original empirical evidence from the sample of managers from publicly listed firms.
2. Most companies going public are relatively young firms with large portion of equity owned by managers. Thus, the interest of managers might be often identified with the interest of pre-IPO shareholders.
3. Calendar-time portfolio approach is sometimes also called Jensen-alpha approach.
4. See section 2.4 in chapter 2.
5. See section 2.3 and 3.2 in chapter 2.
6. The long-term effect of acquisitions on bidding firms typically runs into the problem of measuring abnormal returns in the long period. Most studies indicate poor long-term performance of acquirers. However, the results are sensitive to the sample period and the method of payment. Underperformance is typical for stock bidders while outperformance is more likely in the case of cash acquisitions. This indicates the possibility of managerial market timing ability and valuation driven motives of mergers and acquisitions. See section 2.3 in chapter 7.

7. Compare to section 2.1 and 3.2 of this chapter.
8. There are many competing theories attempting to explain waves in merger activities, including market timing by rational managers, as discussed in section 2.3 in chapter 7.

9 Managerial Practice

1. I am grateful to the team of SW Research Institute www.swresearch.pl for the design of the webpage form of the survey and handling of the responses. I also wish to acknowledge with thanks the administrative efforts by Ms. Krystyna Nowicka.
2. The Friedman test is a nonparametric statistical test developed by the US economist and Nobel Prize winner Milton Friedman. Similar to the parametric repeated measures ANOVA, it is used to detect differences in treatments across multiple test attempts. The procedure involves ranking each row together, then considering the values of ranks by columns. For more information, see Friedman (1937).
3. The Wilcoxon signed-rank test is a nonparametric test used when comparing two related samples, matched samples, or repeated measurements on a single sample to assess whether their population mean ranks differ. See Wilcoxon (1945), and also: Hollander and Wolfe (1999), p. 295.
4. For details, see http://stat.ethz.ch/R-manual/R-patched/library/stats/html/friedman.test.html.

10 Heuristics and Biases among Corporate Managers

1. Information efficiency of the market is often equated with the fact that time series of asset prices follow the random walk model or, more precisely, a slightly less restrictive martingale model. The intuitive line of argument usually put forward in defense of the random character of changes on an efficient market goes as follows: If prices reflect all available information, they should change only when the market receives some news, which, being "new", cannot be expected. Consequently, ensuing price changes should also be unexpected, that is, random. Even though these arguments are commonly accepted, we must remember that market efficiency and the randomness of rates of return do not always have to be equivalent.
2. The analysis of the historical series of daily changes in the WIG20 index in the entire period from the date the index was introduced on April 14, 1994 until the day on which the study was finished (January 11, 2013) shows ex post that the chance of there being five consecutive rising sessions was 3.3 percent. However, the difference between the empirical value and the theoretical value of 3.1 percent was not statistically significant at the level of 0.05. For five consecutive falling sessions, the empirical value equaled the theoretical probability.
3. We checked forecasts of 20 major investment banks published between December 12, 2012, and January 11, 2013. Fourteen analysts predicted that Polish zloty (PLN) will be stronger against the Euro (EUR) at the end of 2013, three analysts forecasted no major change, and only three were pessimistic about the local currency.
4. See section 3.4 in chapter 3 for a detailed discussion on the disposition effect among investors, and section 2.2 in chapter 8 for more information about the disposition effect among corporate managers.

References

Abarbanell, J., Bernard, V. (1992), Tests of Analysts' Overreaction/Underreaction to Earnings Information as an Explanation for Anomalous Stock Price Behavior, *Journal of Finance*, Vol. 47, 3, pp.1181–1207.

Abel, A. (1990), Asset Prices under Habit Formation and Catching Up with the Joneses, *American Economic Review*, Vol. 80, 2, pp. 38–42.

Abreu, D., Brunnermeier, M. (2002), Synchronization Risk and Delayed Arbitrage, *Journal of Financial Economics*, Vol. 66, 2–3, pp. 341–360.

Ackert, L. (1994), Uncertainty and Volatility in Stock Prices, *Journal of Economics and Business*, Vol. 46, 4, pp. 239–253.

Adam, T., Fernando, C., Golubeva, E. (2009), Managerial Biases and Corporate Risk Management, EFA 2009 Accepted Paper, Norwegian School of Economics, Bergen, Norway, SSRN Electronic Paper Collection: http://ssrn.com/abstract=1364533.

Adler, M., Dumas, B. (1983), International Portfolio Choice and Corporation Finance: A Synthesis, *Journal of Finance*, Vol. 38, 3, pp. 925–984.

Agrawal, A., Chen, M. (2004), Analyst Conflicts and Research Quality, Proceedings EFA 2004 Maastricht Meetings Paper No. 1347,Mastricht University, Maastricht, Holland, SSRN Electronic Paper Collection: http://ssrn.com/abstract=559412.

Agrawal, A., Jaffe, J. (2000), The Post-Merger Performance Puzzle, in Cooper, C., Gregory, A. (eds.), *Advances in Mergers and Acquisitions*, Vol. 1.New York, NY: Elsevier Science, pp. 7–41.

Agrawal, A., Jaffe, J., Mandelker, G. (1992), The Post-Merger Performance of Acquiring Firms: A Re-Examination of an Anomaly, *Journal of Finance*, Vol. 47, 4, pp. 1605–1621.

Aktas, N., De Bodt, E., Bollaert, H., Roll, R. (2012), CEO Narcissism and the Takeover Process: From Private Initiation to Deal Completion, *AFA 2012 Chicago Meetings Paper*, SSRN Electronic Paper Collection: http://ssrn.com/abstract=1784322.

Al-Malkawi, H.-A. N, Rafferty M., Pillai, R. (2010), Dividend Policy: A Review of Theories and Empirical Evidence, *International Bulletin* of Business *Administration*, Vol. 9, pp. 171–200.

Albagli, E., Hellwig, Ch., Tsyvinski, A. (2011), Information Aggregation, Investment, and Managerial Incentives, *Cowles Foundation Discussion Papers 1816*, Cowles Foundation for Research in Economics, Yale University, New Haven, CT.

Ali, A., Klein, A., Rosenfeld, J. (1992), Analysts' Use of Information about Permanent and Transitory Earnings Components in Forecasting Annual EPS, *Accounting Review*, Vol. 67, 1, pp. 183–198.

Allais, M. (1953), The Behavior of Rational Man in Risk Situations: A Critique of the Axioms and Postulates of the AmericanSchool, *Econometrica*, Vol. 21, 4, pp. 503–546.

Allen, D.E., Prince, R. (1995), The Winner/Loser Hypothesis: Some Preliminary Australian Evidence on the Impact of Changing Risk, *Applied Economics Letters*, Vol. 2, pp. 280–283.

Alonso, A., Rubio, G. (1990), Overreaction in the Spanish Equity Market, *Journal of Banking and Finance*, Vol. 14, pp. 469–481.

Alpert, M., Raiffa, H. (1982), A Progress Report on the Training of Probability Assessors, in Kahneman, D., Slovic, P., Tversky, A. (eds.), *Judgment under Uncertainty: Heuristics and Biases*. New York: Cambridge University Press, pp. 294–305.

Amihud, Y., Mendelson, H. (1986), Asset Pricing and the Bid-Ask Spread, *Journal of Financial Economics*, Vol. 17, 2, pp. 223–249.

Andrade, G., Mitchell, M., Stafford, E. (2001), New Evidence and Perspectives on Mergers, *Journal of Economics Perspectives*, Vol. 15, 2, pp. 103–120.

Ang, J., Cheng, Y. (2006), Direct Evidence on the Market-Driven Acquisition Theory, *The Journal of Financial Research*, Vol. 29, pp. 199–216.

Angel, J. (1997), Tick Size, Share Prices, and Stock Splits, *The Journal of Finance*, Vol. 52, 2, pp. 655–681.

Antoniou, A., Galariotis, E., Spyrou, S. (2005), Contrarian Profits and the Overreaction Hypothesis: The Case of the Athens Stock Exchange, *European Financial Management*, Vol. 11, 1, pp.71–98.

Antoniou, A., Galariotis, E., Spyrou, S. (2003), Are Contrarian Investment Strategies Profitable in the London Stock Exchange? Where Do These Profits Come from? Proceedings EFMA 2003 Helsinki Meetings, European Financial Management Association, Helsinki, Finland, SSRN Electronic Paper Collection: http://ssrn.com/abstract=391570.

Arghyrou, M., Chortareas, G. (2008), Current Account Imbalances and Real Exchange Rates in the Euro Area, *Review of International Economics*, Vol. 16, pp. 747–764.

Arkes, H., Herren, L., Isen, A. (1988), The Role of Potential Loss in the Influence of Affect on Risk-Taking Behavior, *Organizational Behavior and Human Decision Processes*, Vol. 66, 2, pp. 228–236.

Arrow, K. (1971), *Essays in the Theory of Risk-Bearing*. Amsterdam: North-Holland Publishing Company.

Arshanapalli, B., Coggin, D., Nelson, W. (2002), The January Effect and the Global Value-Growth Premium, *Journal of Investing*, Vol. 11, 4, pp. 15–26.

Asquith, P. (1983), Merger Bids, Uncertainty, and Stockholders Returns, *Journal of Financial Economics*, Vol. 11, 1, pp. 51–83.

Asquith, P., Healy, P., Palepu, K. (1989), Earnings and Stock Splits, *Accounting Review*, Vol. 44, pp. 387–403.

Azfar, O. (1999), Rationalizing Hyperbolic Discounting, *Journal of Economic Behavior & Organization*, Vol. 38, 2, pp. 245–252.

Babenko, I., Tserlukevich, Y., Vedrashko, A. (2012), Insider Purchases and the Credibility of Open Market Share Repurchase Signals, *Journal of Financial and Quantitative Analysis*, Vol. 47, 5, pp. 1059–1088.

Bacmann, J. F., Dubois, M. (1998), Contrarian Strategies and Cross-Autocorrelations in Stock Returns: Evidence from France, SSRN Electronic Paper Collection: http://ssrn.com/abstract=138176.

Bacmann, J.F., Dubois, M., Isakov, D. (2001), Industries, Business Cycle and Profitability of Momentum Strategies: An International Perspective, Proceedings EFMA 2001

Lugano Meetings, European Financial Management Association, Lugano, Switzerland, SSRN Electronic Paper Collection: http://ssrn.com/abstract=264657..

Bagnoli, M, Clement, M., Watts, S. (2004), The Timing of Earnings Announcements Throughout the Day and Throughout the Week, SSRN Electronic Papers Collection: http://ssrn.com/abstract=570247.

Baker, K., Gallagher, P. (1980), Management's View of Stock Splits, *Financial Management*, Vol. 2, pp. 73–77.

Baker, K., Powell, M. (1993), Further Evidence on Managerial Motives For Stock Splits, *Quarterly Journal of Business and Economics*, Vol. 32, 3, pp. 20–31.

Baker, M., Coval, J., Stein, J. (2007), Corporate Financing Decisions when Investors Take the Path of Least Resistance, *Journal of Financial Economics*, Vol. 84, pp. 266–298.

Baker, M., Greenwood, R., Wurgler, J. (2003), The Maturity of Debt Issues and Predictable Variation in Bond Returns, *Journal of Financial Economics*, Vol. 70, pp. 261–291.

Baker, M., Greenwood, R., Wurgler, J. (2009), Catering through Nominal Share Prices, *Journal of Finance*, Vol. 64, 6, pp. 2559–2590.

Baker, H. K., Powell, G. E., Veit, E. T. (2002), Revisiting the dividend puzzle: Do all of the pieces now fit? Review of Financial Economics, Vol. 11, 4, pp. 241–261.

Baker, M., Pan, X., Wurgler, J. (2012), The Effect of Reference Point Prices on Mergers and Acquisitions, *Journal of Financial Economics*, Vol. 106, 1, pp. 49–71

Baker, M., Stein, J., Wurgler, J. (2003), When Does the Market Matter? Stock Prices and the Investment of Equity-Dependent Firms, *Quarterly Journal of Economics*, Vol. 118, pp. 969–1006.

Baker, M., Wurgler, J. (2002), Market Timing and Capital Structure, *Journal of Finance*, Vol. 57, 1, pp. 1–32.

Baker, M., Wurgler, J. (2004a), A Catering Theory of Dividends, *Journal of Finance*, Vol. 59, 3, pp. 1125–1165.

Baker, M., Wurgler, J. (2004b), Appearing and Disappearing Dividends: The Link to Catering Incentives, *Journal of Financial Economics*, Vol. 73, 2, pp. 271–288.

Baker, M. Wurgler, J. (2007), Investor Sentiment in the Stock Market, *Journal of Economic Perspectives*, Vol. 21, 2, pp. 129–152.

Baker, M., Wurgler, J. (2013), Behavioral Corporate Finance: An Updated Survey, in Constantinides, G., Harris, M., Stulz, R. (eds.), *Handbook of Economics of Finance*, Vol. 2A: Corporate Finance. Amsterdam: North Holland, pp. 357–413

Baker, M., Xuan, Y. (2011), Under New Management: Equity Issues and the Attribution of Past Returns, *Harvard Business School Working Paper*, SSRN Electronic Paper Collection: http://ssrn.com/abstract=1376474.

Ball, R., Brown, P. (1968), An Empirical Evaluation of Accounting Income Numbers, *Journal of Accounting Research*, Vol. 6, 2, pp. 159–178.

Ball, R., Kothari, S.P., Shanken, J. (1995), Problems in Measuring Portfolio Performance: An Application to Contrarian Investment Strategies, *Journal of Financial Economics*, Vol. 38, 1, pp. 79–107.

Banerjee, A. (1992), A Simple Model of Herd Behavior, *Quarterly Journal of Economics*, Vol. 107, 3, pp. 797–818.

Banz, R. (1981), The Relationship between Return and Market Value of Common Stocks, *Journal of Financial Economics*, Vol. 9, 1, pp. 3–18.

Barber B., Loeffler D., (1993) "The Dartboard Column: Second-Hand Information and Price Pressure," *Journal of Financial and Quantitative Analysis* 28, June, pp. 273–284.

Barber, B., Lehavy, R., McNichols, M., Treuman, B. (2001), Can Investors Profit from the Prophets? Security Analyst Recommendations and Stock Returns, *Journal of Finance*, Vol. 56, 2, pp. 531–563.

Barber, B., Lehavy, R., McNichols, M., Trueman, B. (2003), Reassessing the Returns to Analysts' Stock Recommendations, *Financial Analysts Journal*, Vol. 59, 2, pp. 16–18.

Barber, B., Lyon, J. (1997), Detecting Long-Run Abnormal Stock Returns: The Empirical Power and Specification of Test Statistics, *Journal of Financial Economics*, Vol. 43, 3, pp. 341–372.

Barber, B., Odean, T. (2000), Trading Is Hazardous to Your Wealth: The Common Stock Investment Performance of Individual Investors, *Journal of Finance*, Vol. 55, 2, pp. 773–806.

Barber, B., Odean, T. (2001), Boys Will Be Boys: Gender, Overconfidence, and Common Stock Investment, *Quarterly Journal of Economics*, Vol. 141, 2, pp. 261–292.

Barber, B., Odean, T. (2002), Online Investors: Do the Slow Die First? *Review of Financial Studies*, Vol. 15, 2, pp. 455–487.

Barber, B., Palmer, D., Wallace, J. (1995), Determinants of Conglomerate and Predatory Acquisitions: Evidence from the 1960s, *Journal of Corporate Finance*, Vol. 1, pp. 283–318.

Barberis, N., Huang, M. (2001), Mental Accounting. Loss Aversion, and Individual Stock Returns, *Journal of Finance*, Vol. 56, 4, pp. 1247–1295.

Barberis, N., Huang, M., Santos, T. (2001), Prospect Theory and Assets Prices, *Quarterly Journal of Economics*, Vol. 116, 1, pp. 1–53.

Barberis, N., Shleifer, A., Vishny, R. (1998), A Model of Investor Sentiment, *Journal of Financial Economics*, Vol. 49, 3, pp. 307–343.

Barberis, N., Thaler, R. (2003), A Survey of Behavioral Finance, in Constantinedes, G., Harris, M., Stulz, R. (eds.), *Handbook of the Economics of Finance*: *Financial Markets and Asset Pricing*, Vol. 1B. Amsterdam: North-Holland, pp. 1051–1121.

Bar-Hillel, M. (1982), Studies of Representativeness, in Kahneman, D., Slovic, P., Tversky, A. (eds.), *Judgment under Uncertainty: Heuristics and Biases*. Cambridge, UK: Cambridge University Press, pp. 69–83.

Bar-Hiller, M., Neter, E. (1996), Why Are People Reluctant to Exchange Lottery Tickets, *Journal of Personality and Social Psychology*, Vol. 70, 1, pp. 17–27.

Barro, R. (1990), The Stock Market and Investment, *Review of Financial Studies*, Vol. 3, pp. 115–131.

Barry, C., S. Brown, (1984), "Differential Information and the Small Firm Effect," *Journal of Financial Economics* 13, pp. 283–294.

Basu, S. (1983), The Relationship between Earnings' Yield, Market Value and Return for NYSE Common Stocks: Further Evidence, *Journal of Financial Economics*, Vol. 12, 1, pp. 129–156.

Beber, A., Fabbri, D. (2012), Who *Times* the Foreign Exchange Market? Corporate Speculation and CEO Characteristics, *Journal of Corporate Finance*, Vol. 18, pp. 1065–1087.

Begg, I. M., Anas, A., Farinacci, S. (1992), Dissociation of Process in Belief: Source Recollection, Statement Familiarity, and the Illusion of Truth, *Journal of Experimental Psychology: General*, Vol. 121, pp. 446–458.

Bell, D. (1982), Regret in Decision Making under Uncertainty, *Operations Research*, Vol. 30, pp. 961–981.

Bell, D. (1985), Disappointment in Decision Making under Uncertainty, *Operations Research*, Vol. 33, pp. 1–27.

Bem, D. (1972), Self-Perception Theory, in Berkowitz, L. (ed.), *Advances in Experimental Social Psychology*, Vol. 6, pp. 1–62.

Benartzi, S. (2001), Excessive Extrapolation and the Allocation of 401(k) Accounts to Company Stock, *Journal of Finance*, Vol. 56, 5, pp. 1747–1764.

Benartzi, S., Michaely, R., Thaler, R., Weld, W. (2009), The Nominal Share Price Puzzle, *Journal of Economic Perspectives*, Vol. 23, 2, pp. 121–142.

Benartzi, S., Thaler, R. (1995), Myopic Loss Aversion and the Equity Premium Puzzle, *Quarterly Journal of Economics*, Vol. 110, 1, pp. 73–92.

Benartzi, S., Thaler, R. (1999), Risk Aversion or Myopia? Choices in Repeated Gambled and Retirement Investments, *Management Science*, Vol. 45, 3, pp. 364–381.

Benartzi, S., Thaler, R. (2001), Naïve Diversification Strategies in Defined Contribution Saving Plans, *American Economic Review*, Vol. 91, 1, pp. 79–98.

Ben-David, I., Graham, J., Harvey, C. (2007), Managerial Overconfidence and Corporate Policies, *NBER Working Paper No. w13711*, SSRN Electronic Paper Collection: http://ssrn.com/abstract=1079308.

Beneish, M. (1991), Stock Prices and the Dissemination of Analysts' Recommendations, *Journal of Business*, Vol. 64, pp. 393–416.

Benzion, U., Rapoport, A., Yagil, J. (1989), Discount Rates Inferred from Decisions: An Experimental Study, *Management Science*, Vol. 35, 3, pp. 270–284.

Berger, P., Ofek, E. (1995), Diversification's Effect on Firm Value, *Journal of Financial Economics*, Vol. 37, pp. 39–65.

Berger, P., Ofek, E. (1996), Bustup Takeovers of Value-Destroying Diversified Firms, *Journal of Finance*, Vol. 51, 3, pp. 1175–1200.

Berger, P., Ofek, E. (1999), Causes and Effects of Corporate Refocusing Programs, *Review of Financial Studies*, Vol. 12, 2, pp. 311–345.

Bergstresser, D., Desai, M., Rauh, J. (2006), Earnings Manipulation, Pension Assumptions, and Managerial Investment Decisions, *The Quarterly Journal of Economics*, Vol. 121, 1, pp. 157–195.

Bergstresser, D., Philippon, T. (2006), CEO Incentives and Earnings Management, *Journal of Financial Economics*, Vol. 80, 3, pp. 511–529.

Berkovitch, E., Narayanan, M. P. (1993), Motives for Takeovers, *Journal of Financial and Quantitative Analysis*, Vol. 28, 3, pp. 347–362.

Bernard, V., Thomas, J. (1989), Post-Earnings-Announcement Drift: Delayed Price Response or Risk Premium? *Journal of Accounting Research*, Vol. 27, Supplement, pp. 1–36.

Bernard, V., Thomas, J. (1990), Evidence that Stock Prices Do Not Fully Reflect the Implications of Current Earnings for Future Earnings, *Journal of Accounting and Economics*, Vol. 13, 4, pp. 305–340.

Bernoulli, D. (1954), Exposition of a New Theory on the Measurement of Risk, *Econometrica*, Vol. 22, 1, pp. 23–36.

Bikhchandani, S., Hirshleifer, D., Welch, I. (1992), A Theory of Fads, Fashion, Custom and Cultural Change as Informational Cascades, *Journal of Political Economy*, Vol. 100, 5, pp. 992–1026.

Bildik, R. (2004), Are Calendar Anomalies Still Alive? Evidence from Istanbul Stock Exchange, SSRN Electronic Paper Collection: http://ssrn.com/abstract=598904.

Black, F. (1972), Capital Market Equilibrium with Restricted Borrowing, *The Journal of Business*, Vol. 45, 3, pp. 444–455.

Black, F. (1986), Noise, *Journal of Finance*, Vol. 41, 3, pp. 529–543.

Black, F., Jensen, M. C., Scholes, M. (1972), The Capital Asset Pricing Model: Some Empirical Tests, in Jensen, M.C. (ed.), *Studies in the Theory of Capital Markets*, New York: Praeger Publishers, pp. 79–121.

Black, F., Scholes, M. (1973), The Pricing of Options and Corporate Liabilities, *Journal of Political Economy*, Vol. 81, pp. 637–654.

Blanchard, O., Giavazzi, F. (2002), Current Account Deficits in the Euro Area. The End of the Feldstein Horioka Puzzle? *Brookings Paper on Economic Activity*, Vol. 2, pp. 147–209.

Blanchard, O., Lopez de Silanes, F., Shleifer, A. (1994), What Do Firms Do with Cash Windfalls? *Journal of Financial Economics*, Vol. 36, 3, pp. 337–360.

Blanchard, O., Rhee, C., Summers, L. (1993), The Stock Market, Profit and Investment, *Quarterly Journal of Economics*, Vol. 108, pp. 115–136.

Bloomfield, R., Leftwich, R., Long, J. (1977), Portfolio Strategies and Performance, *Journal of Financial Economics*, Vol. 5, 11, pp. 201–218.

Bloomfield, R., Libby, R., Nelson, M. (2000), Underreactions, Overreactions and Moderated Confidence, *Journal of Financial Markets*, Vol. 3, pp. 113–137.

Blume, M., Friend, I. (1975), The Asset Structure of Individual Portfolios and Some Implications for Utility Functions, *Journal of Finance*, Vol. 30, 2, pp. 585–603.

Bodurtha, J. N. Jr., Kim, D.S., Lee, C. (1993), Closed-End Country Funds and U.S. Market Sentiment, *Review of Financial Studies*, Vol. 8, 3, pp. 879–918.

Boehme, R., Sorescu, S. (2002), The Long-Run Performance Following Dividend Initiations and Resumptions: Underreaction or Product of Chance? *Journal of Finance*, Vol. 57, 2, pp. 871–901.

Bouwman, C. H. S., Fuller, K., Nain, A. S. (2009), Market Valuation and Acquisition Quality: Empirical Evidence, *Review of Financial Studies*, Vol. 22, pp. 633–679.

Bowen, R., Davis, A., Matsumoto, D. (2002), Emphasis on Street versus GAAP Earnings in Quarterly Press Releases: Determinants, SEC Intervention and Market Reactions, *Accounting Review*, Vol. 80, pp. 1011–1038.

Bradley, M., Desai, A., Kim, E. (1988), Synergy Gains from Corporate Acquisitions and Their Division between the Stockholders of Target and Acquiring Firms, *Journal of Financial Economics*, Vol. 21, 1, pp. 3–40.

Brailsford, T. (1992), A Test for the Winner-Loser Anomaly in the Australian Equity Market: 1958–87, *Journal of Business Finance and Accounting*, Vol. 19, pp. 225–241.

Brainard, W., Tobin, J. (1968), Pitfalls in Financial Model Building, *American Economic Review*, Vol. 58, pp. 99–122.

Branch, B., (1977), A Tax Loss Trading Rule, *Journal of Business*, Vol. 50, 2, pp. 198–207.

Brau, J.,C., Fawcett, S. E. (2006), Initial Public Offerings: An Analysis of Theory and Practice, *Journal of Finance*, Vol. 61, 1, pp. 399–436.

Brav, A., Geczy, C., Gompres, P. (2000), Is the Abnormal Return Following Equity Issuances Anomalous? *Journal of Financial Economics*, Vol. 56, 2, pp. 209–249.

Brav, A., Gompers, P. (1997), Myth or Reality? The Long-Run Underperformance of Initial Public Offerings: Evidence from Venture and Nonventure Capital-Backed Companies, *Journal of Finance*, Vol. 52, 5, pp. 1791–1821.

Brav, A., Graham, J., Harvey, C., Michaely, R. (2005), Payout Policy in the 21st Century, *Journal of Financial Economics*, Vol. 77, 3, pp. 483–527.

Brav, A., Heaton, J. (1998), Did ERISA's Prudent Man Rule Change the Pricing of Dividend Omitting Firms? Working paper, SSRN Electronic Paper Collection: http://ssrn.com/abstract=98568.

Breeden, D. T., (1979), An intertemporal asset pricing model with stochastic consumption and investment opportunities, *Journal of Financial Economics*, 7, pp. 265–296.

Brennan, M. (1971), Capital Market Equilibrium with Divergent Borrowing and Lending Rates, *Journal of Financial and Quantitative Analysis*, Vol. 6, pp. 407–418.

Brennan, M., Schwartz, E. (1985), Evaluating Natural Resource Investments under Uncertainty, *Journal of Business*, Vol. 58, 2, pp. 135–157.

Brennan, M., Xia, Y. (2001), Stock Price Volatility and Equity Premium, *Journal of Monetary Economics*, Vol. 47, 2, pp. 249–283.

Brooks, J. (1987), *The Takeover Game*, 1st ed. New York: E.P. Dutton.

Brooke, E. (2006), Are Investors Influenced by Pro Forma Emphasis and Reconciliations in Earnings Announcements? *The Accounting Review*, Vol. 81, 1, pp. 113–133.

Brouwer, I., Van Der Put, J. (1997), Contrarian Investment Strategies in a European Context, *Journal of Business Finance and Accounting*, Vol. 24, 9–10, pp. 1353–1367.

Brown, K.C., Harlow, W.V., Starks, L. (1996), Of Tournaments and Temptations: An Analysis of Managerial Incentives in the Mutual Fund Industry, *Journal of Finance*, Vol. 51, 1, pp. 85–110.

Brown, L. (1999), Managerial Behavior and the Bias in Analysts' Earnings Forecasts, *Journal of Accounting Research*, Vol. 39, pp. 221–241.

Brown, L. (2001), A Temporal Analysis of Earnings Surprise: Profits versus Losses, *Journal of Accounting Research*, Vol. 39, 2, pp. 221–241.

Brown, L., Higgins, H.N. (2001), Managing Earnings Surprises in the U.S. versus 12 Other Countries, *Journal of Accounting and Public Policy*, Vol. 20, pp. 373–398.

Brown, L., Higgins, H.N. (2005), Managers' Forecast Guidance of Analysts: International Evidence, *Journal of Accounting and Public Policy*, Vol. 24, pp. 280–299.

Brown, P., Keim, D., Kleidon, A., Marsh, T. (1983), Stock Return Seasonalities and the Tax-Loss Selling Hypothesis: Analysis of the Arguments and Australian Evidence, *Journal of Financial Economics*, Vol. 12, 1, pp. 33–88.

Brown, S., Goetzmann, W., Ross, S. (1995), Survival, *Journal of Finance*, Vol. 50, 2, pp. 853–873.

Brown, W., Crabb, P., Haushalter, D. (2006), Are Firms Successful at Selective Hedging? *Journal of Business*, Vol. 79, pp. 2925–2949.

Brunnermeier, M.K. (2001), Asset Pricing under Asymmetric Information: Bubbles, Crashes, Technical Analysis, and Herding. Oxford: Oxford University Press.

Buehler, R., Griffin, D., Ross, M. (2002), Inside the Planning Fallacy: The Causes and Consequences of Optimistic Time Predictions, in Gilovich, T., Griffin, D., Kahneman, D. (eds.), *Heuristics and Biases: The Psychology of Intuitive Judgment*. Cambridge, UK: Cambridge University Press, pp. 250–270.

Burch, T.R., Christie, W.G., Nanda, V.K. (2004), Do Firms Time Equity Offerings? Evidence from the 1930s and 1940s, *Financial Management*, Vol. 33, pp. 5–23.

Burch, T.R., Swaminathan, B. (2001), Are Institutions Momentum Traders? SSRN Electronic Paper Collection: http://ssrn.com/abstract=291643.

Burgstahler, D., Dichev, I. (1997), Earnings Management to Avoid Earnings Decreases and Losses, *Journal of Accounting and Economics*, Vol. 24, 1, pp. 99–126.

Burgstahler, D., Eames, M. (2006), Management of Earnings and Analysts' Forecasts to Achieve Zero and Small Positive Earnings Surprises, *Journal of Business Finance and Accounting*, Vol. 33, 5–6, pp. 633–652.

Busby, J., Pitts, C. (1997), Real Options in Practice: An Exploratory Survey of How Finance Officers Deal with Flexibility in Capital Appraisal, *Management Accounting Research*, Vol. 8, pp. 169–186.

Busenitz, L.W., Barney, J.W. (1997), Differences between Entrepreneurs and Managers in Large Organizations: Biases and Heuristics in Strategic Decision-Making, *Journal of Business Venturing*, Vol. 12, 6, pp. 9–30.

Byun, J., Rozeff, M. (2003), Long-Run Performance after Stock Splits: 1927 to 1996, *Journal of Finance*, Vol. 58, 3, pp. 1063–1085.

Camerer, C. (1995), Individual Decision Making, in Kagel, J., Roth, A. (eds.), *The Handbook of Experimental Economics*. Princeton, NJ: Princeton University Press, pp. 587–703.

Camerer, C. (1998), Bounded Rationality in Individual Decision Making, *Experimental Economics*, Vol.1, 2, pp. 163–183.

Campbell, J. (1991), A Variance Decomposition of Stock Returns, *Economic Journal*, Vol. 101, 405, pp. 157–179.

Campbell, J., Cochrane, J. (1999), By Force of Habit: A Consumption-Based Explanation of Aggregate Stock Market Behavior, *Journal of Political Economy*, Vol. 107, 2, pp. 205–251.

Campbell, J., Goodie, A.S., Foster, J. (2004), Narcissism, Confidence, and Risk Attitude, *Journal of Behavioral Decision Making*, Vol. 20, pp. 297–311.

Campbell, J., Lettau, M., Malkiel, B., Xu, Y. (2001), Have Individual Stocks Became More Volatile? An Empirical Exploration of Idiosyncratic Risk, *Journal of Finance*, Vol. 56, 1, pp. 1–43.

Campbell, J., Lo, A.W., MacKinlay, A.C. (1997), *The Econometrics of Financial Markets*. Princeton, NJ: Princeton University Press.

Campbell, J., Shiller, R. (1988), Stock Prices, Earnings, and Expected Dividends, *Journal of Finance*, Vol. 43, 3, pp. 661–676.

Campbell, J., Vuolteenaho, T. (2004), Inflation Illusion and Stock Prices, *American Economic Review*, Vol. 94, 2, pp. 19–23.

Capaul, C., Rowley, I., Sharpe, W. (1993), International Value and Growth Stock Returns, *Financial Analysts Journal*, Vol. 49, 1, pp. 27–36.

Capstaff, J., Paudyal, K., Rees, W. (1995), The Accuracy and Rationality of Earnings Forecasts by UK Analysts, *Journal of Business Finance and Accounting*, Vol. 22, 1, pp. 69–87.

Capstaff, J., Paudyal, K., Rees, W. (1998), Analysts' Forecast of German Firms' Earnings: A Comparative Analysis, *Journal of International Financial Management and Accounting*, Vol. 9, 2, pp. 83–116.

Chan, H., Faff, R., Kalev, P., Lee, D. (2003), Short-Term Contrarian Investing—Is It Profitable? ... Yes and No, *Journal of Multinational Financial Management*, Vol. 13, 4–5, pp. 385–405.

Chan, K., Chen, N.F. (1991), Structural and Return Characteristics of Small and Large Firms, *Journal of Finance*, Vol. 46, 4, pp. 1467–1484.

Chan, K. (1988), On the Contrarian Investment Strategy, *Journal of Business*, Vol. 61, 2, pp. 14–163.

Chan, L., Hamao, Y., Lakonishok, J. (1991), Fundamentals and Stock Returns in Japan, *Journal of Finance*, Vol. 46, 5, pp. 1739–1765.

Chan, L., Jeegadeesh, N., Lakonishok, J. (1996), Momentum Strategies, *Journal of Finance*, Vol. 51, 5, pp. 1681–1713.

Chang, E., Pinegar, M., Ravichandran, R. (1993), International Evidence on the Robustness of the Day-of-the-Week Effect, *Journal of Financial and Quantitative Analysis*, Vol. 28, 4, pp. 497–513.

Chapman, D. (2002), Does Intrinsic Habit Formation Actually Resolve the Equity Premium Puzzle? *Review of Economic Dynamics*, Vol. 5, 3, pp. 618–645.

Chapman, G., Johnson, E. (1994), The Limits of Anchoring, *Journal of Behavioral Decision Making*, Vol. 7, pp. 223–242.

Chen, H., Jegadeesh, N., Wermers, R. (2002), The Value of Active Mutual Fund Management: An Examination of Stockholdings and Trades of Fund Managers, *Journal of Financial and Quantitative Analysis*, Vol. 35, 3, pp. 343–369.

Chen, H., Singal, V. (2000), What Drives the January Effect? Working Paper, University of Baltimore & Virginia Tech.

Chen, H., Singal, V. (2003), Role of Speculative Short Sales in Price Formation: The Case of the Weekend Effect, *Journal of Finance*, Vol. 58, 2, pp. 685–705.

Cheng, Q., Warfield, T. D. (2005), Equity Incentives and Earnings Management, *The Accounting Review*, Vol. 80, pp. 441–476.

Chinn, M. (2005), *Getting Serious about the Twin Deficits, Council Special Reports No. 10*, Council on Foreign Relations, New York.

Chirinko, R., Schaller, H. (2011), Do Bubbles Lead to Overinvestment? A Revealed Preference Approach, *CESifo Working Paper Series 3491*, CESifo Group Munich.

Chopra, N., Lakonishok, J., Ritter, J. (1992), Measuring Abnormal Performance: Do Stocks Overreact? *Journal of Financial Economics*, Vol. 31, 2, pp. 235–269.

Chopra, N., Lee, C., Shleifer, A., Thaler, R. (1993), Yes, Discounts on Closed-End Funds are a Sentiment Index, *Journal of Finance*, Vol. 48, pp. 801–808.

Chordia, T., Shivakumar, L. (2002), Momentum, Business Cycle, and Time-varying Expected Returns, *Journal of Finance*, Vol. 57, 2, pp. 985–1019.

Chordia, T., Shivakumar, L. (2006), Earnings and Price Momentum, *Journal of Financial Economics*, Vol. 80, 3, pp. 627–656.

Christensen-Szalanski, J., Bushyhead, J. (1981), Physicians' Use of Probabilistic Information in Real Clinical Setting, *Journal of Experimental Psychology: Human Perception and Performance*, 7, pp. 928–935.

Chui, A.C.W., Titman, S., Wei, K.C.J. (2001), Momentum, Legal Systems and Ownership Structure: An Analysis of Asian Stock Markets, SSRN Electronic Paper Collection: http://ssrn.com/abstract=265848.

Ciccone, S. (2011), Investor Optimism, False Hopes and the January Effect, *Journal of Behavioral Finance*, Vol. 12, 3, pp.158–168.

Clare, A., Thomas, S. (1995), The Overreaction Hypothesis and the UK Stock Market, *Journal of Business, Finance and Accounting*, Vol. 22, pp. 961–973.

Cliff, M. (2004), Do Independent Analysts Provide Superior Stock Recommendations? SSRN Electronic Paper Collection: http://ssrn.com/abstract=540123.

Comment, R., Jarrell, G. (1995), Corporate Focus and Stock Returns, *Journal of Financial Economics*, Vol. 37, 1, pp. 67–88.

Conrad, J., Kaul, G. (1993), Long-Term Market Overreaction or Biases in Computed Returns? *Journal of Finance*, Vol. 48, 1, pp. 39–63.

Conrad, J., Kaul, G. (1998), An Anatomy of Trading Strategies, *Review of Financial Studies*, Vol. 11, 3, pp. 489–519.

Conroy, R. M., Harris, R. S., Benet, B. A. (1990), The Effect of Stock Splits on Bid-Ask Spreads, *Journal of Finance*, Vol. 45, 4, pp. 1285–1296.

Constantinides, G. (1990), Habit Formation: A Resolution of the Equity Premium Puzzle, *Journal of Political Economy*, Vol. 98, 3, pp. 519–543.

Constantinides, G. (2002), Rational Asset Prices, *Journal of Finance*, Vol. 57, 4, pp. 1567–1591.

Constantinides, G., Duffie, D. (1996), Asset Pricing with Heterogeneous Consumers, *Journal of Political Economy*, Vol. 104, 2, pp. 219–240.

Cooper, A.C., Woo, C.Y., Dunkelberg, W.C. (1988), Entrepreneurs' Perceived Chances for Success, *Journal of Business Venturing*, Vol. 3, 2, pp. 97–108.

Cooper, I., Kaplanis, E. (1994), Home Bias in Equity Portfolios, Inflation Hedging, and International Capital Market Equilibrium, *Review of Financial Studies*, Vol. 7, 1, pp. 45–60.

Cooper, M., Dimitrov, O., Rau, R. (2001), A Rose.com by Any Other Name, *Journal of Finance*, Vol. 56, 6, pp. 2371–2388.

Cooper, M., Khorana, A., Osobov, I., Patel, A., Rau, R. (2005), Managerial Actions in Response to a Market Downturn: Valuation Effects of Name Changes in the Dot. com Decline, *Journal of Corporate Finance*, Vol. 11, 1–2, pp.319–335.

Cootner, P. (1964), *The Random Character of Stock Market Prices*. Cambridge, MA: MIT Press.

Copeland, T.E. (1979), Liquidity Changes Following Stock Splits, *The Journal of Finance*, Vol. 34, 1, pp. 115–141.

Corman, J., Perles, B., Vancini, P. (1988), Motivational Factors Influencing High-Technology Entrepreneurship, *Journal of Small Business Management*, Vol. 26, 1, pp. 36–42.

Cornett, M., Travlos, N. (1989), Information Effects Associated with Debt-for-Equity and Equity-for-Debt Exchange Offers, *Journal of Finance*. Vol. 44, 2, pp. 451–468.

Coval, J., Moskowitz, T. (1999), Home Bias at Home: Local Equity Preference in Equity Portfolios, *Journal of Finance*, Vol. 54, 6, pp. 2045–2073.

Coval, J., Moskowitz, T. (2001), Geography of Investment: Informed Trading and Asset Prices, *Journal of Political Economy*, Vol. 109, 4, pp. 811–841.

Cowen, A., Groysberg, B., Healy, P. (2006), Which Types of Analyst Firms Make More Optimistic Forecasts? *Journal of Accounting and Economics*, Vol.41, 1–2, pp. 119–146.

Cox, J. C., Ross, S. A., Rubinstein, M. (1979), Option Pricing: A Simplified Approach, *Journal of Financial Economics*, Vol. 7, pp. 229–264.

Croci, E., Petmezas, D., Vagenas-Nanos, E. (2010), Managerial Overconfidence in High and Low Valuation Markets and Gains to Acquisitions, *International Review of Financial Analysis,* Vol. 19, pp. 368–378.

Cross, F. (1973), The Behavior of Stock Prices on Fridays and Mondays, *Financial Analyst Journal*, Vol. 29, 6, pp. 67–69.

Cutler, D., Poterba, J., Summers, L. (1990), Speculative Dynamics and the Role of Feedback Traders, *American Economic Review*, Vol. 80, 2, pp. 63–68.

Dadush, U., Stancil, B. (2010), Europe's Debt Crisis: More than a Fiscal Problem, in Dadush, U. (ed.), *Paradigm Lost. The Euro in Crisis*. Washington, DC: Carnegie Endowment For International Pace, pp. 9–15.

Damodaran, A. (1989), The Weekend Effect in Information Releases: A Study of Earnings and Dividend Announcements, *Review of Financial Studies*, Vol.2, 4, pp. 607–623.

Damodaran, A. (2012),Equity Risk Premiums (ERP): Determinants, Estimation and Implications—The 2012 Edition, New York University, Stern School of Business, New York.

Daniel, K., Hirshleifer, D., Subrahmanyam, A. (1998), Investor Psychology and Security Market Under- and Overreactions, *Journal of Finance*, Vol. 53, 6, pp. 1839–1885.

Daniel, K., Hirshleifer, D., Subrahmanyam, A. (2001), Overconfidence, Arbitrage, and Equilibrium Asset Pricing, *Journal of Finance*, Vol. 56, 3, pp. 921–965.

Daniel, K., Titman, S. (1997), Evidence on the Characteristics of Cross Sectional Variation in Stock Returns, *Journal of Finance*, Vol. 52, 1, pp. 1–33.

Dann, L. (1981), Common Stock Repurchases: An Analysis of Returns to Bondholders and Stockholders, *Journal of Financial Economics*, Vol. 9, pp. 113–138.

Das, S., Levine, C., Sivaramakrishnan, K. (1998), Earnings Predictability and Bias in Analysts' Earnings Forecasts, *Accounting Review*, Vol. 73, 2, pp. 277–294.

Davis, A. K., Piger, J. M., Sedor, L. M. (2011), Beyond the Numbers: Managers' Use of Optimistic and Pessimistic Tone in Earnings Press Releases, SSRN Electronic Paper Collection: http://ssrn.com/abstract=875399.

Davis, J., Fama, E., French, K. (2000), Characteristics, Covariances, and Average Returns: 1929 to 1997, *Journal of Finance*, Vol. 55, 1, pp. 389–406.

Davies, P. L., J. Canes, (1978), "Stock Prices and the Publication of Second-hand Information," *The Journal of Business* 51, pp. 43–56.

Dean, J. (1951), *Capital Budgeting*. New York: Columbia University Press.

Deaux, K., Emswiller, T. (1974), Explanations for Successful Performance on Sex-Linked Tasks: What Is Skill for the Male is Luck for the Female, *Journal of Personality and Social Psychology*, Vol. 29, pp. 80–85.

De Bondt, W. (1993), Betting on Trends: Intuitive Forecast of Financial Risk and Return, *International Journal of Forecasting*, Vol. 9, pp. 355–371.

De Bondt, W. (1998), A Portrait of the Individual Investor, *European Economic Review*, Vol. 42, 3–5, pp. 831–844.

De Bondt, W., Thaler, R. (1985), Does the Stock Market Overreact? *Journal of Finance*, Vol. 40, 3, pp. 793–805.

De Bondt, W., Thaler, R. (1987), Further Evidence on Investor Overreaction and Stock Market Seasonality, *Journal of Finance*, Vol. 42, 3, pp. 557–581.

De Bondt, W., Thaler, R. (1990), Do Security Analyst Overreact? *American Economic Review*, Vol. 80, 2, pp. 52–57.

Dechow, P., Hutton, A., Sloan, R. (2000), The Relation between Analysts' Forecasts of Long-Term Earnings Growth and Stock Price Performance Following Equity Offerings, *Contemporary Accounting Research*, Vol. 17, pp. 1–32.

Degeorge, F., Derrien, F., Womack, K. (2010), Auctioned IPOs: The U.S. Evidence, *Journal of Financial Economics*, Vol. 98, 2, pp.177–194.

Degeorge, F., Patel, J., Zeckhauser, R. (1999), Earnings Management to Exceed Thresholds, *Journal of Business*, Vol. 72, 1, pp. 1–33.

De Jong, A., Duca, E., Dutordoir, M. (2013), Do Convertible Bond Issuers Cater to Investor Demand? *Financial Management*, Vol. 42, 1, pp. 41–78

DellaVigna, S., Pollet, J. (2005), Strategic Release of Information on Friday: Evidence from Earnings Announcements, SSRN Electronic Paper Collection: http://ssrn.com/abstract=586702.

De Long, B., Shleifer, A., Summers, L., Waldmann, R. (1990a), Noise Trader Risk in Financial Markets, *Journal of Political Economy*, Vol. 98, 4, pp. 703–738.

De Long, B., Shleifer, A., Summers, L., Waldmann, R. (1990b), Positive Feedback Investment Strategies and Destabilizing Rational Speculation, *Journal of Finance*, Vol. 45, 2, pp. 379–395.

De Long, B., Shleifer, A., Summers, L., Waldmann, R. (1991), The Survival of Noise Traders in Financial Markets, *Journal of Business*, Vol. 64, 1, pp. 1–19.

Demers, E., Vega, C. (2011), Linguistic Tone in Earnings Announcements: News or Noise? FRB International Finance Discussion Paper No. 951, SSRN Electronic Paper Collection: http://ssrn.com/abstract=1152326.

Derrien, F. (2010), Initial Public Offerings, in Baker, K., Nofsinger, J. (eds.), *Behavioral Finance: Investors, Corporations, and Markets*. New York: John Wiley & Sons, pp. 475–490.

Desai, H., Jain, P. (1997), Long-Run Common Stocks Returns Following Splits and Reverse Splits, *Journal of Business*, Vol. 70, 3, pp. 409–433.

Dhaliwal, D., Erickson, M., Trezevant, R. (1999), A Test of the Theory of Tax Clienteles for Dividend Policies, *National Tax Journal*, Vol. 52, pp. 179–194.

Dhar, R., Zhu, N. (2006), Up Close and Personal: An Individual Level Analysis of the Disposition Effect, *Management Science*, Vol. 52, pp. 726–740.

Dimson, E. (1988), *Stock Market Anomalies*. Cambridge, UK: Cambridge University Press.

Dimson, E., Marsh, P. (1999), Murphy's Law and Market Anomalies, *Journal of Portfolio Management*, Vol. 25, 2, pp. 53–70.

Dimson, E., Marsh, P., Staunton, M. (2009), *Looking to the Long Term*, Credit Suisse Research Institute 2009 Report, Zurich, Switzerland.

Dimson, E., Garthwaite, A., Marsh, P., Staunton, M. (2013), *Credit Suisse Global Investment Returns Yearbook 2013*, Credit Suisse Research Institute 2013 Report, Zurich, Switzerland.

Dimson, E., Minio-Kozerski, C. (1999), Closed-End Funds: A Survey, *Financial Markets, Institutions and Instruments*, Vol. 8, 2, pp. 1–41.

Dissanaike, G. (1994), On the Computation of Returns in Tests of the Stock Market Overreaction Hypothesis, *Journal of Banking and Finance*, Vol. 18, pp. 1083–1094.

Dodd, P., Ruback, R. (1977), Tender Offers and Stockholders Returns, *Journal of Financial Economics*, Vol. 5, pp. 351–373.

Dodonova, A., Khoroshilov, Y. (2005), Applications of Regret Theory to Asset Pricing, Available at SSRN: http://ssrn.com/abstract=301383.

Donaldson, G. (1961), *Corporate Debt Capacity: A Study of Corporate Debt Policy and the Determination of Corporate Debt Capacity*. Boston, MA: Division of Research, Harvard Graduate School of Business Administration.

Dong, M., Hirshleifer, D., Richardson, S., Teoh, S. H. (2006), Does Investor Misvaluation Drive the Takeover Market? *Journal of Finance*, Vol. 61, 2, pp. 725–762.

Dougal, C., Engelberg, J., Parsons, C., Van Wesep, E. (2012), The Path Dependence of Borrowing Costs, SSRN Electronic Paper Collection: http://ssrn.com/abstract =1732559.

Dowling, M., Lucey, B. (2005), The Role of Feelings in Investor Decision-Making, *Journal of Economic Surveys*, Vol. 19, 2, pp. 211–237.

Dravid, A. R. (1987), A Note on the Behavior of Stock Returns around Ex-Dates of Stock Distributions, *Journal of Finance*, Vol. 42, 1, pp. 163–168.

Dyl, E. (1977), Capital Gains Taxation and Year-End Stock Market Behavior, *Journal of Finance*, Vol. 32, 1, pp. 165–175.

Eagles, J. (1994), The Relationship between Mood and Daily Hours of Sunlight in Rapid Cycling Bipolar Illness, *Biological Psychiatry*, Vol. 36, pp. 422–424.

Easterwood, J., Nutt, S. (1999), Inefficiency in Analysts' Earnings Forecasts: Systematic Misreaction or Systematic Optimism? *Journal of Finance*, Vol. 54, 5, pp. 1777–1797.

Easton, P., Harris, T., Ohlson, J. (1992), Aggregate Accounting Earnings Can Explain Most of Security Returns: The Case of Long Return Intervals, *Journal of Accounting and Economics*, Vol. 15, pp. 119–1142.

Eckbo, E. B., Masulis, R. W., Norli,Ø. (2000), Seasoned Public Offerings: Resolution of the New Issues Puzzle, *Journal of Financial Economics*, Vol. 56, 2, pp. 251–291.

Edwards, W. (1968), Conservatism in Human Information Processing, in Klienmutz, B. (ed.), *Formal Representation of Human Judgment*. New York: John Wiley & Sons, pp. 17–52.

Einhorn, H. (1980), Overconfidence in Judgment, *New Directions for Methodology of Social and Behavioral Science*, Vol. 4, pp. 1–16.

Einhorn, H., Hogarth, R. (1978), Confidence in Judgement: Persistence in the Illusion of Validity, *Psychological Review*, Vol. 85, pp. 395–416.

Elliot, J., Philbrick, D., Wiedman, C. (1995), Evidence from Archival Data on the Relation Between Security Analysts, *Contemporary Accounting Research*, Vol. 11, 2, pp. 919–938.

Ellsberg, D. (1961), Risk, Ambiguity, and the Savage Axioms, *Quarterly Journal of Economics*, Vol. 75, 3, pp. 643–669.

Elton, E., Gruber, M., Das, S., Hlavka, M. (1993), Efficiency with Costly Information: A Reinterpretation of Evidence from Managed Portfolios, *Review of Financial Studies*, Vol. 6, 1, pp. 1–22.

Epstein, L., Zin, S. (1989), Substitution, Risk Aversion, and Temporal Behavior of Consumption and Asset Returns: A Theoretical Framework, *Econometrica*, Vol. 57, 4, pp. 937–969.

Epstein, L., Zin, S. (1991), Substitution, Risk Aversion, and Temporal Behavior of Consumption and Asset Returns: An Empirical Analysis, *Journal of Political Economy*, Vol. 99, 2, pp. 263–286.

Erel, I., Julio, B., Kim, W., Weisbach, M. (2010), Macroeconomic Conditions and the Structure of Securities, Working paper, Ohio State University, Columbus.

Erickson, M., Wang, S. (1999), Earnings Management by Acquiring Firms in Stock for Stock Mergers, *Journal of Accounting and Economics*, Vol. 27, pp. 149–176.

Fama, E. (1965), The Behavior of Stock-Market Prices, *Journal of Business*, Vol.38, 1, pp. 34–105.

Fama, E. (1970), Efficient Capital Markets: A Review of Theory and Empirical Work, *Journal of Finance*, Vol. 25, 2, pp. 383–417.

Fama, E. (1998), Market Efficiency, Long-Term Returns, and Behavioral Finance, *Journal of Financial Economics*, Vol. 49, 3, pp. 283–306.

Fama, E., Fisher, L., Jensen, M., Roll, R. (1969), The Adjustment of Stock Prices to New Information, *International Economic Review*, Vol. 10, 1, pp. 1–21.

Fama, E., French, K. (1988), Permanent and Temporary Components of Stock Prices, *Journal of Political Economy*, Vol. 96, 2, pp. 246–273.

Fama, E., French, K. (1992), The Cross-Section of Expected Stock Returns, *Journal of Finance*, Vol. 47, 2, pp.427–465.

Fama, E., French, K. (1993), Common Risk Factors in the Returns of Stocks and Bonds, *Journal of Financial Economics*, Vol. 33, 1, pp. 3–56.

Fama, E., French, K. (1996), Multifactor Explanations of Asset Pricing Anomalies, *Journal of Finance*, Vol. 51, 1, pp. 55–84.

Fama, E., French, K. (2001), Disappearing Dividends: Changing Firm Characteristics Or Lower Propensity To Pay? *Journal of Financial Economics*, Vol. 60, 1, pp. 3–43.

Fama, E., French, K. (2002a), The Equity Premium, *Journal of Finance*, Vol. 57, 2, pp. 637–659.

Fama, E., French, K. (2002b), Testing Tradeoff and Pecking Order Predictions about Dividends and Debt, *Review of Financial Studies*, Vol. 15, pp. 1–37.

Fama, E., French, K. (2012), Size, Value, and Momentum in International Stock Returns, *Journal of Financial Economics*, Vol.105, 3, pp. 457–472.

Fama, E., MacBeth, J.D. (1973), Risk, Return, and Equilibrium: Empirical Tests, *Journal of Political Economy*, Vol. 81, pp. 607–636.

Ferson, W., Constantinides, G. (1991), Habit Persistence and Durability in Aggregate Consumption: Empirical Tests, *Journal of Financial Economics*, Vol. 29, 2, pp. 199–241.

Fischhoff, B. (1982), For Those Condemned to Study the Past: Heuristics and Biases in Hindsight, in Kahneman, D., Slovic, P., Tversky, A. (eds.), *Judgment under Uncertainty: Heuristics and Biases*. Cambridge, UK: Cambridge University Press, pp. 80–98.

Fischhoff, B., Phillips, L.D. (1982), Calibration of Subjective Probabilities: The State of the Art up to 1980, in Kahneman, D., Slovic, P., Tversky, A. (eds.), *Judgment under Uncertainty: Heuristics and Biases*. Cambridge, UK: Cambridge University Press, pp. 80–98, 306–334.

Fischhoff, B., Slovic, P., Lichtenstein, S. (1977), Knowing with Certainty: The Appropriateness of Extreme Confidence, *Journal of Experimental Psychology*, Vol. 3, pp. 552–564.

Fisher, I. (1930), *The Theory of Interest Rates*, London: Macmillan.

Fisher, S. (1994), Asset Trading, Transaction Costs and the Equity Premium, *Journal of Applied Econometrics*, Vol. 9, 4, pp. 71–95.

Flannery, J. F., Rangan, K.P. (2006), Partial Adjustment toward Target Capital Structures, *Journal of Financial Economics,* Vol. 79, 3, pp. 469–506.

Fong, K., Gallagher, D., Gardner, P., Swan, P.(2005), A Closer Examination of Investment Manager Herding Behaviour, SSRN Electronic Paper Collection: http://ssrn.com/abstract=508822.

Forgas, J. (1995), Mood and Judgment: The Affect Illusion Model (Aim), *Psychological Bulletin*, Vol. 117, 1, pp. 39–66.

Foster, G., Olsen, C., Shevlin, T. (1984), Earnings Releases, Anomalies, and the Behavior of Security Returns, *Accounting Review*, Vol. 59, 4, pp. 574–603.

Fox, C., Tversky, A. (1995), Ambiguity Aversion and Comparative Ignorance, *Quarterly Journal of Economics*, Vol. 110, 3, pp. 585–603.

Frank, M.Z., Goyal, V.K. (2003), Testing the Pecking Order Theory of Capital Structure, *Journal of Financial Economics*, Vol. 67, 2, pp. 217–248.

Frankfort-Nachmias, C., Nachmias, D. (2000), *Metody badawcze w naukach społecznych*. Poznań: Wydawnictwo Zysk i Spółka.

Frankfurter, G. M. and Wood, B. Jr. (2003), *Dividend Policy: Theory and Practice*, Amsterdam: Elsevier Academic Press

Franks, J., Harris, R., Titman, S. (1991), The Post-Merger Share Price Performance of Acquiring Firms, *Journal of Financial Economics*, Vol. 29, pp. 81–96.

French, K. (1980), Stock Returns for the Weekend Effect, *Journal of Financial Economics*, Vol. 8, 1, pp. 55–69.

French, K., Poterba, S. (1991), Investor Diversification and International Equity Markets, *American Economic Review*, Vol. 81, 2, pp. 222–226.

Friedman, J. N. (2006), Stock Market Driven Acquisitions: Theory and Evidence, *Working Paper*, Harvard University, Cambridge, MA.

Friedman, M. (1937), The Use of Ranks to Avoid the Assumption of Normality Implicit in the Analysis of Variance, *Journal of the American Statistical Association*, Vol. 32, pp. 675–701.

Friedman, M. (1953), The Case for Flexible Exchange Rates, in M. Friedman, *Essays in Positive Economics*, Chicago, IL: University of Chicago Press, pp. 157–203.

Friedman, M., Savage, L. (1948), The Utility Analysis of Choices Involving Risk, *Journal of Political Economy*, Vol. 56, 4, pp. 279–304.

Frisch, D., Baron, J. (1988), Ambiguity and Rationality, *Journal of Behavioral Decision Making*, Vol. 1, 3, pp. 149–157.

Froot, K., Dabora, E. (1999), How Are Stock Prices Affected by the Location of Trade? *Journal of Financial Economics*, Vol. 53, 2, pp. 189–216.

Fuller, K.,Goldstein, M. (2011), Do Dividends Matter More in Declining Markets? *The Journal of Corporate Finance*, Vol. 17, 3, pp. 457–473.

Galeotti, M., Schiantarelli, F. (1994), Stock Market Volatility and Investment: Do Only Fundamentals Matter? *Economica*, London School of Economics and Political Science, Vol. 61, 242, pp. 147–165.

Gärtner, M., Griesbach, B., Jung, F. (2011), PIGS or Lambs? The European Sovereign Debt Crisis and the Role of Rating Agencies, Universität St. Gallen, St. Gallen, Switzerland, Discussion Paper no. 2011–06.

Garvey, R., Murphy, A. (2004), Are Professional Traders Too Slow to Realize Their Losses, *Financial Analysts' Journal*, Vol. 60, 4, pp. 35–43.

Geczy, C., Minton, B., Schrand, C. (1997),Why Firms Use Currency Derivatives, *Journal of Finance* Vol. 52, 4, pp. 1323–1354.

Gerber, A., Hens, T., Vogt, B. (2002), Rational Investor Sentiment, Working Paper No. 126, Institute for Empirical Research in Economics, University of Zurich, Zurich, Switzerland.

Gibbons, M., Hess, P. (1981), Day of the Week Effects and Asset Returns, *Journal of Business*, Vol. 54, 4, pp. 579–596.

Gider, J., Hackbarth, D. (2010), Financing Decisions, in Baker, K., Nofsinger, J. (eds.), *Behavioral Finance. Investors, Corporations, and Markets*. New York: John Wiley & Sons, pp. 393–412.

Gilbert, D., Krull, D., Malone, P. (1990), Unbelieving the Unbelievable: Some Problems in the Rejection of False Information, *Journal of Personality & Social Psychology*, Vol. 59, pp. 601–613.

Gilchrist, S., Himmelberg, Ch., Huberman, G. (2005), Do Stock Price Bubbles Influence Corporate Investment? *Journal of Monetary Economics*, Vol. 52, 4, pp. 805–827.

Gilovich, T., Griffin, D., Kahneman, D. (2002), *Heuristics and Biases: The Psychology of Intuitive Judgment*. Cambridge, UK: Cambridge University Press.

Gilovich, T., Vallone, R., Tversky, A. (1985), The Hot Hand in Basketball: On the Misperception of Random Sequences, *Cognitive Psychology*, Vol. 17, pp. 295–314.

Gitman, L.J., Forrester, J.R. (1977), A Survey of Capital-Budgeting Techniques Used by Major U.S. Firms, *Financial Management*, Vol. 6, 3, pp. 66–71.

Glaser, M., Weber, M. (2007), Overconfidence and Trading Volume, *Geneva Risk and Insurance Review*, Vol. 32, 1, pp. 1–36.

Gneezy, U. (2005), Updating the Reference Level: Experimental Evidence, *Experimental Business Research*, Vol. 3, pp. 263–284

Goergen, M., Renneboog, L. (2004), Shareholder Wealth Effect of European Domestic and Cross-Border Takeover Bids, *European Financial Management*, Vol. 10, 1, pp. 9–45.

Goetzmann, W., Kumar, A. (2008), Equity Portfolio Diversification, *Review of Finance*, Vol. 12, 3, pp. 433–463.

Gonedes, N.J. (1976), Capital Market Equilibrium for a Class of Heterogeneous Expectations in a Two-Parameter World,*Journal of Finance*, Vol. 31, 2, pp. 1–15.

Gong, G., Louis, H., Sun, A. (2008), Earnings Management and Firm Performance Following Open-Market Repurchases, *Journal of Finance*, Vol. 63, 2, pp. 947–986.

Gort, M. (1969), An Economic Disturbance Theory of Mergers, *The Quarterly Journal of Economics*, MIT Press, Vol. 83, 4, pp. 624–642.

Graham, J., Harvey, C. (2001), The Theory and Practice of Corporate Finance: Evidence from the Field, *Journal of Financial Economics*, Vol. 60, pp. 187–243.

Graham, J., Harvey, C., Puri, M. (2013), Managerial Attitudes and Corporate Actions, *Journal of Financial Economics*, Vol. 109, 1, pp. 103–121.

Graham, J., Harvey, C., Rajgopal, S. (2005), The Economic Implications of Corporate Financial Reporting, *Journal of Accounting and Economics*, Vol. 40, pp. 3–73.

Graham, J., Kumar, A. (2006), Do Dividend Clienteles Exist? Evidence on Dividend Preferences of Retail Investors, *Journal of Finance*, Vol. 61, 3, pp. 1305–1336.

Grether, D. (1980), Bayes' Rule as a Descriptive Model: The Representativeness Heuristic, *Quarterly Journal of Economics*, Vol. 95, 4, pp. 537–557.

Grether, D., Plott, C. (1979), Economic Theory of Choice and the Preference Reversal Phenomenon, *American Economic Review*, Vol. 69, 4, pp. 623–638.

Griffin, D., Tversky, A. (1992), The Weighing of Evidence and the Determinants of Overconfidence, *Cognitive Psychology*, Vol. 24, pp. 411–435.

Griffin, J. (2002), Are the Fama and French Factors Global or Country Specific? *The Review of Financial Studies*, Vol.15, 3, pp. 783–803.

Griffin, J., Martin, S. (2003), Momentum Investing and Business Cycle Risk: Evidence from Pole to Pole, *Journal of Finance*, Vol. 58, 6, pp. 2515–2547.

Grinblatt, M., Han, B. (2005), The Disposition Effect and Momentum, *Journal of Financial Economics*, Vol. 78, pp. 311–339.

Grinblatt, M., Keloharju, M. (2001), What Makes Investors Trade, *Journal of Finance*, Vol. 56, 2, pp. 589–616.

Grinblatt, M., Titman, S., Wermers, R. (1995), Momentum Investment Strategies, Portfolio Performance, and Herding: A Study of Mutual Fund Behavior, *American Economic Review*, Vol. 85, 5, pp. 1088–1105.

Grinstein, Y., Michaely, R. (2005), Institutional Holdings and Payout Policy, *Journal of Finance*, Vol. 60, 3, pp. 1389–1426.

Gropp, J. (2012), Anchoring in Mergers & Acquisitions. An Empirical Study of the European Market, Master Thesis, Copenhagen Business School, available at www .grin.com.

Grundy, B., Martin, S. (2001), Understanding the Nature of the Risk and the Source of the Rewards to Momentum Investing, *Review of Financial Studies*, Vol. 14, 1, pp. 29–78.

Gu, A.Y. (2003), The Declining January Effect: Evidences from the U.S. Equity Markets, *Quarterly Review of Economics and Finance*, Vol. 43, 2, pp. 395–404.

Guedes, J., Opler, T. (1996), The Determinants of Maturity of Corporate Debt Issues, *Journal of Finance*, Vol. 51, 5, pp. 1809–1833.

Guedj, I., Scharfstein, D. (2008), Organizational Scope and Investment: Evidence from the drug Development Strategies of Biopharmaceutical Firms, NBER Working paper, National Bureau of Economic Research, Cambridge, MA.

Gul, F. (1991), A Theory of Disappointment Aversion, *Econometrica*, Vol. 59, 3, pp. 677–686.

Gultekin, M., Gultekin, N. (1983), Stock Market Seasonality: International Evidence, *Journal of Financial Economics*, Vol. 12, 4, pp. 469–481.

Hales, J., Kuang, X., Venkataraman, S. (2011), Who Believes the Hype? An Experimental Investigation of How Language Affects Investor Judgments, *Journal of Accounting Research*, Vol. 49, 1, pp. 223–255.

Haliassos, M., Bertaut, C. (1995), Why Do So Few Hold Stocks? *Economic Journal*, Vol. 105, pp. 1110–1130.

Han, K.C. (1995), The Effects of Reverse Splits on the Liquidity of the Stock, *The Journal of Financial and Quantitative Analysis*, Vol. 30, 1, pp. 159–169.

Hanley, K. (1993), The Underpricing of Initial Public Offerings and the Partial Adjustment Phenomenon, *Journal of Financial Economics*, Vol. 34, pp. 231–250.

Hansen, R., Sarin, A. (1998), Are Analysts Over-Optimistic Around Seasoned Equity Offerings, SSRN Electronic Paper Collection: http://ssrn.com/abstract=140435.

Harbaugh, R. (2002), Skill Reputation, Prospect Theory, and Regret Theory, Working paper, Mimeo, Claremont Colleges, Claremont, CA.

Harford, J. (2005), What drives merger waves? *Journal of Financial Economics*, Vol. 77, 3, pp. 529–560.

Harris, L. (1986), A Transaction Data Study of Weekly and Intradaily Patterns in Stock Returns, *Journal of Financial Economics*, Vol. 16, 1, pp. 99–117.

Harris, L., Gurel, E. (1986), Price and Volume Effects Associated with Changes in the S&P 500 List: New Evidence for the Existence of Price Pressures, *Journal of Finance*, Vol. 41, 4, pp. 815–829.

Haugen, R., Lakonishok, J. (1988), *The Incredible January Effect*. Homewood, IL: Dow Jones-Irwin.

Hawawini, G., Keim, D. (1995), On the Predictability of Common Stock Returns: World-Wide Evidence, in Jarrow, R., Maksimovic, V., Ziemba, W.(eds.), *Finance*. Amsterdam: North-Holland, pp. 82–99.

Hawkins, S., Hastie, R. (1990), Hindsight: Biased Judgments of Past Events After Outcomers Are Known, *Psychological Bulletin*, Vol. 107, pp. 311–327.

Hawkins, S., Hoch, S. (1992), Low-Involvement Learning: Memory Without Evaluation, *Journal of Consumer Research*, Vol. 19, pp. 212–225.

Hayward, M., Hambrick, D. (1997), Explaining the Premiums Paid for Large Acquisitions: Evidence of CEO Hubris, *Administrative Science Quarterly*, Vol. 42,1, pp. 103–129.

Hayward, M., Shepherd, D., Griffin, D. (2006), A Hubris Theory of Entrepreneurship, *Management Science*, Vol. 52, 2, pp. 160–172.

Healy, P., Palepu, K.G. (1988), Earnings Information Conveyed by Dividend Initiations and Omissions, *Journal of Financial Economics*, Vol. 21, pp. 149–176.

Heath, F., Tversky, A. (1991), Preference and Belief: Ambiguity and Competence in Choice Under Uncertainty, *Journal of Risk and Uncertainty*, Vol. 4, pp. 5–28.

Heaton, J. (2002), Managerial Optimism and Corporate Finance, *Financial Management Association*, Vol. 31, 2, pp. 33–45.

Heaton, J., Lucas, D. (1996), Evaluating the Effect of Incomplete Markets on Risk Sharing and Asset Pricing, *Journal of Political Economy*, Vol. 104, 3, pp. 668–712.

Heaton, J., Lucas, D. (1997), Market Frictions, Saving Behavior and Portfolio Choice, *Journal of Macroeconomic Dynamics*, Vol. 1, 1, pp. 76–101.

Henry, E. (2008), Are Investors Influenced by How Earnings Press Releases Are Written? *Journal of Business Communication*, Vol. 45, pp. 363–407.

Heston, S., Rouwenhorst, G., Wessels, R. (1995), The Structure of International Stock Returns and the Integration of Capital Markets, *Journal of Empirical Finance*, Vol. 2, pp. 173–197.

Hillier, D., Marshall, A. (2002), Insider Trading, Tax-Loss Selling, and the Turn-of-the-Year Effect, *International Review of Financial Analysis*, Vol. 11, 1, pp. 73–84.

Hirota, S., Sunder, S. (2002), Stock Market as a 'Beauty Contest': Investor Beliefs and Price Bubbles sans Dividend Anchors, Yale ICF Working Paper No. 02–42; EFA 2003 Annual Conference Paper No. 119. http://ssrn.com/abstract=302393.

Hirota, S., Sunder, S. (2007), Investor Beliefs and Price Bubbles sans Dividend Anchors, *Journal of Economic Dynamics and Control*, Vol. 31, 6, pp. 1875–1909.

Hirschey, M., Richardson, V., Scholz, S. (2000), How "Foolish" Are Internet Investors, *Financial Analysts Journal*, Vol. 56, 1, pp. 62–69.

Hirshleifer, D. (1993), Reputation, Incentives and Managerial Decisions, in Newman, P., Milgate, M., Eatwell, J. (eds.), *The New Palgrave Dictionary of Money and Finance*. New York: Stockton Press, pp. 332–337.

Hirshleifer, D. (2001), Investor Psychology and Asset Pricing, *Journal of Finance*, Vol. 56, 5, pp. 1533–1597.

Hirshleifer, D., and Teoh, S. H., (2003), "Limited Attention, Information Disclosure, and Financial Reporting," *Journal of Accounting and Economics*, 36(1–3), December, pp. 337–386.

Hirshleifer, D., Low, A., Teoh, S.H. (2012), Are Overconfident CEOs Better Innovators? *Journal of Finance*, Vol. 67, 4, pp. 1457–1498.

Hirshleifer, D., Shumway, T. (2003), Good Day Sunshine: Stock Returns and the Weather, *Journal of Finance*, Vol. 58, 3, pp.1009–1033.

Ho, T., Michaely, R. (1988), Information Quality and Market Efficiency, *Journal of Financial and Quantitative Analysis*, Vol. 23, 1, pp. 53–70.

Holinski, N., Kool, C., Muysken, J. (2010), Origins of Persistent Macroeconomic Imbalances in the Euro Area, RM/10/026, Maastricht, Maastricht University School of Business and Economics.

Hollander, M., Wolfe, D. (1999), *Nonparametric Statistical Methods*, Second Edition, John Wiley & Sons Series in Probability and Statistics. New York: John Wiley & Sons.

Hong, H., Lim, T., Stein, J. (2000), Bad News Travels Slowly: Size, Analyst Coverage and the Profitability of Momentum Strategies, *Journal of Finance*, Vol. 55, 1, pp. 265–295.

Hong, H., Stein, J. (1999), A Unified Theory of Underreaction, Momentum Trading and Overreaction is Asset Markets, *Journal of Finance*, Vol. 54, 6, pp. 2143–2184.

Hong, H., Wang, J., Yu, J. (2008), Firms as Buyers of Last Resort, *Journal of Financial Economics*, Vol. 88, 1, pp. 119–145.

Horowitz, J., Loughran, T., Savin, N.E. (2000), The Disappearing Size Effect, *Research in Economics*, Vol. 1, pp. 83–100.

Howarth, E., Hoffman, M. (1984), A Multidimensional Approach to the Relationship between Mood and Weather, *British Journal of Psychology*, Vol. 75, 2, pp. 15–23.

Howell, S., Jägle, A. (1997), Laboratory Evidence on How Managers Intuitively Value Real Growth Options, *Journal of Business Finance and Accounting*, Vol. 24, pp. 915–935.

Huang, R., Ritter, J. (2009), Testing Theories of Capital Structure and Estimating the Speed of Adjustment, *Journal of Financial and Quantitative Analysis*, Vol. 44, pp. 237–271.

Hubbart, G., Palia, D. (1999), A Re-Examination of the Conglomerate Merger Wave in the 1960s: An Internal Capital Market View, *Journal of Finance*, Vol. 54, 3, pp. 1131–1152.

Huberman, G. (2001), Familiarity Breeds Investment, *Review of Financial Studies*, Vol. 14, 3, pp. 659–680.

Huberman, G., Kandel, S. (1987), Mean-Variance Spanning, *Journal of Finance*, Vol. 42, 3, pp. 873–888.

Huberman, G., Regev, T. (2001), Contagious Speculation and a Cure for Cancer: A Nonevent that Made Stock Prices Soar, *Journal of Finance*, Vol. 56, 1, pp. 387–396.

Huddart, S., Lang, M., Yetman, M. (2005), Psychological Factors, Stock Price Paths, and Trading Volume, SSRN Electronic Papers Collection: http://ssrn.com/abstract=353749.

Ibbotson, R., Jaffe, J. (1975), "Hot Issue" Markets, *Journal of Finance*, Vol. 25, 4, pp. 1027–1042.

Ibbotson, R., Sindelar, J., Ritter, J. (1988), Initial Public Offerings, *Journal of Applied Corporate Finance*, Vol. 1, pp. 37–45.

Ibbotson, R., Sindelar, J., Ritter, J. (1994), The Market's Problems with the Pricing of Initial Public Offerings, *Journal of Applied Corporate Finance*, Vol. 7, pp. 66–74.

Ikenberry, D., Lakonishok, J., Vermaelen, T. (1995), Market Underreaction to Open Market Share Repurchases, *Journal of Financial Economics*, Vol. 39, 2–3, 181–208.

Ikenberry, D., Ramnath, S. (2002), Underreaction to self-selected News Events: The Case of Stock Splits, *Review of Financial Studies*, Vol. 15, 2, pp. 489–527

Ikenberry, D., Rankine, G., Stice, E. (1996), What Do Stock Splits Really Signal? *Journal of Financial and Quantitative Analysis*, Vol. 31, 3, pp. 357–375.

Irvine, P. (2004), Analysts' Forecasts and Brokerage-Firm Trading, *The Accounting Review*, Vol. 79, 1, pp. 125–149.

Irvine, P., Nathan, S., Simko, P. (1998), The Relation between Securities Firms' Mutual Fund Equity Holdings and their Analysts' Earnings Forecasts, SSRN Electronic Papers Collection: http://ssrn.com/abstract=74388.

Jaffe, J., Keim, D., Westerfield, R. (1989), Earning Yields, Market Values, and Stock Returns, *Journal of Finance*, Vol. 44, 1, pp. 135–148.

Jaffe, J., Westerfield, R. (1985), The Week-End Effect in Common Stock Returns: The International Evidence, *Journal of Finance*, Vol. 40, 2, pp. 433–454.

Jain, B., Kini, O. (1994), The Post-Issue Operating Performance of IPO Firms, *Journal of Finance*, Vol. 49, pp. 1699–1726.

Jegadeesh, N. (1990), Evidence of Predictable Behavior of Security Returns, *Journal of Finance*, Vol. 45, 3, pp. 881–898.

Jegadeesh, N., Kim, J., Krische, S., Lee, C. (2004), Analyzing the Analysts: When Do Recommendations Add Value? *Journal of Finance*, Vol. 59, 3, pp.1083–1124.

Jegadeesh, N., Titman, S. (1993) Returns to Buying Winners and Selling Losers: Implications for Stock Market Efficiency, *Journal of Finance*, Vol. 48, 1, pp. 65–91.

Jegadeesh, N., Titman, S. (1995), Overreaction, Delayed Reaction, and Contrarian Profits, *Review of Financial Studies*, Vol. 8, 4, pp. 973–993.

Jegadeesh, N., Titman, S. (2001), Profitability of Momentum Strategies: An Evaluation of Alternative Explanations, *Journal of Finance*, Vol. 56, 2, pp. 699–720.

Jegadeesh, N., Titman, S. (2002), Cross-Sectional and Time Series Determinants of Momentum Returns, *Review of Financial Studies*, Vol. 15, 1, pp. 143–158.

Jensen, M. (1986), Agency Costs of Free Cash Flow, Corporate Finance and Takeovers, *American Economic Review*, Vol. 76, 2, pp. 323–329.

Jensen, M., Ruback, R. (1983), The Market For Corporate Control: The Scientific Evidence, *Journal of Financial Economics*, Vol. 11, 1, pp. 17–31.

Jensen, M., Meckling, W.H. (1976), Theory of the Firm: Managerial Behaviour, Agency Costs and Ownership Structure, *Journal of Financial Economics,* Vol. 3, 4, pp. 305–360.

Jiraporn, P., Miller, G., Yoon, S., Kim, Y. (2008), Is Earnings Management Opportunistic or Beneficial? An Agency Theory Perspective, *International Review of Financial Analysis*, Vol. 17, pp. 622–634.

John, K., Liu, Y., Taffler, R. (2011), It Takes Two for Tango: Overpayment and Value Destruction in M&A Deals, BAFA 2011 Conference Presentation Paper, University of Sheffield, Sheffield, UK.

Johnson, E., Tversky, A. (1983), Affect, Generalization, and Perception of Risk, *Journal of Personality and Social Psychology*, Vol. 45, pp. 20–31.

Jung, K., Kim, Y., Stulz, R. (1996), Timing, Investment Opportunities, Managerial Discretion, and the Security Issue Decision, *Journal of Financial Economics,* Vol. 42, 2, pp. 159–185.

Kadapakkam, P.R., Krishnamurthy, S., Tse, Y. (2005), Stock Splits, Broker Promotion, and Decimalization, *Journal of Financial and Quantitative Analysis*, Vol. 40, pp. 873–895.

Kahneman, D., Knetsch, J. L., Thaler, R. (1990), Experimental Tests of the Endowment Effect and the Coase Theorem, *Journal of Political Economy*, Vol. 98, 6, pp. 1325–1248.

Kahneman, D., Knetsch, J. L., Thaler, R. (1991), The Endowment Effect, Loss Aversion, and the Status Quo Bias, *Journal of Economic Perspectives*, Vol. 5, 1, pp. 193–206.

Kahneman, D., Lovallo, D. (1993), Timid Choices and Bold Forecasts: A Cognitive Perspective on Risk Taking, *Management Science*, Vol. 39, 1, pp. 17–31.

Kahneman, D., Riepe, M. (1998), Aspects of Investor Psychology, *Journal of Portfolio Management*, Vol. 24, 4, pp. 52–65.

Kahneman, D., Slovic, P., Tversky, A. (1982), *Judgment under Uncertainty: Heuristics and Biases*. Cambridge, UK: Cambridge University Press.

Kahneman, D., Tversky, A. (1973), On the Psychology of Prediction, *Psychological Review*, Vol. 80, pp. 237–251.

Kahneman, D., Tversky, A. (1974), Judgment under Uncertainty: Heuristics and Biases, *Science*, Vol. 185, pp. 1124–1131.

Kahneman, D., Tversky, A. (1979), Prospect Theory: An Analysis of Decision under Risk, *Econometrica*, Vol. 47, 2, pp. 263–292.

Kahneman, D., Tversky, A. (1982), Evidential Impact of Base Rates, in Kahneman, D., Slovic, P., Tversky, A. (eds.), *Judgment under uncertainty: Heuristics and biases*. Cambridge, UK: Cambridge University Press.

Kahneman, D., Tversky, A. (1984), Choices, Values, and Frames, *American Psychologist*, Vol. 39, 4, pp. 341–350.

Kahneman, D., Tversky, A. (2000), *Choices, Values, and Frames*. Cambridge, UK: Cambridge University Press.

Kalay, A., Kornlund, M. (2012), The Market Reaction to Stock Splits Announcements: Earnings Information after All, SSRN Electronic Paper Collection: http://ssrn.com /abstract=1027543.

Kanaryan, K., Lyroudi, K., Patev, G. (2004), The Day of the Week Effect in the Central European Transition Stock Markets. Tsenov Academy of Economics Finance and Credit Working Paper No. 03–06, SSRN Electronic Paper Collection: http://ssrn .com/abstract=434501.

Kang, J., Stulz, R. (1997), Why Is There a Home Bias? An Analysis of Foreign Portfolio Equity Ownership in Japan, *Journal of Financial Economics*, Vol. 46, 1, pp. 3–28.

Karlsson, A., Norden, L. (2007), Home Sweet Home: Home Bias and International Diversification among Individual Investors, *Journal of Banking and Finance*, Vol. 31, 2, pp. 317–333.

Kaul, A., Mehrotra, V., Morck, R. (2000), Demand Curves for Stocks Do Slope Down: New Evidence from an Index Weights Adjustment, *Journal of Finance*, Vol. 55, 2, pp. 893–912.

Kaustia, M. (2004), Market-Wide Impact of the Disposition Effect: Evidence from IPO Trading Volume, *Journal of Financial Markets*, Vol. 7, 2, pp. 207–235.

Kayhan, A., Titman, S. (2007), Firms' Histories and Their Capital Structures, *Journal of Financial Economics*, Elsevier, Vol. 83, 1, pp. 1–32.

Keim, D. (1983), Size-Related Anomalies and Stock Return Seasonality: Further Empirical Evidence, *Journal of Financial Economics*, Vol. 12, 1, pp. 13–32.

Keim, D., Stambaugh, R. (1984), A Further Investigation of the Weekend Effect in Stock Returns, *Journal of Finance*, Vol. 39, 3, pp. 819–835.

Keren, G. (1991), Calibration and Probability Judgments: Conceptual and Methodological Issues, *Acta Psychologica*, Vol. 77, pp. 217–273.

Keynes, J.M. (1936), The General Theory of Employment, Interest and Money. London: Macmillan.

Kidd, J. (1970), The Utilization of Subjective Probabilities un Production Planning, *Acta Psychologica*, Vol. 34, pp. 338–347.

Kim, K., Nofsinger, J. (2005), Institutional Herding, Business Groups, and Economic Regimes: Evidence from Japan, *Journal of Business*, Vol. 78, 1, pp. 213–242.

Kim, S., Klein, A., Rosenfeld, J. (2008), Return Performance Surrounding Reverse Stock Splits: Can Investors Profit? *Financial Management*, Vol. 37, 2, pp. 173–192.

Kindleberger, C., Aliber, R. Z. (2011), *Manias, Panics, and Crashes: A History of Financial Crises*, 6th edition, New York: Palgrave Macmillan.

King, B., (1966), Market and Industry Factors in Stock Price Behavior, *Journal of Business*, Vol. 39, 1, supplement, pp. 139–190.

Kilka, M., Weber, M. (2000), Home Bias in International Stock Return Expectations, Working Paper, University of Manheim, Manheim, Germany.

Kirby, K., Marković, N. (1995), Modeling Myopic Decisions: Evidence for Hyperbolic Delay-Discounting within Subjects and Amounts, *Organizational Behavior and Human Decision Processes*, Vol. 64, 1, pp. 22–30.

Kiyoshi, K. (1985), Seasonal and Size Anomalies in the Japanese Stock Market, *Journal of Financial and Quantitative Analysis*, Vol. 20, 2, pp. 223–245.

Kleidon, A. (1986), Anomalies in Financial Economics: Blueprint for Change? *Journal of Business*, Vol. 59, 4, pp. 469–499.

Klein, P. (2001), Were the Acquisitive Conglomerates Inefficient? *RAND Journal of Economics*, Vol. 32, pp. 745–761.

Knetsch, J. L. (1989), The Endowment Effect and Evidence of Nonreversible Indifference Curves, *American Economic Review*, Vol. 79, 5, pp. 1277–1284.

Knetsch, J. L., Sinden, J. A. (1984), Willingness to Pay and Compensation Demanded: Experimental Evidence of an Unexpected Disparity in Measures of Value, *Quarterly Journal of Economics*, Vol. 99, 4, pp. 507–521.

Kocherlakota, N. (1996), The Equity Premium: It's Still a Puzzle, *Journal of Economic Literature*, Vol. 34, 1, pp. 42–71.

Koellinger, Ph., Minniti, M., Schade, Ch. (2007), I Think I Can, I Think I Can: Overconfidence and Entrepreneurial Behavior, *Journal of Economic Psychology*, Vol. 28, 4, pp. 502–527.

Konieczka, P., Szyszka, A. (2013), More Evidence on Dividend Catering Policy, Working paper, Warsaw School of Economics, Warsaw.

Koski, J. L. (2007), Does Volatility Decrease after Reverse Stock Splits? *The Journal of Financial Research*, Vol. 30, 2, pp. 217–235.

Kothari, S.P., Sloan, R. (1992), Information in Prices about Future Earnings: Implications for Earnings Response Coefficients, *Journal of Accounting and Economics*, Vol. 15, pp. 143–171.

Kramer, W., Runde, R. (1997), Stocks and the Weather: An Exercise in Data Mining or yet Another Capital Market Anomaly? *Empirical Economics*, Vol. 22, 4, pp. 637–641.

Kraus, A., Litzenberger, H. (1973), A State-Preference Model of Optimal Financial Leverage, *Journal of Finance*, Vol. 28, 4, pp. 911–922.

Krische, S. (2005), Investors' Evaluations of Strategic Prior-Period Benchmark Disclosures in Earnings Announcements, *The Accounting Review*, Vol. 80, 1, pp. 243–268.

Krische, S., Lee, C. (2001), The Information Content of Analyst Stock Recommendations, Parker Center for Investment Research Working Paper.

Kroll, Y., Levy, H., Rapoport, A. (1988), Experimental Tests of the Separation Theorem and the Capital Asset Pricing Model, *American Economics Review*, Vol. 78, 3, pp. 500–519.

Krueger, P., Landier, A., Thesmar, D. (2012), The WACC Fallacy: The Real Effects of Using a Unique Discount Rate, *AFA 2012 Chicago Meeting Paper*, SSRN Electronic Paper Collection: http://ssrn.com/abstract=1764024.

Kryzanowski, L., Zhang, H. (1992), The Contrarian Investment Strategy Does Not Work in Canadian Markets, *Journal of Financial and Quantitative Analysis*, Vol. 27, 3, pp. 383–395.

Kroll, Y., Levy, H., Rapoport, A. (1988), Experimental Tests of the Separation Theorem and the Capital Asset Pricing Model, *American Economic Review*, Vol. 78, pp. 500–519.

Kwok-Wah Fung, A. (1999), Overreaction in the Hong Kong Stock Market, *Global Finance Journal*, Vol. 10, 2, pp. 223–230.

Lakonishok, J., Lev, B. (1987), Stock Splits and Stock Dividends: Why, Who and When, *Journal of Finance*, Vol. 42, 4, pp. 913–932.

Lakonishok, J., Maberly, E. (1990), The Weekend Effect: Trading Patterns of Individual and Institutional Investors, *Journal of Finance*, Vol. 45, 1, pp. 231–243.

Lakonishok, J., Shleifer, A., Thaler, R., Vishny, R. (1991), Window Dressing by Pension Fund Managers, *American Economic Review*, Vol. 81, 2, pp. 227–231.

Lakonishok, J., Shleifer, A., Vishny, R. (1992), The Impact of Institutional Trading on Stock Prices, *Journal of Financial Economics*, Vol. 32, 1, pp. 23–43.

Lakonishok, J., Shleifer, A., Vishny, R. (1994), Contrarian Investment, Extrapolation, and Risk, *Journal of Finance*, Vol. 49, 5, pp. 1541–1578.

Lakonishok, J., Smidt, S. (1988), Are Seasonal Anomalies Real? A Ninety-Year Perspective, *Review of Financial Studies*, Vol. 4, pp. 403–425.

Lakonishok, J., Vermaelen, T. (1990), Anomalous Price Behavior around Repurchase Tender Offers, *Journal of Finance*, Vol. 45, 2, pp. 455–477.

Lamont, O., Thaler, R. (2003), Can the Market Add and Subtract? Mispricing in Tech Stock Carve-Outs, *Journal of Political Economy*, Vol. 111, 2, pp. 227–269.

Lamoureux, C. G., Poon, P. (1987), The Market Reaction to Stock Splits, *Journal of Finance*, Vol. 42, 5, pp. 1347–1370.

Lang, L., Stulz, R. (1994), Tobin's q, Corporate Diversification, and Firm Performance, *Journal of Political Economy*, Vol. 102, 6, pp. 1248–1280.

Langer, E. (1975), Illusion of Control, *Journal of Personality and Social Psychology*, Vol. 32, pp. 311–328.

Langer, E., Roth, J. (1975), Heads I Win Tails It's Chance: The Illusion of Control as a Function, *Journal of Personality and Social Psychology*, Vol. 32, pp. 951–955.

Lanstein, R., Reid, K., Rosenberg, B. (1985), Persuasive Evidence of Market Inefficiency, *Journal of Portfolio Management*, Vol. 11, pp. 9–17.

La Porta, R. (1996), Expectations and the Cross-Section of Stock Returns, *Journal of Finance*, Vol. 51, 5, pp. 1715–1742.

La Porta, R., Lakonishok, J., Shleifer, A., Vishny, R. (1997), Good News for Value Stocks: Further Evidence on Market Efficiency, *Journal of Finance*, Vol. 52, 2, pp. 859–874.

Lauterbach, B., Reisman, H. (2004), Keeping Up with the Joneses and the Home Bias, *European Financial Management*, Vol. 10, pp. 225–234.

Leary, M., Roberts, M. (2005), Do Firms Rebalance Their Capital Structures? *Journal of Finance*, Vol. 60, 6, pp. 2575–2619.

Lee, C., Shleifer, A., Thaler, R. (1990), Anomalies: Closed-End Mutual Funds, *Journal of Economic Perspectives*, Vol. 4, pp. 153–164.

Lee, C., Shleifer, A., Thaler, R. (1991), Investor Sentiment and the Closed-End Fund Puzzle, *Journal of Finance,* Vol. 46, 1, pp. 76–110.

Lee, I. (1997), Do Firms Knowingly Sell Overvalued Equity? *Journal of Finance*, Vol. 52, 4, pp. 1439–1466.

Lehmann, B. (1990), Fads, Martingales, and Market Efficiency, *Quarterly Journal of Economics*, Vol. 105, 1, pp. 1–28.

Lenney, E. (1977), Women's Self-Confidence in Achievement Settings, *Psychological Bulletin*, 84, pp. 1–13.

Lerner, J. (1994), Venture Capitalists and the Decision to Go Public, *Journal of Financial Economics*, Vol. 35, pp. 293–316.

LeRoy, S., Porter, R. (1981), The Present Value Relation: Tests Based on Implied Variance Bounds, *Econometrica*, Vol. 49, pp. 555–674.

Levis, M., Liodakis, M. (2001), Contrarian Strategies and Investor Expectations: The U.K. Evidence, *Financial Analysts Journal*, Vol. 57, 5, pp. 43–57.

Levis, M., Thomas, D. (1995), Investment Trust IPOs: Issuing Behavior and Price Performance. Evidence from the London Stock Exchange, *Journal of Banking and Finance*, Vol. 19, pp. 1437–1458.

Levy, H., Sarnat, M. (1970), International Diversification of Investment Portfolios, *American Economic Review*, Vol. 60, pp. 668–675.

Lewellen, J., Shanken, J. (2002), Learning, Asset-Pricing Tests, and Market Efficiency, *Journal of Finance*, Vol. 57, 3, pp. 1113–1145.

Lewis, W.W. (2004), The Power of Productivity: Wealth, Poverty, and the Threat to Global Stability. Chicago: The University of Chicago Press.

Lewis, K. (1999), Trying to Explain Home Bias in Equities and Consumption, *Journal of Economic Literature*, Vol. 37, pp. 571–608.

Li, W., Lie, E. (2006), Dividend Changes and Catering Incentives, *Journal of Financial Economics*, Vol. 80, 2, pp. 293–308.

Li, H., Xu, Y. (2002), Survival Bias and the Equity Premium Puzzle, *Journal of Finance*, Vol. 57, 5, pp. 1981–1995.

Libby, R., Bloomfield, R., Nelson, M. (2002), Experimental Research in Financial Accounting, *Accounting Organizations and Society*, Vol. 27, 8, pp. 775–810.

Lichtenstein, S., Fischhoff, B. (1977), Do Those Who Know More Also Know More about How Much They Know? *Organizational Behavior and Human Performance*, Vol. 20, pp. 159–183.

Lichtenstein, S., Fischhoff, B., Phillips, L. (1982), Calibration of Probabilities: The State of the Art to 1980, in Kahneman, D., Slovic, P., Tversky, A. (eds.), *Judgment under Uncertainty: Heurestics and Biases.* New York: Cambridge University Press, pp. 306–334.

Lichtenstein, S., Slovic, P. (1971), Reversals of Preference between Bids and Choices in Gambling Decisions, *Journal of Experimental Psychology*, 89, 1, pp. 46–55.

Lichtenstein, S., Slovic, P. (1973), Response-Induced Reversals of Preference in Gambling: An Extended Replication in Las Vegas, *Journal of Experimental Psychology*, Vol. 101, 11, pp. 16–20.

Liew, J., Vassalou, M. (2000), Can Book-to-Market, Size and Momentum Be Risk Factors that Predict Economic Growth? *Journal of Financial Economics*, Vol. 57, 2, pp. 221–246.

Lim, T. (2001), Rationality and Analysts' Forecast Bias, *Journal of Finance*, Vol. 56, 1, pp. 369–385.

Lindenberg, E. (1979), Capital Market Equilibrium with Price Affecting Institutional Investors, in: Elton, E. J., Gruber M. J., *Portfolio Theory 25 Years Later*, Amsterdam: North-Holland.

Lintner, J. (1962). Dividends, Earnings, Leverage, Stock Prices and the supply of Capital to Corporations, *The Review of Economics and Statistics*, 44, 3, pp. 243–69.

Lintner, J. (1965), Security Prices, Risk, and Maximal Gains from Diversification, *Journal of Finance*, Vol. 20, pp. 587–615.

Lintner, J. (1969), The Aggregation of Investor's Diverse Judgements and Preferences in Purely Competitive Security Markets, *Journal of Financial and Quantitative Analysis*, Vol. 4, pp. 347–400.

Lintner, J. (1971), Expectations, Mergers and Equilibrium in Purely Competitive Securities Markets, *The American Economic Review*, Vol. 2, 5, pp. 101–111.

Liu, P., S. Smith, and A. Syed, (1990), "Stock Price Reactions to the Wall Street Journal's Securities Recommendations," *Journal of Financial and Quantitative Analysis* 25, September, pp. 399–410.

Liu, Y. (2009), CEO Narcissism in M&A Decision-Making and Its Impact on Firm Performance, Doctorate Thesis, The University of Edinburgh.

Liu, Y., Ning, Y., Davidson, W. (2010), Earnings Management Surrounding New Debt Issues, *Financial Review*, Vol. 45, 3, pp. 659–681.

Ljungqvist, A.,Wilhelm, W., Jr. (2005), Does Prospect Theory Explain IPO Market Behavior? *Journal of Finance*, Vol. 60, 4, pp. 1759–1790.

Lo, A.W., MacKinlay, A.C. (1988), Stock Prices Do Not Follow Random Walks: Evidence from the Simple Specification Test, *Review of Financial Studies*, Vol. 1, 1, pp. 41–66.

Lo, A.W., MacKinlay, A.C. (1990), When Are Contrarian Profits Due to Stock Market Overreaction? *Review of Financial Studies*, Vol. 3, 2, pp. 175–205.

Loewenstein, G. (1988), Frames of Mind in Intertemporal Choice, *Management Science*, Vol. 34, pp. 200–214.

Loewenstein, G., Hsee, C., Weber, E., Welsh, N. (2001), Risk as Feelings, *Psychological Bulletin*, Vol. 127, 2, pp. 267–286.

Loewenstein, G., Kahneman, D. (1991), Explaining the Endowment Effect, *Working Paper*, Carnegie Mellon University, Pittsburgh, PA.

Loewenstein, G., Prelec, D. (1992), Anomalies in Intertemporal Choice, *Quarterly Journal of Economics*, Vol. 107, 2, pp. 573–597.

Loewenstein, G., Prelec, D. (1993), Preferences for Sequences of Outcomes, *Psychological Review*, Vol. 100, 1, pp. 91–108.

Long, J. B., Jr. (1978), The Market Valuation of Cash Dividends: A Case to Consider, *Journal of Financial Economics*, Vol. 6, 2–3, pp. 235–264.

Longstaff, F. A., Schwartz, E. (2001), Valuing American Options by Simulation: A Simple Least-Squares Approach, *Review of Financial Studies*, Vol. 14, 1, pp. 113–147.

Loomes, G., Sugden, R. (1982), Regret Theory: An Alternative Theory of Rational Choice under Uncertainty, *Economic Journal*, Vol. 92, pp. 805–824.

Lord, Lepper, Ross (1979), Biased Assimilation and Attitude Polarization: The Effects of Prior Theories on Subsequently Considered Evidence, *Journal of Personality and Social Psychology*, Vol. 37, pp. 2098–2110.

Lovallo, D., Kahneman, D. (2003), Delusions of Success. How Optimism Undermines Executives' Decisions, *Harvard Business Review*, Vol. 81, 7, pp. 56–63.

Lougee, B. A., Marquardt, C.A. (2004), Earnings Informativeness and Strategic Disclosure: An Empirical Examination of "Pro forma" Earnings, *Accounting Review*, Vol. 79, 3, pp. 769–795.

Loughran, T., Ritter, J., Rydqvist, K. (1994), Initial Public Offerings: International Insights, *Pacific-Basin Finance Journal*, Vol. 2, 2–3, pp. 165–199.

Loughran, T., Ritter, J. (1995), The New Issue Puzzle, *Journal of Finance*, Vol. 50, 1, pp. 23–51.

Loughran, T., Ritter, J. (1996), Long-Term Market Overreaction: The Effect of Low-Priced Stock, *Journal of Finance*, Vol. 51, 5, pp. 1959–1970.

Loughran, T., Ritter, J. (2000), Uniformly Least Powerful Tests of Market Efficiency, *Journal of Financial Economics*, Vol. 55, 3, pp. 361–389.

Loughran, T., Ritter, J. (2002), Why Don't Issuers Get Upset about Leaving Money on the Table in IPOs?*Review of Financial Studies*, Vol. 15, pp. 413–443.

Loughran, T., Vijh, A. (1997), Do Long-Term Shareholders Benefit from Corporate Acquisitions? *Journal of Finance*, Vol. 52, 5, pp. 1765–1790.

Lucas, D. (1994), Asset Pricing with Undiversifiable Income Risk and Short Sale Constrains: Deepening the Equity Premium Puzzle, *Journal of Monetary Economics*, Vol. 34, pp. 325–341.

Lundenberg, M., Fox, P., Punccohar, J. (1994), Highly Confident but Wrong: Gender Differences and Similarities in Confidence Judgments, *Journal of Educational Psychology*, Vol. 86, pp. 114–121.

Loughran, T., Ritter, J. (2002), Why Don't Issuers Get Upset about Leaving Money on the Table in IPOs? *Review of Financial Studies*, Vol. 15, 2, pp. 413–443.

Lynch, A., Mendenhall, R. (1997), New Evidence on Stock Price Effects Associated with Changes in the S&P 500 Index, *Journal of Business*, Vol. 70, 3, pp. 351–383.

Malkiel, B. (2007), A Random Walk Down Wall Street: The Time-Tested Strategy for Successful Investing. New York: W. W. Norton & Company.

Malmendier, U., Tate, G. (2005a), CEO Overconfidence and Corporate Investment, *Journal of Finance* Vol. 60, 6, pp. 2661–2700.

Malmendier, U., Tate, G. (2005b), Does Overconfidence Affect Corporate Investment? CEO Overconfidence Measures Revisited, *European Financial Management*, Vol. 11, pp. 649–659.

Malmendier, U., Tate, G. (2008), Who Makes Acquisitions? CEO Overconfidence and the Market's Reaction, *Journal of Financial Economics*, Vol. 89, pp. 20–43.

Malmendier, U., Tate, G., Yan, J. (2011), Overconfidence and Early-life Experiences: The Effect of Managerial Traits on Corporate Financial Polices, *Journal of Finance*, Vol. 66, 5, pp. 1687–1733.

Mankiw, N., Zeldes, S. (1991), The Consumption of Stockholders and Nonstockholders, *Journal of Financial Economics*, Vol. 29, pp. 97–112..

March, G., Shapira, Z. (1987), Managerial Perspectives on Risk and Risk Taking, *Management Science*, Vol. 33,11, pp. 1404–1418.

Markides, C. (1992), The Economics Characteristics of De-diversifying Firms, *British Journal of Management*, Vol. 3, 2, pp. 91–100.

Markowitz, H. (1952), Portfolio Selection, *Journal of Finance*, Vol. 7, 1, pp. 77–91.

Marsh, P. (1982), The Choice between Equity and Debt: An Empirical Study, *Journal of Finance*, Vol. 37, 1, pp. 121–144.

Marsh, T., Merton, R. (1986), Dividend Variability and Variance Bounds Tests for the Rationality of Stock Market Prices, *American Economic Review*, Vol. 76, 3, pp. 483–499.

Martell, T.F., Webb, G.P. (2008), The Performance of Stocks That Are Reverse Split, *Review of Quantitative Finance and Accounting*, Vol.30, pp. 253–279.

Masulis, R. (1980), The Effects of Capital Structure Change on Security Prices: A Study of Exchange Offers, *Journal of Financial Economics*, Vol. 8, 2, pp. 139–178.

Matsumoto, D. (2002), Management Incentives to Avoid Negative Earnings Surprises, *Accounting Review*, Vol. 77, 3, pp. 483–515.

Matsusaka, J.G. (1993), Takeover Motives During the Conglomerate Merger Wave, *RAND Journal of Economics*, Vol. 24, pp. 357–379.

Mayers, D. (1972), Non Marketable Assets and Capital Market Equilibrium under Uncertainty, in Jensen, M. (ed.), *Studies in the Theory of Capital Markets*. New York: Pragaeger, pp. 223–248.

McDonald, R., Siegel, D. (1985), Investment and the Valuation of Firms When There Is an Option to Shut Down, *International Economic Review*, Vol.26, pp. 331–349.

McDonald, R., Siegel, D. (1986), The Value of Waiting to Invest, *Quarterly Journal Economics*, Vol. 101, pp. 707–727.

McKinsey Global Institute (2008), Mapping Global Capital Markets: Fourth Annual Report, available on-line http://www.mckinsey.com/insights/global_capital_markets/mapping_global_capital_markets_fourth_annual_report.

McLean, R.D., Zhao, M. (2013), The Business Cycle, Investor Sentiment, and Costly External Finance, *Journal of Finance,* forthcoming.

McQueen, G., Thorley, S. (1994), Bubbles, Stock Returns, and Duration Dependence, *Journal of Financial and Quantitative Analysis*, Vol. 29, pp. 379–401.

Mehra, R. (2003), The Equity Premium: Why Is It a Puzzle? *Financial Analysts Journal*, Vol. 59, 1, pp. 54–69.

Mehra, R., Prescott, E. (1985), The Equity Premium Puzzle, *Journal of Monetary Economics*, Vol. 15, 2, pp. 145–161.

Mehra, R., Prescott, E. (1988), The Equity Premium Puzzle: A Solution? *Journal of Monetary Economics*, Vol. 22, 1, pp. 133–136.

Mellers, B., Schwartz, A., Cooke, A. (1998), Judgment and Decision Making, *Annual Review of Psychology*, Vol. 49, pp. 447–477.

Mello, A., Parsons, J. (2000), Hedging and Liquidity, *Review of Financial Studies*, Vol. 13, pp. 127 – 153.

Menyah, K. (1999), New Evidence on the Impact of Size and Taxation on the Seasonality of UK Equity Returns, *Review of Financial Economics*, Vol. 8, 1, pp. 11–24.

Merrow, E. W., Phillips, K. E., Myers, C. (1981), Understanding Cost Growth and Performance Shortfalls in Pioneer Process Plants, The Rand Corporation, Santa Monica.

Merton, R. C. (1973a), An Intertemporal Capital Asset Pricing Model, *An Intertemporal Capital Asset Pricing Model Econometrica*, Vol. 41, 5, pp. 867–887.

Merton, R. C. (1973b), Theory of Rational Option Pricing, *Bell Journal of Economics and Management Science*, Vol. 4, 1, pp. 141–183.

Mian, S. (1996), Evidence on Corporate Hedging Policy, *Journal of Financial and Quantitative Analysis*, Vol. 31, pp. 419–439.

Michaely, R., Roberts, M. (2012), Corporate Dividend Policies: Lessons from Private Firms, *Review of Financial Studies*, Vol. 25, pp. 711–746.

Michaely, R., Thaler, R., Womack, K. (1995), Price Reactions to Dividend Initiations and Omissions: Overreaction or Drift? *Journal of Finance*, Vol. 50, 2, pp. 573–608.

Michaely, R., Womack, K. (1999), Conflict of Interest and the Creditability of Underwriter Analyst Recommendations, *Review of Financial Studies*, Vol. 12, 4, pp. 653–686.

Mikkelson, W. H., Partch, M. M., Shah, K. (1997), Ownership and Operating Performance of Companies that Go Public, *Financial Economics*, Vol. 44, 3, pp. 281–307.

Milgrom, P., Stockey, N. (1982), Information, Trade, and Common Knowledge, *Journal of Economic Theory*, Vol. 22, 1, pp. 17–27.

Miller, M. H., Modigliani, F. (1961), Dividend Policy, Growth and the Valuation of Shares, *Journal of Business*, Vol. 34, pp. 411–433.

Miller, D., Ross, M. (1975), Self-Serving Bias in Attribution of Causality: Fact or Fiction? *Psychological Bulletin*, Vol. 82, pp. 213–225.

Miller, K., Shapira, Z. (2004), An Empirical Test of Heuristics and Biases Affecting Real Options Valuation, *Strategic Management Journal*, Vol. 25, 3, pp. 269–284.

Mitchell, M., Pulvino, T., Stafford, E. (2002), Limited Arbitrage in Equity Markets, *Journal of Finance*, Vol. 57, 2, pp. 551–584.

Mitchell, M., Stafford, E. (2000), Managerial Decisions and Long-Term Stock Price Performance, *Journal of Business*, Vol. 73, 3, pp. 287–329.

Modigliani, F., Cohn, R. (1979), Inflation, Rational Valuation and the Market, *Financial Analysts Journal*, Vol. 35, 3, pp. 24–44.

Modigliani, F., Miller, M. H. (1958), The Cost of Capital, Corporate Finance and the Theory of Investment, *American Economic Review*, Vol. 48, pp. 261–297.

Modigliani, F., Miller, M. H. (1963), Corporate Income Taxes and the Cost of Capital: A Correction, *American Economic Review*, Vol. 53, pp. 433–443.

Moeller, S., Schlingemann, F., Stulz, R. (2005), Wealth Destruction on a Massive Scale? A Study of Acquiring-Firms Returns in the Recent Merger Wave, *Journal of Finance*, Vol. 60, 2, pp. 757–782.

Monnin, P. (2004), Are Stock Markets Really Like Beauty Contests? Empirical Evidence of Higher Order Belief's Impact on Asset Prices, Working Paper No. 202, Institute for Empirical Research in Economics, University of Zurich, Zurich, Switzerland.

Montgomery, H. (1997). Naturalistic Decision Making. Proceedings of the Subjective Probability, Utility and Decision Making conference, University of Mannheim, Mannheim, Germany.

Morck, R., Shleifer, A., Vishny, R. (1990), The Stock Market and Investment: Is the Market a Sideshow? *Brookings Papers on Economic Activity*, Vol. 2, pp. 157–215.

Morse, A., Shive, S. (2011), Patriotism in Your Portfolio, *Journal of Financial Markets*, Vol. 14, pp. 411–440.

Moskowitz, T., Grinblatt, M. (1999), Do Industries Explain Momentum, *Journal of Finance*, Vol. 54, 4, pp. 1249–1290.

Mossin, J. (1966), Equilibrium in a Capital Asset Market, *The Econometric Society*, Vol. 34, pp. 768–783.

Myers, S., Majluf, N. (1984), Corporate Financing and Investment Decisions When Firms Have Information that Investors Do Not Have, *Journal of Financial Economics*, Vol. 13, pp.187–221.

Myers, S., Shyam-Sunder, L. (1999), Testing Static Tradeoff against Pecking Order Models of Capital Structure, *Journal of Financial Economics*, Vol. 51, 2, pp. 219–244.

Nagel, S. (2005), Short Sales, Institutional Investors and the Cross-Section of Stock Returns, *Journal of Financial Economics*, Vol. 78, 2, pp. 277–309.

Neale, M., Bazerman, M. (1990), *Cognition and Rationality in Negotiation*. New York: Free Press.

Neumann J., Morgenstern, O. (1944), *Theory of Games and Economic Behavior*. Princeton, NJ: Princeton University Press.

Newman, J., Wolff, W., Hearst, E. (1980), The Feature-Positive Effect in Adult Human Subjects, *Journal of Experimental Psychology: Human Learning and Memory*, Vol. 6, pp. 630–650.

Nisbett, R., Wilson, T. (1977a), The Halo Effect: Evidence for Unconscious Alternation of Judgments, *Journal of Personality and Social Psychology*, Vol. 35, pp. 250–256.

Nisbett, R., Wilson, T. (1977b), Telling More than We Can Know: Verbal Reports on Mental Processes, *Psychological Review*, Vol. 84, pp. 231–259.

Nofsinger, J. (2001), Investment Madness. How Psychology Affects Your Investing. London: Prentice Hall.

Northcraft, G., Neale, M. (1987), Experts, Amateurs, and Real Estate: An Anchoring-and-Adjustment Perspective on Property Pricing Decisions, *Organizational Behavior and Human Decision Process*, Vol. 39, pp. 84–97.

Odean, T. (1998a), Are Investors Reluctant to Realize Their Losses? *Journal of Finance*, Vol. 53, 5, pp. 1775–1798.

Odean, T. (1998b), Volume, Volatility, Price, and Profit When All Traders Are Above Average, *Journal of Finance*, Vol. 53, 6, pp. 1887–1934.

Odean, T. (1999), Do Investors Trade Too Much? *American Economic Review*, Vol. 89, 5, pp. 1279–1298.

Oliver, B. (2005), The Impact of Managerial Confidence on Capital Structure, Australian National University Working Paper, SSRN Electronic Paper Collection: http://ssrn.com/abstract=791924.

Olsen, R. (1997), Investment Risk: The Experts' Perspective, *Financial Analysts Journal*, Vol. 53, 2, pp. 62–66.

Olsen, R., Troughton, G. (2000), Are Risk Premium Anomalies Caused by Ambiguity? *Financial Analysts Journal*, Vol. 56, 2, pp. 24–31.

O'Neal, E. (2000), Industry Momentum and Sector Mutual Funds, *Financial Analysts Journal*, Vol. 56, 4, pp. 37–49.

Oskamp, S. (1962), The Relationship of Clinical Experience and Training Methods to Several Criteria of Clinical Prediction, *Psychological Monographs*, Vol. 76, No.547, pp. 1–27.

Oskamp, S. (1982), Overconfidence in Case-Study Judgments, in Kahneman, D., Slovic, P., Tversky, A., *Judgment under Uncertainty: Heuristics and Biases*. Cambridge, UK: Cambridge University Press, pp. 287–293

Pagano, M., Panetta, F., Zingales, L. (1998), Why Do Firms Go Public? An Empirical Analysis, *Journal of Finance*, Vol. 53, 1, pp. 27–64.

Pastor, L., Stambaugh, R. (2003), Liquidity Risk and Expected Stock Returns, *Journal of Political Economy*, Vol. 111, pp. 642–685.

Patz, D. H.(1989), UK Analysts' Earnings Forecasts, *Accounting and Business Research*, Vol. 19, pp. 267–275.

Perez-Gonzales, F. (2002), Large Shareholders and Dividends: Evidence from U.S. Tax Reforms, SSRN Electronic Paper Collection: http://ssrn.com/abstract=337640.

Persinger, M. (1975), Lag Responses in Mood Reports to Changes in Weather Matrix, *International Journal of Biometeorology*, Vol. 19, 2, pp. 108–114.

Petty, R., Gleicher, F., Baker, S. (1991), Multiple Roles for Affect in Persuasion, in Forgas, J. (ed.), *Emotion and Social Judgments*. Oxford: Pergamon, pp. 181–200.

Peyer, U., Vermaelen, T. (2009), The Nature and Persistence of Buyback Anomalies, *Review of Financial Studies*, Vol. 22, 4, pp.1693–1745.

Pilotte, E. (1997), Earnings and Stock Splits in the Eighties, *Journal of Financial and Strategic Decisions*, Vol. 10, 2, pp. 37–47.

Pinegar, J.M., Lease, R.C. (1986), The Impact of Preferred-for-Common Exchange Offers on Firm Value, *Journal of Finance*, Vol. 41, 4, pp. 795–814.

Plotnicki, M., Szyszka, A. (2013), IPO Market Timing: The Evidence of the Disposition Effect among Corporate Managers, Working paper, SSRN Electronic Paper Collection: http://ssrn.com/abstract=2227503.

Polk, Ch., Sapienza, P. (2009), The Stock Market and Corporate Investment: A Test of Catering Theory, *Review of Financial Studies*, Vol. 22, pp. 187–217.

Polkovnichenko, V. (2005), Household Portfolio Diversification: A Case For Rank Dependant Preferences, *Review of Financial Studies*, Vol. 18, 4, pp. 1468–1502.

Pound, J., Zeckhauser, R. (1990), Clearly Heard on the Street: The Effect of Takeover Rumors on Stock Prices, *Journal of Business*, Vol. 63, 3, pp. 291–308.

Poterba, J., Summers, L. (1988), Mean Reversion in Stock Prices: Evidence and Implications, *Journal of Financial Economics*, Vol. 22., 1, pp. 27–60.

Rajan, R., Servaes, H. (1997), Analyst Following of Initial Public Offerings, *Journal of Finance*, Vol. 52, 2, pp. 507–529.

Ranguelova, E. (2001), Disposition Effect and Firm Size: New Evidence on Individual Investor Trading Activity, SSRN Electronic Paper Collection: http://ssrn.com/abstract=293618.

Rashes, M. (2001), Massively Confused Investors Making Conspicuously Ignorant Choices, *Journal of Finance*, Vol. 56, pp. 1911–1928.

Rau, R., Vermaelen, T. (1998), Glamour, Value and the Post-Acquisition Performance of Acquiring Firms, *Journal of Financial Economics*, Vol. 49, 2, pp. 223–253.

Ravenscraft, D., Scherer, F. (1987), *Mergers, Sell-Offs, and Economic Efficiency*. Washington, DC: Brookings Institution Press.

Read, P., Loewenstein, G., Rabin, M. (1999), Choice Bracketing, *Journal of Risk and Uncertainty*, 19, pp. 171–197.

Reber, R., Schwarz, N. (1999), Effects of Perceptual Fluency on Judgments of Truth, *Consciousness and Cognition*, Vol. 8, pp. 338–342.

Reinganum, M. (1981), Misspecifiaction of Capital Asset Pricing: Empirical Anomalies Based on Earnings Yields and Market Values, *Journal of Financial Economics*, Vol. 9, 1, pp. 19–46.

Reinganum, M. (1983), The Anomalous Stock Market Behavior of Small Firms in January: Empirical Tests for Tax-Loss Selling Effects, *Journal of Financial Economics*, Vol. 12, 1, pp. 89–104.

Reinganum, M., Shapiro, A. (1987), Taxes and Stock Market Seasonality: Evidence from the London Stock Exchange, *Journal of Business*, Vol. 60, 2, pp. 281–295.

Reitz, T. (1988), The Equity Risk Premium: A Solution, *Journal of Monetary Economics*, Vol. 22, pp. 117–131.

Rhodes-Kropf, M., Viswanathan, S. (2004), Market Valuation and Merger Waves, *Journal of Finance*, Vol. 59, 6, pp. 2685–2718.

Rhodes-Kropf, M., Robinson, D. T., Viswanathan, S. (2005), Valuation Waves and Merger Activity: The Empirical Evidence, *Journal of Financial Economics*, Vol. 77, 3, pp. 561–603.

Ritter, J. (1984), The "Hot Issue" Market of 1980, *Journal of Business*, Vol. 57, 2, pp. 215–240.

Ritter, J. (1988), The Buying and Selling Behavior of Individual Investors at the Turn of the Year, *Journal of Finance*, Vol. 43, 3, pp. 701–717.

Ritter, J. (1991), The Long-Run Performance of Initial Public Offerings, *Journal of Finance*, Vol. 46, 1, pp. 3–27.

Ritter, J. (2003), Differences between American and European IPO Markets, *European Financial Management*, Vol. 9, 4, pp. 421–434.

Ritter, J., Warr, R. (2002), The Decline of Inflation and the Bull Market of 1982–1999, *Journal of Financial and Quantitative Analysis*, Vol. 37, 1, pp. 29–63.

Roberts, H. (1967), Statistical versus Clinical Prediction of the Stock Market. Unpublished Manuscript, Center for Research in Security Prices, University of Chicago.

Rode, C., Cosmides, L., Hell, W., Tooby, J. (1999), When and Why Do People Avoid Unknown Probabilities in Decisions under Uncertainty? Testing Some Predictions from Optimal Foraging Theory, *Cognition*, Vol. 72, 3, pp. 269–304.

Rogalski, R. (1984a), A Further Investigation of the Weekend Effect in Stock Returns: Discussion, *Journal of Finance*, Vol. 39, 3, pp. 835–837.

Rogalski, R. (1984b), New Findings Regarding Day-of-the-Week Returns over Trading and Non-Trading Periods: A Note, *Journal of Finance*, Vol. 39, 5, pp. 1603–1614.

Roll, R. (1981), A Possible Explanation of the Small Firm Effect, *Journal of Finance*, Vol. 36, 3, pp. 879–888.

Roll, R. (1983), Vas ist das? The Turn-of-the-year Effect and the Return Premia of small firms, *Journal of Portfolio Management*, Vol. 9, 2, pp. 18–28.

Roll, R. (1986), The Hubris Hypothesis of Corporate Takeovers, *The Journal of Business*, Vol. 59, 2, pp. 97–216.

Rosenthal, L., Young, C. (1990), The Seemingly Anomalous Price Behaviour Royal Dutch/Shell and Unilever N.V./PLC, *Journal of Financial Economics*, Vol. 26, 1, pp. 123–141.

Rosenzweig, P. (2007), The Halo Effect: … and the Eight Other Business Delusions That Deceive Managers. New York: Free Press.

Ross, S. (1976), The Arbitrage Theory of Capital Asset Pricing, *Journal of Economic Theory*, Vol. 13, 3, pp. 341–360.

Rouwenhorst, G. (1998), International Momentum Strategies, *Journal of Finance*, Vol. 53, 1, pp. 267–284.

Rouwenhorst, G. (1999), European Equity Markets and the EMU, *Financial Analysts Journal*, Vol. 55, 3, pp. 57–65.

Rovenpor, J. (1993), The Relationship between Four Personal Characteristics of Chief Executive Officers and Company Merger and Acquisition Activity, *Journal of Business and Psychology*, Vol. 8, 1, pp. 27–55.

Rozeff, M., Kinney, W. (1976), Capital Market Seasonality: The Case of Stock Returns, *Journal of Financial Economics*, Vol. 3, 4, pp. 379–402.

Rubinstein, M., (1976), The valuation of uncertain income streams and the pricing of options, *Bell Journal of economics and Management Science*, 7, pp. 407–425.

Sadique, S., In F., Veeraraghavan, M. (2008), The Impact of Spin and Tone on Stock Returns and Volatility: Evidence from Firm-Issued Earnings Announcements and the Related Press Coverage, Working paper, SSRN Electronic Paper Collection: http://ssrn.com/abstract=1121231.

Samuelson, P. (1937), A Note on Measurement of Utility, *Review of Economic Studies*, Vol. 4, pp. 155–161.

Samuelson, W., Zeckhauser, R. (1988), Status Quo Bias in Decision Making, *Journal of Risk and Uncertainty*, Vol. 1, pp. 7–59.

Saunders, E. (1993), Stock Prices and Wall Street Weather, *American Economic Review*, Vol. 83, 5, pp. 1337–1345.

Savage, L. (1954), *The Foundations of Statistics*. New York: John Wiley & Sons.

Savor, P., Lu, Q. (2009), Do Stock Mergers Create Value for Acquirers? *The Journal of Finance*, Vol. 64, 3, pp. 1061–1097.

Scarpetta, S., Hemmings, P., Tressel, T., Woo, J. (2002), The Role of Policy and Institutions for Productivity and Firm Dynamics: Evidence from Micro and Industry Data, OECD Economics Department Working Paper No. 329, Paris.

Schipper, K., Thompson, R. (1983), Evidence on the Capitalized Value of Merger Activity for Merging Firms, *Journal of Financial Economics*, Vol. 11, 1–4, pp. 85–119.

Schrand, C., Walther, B. (2000), Strategic Benchmarks in Earnings Announcements: The Selective Disclosure of Prior-Period Earnings Components, *The Accounting Review*, Vol. 75, 2, pp. 151–177.

Schultz, P. (2003), Pseudo Market Timing and the Long-Run Underperformance of IPOs, *Journal of Finance*, Vol. 58, 2, pp. 483–516.

Schwarz, N., Clore, G. (1983), Mood, Misattribution, and Judgments of Well-Being: Informative and Directive Functions of Affective States, *Journal of Personality and Social Psychology*, 45, pp. 513–523.

Schwert, W. (2003), Anomalies and Market Efficiency, in Constantinides, G. M., Harris, M., Stulz, R. M. (eds.), *Handbook of the Economics of Finance*, Vol. 1. Amsterdam: North Holland, chap. 15, pp. 939–974.

Scowcroft A., Sefton J. (2005), Understanding Momentum, *Financial Analysts Journal*, Vol. 61, 2, pp. 64–83

Seida, J. (2001), Evidence of Tax-Clientele-Related Trading Following Dividend Increases, *Journal of the American Taxation Association*, Vol. 23, 1, pp. 1–21.

Shafir, E., Diamond, P., Tversky, A. (1997), Money Illusion, *Quarterly Journal of Economics*, Vol. 112, 2, pp. 341–374.

Shapira, Z., March, G. (1987), Managerial Perspectives on Risk and Risk Taking, *Management Science*, Vol. 33, 11, pp. 1404–1418.

Shapira, Z., Venezia, I. (2001), Patterns of Behavior of Professionally Managed and Independent Investors, *Journal of Banking & Finance*, Vol. 25, 8, pp. 1573–1587.

Sharfstein, D., Stein, J. (1990), Herd Behavior and Investment, *American Economic Review*, Vol. 80, 3, pp. 465–479.

Sharpe, W. (1964), Capital Asset Prices: A Theory of Market Equilibrium under Conditions of Risk, *Journal of Finance*, Vol. 19, 3, pp. 425–442.

Sharpe, W. (1970), *Portfolio Theory and Capital Markets*. New York: McGraw-Hill.

Shefrin, H. (2000), Beyond Greed and Fear: Understanding Behavioral Finance and the Psychology of Investing. Boston, MA: Harvard Business School Press.

Shefrin, H. (2001), Behavioral Corporate Finance, *Journal of Applied Corporate Finance*, Vol. 14, 3, pp. 113–126.

Shefrin, H. (2005), *Behavioral Corporate Finance. Decisions that Create Value*. New York: McGraw-Hill Irwin, International Edition.

Shefrin, H. (2010), How Psychological Pitfalls Generated the Global Financial Crisis, in Siegel, L.B. (ed.), *Voices of Wisdom: Understanding the Global Financial Crisis*. Research Foundation of CFA Institute, Charlottesville, VA

Shefrin, H., Statman, M. (1984), Explaining Investor Preference for Cash Dividends, *Journal of Financial Economics*, Vol. 13, 2, pp. 253–282.

Shefrin, H., Statman, M. (1985), The Disposition to Sell Winners Too Early and Ride Losers Too Long: Theory and Evidence, *Journal of Finance*, Vol. 40, 3, pp. 777–790.

Shefrin, H., Statman, M. (1988), Noise Trading and Efficiency in Behavioral Finance, Working Paper, Leavey School of Business, Santa Clara University, Santa Clara, CA.

Shefrin, H., Statman, M. (2000), Behavioral Portfolio Theory, *Journal of Financial and Quantitative Analysis*, Vol. 35, 2, pp. 127–151.

Shiller, R. (1981), Do Stock Prices Move Too Much to Be Justified by Subsequent Changes in Dividends? *American Economic Review*, Vol. 71, pp. 421–436.

Shiller, R. (1990), Market Volatility and Investor Behavior, *American Economics Review*, Vol. 80, 2, pp. 58–62.

Shiller, R. (2000), *Irrational Exuberance*. Princeton, NJ: Princeton University Press.

Shleifer, A. (1986), Do Demand Curves for Stock Slope Down, *Journal of Finance*, Vol. 41, 3, pp. 579–590.

Shleifer, A. (2000), Inefficient Markets: An Introduction to Behavioral Finance. Oxford, UK: Oxford University Press.

Shleifer, A., Summers, L. (1990), The Noise Trader Approach to Finance, *Journal of Economic Perspectives*, Vol. 4, 2, pp. 19–33.

Shleifer, A., Vishny, R. (1997), The Limits of Arbitrage, *Journal of Finance*, Vol. 52, 1, pp. 35–55.

Shleifer, A., Vishny, R. (2003), Stock Market Driven Acquisition, *Journal of Financial Economics*, Vol. 70, 3, pp. 295–311.

Sias, R. (2004), Institutional Herding, *The Review of Financial Studies*, Vol. 17, 1, pp. 165–206.

Sieber, J. (1974), Effects on Decision Importance on Ability to Generate Warranted Subjective Uncertainty, *Journal of Personality and Social Psychology*, Vol. 30, 5, pp. 688–694.

Siegel, J. (1992), The Equity Premium Puzzle: Stock and Bonds Returns Since 1802, *Financial Analysts Journal*, Vol. 48, 1, pp. 28–38.

Simon, H. (1955), A Behavioral Model of Rational Choice, *Quarterly Journal of Economics*, Vol. 69, pp. 99–118.

Skinner, D., Sloan, R. (2002), Earnings Surprises, Growth Expectations, and Stock Returns: Don't Let an Earnings Torpedo Sink Your Portfolio, *Review of Accounting Studies*, Vol. 7, pp. 289–312.

Skurnik, I., Yoon, C., Park, D.C., Schwarz, N. (2005), How Warnings about False Claims Become Recommendations, *Journal of Consumer Research*, Vol. 31, pp. 713–724.

Sloan, R. (1996), Do Stock Prices Fully Reflect Information in Accruals and Cash Flows about Future Earnings, *Accounting Review*, Vol. 73, 2, pp. 289–315.

Smirlock, M., Starks, L. (1986), Day-of-the-Week and Intraday Effects in Stock Returns, *Journal of Financial Economics*, Vol. 17, pp. 197–210.

Soffer, L., Walther, B. (2000), Returns Momentum, Returns Reversals and Earnings Surprises, SSRN Electronic Paper Collection: http://ssrn.com/abstract=212368.

Spiess, K., Affleck-Graves, J. (1995), Underperformance in Long-Run Stock Returns Following Seasoned Equity Offerings, *Journal of Financial Economics*, Vol. 38, 3, pp. 243–267.

Stael von Holstein, C.A. S. (1972), Probability Forecasting: An Experiment Related to the Stock Market, *Organizational Behavior and Human Performance*, Vol. 8, pp.139–158.

Stanley, M., Block, S. (1984), A Survey of Multinational Capital Budgeting, *Financial Review*, Vol. 19, 1, pp. 36–54.

Statman, M. (1987), How Many Stocks Make a Diversified Portfolio? *Journal of Financial and Quantitative Analysis*, Vol. 35, pp. 353–363.

Statman, M. (2002a), How Much Diversification is Enough? SSRN Electronic Paper Collection, http://ssrn.com/abstract=365241.

Statman, M. (2002b), Lottery Players/Stock Traders, *Financial Analysts Journal*, Vol. 58, 1, pp. 14–21.

Statman, M. (2004), Diversification Puzzle, *Financial Analysts Journal*, Vol. 60, pp. 44–53.

Statman, M. (2007), Socially Responsible Investment, *Journal of Investment Consulting*, Vol. 8, 2, pp. 17–32.

Statman, M., Sepe, J. F. (1989), Project Termination Announcements and the Market Value of the Firm, *Financial Management*, Vol. 18, pp. 74–81.

Statman, M., Thorley, S., Vorkink, K. (2006), Investor Overconfidence and Trading Volume, *Review of Financial Studies*, Vol. 19, pp. 1531–1565.

Statman, M., Tyebjee, T.T. (1985), Optimistic Capital Budgeting Forecasts: An Experiment, *Financial Management*, Vol. 14, pp. 27–33.

Stein, J. (1996), Rational Capital Budgeting in an Irrational World, *Journal of Business*, Vol. 69, 4, pp. 429–455.

Stephan, E., Kiell, G. (2000), Decision Processes in Professional Investors: Does Expertise Moderate Judgment Biases? in Hoelzl, E. (ed.), Fairness and competition. Proceedings of the IAREP/SABE Conference, WUV Universitaetsverlag, Vienna, Austria.

Stice, E. (1991), The Market Reaction to 10-K and 10-Q Filings and to Subsequent The Wall Street Journal Earnings Announcements, *Accounting Review*, Vol. 66, pp. 42–45.

Stickel, S.E. (1995), The Anatomy of the Performance of Buy and Sell Recommendations, *Financial Analysts Journal*, Vol. 51, pp. 25–39.

Strack, F., Mussweiler, T. (1997), Explaining the Enigmatic Anchoring Effect: Mechanism of Selective Accessibility, *Journal of Personality and Social Psychology*, Vol. 73, 3, pp. 437–446.

Strickland, L., Lewicki, R., Katz, A. (1966), Temporal Orientation and Perceived Control as Determinants of Risk-Taking, *Journal of Experimental Social Psychology*, Vol. 2, pp. 143–151.

Strong, N., Xu, X. (2003), Understanding the Equity Home Bias: Evidence Form Survey Data, *Review of Economics and Statistics*, Vol. 85, 2, pp. 307–312.

Stultz, R. (1984), Optimal Hedging Policies, *Journal of Financial and Quantitative Analysis* Vol. 19, pp.127–140.

Stulz, R. (1996), Rethinking Risk Management, *Journal of Applied Corporate Finance*, Vol. 9, pp.8–24.

Svenson, O. (1981), Are We All Less Risky and More Skillful than Our Fellow Drivers? *Acta Psychologica*, Vol. 47, pp. 143–148.

Swinkels, L. (2002), International Industry Momentum, *Journal of Asset Management*, Vol. 3, 2, pp. 124–141.

Szyszka, A. (2001), CAPM—A Satisfactory Theory of Asset Pricing or An Idealistic Myth? in Janc, A. (ed.), *Economy in Transition. Problems, Ideas, Solutions*. Poznan: Poznan University of Economics Press.

Szyszka, A. (2002), Quarterly Financial Reports and the Stock Price Reaction at the Warsaw Stock Exchange, EFA 2002 Berlin Meetings Discussion Paper, SSRN Electronic Paper Collection: http://ssrn.com/abstract=295299.

Szyszka A. (2003), *Efektywność Giełdy Papierów Wartościowych w Warszawie na tle rynków dojrzałych* [Efficiency of the Warsaw Stock Exchange against mature markets], Poznań: Poznan University of Economics Press.

Szyszka, A. (2006), Zjawisko kontynuacji stóp zwrotu na Giełdzie Papierów Wartościowych w Warszawie [Momentum at the Warsaw Stock Exchange], *Bank i Kredyt*, nr 8/2006, pp. 37–49.

Szyszka, A. (2007), *Wycena papierów wartościowych na rynku kapitałowym w świetle finansów behawioralnych* [A Behavioral Finance Perspective on Valuation of Securities in the Capital Market]. Poznań: Poznan University of Economics Press.

Szyszka, A. (2010), Belief and Preference Based Models, in Baker, H. K., Nofsinger, J. (eds.), *Behavioral Finance. Investors, Corporations, and Markets*. Hoboken, NJ: John Wiley & Sons, pp. 351–372.

Szyszka, A., Zaremba, A. (2011), The Buyback Anomaly on the Polish Capital Market, SSRN Electronic Paper Collection: http://ssrn.com/abstract=2240303.

Szyszka, A., Zielonka, P. (2007), The Disposition Effect Demonstrated on IPO Trading Volume, *ICFAI Journal of Behavioral Finance*, Vol. IV, 3, Sep-2007 Issue, pp. 40–48.

Taft, R. (1955), The Ability to Judge People, *Psychological Bulletin*, Vol. 52, pp. 1–23.

Tambiah, S. (1990), Magic, Science, Religion, and the Scope of Rationality. Cambridge, UK: Cambridge University Press.

Tan, H. T., Libby, R., Hunton, J. E. (2002), Analysts' Reactions to Earnings Pre-Announcement Strategies, *Journal of Accounting Research*, Vol. 40, 1, pp. 223–246.

Taylor, S. (1982), The Availability Bias in Social Perception and Interaction, in Kahneman, D., Slovic, P., Tversky, A. (eds.), *Judgment under Uncertainty: Heuristics and Biases*. Cambridge, UK: Cambridge University Press.

Taylor, S., Brown, J. (1988), Illusion and Well-Being: A Social Psychological Perspective on Mental Health, *Psychological Bulletin*, Vol. 103, pp. 193–210.

Teoh, S. H., Welch, I., Wong, T. J. (1998a), Earnings Management and the Long-Run Market Performance of Initial Public Equity Offerings, *Journal of Finance*, Vol. 53, 6, pp. 1935–1974.

Teoh, S. H., Welch, I., Wong, T. J. (1998b), Earnings Management and the Under-performance of Seasoned Equity Offerings, *Journal of Financial Economics*, Vol. 50, 1, pp. 63–99.

Thaler, R. (1980), Toward a Positive Theory of Consumer Choice, *Journal of Economic Behavior and Organization*, Vol. 39, pp. 36–90.

Thaler, R. (1981), Some Empirical Evidence on Dynamic Inconsistency, *Economic Letters*, Vol. 81, pp. 201–207.

Thaler, R. (1985), Mental Accounting and Consumer Choice, *Marketing Science*, Vol. 4, pp. 199–214.

Thaler, R. (1990), Savings, Fungibility, and Mental Accounts, *Journal of Economic Perspective*, Vol. 4, 1, pp. 193–205.

Thaler R. (1999), Mental Accounting Matters, *Journal of Behavioral Decision Making*, 12, pp. 183–206

Thaler, R., Johnson, E. (1990), Gambling with the House Money and Trying to Break Even: The Effects of Prior Outcomes on Risky Choice, *Management Science*, Vol. 36, 6, pp. 643–661.

Thorndike, E.L. (1920), A Constant Error in Psychological Rating, *Journal of Applied Psychology*, Vol. 4, pp. 25–29.

Titman, S. (1985), Urban Land Prices under Uncertainty, *American Economic Review*, Vol. 75, pp. 505–514.

Tiwana, A., Wang, J., Keil, M., Ahluwalia, P. (2007), The Bounded Rationality Bias in Managerial Valuation of Real Options: Theory and Evidence from IT Projects, *Decision Sciences*, Vol. 38, 1, pp. 157–181.

Tkac, P. (1999), A Trading Volume Benchmark: Theory And Evidence, *Journal of Financial and Quantitative Analysis*, Vol. 34, 1, pp. 89–114.

Trahan, E., Gitman, L. (1995), Bridging the Theory-Practice Gap in Corporate Finance: A Survey of Chief Financial Officers, *Quarterly Review of Economics and Finance*, Vol.35, pp. 73–87.

Trombley, M. (1997), Stock Prices and Wall Street Weather: Additional Evidence, *Quarterly Journal of Business and Economics*, Vol. 36, 3, pp. 11–21.

Trueman, B. (1988), A Theory of Noise Trading in Security Markets, *Journal of Finance*, Vol. 43, 1, pp. 83–95.

Tufano, P. (1996), Who Manages Risk? An Empirical Examination of Risk Management Practices in the Gold Mining Industry, *Journal of Finance*, Vol. 51, pp. 1097–1137.

Tumarkin, R., Whitelaw, R. (2001), News or Noise? Internet Postings and Stock Prices, *Financial Analysts Journal*, Vol. 57, 3, pp. 41–51.

Tvede, L. (2002), *The Psychology of Finance: Understanding the Behavioural Dynamics of Markets*, Rev. ed. New York: John Wiley & Sons.

Tversky, A. (1969). Intransitivity of preferences. *Psychological Review, 76*, pp. 31–48.

Tversky, A., Kahneman, D. (1973), Availability: A Heuristic for Judging Frequency and Probability, *Cognitive Psychology*, Vol. 5, pp. 207–232.

Tversky, A., Kahneman, D. (1974), Judgment under Uncertainty: Heuristics and Biases, *Science*, Vol. 185, pp. 1124–1131.

Tversky, A., Kahneman, D. (1981), The Framing of Decisions and the Psychology of Choice, *Science*, 221, pp. 453–458.

Tversky, A., Kahneman, D. (1982), Judgments of and by Representativeness, in Kahneman, D., Slovic, P., Tversky, A. (eds.), *Judgment under Uncertainty: Heuristics and Biases*. Cambridge, UK: Cambridge University Press, pp. 84–98.

Tversky, A., Kahneman, D. (1986), Rational Choice and the Framing Decisions, *Journal of Business*, Vol. 59, 4, pp. 5251–5278.

Tversky, A., Kahneman, D. (1992), Advances in Prospect Theory: Cumulative Representation of Uncertainty, *Journal of Risk and Uncertainty*, Vol. 5, 4, pp. 297–323.

Tversky, A., Thaler, R. (1990), Preference Reversals, *Journal of Economic Perspectives*, Vol. 4, 2, pp. 201–211.

Tykocinski, O., Pittman, T. (1998), The Consequences of Doing Nothing: Inaction Inertia as Avoidance of Anticipated Counterfactual Regret, *Journal of Personality and Social Psychology*, Vol. 75, pp. 607–616.

Van Gelderen, M., Thurik, R., Bosma, N. (2005), Success and Risk Factors in Pre-Startup Phase, *Small Business Economics*, Vol. 24, p. 265–380.

Vafeas, N. (2001), Reverse Stock Splits and Earnings Performance, *Accounting and Business Research*, Vol. 31, 3, pp. 191–202.

Vermaelen, T. (1981), Common Stock Repurchases and Market Signaling, *Journal of Financial Economics*, Vol. 9, pp. 139–183

Vermaelen, T. (1984), Repurchase Tender Offers, Signalling, and Managerial Incentives, *Journal of Financial and Quantitative Analysis*, Vol. 19, pp. 163–181.

Vermaelen, T., Verstringe, M. (1986), Do Belgians Overreact? Working Paper, Catholic University of Louvain, Louvain, Belgium.

Verter, G. (2002), "Timing merger waves," Working paper of Harvard University, Cambridge, MA.

Von Neumann, J., Morgenstern, O. (1944), *Theory of Games and Economic Behavior*, Princeton University Press, Princeton, NJ.

Von Neumann, J., Morgenstern, O. (1947), *Theory of Games and Economic Behavior*, 2nd ed. Princeton, NJ: Princeton University Press.

Wachtel, S. (1942), Certain Observations on Seasonal Movements in Stock Prices, *Journal of Business*, Vol. 15, 2, pp. 184–193.

Warnock, F., Warnock, V. (2005), International Capital Flows and U.S. Interest Rates, *International Finance Discussion Papers*, No. 840, Board of Governors of the Federal Reserve System, Washington DC.

Wason, P. (1966), Reasoning, in Foss, B. (ed.), *New Horizons in Psychology*, Harmondsworth: Penguin, pp. 131–151.

Weber, M., Camerer, C. (1998), The Disposition Effect in Securities Trading: An Experimental Analysis, *Journal of Economic Behavior & Organization*, Vol. 33, 2, pp.167–185.

Weil, P. (1989), The Equity Premium Puzzle and the Risk-Free Rate Puzzle, *Journal of Monetary Economics*, Vol. 24, 3, pp. 401–421.

Weinstein, N. (1980), Unrealistic Optimism about Future Life Events, *Journal of Personality and Social Psychology*, Vol. 39, pp. 806–820.

Weiss, K. (1989), The Post-Offerings Price Performance of Closed-End Funds, *Financial Management*, Vol. 18, 3, pp. 57–67.

Weiss, K., Lee, C., Seguin, P. (1996), The Marketing of Closed-End Fund IPOs: Evidence from Transaction Data, *Journal of Financial Intermediation*, Vol. 5, 1, pp. 127–159.

Welch, I. (2000), Herding among Security Analysts, *Journal of Financial Economics*, Vol. 58, pp. 369–396.

Welch, I. (2004), Stock Returns and Capital Structure, *Journal of Political Economy*, Vol. 112, pp. 106–131.

West, K. (1988), Bubbles, Fads and Stock Price Volatility Tests: A Partial Evaluation, *Journal of Finance*, Vol. 43, 3, pp. 639–660.

Wilcoxon, F. (1945), Individual Comparisons by Ranking Methods, *Biometrics Bulletin*, Vol. 1, 6, pp. 80–83.

Womack, K. (1996), Do Brokerage Analysts' Recommendation Have Investment Value? *Journal of Finance*, Vol. 51, 1, pp. 137–167.

Woolridge, J. R., Chambers, D. R. (1983), Reverse Splits and Shareholder Wealth, *Financial Management*, Vol. 12, pp. 5–15.

Wright, W., Bower, G. (1992), Mood Effects on Subjective Probability Assessment, *Organizational Behavior and Human Decision Processes*, Vol. 52, pp. 276–291.

Wurgler, J., Zhuravskaya, E. (2002), Does Arbitrage Flatten Demand Curves for Stocks? *Journal of Business*, Vol. 75, 4, pp. 583–608.

Yates, J.F. (1990), *Judgment and Decision Making*. Englewood, NJ: Prentice Hall.

Zhang, C., Jacobsen, B. (2013), Are Monthly Seasonals Real? A Three Century Perspective, *Review of Finance*, forthcoming.

Name Index

Subject Index

CPSIA information can be obtained at www.ICGtesting.com
Printed in the USA
LVOW10*2201270614

392131LV00002B/25/P